# THE ULTIMATE LAUGHTER BOOK

**THREE BOOKS IN ONE!**

Laughter, the Best Medicine®

Laughter Really Is the Best Medicine®

Laughter Still Is the Best Medicine®

# Reader's digest

The Reader's Digest Association, Inc. • New York, NY/Montreal

A READER'S DIGEST BOOK
Copyright ©2014 The Reader's Digest Association, Inc.

Reader's Digest and Laughter the Best Medicine are registered trademarks of
The Reader's Digest Association, Inc.

ISBN  978-1-62145-202-7

*The Ultimate Laughter Book* comprises three books previously published by Reader's Digest:

*Laughter, the Best Medicine*® (ISBN 978-0-89577-977-9)
*Laughter Really Is the Best Medicine*® (ISBN 978-1-60652-204-2)
*Laughter Still Is the Best Medicine*® (ISBN 978-1-62145-137-2)

Cover and spot illustrations: George McKeon and Travis Foster

Cartoon Credits (alphabetically by artist):
*Laughter, the Best Medicine*: ©1997 Charles Barsotti from The Cartoon Bank™, Inc: 195; ©1997
Frank Cotham from The Cartoon Bank™, Inc: 18, 42, 50, 62, 131, 143, 149, 163, 169, 172, 185, 187, 193;
©1997 Leo Cullum from The Cartoon Bank™, Inc: 47, 77, 94, 115, 144, 160, 174, 180, 190; ©1997 Boris
Drucker from The Cartoon Bank™, Inc: 101; ©1997 Joseph Farris from The Cartoon Bank™, Inc:
57, 91, 165; ©1997 Mort Gerberg from The Cartoon Bank™, Inc: 205, 211; ©1997 Ted Goff from The
Cartoon Bank™, Inc: 28; ©1997 William Haefeli from The Cartoon Bank™, Inc: 37; ©1997 Glen
Lelievre from The Cartoon Bank™, Inc: 151; ©1997 Arnie Levin from The Cartoon Bank™, Inc: 201;
Robert Mankoff ©1984 from The New Yorker Magazine, Inc: 64; Robert Mankoff ©1988 from The
New Yorker Magazine, Inc: 139; Robert Mankoff ©1995 from The New Yorker Magazine, Inc: 118;
©1997 Robert Mankoff from The Cartoon Bank™, Inc: 13, 24, 39, 45, 183; ©1997 Jerry Marcus from
The Cartoon Bank™, Inc: 83, 87, 97; ©1997 J. P. Rini from The Cartoon Bank™, Inc: 71, 107, 110, 176,
199; ©1997 Bernhard Schoenbaum from The Cartoon Bank™, Inc: 214; ©1997 Phil Somerville from
The Cartoon Bank™, Inc: 7; ©1997 Peter Steiner from The Cartoon Bank™, Inc: 85, 129; ©1997
Mick Stevens from The Cartoon Bank™, Inc: 81, 157; ©1997 P. C. Vey from The Cartoon Bank™,
Inc: 103; ©1997 Bob Zahn from The Cartoon Bank™, Inc: 33, 67, 74, 122, 208; ©1997 Jack Ziegler
from The Cartoon Bank™, Inc: 11, 15, 22, 53, 125, 136, 146, 152

*Laughter Really Is the Best Medicine:* John Caldwell: 218, 224, 227, 235, 266, 311, 374, 393, 408;  Dave
Carpenter: 230, 247, 257, 297, 303, 314, 353, 368, 379, 387, 390, 417;  Roy Delgado: 223, 253, 265, 271,
284, 298, 313, 330, 341, 362, 400, 423; Mike Lynch: 248, 260, 275, 276, 289, 322, 335, 405;  Scott Arthur
Masear: 238, 319, 348, 394, 397; Dan Reynolds: 281, 292, 327, 361, 367, 382, 413, 420, 427;  Harley
Schwadron: 242, 306, 336, 344, 356, 371

*Laughter Still Is the Best Medicine:* Ian Baker: 548, 628; John Caldwell: 430, 485, 502, 532, 574, 584,
605; Dave Carpenter: 453, 520; Roy Delgado: 468, 510, 537, 593, 633; Ralph Hagen: 456, 465, 493,
545, 597; Mike Lynch: 517, 540; Scott Arthur Masear: 435, 568, 571; Harley Schwadron: 496, 560, 579;
Steve Smeltzer: 448, 557; Thomas Bros.: 438, 472, 488, 507, 527, 588, 600, 612, 617, 636; Kim Warp:
481; Elizabeth Westley & Steven Mach: 443, 477, 553, 625

We are committed to both the quality of our products and the service we provide to our
customers. We value your comments, so please feel free to contact us.
  The Reader's Digest Association, Inc.
  Adult Trade Publishing
  44 South Broadway
  White Plains, NY 10601

For more Reader's Digest products and information, visit our website:
  www.rd.com (in the United States)
  www.readersdigest.ca (in Canada)

Printed in China

3  5  7  9  10  8  6  4  2

# CONTENTS

# Laughter

## THE BEST
## MEDICINE®

A Laugh-Out-Loud
Collection of our
Funniest Jokes,
Quotes, Stories
& Cartoons

# Contents

# A Note from the Editors

**W**hat's your handicap these days?" one golfer asked his companion.

"I'm a scratch golfer . . . I write down all my good scores and scratch out all my bad ones."

So relates Charles Schulz, the much-loved creator of the comic strip, *Peanuts*. Schulz is just one of the many funny folks, both professional and everyday, whose jokes appear in *Laughter, The Best Medicine*®, this year celebrating 50 years of monthly funny business in *Reader's Digest*. It is the column's vast supply of homey humor that supplied this book with an unbeatable collection.

What has made *Laughter, The Best Medicine* so popular for so long? In part, the answer lies in the department's consistent ability to pinpoint—and poke fun at—the facts and foibles of daily life. Nothing is sacred—from politics, religion, technology, doctors and lawyers, to sports, pets, children, and relationships. Add to this the quality of contributors—professional comedians, joke writers, and best of all, readers themselves—and you have a winning, winsome feature that readers look forward to month after month.

You can tell a lot about people and their times by what makes them laugh. A look through 50 years of *Laughter, The Best Medicine* offers us a glimpse of the past while tickling us in the present. Remember when knock-knock jokes were the rage? How about riddles and puns? Today's hot commodities in the humor department tend to be top ten lists and computer comedy.

While there is much more to The Digest than its jokes, its regular offerings of comic relief serve a noble and delightful purpose that has been captured in this book. Letters of thanks pour in weekly from readers who rely on *Laughter, The Best Medicine* to lift their spirits, put a twinkle in their eye or simply call up a chuckle or two after a hard day at home or the office, working or watching the kids. As you take a break from your daily business, browse through the following pages and prepare for a treat. We think you'll find that, after all is said and done, laughter really is the best medicine.

*—The Editors*

*"Oh, Richard, the possibilities."*

# People

# Courting Troubles

**A** man is taking a woman home from their first date, and he asks if he can come inside. "Oh, no," she says. "I never ask a guy in on the first date."

"Okay," the man replies, "how about the last date?"

—HEIDI MOSELEY

**T**ammy: "I'm not looking to get involved with one particular guy right now, Al."

Al: "Well, luckily for you, Tammy, I'm not exactly known for being particular."

—J. C. DUFFY, UNIVERSAL PRESS SYNDICATE

**M**other to daughter: "What kind of a person is your new friend? Is he respectable?"

"Of course he is, Mum. He's thrifty, doesn't drink or smoke, has a very steady wife and three well-behaved children."

—LEA BERNER

**H**ow was your date last night, Billy?" his friend asked.

"Fabulous. We went to the concert, had a bite to eat, and then we drove around for a while until I found a nice dark spot to park. I asked her for a kiss, and she said that first I'd have to put the top down on the car. So I worked for an hour getting the top down—"

"An hour?" interrupted his pal. "I can put my top down in three minutes."

"I know," said Billy. "But you have a convertible."

—PHIL HARTMAN IN *OHIO MOTORIST*

*"Who said anything about marriage? What I'm offering is an array of mutual funds, variable annuities and life insurance."*

**W**hile riding a bus, I overheard one woman ask another, with great curiosity, "Well, what happened on your date with dashing Prince Lancelot?"

"Yuk!" was the disillusioned reply. "He was more like disgusting Prince Lust-a-lot—and I was the one who needed the suit of armor!"

—T. HOWIE

**A** college friend was going to meet a young lady he knew.
"An old flame?" I asked.
He winked and said, "More like an unlit match."

—MICHAEL HARTLAND

A bachelor, just turned 40, began feeling desperate. "I went to a singles bar," he told a friend, "walked over to this 20-year-old woman and asked, 'Where have you been all my life?' She said, 'Teething.'"

—MACK McGINNIS IN *QUOTE*

Professor to a student: "Can you think of a solution to end unemployment?"

"Yes, sir! I'd put all the men on one island and the women on another."

"And what would they be doing then?"

"Building boats!"

—SOMEN GUHA

To impress his date, the young man took her to a very chic Italian restaurant. After sipping some fine wine, he picked up the menu and ordered. "We'll have the *Giuseppe Spomdalucci*," he said.

"Sorry, sir," said the waiter. "That's the proprietor."

—JIM STARK

I'm not saying her fiancé is cheap," whispered the office gossip. "But every time I get close to her engagement ring, I have an overwhelming desire for some Cracker Jack."

—QUOTED BY JAMES DENT IN THE CHARLESTON, W.VA., *GAZETTE*

She answered the phone to hear a repentant voice. "I'm sorry, darling," he said. "I have thought things over and you *can* have the Rolls-Royce as a wedding present, we *will* move to the Gold Coast, and your mother *can* stay with us. Now will you marry me?"

"Of course I will," she said. "And who is this speaking?"

—*THE ROTARIAN*

**S**triking up a conversation with the attractive woman seated beside him on a coast-to-coast flight, a would-be Romeo asked, "What kind of man attracts you?"

"I've always been drawn to Native American men," she replied. "They're in harmony with nature."

"I see," said the man, nodding.

"But, then, I really go for Jewish men who put women on a pedestal, and I can rarely resist the way Southern gentlemen always treat their ladies with respect."

"Please allow me to introduce myself," said the man. "My name is Tecumseh Goldstein, but all my friends call me Bubba."

—Matthew W. Boyle

**D**onna: "He's so romantic. Every time he speaks to me he starts with, 'Fair lady.' "

Tina: "Romantic, my eye. He used to be a bus driver."

—Steve Jenks

**W**hat am I supposed to do?" a young man looking to get married asked his friend. "Every woman I bring home to meet my parents, my mother doesn't like."

"Oh, that's easy," his pal replied. "All you have to do is find someone who's just like your mother."

"I did that already," he said, "and that one my father didn't like."

—Minnie Herman

**A** bachelor asked the computer to find him the perfect mate: "I want a companion who is small and cute, loves water sports, and enjoys group activities."

Back came the answer: "Marry a penguin."

—Rainbow

An 85-year-old widow went on a blind date with a 90-year-old man. When she returned to her daughter's house later that night, she seemed upset. "What happened, Mother?" the daughter asked.

"I had to slap his face three times!"

"You mean he got fresh?"

"No," she answered. "I thought he was dead!"

—Warren Holl

## Altar Egos

The groom and his best man were sitting together at a table, playing poker in a small room at the back of the church. Their jackets were off, their sleeves rolled up and each man was viewing the cards he had been dealt. The door suddenly swung open, and the angry bride came barging in.

"What do you two think you're doing here? The ceremony is about to begin!" screamed the bride.

"Honey," replied the groom, "you know it's bad luck for the groom to see the bride before the wedding!"

—Robert Halstead

At an Italian wedding ceremony, the priest asked the bride, "Do you take Franco Giuseppe Antonio to be your husband?"

Looking confused, she said, "Father, there's a mistake. I'm only marrying Frank."

—L. C.

How lovely you look, my dear!" gushed a wedding guest to the bride. And then she whispered, "Whatever happened to that dizzy blonde your groom used to date?"

"I dyed my hair," replied the bride.

—Kevin Benningfield in Louisville, Ky., Courier-Journal

**A** Cockney asked a Roman Catholic coworker's help in choosing a bride. "I'm torn between Betty and Maria," he said. "'Ow do you Catholics make decisions?"

"I go to church," said his pal. "Then I look up and pray, and the answer comes to me."

Next day the Cockney was all excited. "I did what you told me, mate, and the answer was given to me!"

"What happened?"

"I went to your church, knelt in prayer, looked up and there it was! Written in gold, 'igh above a stained-glass window."

"What did it say?"

"It said, 'ave Maria."

—*The Jokesmith*

**O**verheard: "Marriage is nature's way of keeping people from fighting with strangers."

—*Alan King*

**A**ttending a wedding for the first time, a little girl whispered to her mother, "Why is the bride dressed in white?"

"Because white is the color of happiness," her mother explained. "And today is the happiest day of her life."

The child thought about this for a moment. "So why is the groom wearing black?"

—*Jerry H. Simpson Jr.*

**W**hy did you marry your husband?" asked the neighborhood gossip. "You don't seem to have much in common."

"It was the old story of opposites attracting each other," explained the wife. "I was pregnant and he wasn't."

—*Parts Pups*

After issuing driver's licenses for 20 years, a clerk was transferred to the marriage license bureau. Almost at once, he was in trouble. Young couples were leaving his desk red-faced and angry. His supervisor asked what was wrong.

"I can't seem to help it," muttered the dismayed clerk. "I just can't get out of the habit of asking whether they want the license for business or for pleasure."

—FRANK SCHAFF

Two neighbors were talking over the back fence. "I went to a wedding this weekend," said one, "but I don't think the marriage will last."

"Why not?" asked the other.

"Well, when the bride said 'I do,' the groom said, 'Don't use that tone of voice with me.' "

—GARY APPLE IN SPEAKER'S IDEA FILE

I had almost made up my mind to attend my friend's wedding when my attention was drawn to the last sentence of the wedding invitation. In bold letters it stated, "Please avoid presence."

—ROBBY ABRAHAM

A man fond of weddings was being married for a fourth time. The groom seemed very moved as he stood at the altar with his new bride, and as he stood dabbing his eyes after the ceremony, his concerned best man asked him why he was so emotional.

"Well," replied the groom, "it just occurred to me that this could be my last wedding."

—BERTE GODERSTAD

# For Better or Perverse

A husband and wife drove for miles in silence after a terrible argument in which neither would budge. The husband pointed to a mule in a pasture.

"Relative of yours?" he asked.

"Yes," she replied. "By marriage."

—Bobbie Mae Cooley in *The American Legion Magazine*

Executive overheard talking to a friend: "My wife tells me I don't display enough passion. Imagine! I have a good mind to send her a memo."

—*Speaker's Idea File*

Let's get one thing straight," the newlywed said to her husband. "I'm not cleaning up after you. I'm a career woman. That means I pay other people to do housework. Got it?"

"How much?"

"Eight dollars an hour. Take it or leave it."

—Bill Holbrook, King Features Syndicate

Did you hear about the dentist who married a manicurist? They fought tooth and nail.

—Joan McCourt

John, an avant-garde painter, got married. Someone asked the bride a few weeks after the wedding, "How's married life, Helen?"

"It's great," she answered. "My husband paints, I cook; then we try to guess what he painted and what I cooked."

—Mrs. Istvan Pap

Three Frenchmen were trying to define *savoir-faire*. "If I go home," said Alphonse, "and find my wife with another man, say 'Excuse me' and leave, that is savoir-faire."

"No," replied Pierre, "if I go home and find my wife with another man, and say 'Excuse me, please continue,' that is savoir-faire."

"*Au contraire*," said Jacques, "if I go home and find my wife with another man and say 'Excuse me, please continue,' and he can continue, then he has savoir-faire."

—QUOTED BY SUSIE TELTSER-SCHWARZ IN
*NITE LIGHTS*

Arnold complained to a coworker that he didn't know what to get his wife for her birthday. "She already has everything you could think of, and anyway, she can buy herself whatever she likes."

"Here's an idea," said the coworker. "Make up your own gift certificate that says, 'Thirty minutes of great loving, any way you want it.' I guarantee she'll be enchanted."

The next day, Arnold's coworker asked, "Well? Did you take my suggestion?"

"Yes," said Arnold.

"Did she like it?"

"Oh, yes! She jumped up, kissed me on the forehead, and ran out the door yelling, 'See you in 30 minutes!' "

—TOM MATTHEWS

Kevin: "My wife and I argue a lot. She's very touchy—the least little thing sets her off."

Christopher: "You're lucky. Mine is a self-starter."

—RON DENTINGER IN THE
DODGEVILLE, WIS., *CHRONICLE*

*"Look, I know its not perfect, but, by and large, the jury system has worked very well for our marriage."*

The judge was trying to change the mind of a woman filing for divorce. "You're 92," he said. "Your husband's 94. You've been married for 73 years. Why give up now?"

"Our marriage has been on the rocks for quite a while," the woman explained, "but we decided to wait until the children died."

—QUOTED BY JOYCE BROTHERS

John, I can see that all your buttons are sewed on perfectly. You must be married!"

"That's right. Sewing on buttons was the first thing my wife taught me on our honeymoon."

—*Chayan*

A doctor and his wife were having a big argument at breakfast. "You aren't so good in bed either!" he shouted and stormed off to work. By midmorning, he decided he'd better make amends and phoned home. After many rings, his wife picked up the phone.

"What took you so long to answer?"

"I was in bed."

"What were you doing in bed this late?"

"Getting a second opinion."

—EDWARD B. WORBY

I was relaxing in my favorite chair on Sunday," said one office worker to another, "reading the newspaper, watching a ball game on TV and listening to another on the radio, drinking beer, eating a snack, and scratching the dog with my foot—and my wife has the nerve to accuse me of just sitting there doing nothing!"

—LOLA BRANDLI

Congratulating a friend after her son and daughter got married within a month of each other, a woman asked, "What kind of boy did your daughter marry?"

"Oh, he's wonderful," gushed the mother. "He lets her sleep late, wants her to go to the beauty parlor regularly, and insists on taking her out to dinner every night."

"That's nice," said the woman. "What about your son?"

"I'm not so happy about that," the mother sighed. "His wife sleeps late, spends all her time in the beauty parlor, and makes them eat take-out meals!"

—SABEEN

First man: I can't think what to get my wife for Christmas. If I give her something practical, I know she'll burst into tears.

Second man: In that case, buy her some handkerchiefs.

—MUSTAFA AMMI

"The guys down at the bowling alley figure the delivery man has seduced every woman on our street except one," Harvey told his wife.

She thought for a moment. "I'll bet it's that snooty Mrs. Jenkins."

—G. L. Gaukroger

Over breakfast one morning, a woman said to her husband, "I bet you don't know what day this is."

"Of course I do," he indignantly answered, going out the door on his way to the office.

At 10 AM, the doorbell rang, and when the woman opened the door, she was handed a box containing a dozen long-stemmed red roses. At 1 PM, a foil-wrapped, two-pound box of her favorite chocolates arrived. Later, a boutique delivered a designer dress.

The woman couldn't wait for her husband to come home. "First the flowers, then the candy, and then the dress!" she exclaimed. "I've never spent a more wonderful Groundhog Day in my whole life!"

—Eva C. Bean

I was talking with an elderly relative who had just celebrated his 55th wedding anniversary. "Are there any secrets between you two?" I asked. "Do you ever hide anything from each other?"

"Well, yes," replied the old man with a sly smile. "I have ten thousand dollars in a bank that Mary doesn't know about. And she has ten thousand in a bank that I don't know about."

—James A. Sanaker

A couple walking in the park noticed a young man and woman sitting on a bench, passionately kissing.

"Why don't you do that?" said the wife.

"Honey," replied her husband, "I don't even know that woman!"

—Gary R. Handley

A man had just presented his wife with the fox coat she had been coaxing and cajoling him to buy her for weeks. Now he was perplexed to see her examining it with a sad look.

"What's the matter, sweetheart? Don't you like the coat?" he asked.

"I love it," she answered. "It's just that I was feeling sorry for the poor little creature who was skinned alive so that I could have the pleasure of wearing this coat."

"Why, thank you," said the husband.

—AMAL KHALIDI

I've finally found a way to get money out of my husband," a woman told her friend. "We were arguing last night, and I told him I was going home to Mother. He gave me the fare."

—CHARLES DONNE

# Why Some Species Eat Their Young

A man was walking along a street when from the other side of a wall he heard someone shout, "Fifty-two!"

He stopped, and again he heard, "Fifty-two!"

Unable to overcome his curiosity, the man stood on a box that he found at the spot, peeked over, and a boy hit him with a handful of clay and shouted, "Fifty-three!"

—JULIO CESAR DA CRUZ

Wife: "Donald, when was the last time we received a letter from our son?"

Husband: "Just a second, honey, I'll go look in the checkbook."

—*Die Weltwoche*

*"Wait a minute! I smell toys."*

Edgar, father of nine, reflected on how he had mellowed over the years: "When the firstborn coughed or sneezed, I called the ambulance. When the last one swallowed a dime, I just told him it was coming out of his allowance."

—Jean Short

My mother always told me I wouldn't amount to anything because I procrastinate," says comedian Judy Tenuta. "I told her, 'Just wait.'"

Mummy has no idea how to raise children," said the child to his father.

"How can you say such a thing?" replied the father.

"Well, Mummy always sends me to bed at night when I'm not sleepy, and wakes me up in the morning when I am."

—SANDOR SZABO

The young wife found her husband at their baby's crib, a mixture of emotions spreading over his face. She slipped her arms around him. "A penny for your thoughts," she said, her eyes glistening.

"For the life of me," he replied, "I can't see how anybody can make a crib like this for $84.97."

—H. B. MCCLUNG

A little girl asked her mother for ten cents to give to an old lady in the park. Her mother was touched by the child's kindness and gave her the required sum.

"There you are, my dear," said the mother. "But, tell me, isn't the lady able to work any more?"

"Oh yes," came the reply. "She sells sweets."

—HARILLON AND SUZANNE LECLERCQ

A couple, desperate to conceive a child, went to their priest and asked him to pray for them. "I'm going on a sabbatical to Rome," he replied, "and while I'm there, I'll light a candle for you."

When the priest returned three years later, he went to the couple's house and found the wife pregnant, busily attending to two sets of twins. Elated, the priest asked her where her husband was so that he could congratulate him.

"He's gone to Rome," came the harried reply, "to blow that candle out."

—ELIZABETH BENOIT

Betsy: "If you have $2, and you ask your father for $4, how much will you have?"
Billy: "Two dollars."
Betsy: "You don't know your math."
Billy: "You don't know my father."

—LISA McNEASE

My Mary is so smart, she walked when she was eight months old," bragged one woman.
"You call that intelligent?" challenged her companion. "When my Cindy was that old, she let us carry her."

—ARD-JAN DANNENBERG

A girl watched, fascinated, as her mother smoothed cold cream on her face. "Why do you do that?" she asked.
"To make myself beautiful," said the mother, who began removing the cream with a tissue.
"What's the matter?" asked the girl. "Giving up?"

—NANCY C. BELL

Seven-year-old John had finished his summer vacation and gone back to school. Two days later his teacher phoned his mother to tell her that John was misbehaving.
"Wait a minute," she said. "I had John here for two months and I never called you once when he misbehaved."

—F. TRACEY

But, dear," said the mother to her little kid, "I didn't hear you cry when you cut your finger!"
"What's the use of crying? I thought you were outside the house."

—HANI RUSHDI GHEBRI BESHAY

Mrs. Smith was preparing dinner when little Brad came into the kitchen. "What has mama's darling been doing all day?"

"I've been playing mailman," replied Brad.

"Mailman?" asked the mother. "How could you do that when you had no letters?"

"I had a whole bunch of letters," said Brad. "I found them in that old trunk up in the attic, all tied up with ribbon. I put one in every mailbox on the street."

—H. B. McClung

I was a very unpopular child," says comedian Rita Rudner. "I had only two friends. They were imaginary. And they would only play with each other."

# The Rogue's Calorie

Horace grabbed his plate and walked up to the party buffet for the fourth time. "Aren't you embarrassed to go back for so many helpings?" asked his wife.

"Not a bit," Horace replied. "I keep telling them it's for you."

—Elinor Filice in *Woman's World*

Heard about the new diet? You eat whatever you want whenever you want, and as much as you want. You don't lose any weight, but it's really easy to stick to.

—George J. Tricker

Comic J. Scott Homan said he'd been trying to get in shape doing 20 sit-ups each morning. "That may not sound like a lot, but you can only hit that snooze alarm so many times."

—Atlanta *Journal-Constitution*

**D**on't tell me to reduce, Doc," said the man after his examination. "I just can't take those diets."

"No problem," said the doctor. "I'm prescribing an exercise machine."

"Really? What kind?"

"A rack. For your weight, you should be a foot and a half taller."

—GENE NEWMAN

**D**arn!" the man said to his pal while weighing himself in a drug-store. "I began this diet yesterday, but the scale says I'm *heavier.* Here, Norm, hold my jacket. . . . It *still* says I'm heavier. Here, hold my Twinkies."

—KEVIN FAGAN,
United Features Syndicate

**H**ow do you account for your longevity?" asked the reporter on Harvey's 110th birthday.

"You might call me a health nut," Harvey replied. "I never smoked. I never drank. I was always in bed and sound asleep by 10 o'clock. And I've always walked three miles a day, rain or shine."

"But," said the reporter, "I had an uncle who followed that exact routine and died when he was 62. How come it didn't work for him?"

"All I can say," replied Harvey, "is that he didn't keep it up long enough."

—QUOTED IN *Lutheran Digest*

**Q**: How do you get a man to do sit-ups?
A: Put the remote control between his feet.

—KATIE KENDRICK

**"That weight I lost . . . I found it!"**

**A**re the slimming exercises doing you any good?" a man asked his beer-bellied colleague. "Can you touch your toes now?"

"No, I can't touch them," the other replied, "but I'm beginning to see them."

—FRITZ HEIDI

The doctor told Uncle Fudd that if he ran five miles a day for 300 days, he would lose 75 pounds. At the end of 300 days, Uncle Fudd called the doctor to report he had lost the weight, but he had a problem.

"What's the problem?" asked the doctor.

"I'm 1,500 miles from home."

—H. B. McClung

I never eat food with additives or preservatives," boasted a health fanatic. "And I never touch anything that's been sprayed or fed chemical grain."

"Wow, that's wonderful," her friend marveled. "How do you feel?"

"Hungry," she moaned.

—S. Bader in *Woman's World*

Did you hear about the man who was arrested for paying his check at a cafeteria with a counterfeit 10-dollar bill?

He had been served decaffeinated coffee with a nondairy creamer and an artificial sweetener.

—Aldo Cammarota

There's a new garlic diet around. You don't lose weight, but you look thinner from a distance.

—Red Shea on *The Tommy Hunter Show*, TNN, Nashville

Those three hams you sold me last month were delicious," the woman told her butcher.

"If you want more, I still have 10 of the same quality."

"Give me your word they're from the same pig, and I'll take three of them."

—*Almanaque Bertrand*

When short hemlines came back into fashion, a woman dug an old miniskirt out of her closet. She tried it on, but couldn't figure out what to do with the other leg.

—ASHLEY COOPER IN THE CHARLESTON, S.C.,
*News and Courier*

Man to clerk in video store: "I'd like to exchange this diet-and-workout tape for one on self-acceptance."

—KEVIN FAGAN,
United Features Syndicate

# We're Only Human

George Burns punctuated this story with a flick of his cigar. "A woman said to me, 'Is it true that you still go out with young girls?' I said yes, it's true. She said, 'Is it true that you still smoke 15 to 20 cigars a day?' I said yes, it's true. She said, 'Is it true that you still take a few drinks every day?' I said yes, it's true.

"She said, 'What does your doctor say?' I said, 'He's dead.' "

In New York City," notes comedian Jay Leno, "they're handing out condoms to high-school students. Gee, I thought it was a big day when I got my class ring!"

At a party several young couples were discussing the difficulties of family budgets. "I really don't want a lot of money," said one yuppie. "I just wish we could afford to live the way we're living now."

—*The Lion*

My parents are the epitome of abstinence," the boy explains to his schoolmates.

"They don't smoke, they don't drink, and my sister and I are adopted children."

—*Weltwoche*

Two men were sitting by the swimming pool at a nudist colony when they noticed a beautiful young woman walking toward the pool. Her tan lines traced the outline of a tiny bathing suit with elaborately crisscrossed straps across the back.

"Mmm," one of the men said wistfully, "I'll bet she looks great in that suit."

—Barbara Hadley, quoted by Patricia McLaughlin in the Philadelphia *Inquirer Magazine*

A 90-year-old man checked into a posh hotel to celebrate his birthday. As a surprise, some friends sent a call girl to his room. When the man answered his door, he saw before him a beautiful young woman. "I have a present for you," she said.

"Really?" replied the bewildered gent.

"I'm here to give you super sex," she said in a whisper.

"Thanks," he said thoughtfully. "I'll take the soup."

—Dorian Goldstein

Two friends are talking about their reading:

"I'm fascinated by medical publications. A friend of mine treated herself, using articles she read in the journals."

"You're speaking of her in the past tense. Did she die?"

"Unfortunately."

"Of what?"

"A typographical error."

—Maurice Ooghe

**Q**: What's the definition of a bachelor pad?

A: All the house plants are dead, but there's something growing in the refrigerator.

—Marshall Williams in *The Los Angeles Times*

**A** woman sat down on a park bench, glanced around and decided to stretch out her legs on the seat and relax. After a while, a beggar came up to her and said, "Hello, luv, how's about us going for a walk together?"

"How dare you," retorted the woman, "I'm not one of your cheap pickups!"

"Well then," said the tramp, "what are you doing in my bed?"

—Alzira Infante de la Cerda

**T**o gain self-confidence, you must avoid using negative words such as *can't* and *not*," the counselor advised the young woman. "Do you think you could do that?"

"Well, I can't see why not."

—Greg Evans, North American Syndicate

Overheard: "I'm trying to keep up with the Joneses, but every time I catch up, they just refinance!"

—DAVID A. SNELL

The best thing about getting older is that you gain sincerity," says Tommy Smothers. "Once you learn to fake that, there's nothing you can't do."

Did you hear about the self-help group for compulsive talkers? It's called On & On Anon.

—SALLY DAVIS

Bill: "Why the glum look?"
Stan: "I just don't understand today's world. My son wears an earring. My daughter has a tattoo. My wife makes twice what I do."
Bill: "So what are you going to do?"
Stan: "I'm thinking of going home to my father."

—*American Speaker*

Heard at a bus stop:
"Hello, Lily, how are you? What have you done to your hair? It looks like a wig."
"Yes, it is a wig."
"Really, how wonderful! It looks just like real hair."

—GANESH V.

One woman was talking to another on the telephone:
"I ran into an old friend from high school the other day and she looked marvelous! She hadn't gained an ounce, and she didn't have a single wrinkle—so I ran into her again."

—*Shoebox Greetings*

*"Dear, did something happen at the office?"*

# The Professions

# Open Wide and Say Ha!

**T**hree doctors were on their way to a convention when their car had a flat. They got out and examined the tire. The first doctor said, "I think it's flat."

The second doctor examined it closely and said, "It sure looks flat."

The third doctor felt the tire and said, "It feels like it's flat."

All three nodded their heads in agreement. "We'd better run some tests."

—Denise Bright

**A** woman and her husband interrupted their vacation to go to a dentist. "I want a tooth pulled, and I don't want Novocain because I'm in a big hurry," the woman said. "Just extract the tooth as quickly as possible, and we'll be on our way."

The dentist was quite impressed. "You're certainly a courageous woman," he said. "Which tooth is it?"

The woman turned to her husband and said, "Show him your tooth, dear."

—*Portals of Prayer*

**P**atient: "This hospital is no good. They treat us like dogs."
Orderly: "Mr. Jones, you know that's not true. Now, roll over."

—Anne Wolosyn

**A** physician went to heaven and met God, who granted him one question. So the physician asked, "Will health-care reform ever occur?"

"I have good news and bad news," God replied. "The answer is yes, but not in my lifetime."

—Stephen Huber, MD, in *Medical World News*

**A** patient was anxious after a prolonged bedside discussion by hospital doctors. The head doctor even came to see him.

"There must be a lot of doubt about what is wrong with me," the patient told the doctor.

"Where did you get that idea?" the doctor replied.

"All the other doctors disagreed with you, didn't they?"

"To some extent, but don't worry," said the doctor consolingly. "In a similar case, I stood firm on my diagnosis—and the postmortem proved me right!"

—ABBAS ALI ZAHID

**A** woman accompanied her husband when he went for his annual checkup. While the patient was getting dressed, the doctor came out and said to the wife, "I don't like the way he looks."

"Neither do I," she said. "But he's handy around the house."

—MERRITT K. FREEMAN in *Y. B. News*

**A** jungle witch doctor was called to treat a man with a high fever. He made a medicine with the eye of a toad, the liver of a snake, the heart of a rat, six black beetles and half a cockroach, all mixed together with slime from the local river.

The next day he went to see his patient and found him no better. "Oh dear," said the witch doctor. "Maybe you had better try a couple of aspirins."

—CHARISMA B. RAMOS

**A** guy spots his doctor in the mall. He stops him and says, "Six weeks ago when I was in your office, you told me to go home, get into bed and stay there until you called. But you never called."

"I didn't?" the doctor says. "Then what are you doing out of bed?"

—RON DENTINGER in the Dodgeville, Wis., *Chronicle*

**"The dentist will see you in a moment."**

**A**fter giving a woman a full medical examination, the doctor explained his prescription as he wrote it out. "Take the green pill with a glass of water when you get up. Take the blue pill with a glass of water after lunch. Then just before going to bed, take the red pill with another glass of water."

"Exactly what is my problem, Doctor?" the woman asked.

"You're not drinking enough water."

—*Quote*

"Doctor," the man said to his ophthalmologist, "I was looking in the mirror this morning, and I noticed that one of my eyes is different from the other!"

"Oh?" replied the doctor. "Which one?"

—Jerry H. Simpson Jr.


A man called his doctor's office for an appointment. "I'm sorry," said the receptionist, "we can't fit you in for at least two weeks."

"But I could be dead by then!"

"No problem. If your wife lets us know, we'll cancel the appointment."

—Ron Dentinger in the Dodgeville, Wis., *Chronicle*


The woman went to a dentist to have her false teeth adjusted for the fifth time. She said they still didn't fit. "Well," said the dentist, "I'll do it again this time, but no more. There's no reason why these shouldn't fit your mouth easily."

"Who said anything about my mouth?" the woman answered. "They don't fit in the glass!"

—*The Speaker's Handbook of Humor,*
edited by Maxwell Droke


The hospital patient was worried. "Are you sure it's pneumonia, Doctor?" he asked. "I've heard of cases where a doctor treated a patient for pneumonia, and he ended up dying of something else."

"Don't worry," said the doctor. "When I treat a patient for pneumonia, he dies of pneumonia."

—Winston K. Pendleton,
*Funny Stories, Jokes and Anecdotes*

# It's the Law!

The law professor was lecturing on courtroom procedure.

"When you are fighting a case and have the facts on your side, hammer away at the facts. If you have the law on your side, hammer away with the law."

"But what if you have neither the facts nor the law on your side?"

"In that case," said the professor, "hammer away on the table."

—*The Rotarian*

What possible excuse can you give for acquitting this defendant?" the judge shouted at the jury.

"Insanity, Your Honor," replied the foreman.

"All 12 of you?"

—Martha J. Beckman in *Modern Maturity*

You admit having broken into the dress shop four times?" asked the judge.

"Yes," answered the suspect.

"And what did you steal?"

"A dress, Your Honor," replied the suspect.

"One dress?" echoed the judge. "But you admit breaking in four times!"

"Yes, Your Honor," sighed the suspect. "But three times my wife didn't like the color."

—*The Jewish Press*

And did you hear about the lawyer who didn't like what the restaurant offered? He asked for a change of menu.

—Bill Nelson in the Milwaukee *Journal*

**"It's a deal, but just to be on the safe side let's have our lawyers look at this handshake."**

**A** young executive stomped into the elevator, obviously upset. "What's the matter?" asked a businessman standing there.

"Nepotism!" shouted the first man. "My boss just bypassed me and made his nephew office manager!"

"I see," the other said, handing over his business card. "If you need legal advice, please call me."

The young man glanced at the card: "O'Brien, O'Brien, O'Brien and O'Brien, Attorneys at Law."

—Norman F. Pihaly

The lawyer was cross-examining a witness. "Isn't it true," he bellowed, "that you were given $500 to throw this case?"

The witness did not answer. Instead, he just stared out the window as though he hadn't heard the question. The attorney repeated himself, again getting the same reaction—no response.

Finally, the judge spoke to the witness, "Please answer the question."

"Oh," said the startled witness, "I thought he was talking to you."

—*Sunshine* Magazine

A man visiting a graveyard saw a tombstone that read: "Here lies John Kelly, a lawyer and an honest man."

"How about that!" he exclaimed. "They've got three people buried in one grave."

—Louise Mayer in *Capper's*

Your Honor," began the defense attorney, "my client has been characterized as an incorrigible bank robber, without a single socially redeeming feature. I intend to disprove that."

"And how will you accomplish this?" the judge inquired.

"By proving beyond a shadow of a doubt," replied the lawyer, "that the note my client handed the teller was on recycled paper."

—R. C. Shebelski

Before a burglary trial, the judge explained to the defendant, "You can let me try your case, or you can choose to have a jury of your peers."

The man thought for a moment. "What are peers?" he asked.

"They're people just like you—your equals."

"Forget it," retorted the defendant. "I don't want to be tried by a bunch of thieves."

—Joey Adams

**"Your Honor, the relevance of this line of questioning
will become apparent in a moment."**

I'll need to see your license and registration," says the highway patrolman after stopping a middle-aged couple. "You were speeding."

"But, officer," says the husband, "I was way under the speed limit."

"Sir, you were doing 63 in a 55 zone."

"I was not speeding!" insists the man. "Your radar gun must be broken."

At this point, the wife leans over. "It's no use arguing with him, officer," she says apologetically. "He always gets this stubborn when he's been drinking."

—LISA MALLETTE

In darkest night, a policeman watches a staggering man trying in vain to unlock a door.

"Is this your home, after all?" the policeman asks.

"Sure, I'll prove it to you if you help me."

Inside, the man explains, "You see, this is my bedroom. And this is my wife."

"And who is the man next to her?" the policeman wants to know.

"That's me!"

—RENÉ GUYER

A junior partner in a law firm called his staff in for a meeting. "I have good news and bad news," he said, grinning. "Which do you want first?" The staff groaned, and agreed they'd better get the bad news first. "Okay," said the junior partner, "we are going to downsize. Half of you won't be here tomorrow. And the others may stay at a substantial reduction in salary."

The staff stood in horrified shock. Finally, one asked in a trembling voice, "What's the good news?"

The boss beamed. "I've been made a *full* partner!"

—*The Jokesmith*

# Shrink Rap

Hello, welcome to the Psychiatric Hotline.

"If you are obsessive-compulsive, please press 1 repeatedly.

"If you are co-dependent, please ask someone to press 2.

"If you have multiple personalities, please press 3, 4, 5 and 6.

"If you are paranoid-delusional, we know who you are and what you want. Just stay on the line until we can trace the call.

"If you are schizophrenic, listen carefully and a little voice will tell you which number to press.

"If you are manic-depressive, it doesn't matter which number you press. No one will answer."

—Jacquelyn Mayerhofer

The psychiatrist was interviewing a first-time patient. "You say you're here," he inquired, "because your family is worried about your taste in socks?"

"That's correct," muttered the patient. "I like wool socks."

"But that's perfectly normal," replied the doctor. "Many people prefer wool socks to those made from cotton or acrylic. In fact, I myself like wool socks."

"You DO?" exclaimed the man. "With oil and vinegar or just a squeeze of lemon?"

—Phyllis Thatcher

Psychiatrist: "Why can't you sleep at night?"
Patient: "Because I'm trying to solve all the world's problems."
Psychiatrist: "Ever get them solved?"
Patient: "Almost every time."
Psychiatrist: "Then why can't you sleep?"
Patient: "The ticker-tape parades they hold for me keep me awake."

—*Funny, Funny World*

*"Get me a psychiatrist, preferably one with military experience."*

**P**sychiatrist to patient: "You have nothing to worry about—anyone who can pay my bills is certainly not a failure."

—Lea Berner

**Q:** Why is psychoanalysis a lot quicker for men than for women?
A: When it's time to go back to their childhood, they're already there.

—Martha J. Kielek

**D**on't worry," a patient told his psychiatrist. "I'll pay every cent I owe or my name isn't Alexander the Great!"

—*The Return of the Good Clean Jokes*, compiled by Bob Phillips

**I**s it true that Natalie's son is seeing a psychiatrist?" a woman asked her friend.
"That's what I heard," she answered.
"So what's his problem?"
"The doctor says that what he has is a terrible Oedipus complex."
"Oedipus-schmoedipus—as long as he loves his mother."

—Leo Rosten, *Hooray for Yiddish*

**T**hree women started boasting about their sons. "What a birthday I had last year!" exclaimed the first. "My son, that wonderful boy, threw me a big party in a fancy restaurant. He even paid for plane tickets for my friends."
"That's very nice, but listen to this," said the second. "Last winter, my son gave me an all-expenses-paid cruise to the Greek islands. First class."
"That's nothing!" interrupted the third. "For five years now, my son has been paying a psychiatrist $150 an hour, three times a week. And the whole time he talks about nothing but me."

—*Current Comedy*

An unhappy man told his friend that he was seeing a psychiatrist about his marital problems. The shrink told him that his wife probably didn't mean the cruel things she was saying about him.

"My doctor said I have a persecution complex," the patient told his friend.

"Really? And what do you think?" the friend asked.

"That's what I expected he'd say," the man replied. "The guy hates me."

—Ron Dentinger in the Dodgeville, Wis., *Chronicle*

Jackson went to a psychiatrist. "Doc," he said, "I've got trouble. Every time I get into bed I think there's somebody under it. I get under the bed, I think there's somebody on top of it. Top, under, top, under. I'm goin' crazy!"

"Just put yourself in my hands for two years," said the shrink. "Come to me three times a week, and I'll cure you."

"How much do you charge?"

"A hundred dollars per visit."

"I'll think about it."

Jackson never went back. Six months later he met the doctor on the street. "Why didn't you ever come to see me again?" asked the psychiatrist.

"For a hundred bucks a visit? A bartender cured me for 10 dollars."

"Is that so! How?"

"He told me to cut the legs off the bed."

—Larry Wilde, *The Ultimate Jewish Joke Book*

John, having completed a course of analysis with his psychiatrist, to friend: "I always thought I was indecisive."

Friend: "And now?"

John: "I'm not so sure."

—Mrs. P. J. Wood

# Tricks of the Trades

**A**n inexperienced real-estate salesman asked his boss if he could refund the deposit to an angry customer who had discovered that the lot he had bought was under water.

"What kind of salesman are you?" the boss scolded. "Get out there and sell him a boat."

—FELIX TESARSKI

**T**he reading material at the barber shop consisted entirely of murder stories, mysteries, thrillers, and ghost tales.

When I asked the barber if he wanted to terrify his customers he replied, "No sir. These books make the customers' hair stand up and then it becomes easier to trim and cut."

—N. RAVI

After being laid off from five different jobs in four months, Arnold was hired by a warehouse. But one day he lost control of a forklift and drove it off the loading dock. Surveying the damage, the owner shook his head and said he'd have to withhold 10 percent of Arnold's wages to pay for the repairs. "How much will it cost?" asked Arnold.

"About $4,500," said the owner.

"What a relief!" exclaimed Arnold. "I've finally got job security!"

—DAVID E. SEES

Pete was telling a friend that he had just lost his job. "Why did the foreman fire you?" the friend asked in surprise.

"Oh," Pete said, "you know how foremen are. They stand around with their hands in their pockets watching everybody else work."

"We all know that," replied his friend. "But why did he let you go?"

"Jealousy," answered Pete. "All the other workers thought I was the foreman."

—*Sunshine* Magazine

A professor of English and the editor of the local newspaper had many friendly arguments. One Friday evening the professor was walking out of a local club with a bottle of whiskey wrapped in that day's newspaper.

"Oh!" said the editor, who was walking past. "Looks like there's something interesting in that paper."

"Aye," replied the professor. "It's the most interesting item that's been in it all week."

—ARTHUR FULLER

How's your new job at the factory?" one guy asked another.

"I'm not going back there."

"Why not?"

"For many reasons," he answered. "The sloppiness, the shoddy workmanship, the awful language—they just couldn't put up with it."

—MELL LAZARUS,
Creators Syndicate

A businessman was dining at a fancy restaurant and, so the story goes, met Lee Iacocca by the phone booth. "Mr. Iacocca," he gushed, "*the* American business hero! I've studied your career, and any success I've had comes from emulating you. Would you do me a favor? I'm with some colleagues. Please come by my table, say 'Hello, Harry,' and let me introduce you. It would mean so much to me."

Iacocca agreed. He waited for the man to sit down and then walked toward his table.

"Holy smoke!" cried one of Harry's friends. "It's Lee Iacocca, and he's heading this way!"

"Hello, Harry!" Iacocca said. "Introduce me to your friends."

Harry looked at him blankly. "Come back later, Lee," he said. "We're trying to have lunch."

—*The Jokesmith*

Approaching a passer-by, a street person asked, "Sir, would you give me a hundred dollars for a cup of coffee?"

"That's ridiculous!" the man replied.

"Just a yes or no, fella," the beggar growled. "I don't need a lecture about how to run my business."

—*Playboy*

I hear the boys are gonna strike," one worker told another.

"What for?" asked the friend.

"Shorter hours."

"Good for them. I always did think 60 minutes was too long for an hour."

—Tal D. Bonham, *The Treasury of Clean Country Jokes*

Bill attended a party where he met an old acquaintance. "Hello, Sam," he said. "How's your clothing business? I heard you lost a lot on that fall shipment of dresses."

"That's right," Sam responded.

"And you almost went bankrupt."

"That's true too."

"But I understand you made a big profit on another shipment and wound up having a pretty good season after all."

"That's correct. Then I guess you heard all about it, Bill."

"Yeah," Bill answered, "but this is the first time I'm hearing all the details."

—*Myron Cohen's Big Joke Book*

Three businessmen were having dinner at a club. When it came time to pay the check, each grabbed for it.

"It's a business expense," said one.

"I'll pay," said the second. "I'm on cost plus."

"Let me have it," argued the third. "I'm filing for bankruptcy next week."

—Joey Adams

*"I've stopped going out at night. Too dangerous."*

Ned took a job working alone in Canada's far frozen north. "Here's your emergency survival kit," said his boss. "It contains a box of flares, a radio, and a deck of cards."

"What are the cards for?" Ned asked.

"In case the flares don't work and the radio freezes up," replied the boss, "just take out the cards and play solitaire. In about 10 seconds someone will tap you on the shoulder and say, 'Put the red 9 on the black 10.' "

—Kevin Hilgers in *One to One*

Football player's wife: "I hate it when my husband calls leftovers 'replays.' "

TV executive's wife: "My husband calls them 'reruns.' "

Mortician's wife: "Be grateful. My husband refers to them as 'remains.' "

—Leslie Baranowsky

A very successful businessman had a meeting with his new son-in-law. "I love my daughter, and now I welcome you into the family," said the man. "To show you how much we care for you, I'm making you a 50-50 partner in my business. All you have to do is go to the factory every day and learn the operation."

The son-in-law interrupted. "I hate factories. I can't stand the noise."

"I see," replied the father-in-law. "Well, then you'll work in the office and take charge of some of the operations."

"I hate office work," said the son-in-law. "I can't stand being stuck behind a desk."

"Wait a minute," said the father-in-law. "I just made you half-owner of a money-making organization, but you don't like factories and won't work in an office. What am I going to do with you?"

"Easy," said the young man. "Buy me out."

—*Gene Perrett's Funny Business*

# The Armed Farces

During our basic army training, a sergeant was telling us how a submachine gun sprayed bullets. He drew a circle on a blackboard and announced that it had 260 degrees.

"But, sergeant, all circles have 360 degrees," someone called out.

"Don't be stupid," the sergeant roared. "This is a small circle."

—C. A. SUTTON

A tail gunner was being court-martialed. "What did you hear in your headset?" demanded a superior officer.

"Well," replied the airman, "I heard my squadron leader holler, 'Enemy planes at 5 o'clock!' "

"What action did you take?" persisted another officer.

"Why, sir," replied the gunner, "I just sat back and waited. It was only 4:30."

—JERRY LIEBERMAN, *3,500 Good Jokes for Speakers*

During a training exercise, an army unit was late for afternoon inspection. "Where are those camouflage trucks?" the irate colonel barked.

"They're here somewhere," replied the sergeant, "but we can't find 'em."

—L. DOWNING

What's the matter with you, lad?"

"Typhoid fever, Sergeant."

"That illness either kills you or leaves you an idiot. I know because I've had it!"

—ANA MARIA SANTOS

Through the pitch-black night, the captain sees a light dead ahead on a collision course with his ship. He sends a signal: "Change your course 10 degrees east."

The light signals back: "Change yours, 10 degrees west."

Angry, the captain sends: "I'm a navy captain! Change your course, sir!"

"I'm a seaman, second class," comes the reply. "Change your course, sir."

Now the captain is furious. "I'm a battleship! I'm not changing course!"

There's one last reply. "I'm a lighthouse. Your call."

—Dan Bell

A sergeant put this problem to a recruit: "Suppose it's wartime. You're walking in the woods, and you suddenly come up against 10 of the enemy. What would you do?"

After a moment's silence the recruit's face brightened, and he replied, "Surround them, Sergeant."

—E. Meutstege

While conducting a routine inspection, the colonel arrived at the mess hall door where he met two KPs with a large soup kettle.

"Let me taste that," the colonel snapped.

One of the men fetched a big spoon and handed it respectfully to the CO, who plunged the ladle into the pot and took a large mouthful of the steaming liquid, smacking his lips critically.

Then he let out a roar that could be heard back at headquarters. "Do you call that soup?" he bellowed.

"No, sir," explained one of the KPs. "It's dishwater we were just throwing out."

—James Mutch

Top brass from the Army, Navy, and Marine Corps were arguing about who had the bravest troops. They decided to settle the dispute using an enlisted man from each branch.

The army general called a private over and ordered him to climb to the top of the base flagpole while singing "The Caissons Go Rolling Along," then let go with both hands, and salute. The private quickly complied.

Next, the admiral ordered a sailor to climb the pole, polish the brass knob at the top, sing "Anchors Aweigh," salute smartly, and jump off. The sailor did as he was told and landed on the concrete below.

Finally the marine was told to do exactly as the army and navy men had done, but in full battle gear, pack filled with bricks, loaded weapon carried high. He took one look at the marine general and said, "You're out of your mind, sir!"

The marine commander turned to the others. "Now *that's* guts!"

—RICHARD BECTON


One hazard of wartime training in England was that road signs were removed when invasion seemed imminent. A cartoon in an English newspaper during the invasion scare of 1940 pictured two German paratroopers scanning a map at a railway station. Over their heads was the one remaining sign: Gentlemen.

"I can't find this place on the map," says one to the other.

—STROME GALLOWAY in *Legion*


It happened that the platoon leader forgot the expression "Mark time." Without losing his composure, he faced his platoon and shouted, "Ten-shut! Pretend to go but don't; pretend to go but don't; pretend to go but don't . . . ."

—SYLVIA MENDES DE ABREU

*"You're lucky. You never have to worry about having a bad clothes day."*

During a simulated attack, the troops have to defend themselves against an imaginary enemy, as the sergeant calls it. Bawling out orders, he notices that one recruit shows little response.

"You there," the sergeant shouts, "the imaginary enemy is advancing, and you're caught in the crossfire. Action!"

The recruit takes two steps to one side.

"What are you doing, man?" yells the sergeant, purple with fury.

"I'm taking shelter behind an imaginary tree, Sergeant," answers the recruit calmly.

—MICHEL VAN KERCKHOVEN

# Office Antics

**O**ne winter morning, an employee explained why he had shown up for work 45 minutes late. "It was so slippery out that for every step I took ahead, I slipped back two."

The boss eyed him suspiciously. "Oh, yeah? Then how did you ever get here?"

"I finally gave up," he said, "and started for home."

—ERIC WIGHT

**S**ay, Bill," a man said to his pal, "how do you like your new job?"

"It's the worst job I ever had."

"How long have you been there?"

"About three months."

"Why don't you quit?"

"No way. This is the first time in 20 years that I've looked forward to going home."

—JIM YOUNG

**E**mployee: "The stress my boss puts me under is killing me. I have migraines, my blood pressure is going through the roof, I can't sleep at night, I just found out I have an ulcer, and as long as I stay in this job, the only question is whether I'll have a stroke or a heart attack."

Friend: "So why don't you quit?"

Employee: "I have a great health plan."

—RICHARD JEROME in *The Sciences*

**A** lot of people complain about their dumb boss," says Joey Adams. "What they don't realize is that they'd be out of a job if their dumb boss were any smarter."

MANKOFF

*"Miss Bremmer, get me whatever coast I'm not on."*

**D**exter had just returned from two weeks of vacation. He asked his boss for two more weeks off to get married.

"What!" shouted the boss. "I can't give you more time now. Why didn't you get married while you were off?"

"Are you nuts?" replied Dexter. "That would have ruined my entire vacation!"

—H. B. McClung

**S**ign on company bulletin board: "This firm requires no physical-fitness program. Everyone gets enough exercise jumping to conclusions, flying off the handle, running down the boss, flogging dead horses, knifing friends in the back, dodging responsibility, and pushing their luck."

*—Financial Times*

**T**he stenographer who had worked for nine years in our firm got a job elsewhere and approached the personnel officer for a certificate of experience.

"Make it out for 10 years," the steno suggested.

"But you've worked for only nine years," the personnel officer pointed out.

"But, sir," replied the steno, "what about my overtime?"

—P. R. Mohanan

**O**ne payday, an employee received an unusually large check. She decided not to say anything about it. The following week, her check was for less than the normal amount, and she confronted her boss.

"How come," the supervisor inquired, "you didn't say anything when you were overpaid?"

Unruffled, the employee replied, "Well, I can overlook one mistake—but not two in a row!"

*—Farmers Independent*

**T**he owner of a big electronics firm called in his personnel director. "My son will be graduating from college soon and needing a job. He's going to be your new assistant, but he's *not* to be shown any favoritism. Treat him just as you would any other son of mine."

—Quoted in *The Rotarian*

# Gag-riculture

**A** cowboy applied for an insurance policy. "Have you ever had any accidents?" asked the agent.

"Nope," said the cowboy, "though a bronc did kick in two of my ribs last year, and a couple of years ago a rattlesnake bit my ankle."

"Wouldn't you call those accidents?" replied the puzzled agent.

"Naw," the cowboy said, "they did it on purpose."

—*Our Daily Bread*

**B**ecause of the shortage of jobs in town, a boy appeared for work on a farm. The foreman decided to give him a try and told him to milk a cow, equipping him with a stool and a bucket.

An hour later the boy returned dirty and sweaty, the bucket in one hand and the broken stool in the other.

"Extracting the milk was easy," he explained. "The worst part was getting the cow to sit on the stool!"

—Miguel José de Oliveria Neto

**W**illie and Ray, a couple of farmers, met at the town hardware store on Saturday. "Had some problems with my herd," lamented Willie. "My prize bull was impotent. But the vet came and gave him some special medicine, and now he seems to be doing fine."

The next week, Ray met Willie again. "My bull's had problems too," said Ray. "What was that medicine the vet prescribed?"

"I don't know," answered Willie. "But it tastes like chocolate."

—William L. Heartwell, Jr.

**V**an der Merwe was carrying a box when he met his friend. "Guess how many chickens I have in this box and I'll give you both of them," he said.

—*Personality*, Durban

"You want a sign that reads 'The world ends tomorrow' . . .
when do you have to have it?"

# Religion

## IN GOOD SPIRITS 68

## COLLARED 72

## YOU SHOULD DIE LAUGHING 76

# In Good Spirits

When Adam came home in the small hours of the morning, Eve was jealous. "But in all of creation," Adam reasoned, "there's no one but you and me." Mollified, Eve snuggled up to him. Still, when he fell asleep, she very carefully counted his ribs.

—BILL SROKA

I used to practice meditation on an old mat. My wife was not happy about the worn-out mat.

One day I found the rug missing from its usual place.

"Where is it?" I asked her sternly.

"It has achieved nirvana," she retorted.

—ANIL BHARTI

A Christian in ancient Rome was being pursued by a lion. He ran through the city streets and into the woods, dodging back and forth among the trees. Finally it became obvious that it was hopeless—the lion was going to catch him. So he turned suddenly, faced the beast and dropped to his knees. "Lord," he prayed desperately, "make this lion a Christian."

Instantly the lion dropped to its knees and prayed, "For this meal of which I am about to partake. . . ."

—VAUNA J. ARMSTRONG

My mother always told me God hears every prayer," says comedian Mary Armstrong. "If I'd pray really hard for something and nothing happened, she would say, 'Sometimes God's answer is no.' But what if God just doesn't answer right away? You could be 42, your needs will have changed, and all of a sudden you look out at your front yard one morning and there's a Shetland pony!"

An impassioned minister was visiting a country church and began his address with a stirring reminder: "Everybody in this parish is going to die."

The evangelist was discomfited to notice a man in the front pew who was smiling broadly. "Why are you so amused?" he asked.

"I'm not in this parish," replied the man. "I'm just visiting my sister for the weekend."

—ROGER DELAHUNTY

Sol strictly observed Jewish dietary laws. But one day he went to a restaurant by himself and noticed roast pig on the menu. *Just once, I'd like to try it*, he thought, and placed his order.

The pig was brought to his table with an apple in its mouth. Just then, Sol looked up, and there was a member of his synagogue staring at him. "So I ordered a baked apple," said Sol innocently. "Who knew how they'd serve it?"

—RUTH SCHWARTZ

A Texan traveled to England on vacation. While there, he attended a religious service and was amazed at how quiet and reserved it was. Not one word was spoken out of turn. All of a sudden he heard the minister say something he really liked. "Amen!" he shouted. Everyone in the church turned and stared, and the usher came running down the aisle.

"You must not talk out loud," admonished the usher.

"But," protested the Texan, "I've got religion!"

"Well," said the usher, "you did not get it here."

—DOROTHY STARLING

Did you hear about the insomniac dyslexic agnostic? He stayed up all night wondering if there really was a dog.

—DANIEL J. KLAIMAN

A preacher was asked to give a talk at a women's health symposium. His wife asked about his topic, but he was too embarrassed to admit that he had been asked to speak about sex. Thinking quickly, he replied, "I'm talking about sailing."

"Oh, that's nice," said his wife.

The next day, at the grocery store, a young woman who had attended the lecture recognized the minister's wife. "That was certainly an excellent talk your husband gave yesterday," she said. "He really has a unique perspective on the subject." Somewhat surprised, the minister's wife replied, "Gee, funny you should think so. I mean, he's only done it twice. The first time he threw up, and the second time, his hat blew off."

—D. E. Norling

A small town's only barber was known for his arrogant, negative attitude. When one of his customers mentioned he'd be going to Rome on vacation and hoped to meet the pope, the barber's reaction was typical. "You?" he said. "Meet the pope? Don't make me laugh! The pope sees kings and presidents. What would he want with you?"

A month later, the man returned for another haircut. "How was Rome?" asked the barber.

"Great! I saw the pope!"

"From St. Peter's Square, I suppose, with the rest of the crowd," said the barber.

"Yes, but then two guards came up, said the pope wanted to meet me, and took me right into his private apartment in the Vatican."

"Really?" the barber asked. "What did he say?"

"He said, 'Who gave you that lousy haircut?' "

—Quoted in Chelmsford, Mass.,
*All Saints Church Newsletter*

"My dad says Mom is a pagan because she serves
burnt offerings for dinner."

Two fellows, Murphy and Clancy, were walking past the church when Murphy said, "I haven't been to confession for a while. I believe I'll go in and get absolution." Murphy went into the confessional and acknowledged having his way with a lady.

"I know you by your voice, Murphy, and this is not the first time this has happened," said the priest. "I want to know the lady's name."

"It's not proper you should ask, and I'll not be telling you!"

"If you want absolution, you'll be telling me. Was it O'Reilly's sister?" Murphy refused to answer. "I'll ask again. Was it the widow Harrington?" Again, Murphy wouldn't reply. "One more time I'll ask: was it the Flanagan girl?"

"For the third time, I'll not be telling you!" said Murphy.

"Then you'll get no absolution from me. Out with you!"

His friend Clancy was waiting. "Well, did you get absolution?"

"No," said Murphy with a smile. "But I got three good leads!"

—WEBB CASTOR

God: "Whew! I just created a 24-hour period of alternating light and darkness on Earth."

Angel: "What are you going to do now?"

God: "Call it a day."

—DAVE COVERLY, Creators Syndicate

## Collared

At a wedding reception, a priest and a rabbi met at the buffet table. "Go ahead," said the priest, "try one of these delicious ham sandwiches. Overlooking your divine rule just this once won't do you any harm."

"That I will do, dear sir," the rabbi replied, "on the day of your wedding!"

—KIM DUBOIS

The newly appointed priest was being briefed by the housekeeper on problems in the rectory that required immediate attention.

"Your roof needs repair, Father," she said. "Your water pressure is bad and your furnace is not working."

"Now, Mrs. Kelly," the priest allowed, "you've been the housekeeper here five years, and I've only been here a few days. Why not say *our* roof and *our* furnace?"

Several weeks later, when the pastor was meeting with the bishop and several other priests, Mrs. Kelly burst into the office terribly upset. "Father, Father," she blurted, "there's a mouse in our room and it's under our bed!"

—Doris Cypher

And did you hear about the bishop who hired a secretary who had worked for the Pentagon? She immediately changed his filing system to "Sacred" and "Top Sacred."

—Ira N. Briggs

The young couple invited their parson for Sunday dinner. While they were in the kitchen preparing the meal, the minister asked their son what they were having. "Goat," the little boy replied.

"Goat?" replied the startled man of the cloth. "Are you sure about that?"

"Yep," said the youngster. "I heard Pa say to Ma, 'Might as well have the old goat for dinner today as any other day.'"

—Pamela D. McManus

In a booming voice, a cantor bragged to his congregation, "Two years ago, I insured my voice with Lloyd's of London for $750,000."

The crowded room was hushed. Suddenly, an elderly woman spoke. "So," she said, "what did you do with the money?"

—Joseph Telushkin, *Jewish Humor*

*"Your sermon helped me understand my soaps better."*

A young vicar about to deliver his first sermon asked the advice of a retired minister on how to capture the congregation's attention.

"Start with an opening line that's certain to grab them," the cleric told him. "For example: Some of the best years of my life were spent in the arms of a woman."

He smiled at the young vicar's shocked look before adding, "She was my mother."

The next Sunday the vicar nervously clutched the pulpit rail before the congregation and stated, "Some of the best years of my life were spent in the arms of a woman."

He was pleased at the instant reaction—then panic-stricken. "But for the life of me, I can't remember who she was!"

—GIL HARRIS

A pastor was preaching an impassioned sermon on the evils of television. "It steals away precious time that could be better spent on other things," he said, advising the congregation to do what he and his family had done. "We put our TV away in the closet."

"That's right," his wife mumbled, "and it gets awfully crowded in there."

—SHERRI DORMER

The minister was sick, and a pastor noted for his never-ending sermons agreed to fill in. When he stood up in the pulpit, he was annoyed to find only 10 worshipers present, including the choir. Afterward he complained to the sexton. "That was a very small turnout," he said. "Weren't they informed that I was coming?" "No," replied the sexton, "but word must have leaked out!"

—*Sunday Post*

The minister selected a 50-cent item at a convenience store but then discovered he didn't have any money with him.

"I could invite you to hear me preach in return," he said jokingly to the clerk, "but I'm afraid I don't have any 50-cent sermons."

"Perhaps," suggested the clerk, "I could come twice."

—GEORGE DOLAN in
Fort Worth *Star-Telegram*

While other people go to church every Sunday morning, Charles, a farmer, likes to sit in the village restaurant drinking wine.

One day the priest said to him, "Charles, I'm afraid we shall not see each other in heaven."

A worried Charles replied, "But, Father, what on earth have you done?"

—AIDA C. FUDOT

A preacher's new car broke down just after his Sunday service. Monday morning he managed to drive the vehicle to the town's one garage for repairs. "I hope you'll go easy on the cost," he told the mechanic. "After all, I'm just a poor preacher."

"I know," came the reply. "I heard you preach yesterday."

—*Lutheran Digest*

Unbeknown to most of the congregation, the new minister enjoyed an occasional bottle of wine. One church member, aware of this, presented the clergyman with a bottle of Bordeaux. But the gift had a string attached. The minister would have to say thank you from the pulpit.

At the conclusion of the next service, the minister made the announcements, then said, "And I want to thank my friend for giving the fine fruit, and for the spirit in which it was given."

—R. L. FINDLEY

A guru who claimed he survived on air started a cult. When some skeptics caught him munching a hamburger and french fries, the pseudo-psychic said, "You can't call this food."

—MARK PLUMMER in *The Indian Post*

# You Should Die Laughing

Surprised to see an empty seat at the Super Bowl, a diehard fan remarked about it to a woman sitting nearby.

"It was my husband's," the woman explained, "but he died."

"I'm very sorry," said the man. "Yet I'm really surprised that another relative, or friend, didn't jump at the chance to take the seat reserved for him."

"Beats me," she said. "They all insisted on going to the funeral."

—*Coffee Break*

**"Remember me? Bangor, Maine. Moose season, 1971."**

**A** young couple had a fatal car accident on the way to their wedding. When they met St. Peter at the Pearly Gates, they asked if it was possible for them to marry in heaven. He said he would make some inquiries and get back to them.

A year later, St. Peter found the couple and told them they could get married. "Could we get a divorce if it doesn't work out?" they wanted to know.

"Good grief!" St. Peter exclaimed. "It took me a whole year to find a preacher up here—and now you want me to find a lawyer."

—DEE MCDONALD

An attorney died and went to heaven. As he approached the Pearly Gates, he noticed an orchestra playing and thousands of angels cheering. St. Peter himself rushed over to shake the lawyer's hand. "This is quite a reception," marveled the new arrival.

"You're very special," St. Peter explained. "We've never had anyone live to be 130 before."

The attorney was puzzled. "But I'm only 65."

St. Peter thought for a moment. "Oh," he said, "we must have added up your billing hours."

—DAVID MICUS

When her late husband's will was read, a widow learned he had left the bulk of his fortune to another woman. Enraged, she rushed to change the inscription on her spouse's tombstone.

"Sorry, lady," said the stonecutter. "I inscribed 'Rest in Peace' on your orders. I can't change it now."

"Very well," she said grimly. "Just add 'Until We Meet Again.'"

—ROBERT E. CANTELL

Two ministers died and went to heaven. St. Peter greeted them and said, "Your condos aren't ready yet. Until they're finished, you can return to earth as anything you want."

"Fine," said the first minister. "I've always wanted to be an eagle soaring over the Grand Canyon."

"And I'd like to be a real cool stud," said the second.

Poof! Their wishes were granted.

When the condos were finished St. Peter asked an assistant to bring back the two ministers. "How will I find them?" the man said.

"One is soaring over the Grand Canyon," St. Peter replied. "The other may be tough to locate. He's somewhere in Detroit—on a snow tire."

—DONNA S. TIPTON

After a preacher died and went to heaven, he noticed that a New York cabdriver had been given a higher place than he had. "I don't understand," he complained to St. Peter. "I devoted my entire life to my congregation."

"Our policy is to reward results," explained St. Peter. "Now what happened, Reverend, whenever you gave a sermon?"

The minister admitted that some in the congregation fell asleep.

"Exactly," said St. Peter. "And when people rode in this man's taxi, they not only stayed awake, they *prayed*."

—Quoted by RAYMOND A. HEIT

Two guys, Jimmy and Johnny, were standing at heaven's gate, waiting to be interviewed by St. Peter.

Jimmy: "How did you get here?"

Johnny: "Hypothermia. You?"

Jimmy: "You won't believe it. I was sure my wife was cheating on me, so I came home early one day hoping to find the guy. I accused my wife of unfaithfulness and searched the whole house without any luck. Then I felt so bad about the whole thing I had a massive heart attack."

Johnny: "Oh, man, if you had checked the walk-in freezer, we'd both be alive."

—FAIZ RAHMAN

A man asked an acquaintance how his wife was; then, suddenly remembering that she had died, he blurted out, "Still in the same cemetery?"

—MAURO BORBA COLLETES ALVES

"They say when you die you see a bright light at the end of a tunnel," notes comedian Ed Marques. "I think my father will see the light, then flip it off to save electricity."

—*Comic Strip Live*, FOX TV

**A** gold miner died and went to heaven. At the gate, St. Peter asked, "What have you done in your life?"

When the man gave his occupation, St. Peter explained that there was already a surplus of miners in heaven. "May I stay if I get rid of the others?" the fellow inquired.

St. Peter agreed. Once in, the miner wandered around until he saw a couple of familiar faces. He whispered that there was a gold strike in hell. Soon, the place was empty of miners.

But a while later, the miner asked St. Peter for permission to leave. "Even if I did start the rumor," he said, "there just might be something to it!"

—*Modern Gold Miner & Treasure Hunter*

**T**he day after Mrs. Zelkin's funeral, the rabbi dropped in to console the widower. To his astonishment he saw the bereaved on the sofa kissing a dazzling redhead.

"Zelkin!" roared the rabbi. "Your beloved wife is not even cold in her grave, and already you're—"

Mr. Zelkin cried, "In my grief, should I know what I'm doing?"

—Leo Rosten, *Hooray for Yiddish!*

**N**inety-year-old Sam bought a hairpiece, had a face lift and worked out at the gym for six months. Then he found a widow half his age to take to dinner. As they got out of his sports car, Sam was struck by lightning and died. At the Gate of Heaven, he ran up to God and asked, "Why me?"

"Oh, Sam," replied God. "I didn't recognize you!"

—Nancy Harrison

**O**verheard: "My greatest fear is that I will be standing behind Mother Teresa in the Final Judgment line and I'll hear God tell her, 'You know, you should have done more.' "

—*The Jokesmith*

**"Sorry, bub. You're not in the database."**

A Texas oilman died and went to heaven. After a few days, his bragging was getting on St. Peter's nerves. No matter what part of paradise he was shown, the oilman claimed it failed to measure up to Texas. Finally St. Peter took him to the edge of heaven so he could look straight into hell. "Have you got anything like that in Texas?" the saint demanded.

"No," the oilman replied. "But I know some ol' boys down in Houston who can put it out."

—Dana Conner

St. Peter halted a man at the entrance to heaven. "You've told too many lies to be permitted in here," he said.

"Have a heart," replied the man. "Remember, you were once a fisherman yourself."

—HAROLD HELFER in *Catholic Digest*

An angel appears at a faculty meeting and tells the dean that in return for his unselfish and exemplary behavior, the Lord will reward him with his choice of infinite wealth, wisdom, or beauty. Without hesitating, the dean selects infinite wisdom.

"Done!" says the angel, and disappears in a cloud of smoke and a bolt of lightning. Now, all heads turn toward the dean, who sits surrounded by a faint halo of light. At length, one of his colleagues whispers, "Say something."

The dean sighs and says, "I should have taken the money."

—BETSY DEVINE and JOEL E. COHEN,
*Absolute Zero Gravity*

Three men died and went to heaven. Upon their arrival, St. Peter asked the first if he had been faithful to his wife. The man admitted to two affairs during his marriage. St. Peter told him that he could receive only a compact car to drive in heaven.

Then St. Peter asked the second man if he had been faithful to his wife, and the man admitted to one affair. St. Peter told him he would be given a midsize car to drive.

The third man was asked about his faithfulness, and he told St. Peter he had been true to his wife until the day he died. St. Peter praised him and gave him a luxury car.

A week later the three men were driving around, and they all stopped at a red light. The men in the compact and midsize cars turned to see the man in the luxury car crying. They asked him what could possibly be the matter—after all, he was driving a luxury car.

"I just passed my wife," he told them. "She was on a skateboard."

—BOBI GORIA

*"That's it? 'Keep my head down?'"*

# Sports

# Fast Pitches

The national pastime of Tahiti is making love," says Bob Hope. "But we, silly fools, picked baseball."

After the rookie pitcher walked a third straight batter, the manager strolled to the mound. "Son," he told the southpaw, "I think you've had enough."

"But look who's coming to bat," whined the rookie. "I struck this guy out the last time he was up."

"Yeah, I know," said the manager. "But this is still the same inning."

—*Sunshine* Magazine

During a baseball game, a woman kept shouting threats at the umpire. No matter what happened on the field, she continually yelled, "Kill the umpire!" This went on for an hour. "Lady," another fan called out, "the umpire hasn't done anything wrong."

"He's my husband," she replied. "Last night he came home with lipstick on his collar. Kill the umpire!"

—*Milton Berle's Private Joke File*

Robert Orben says: "My wife claims I'm a baseball fanatic. She says all I ever read about is baseball. All I ever talk about is baseball. All I ever think about is baseball. I told her she's way off base."

Pitchers say the split-finger fastball is like sex," writes George Will. "When it's good, it's terrific, and when it's bad, it's still pretty good."

—*Men at Work*

"My man called for a fastball and your man threw a slider."

A rookie pitcher was struggling at the mound, so the catcher walked up to have a talk with him. "I've figured out your problem," he told the young southpaw. "You always lose control at the same point in every game."

"When is that?"

"Right after the national anthem."

—JEFF MACNELLY, Tribune Media Services

I have to cut down on hot dogs and beer," one bleacher bum said to another.

"Why's that?"

"Can't you see? I'm starting to get a ballpark figure."

—*The American Legion Magazine*

The morning of a New York Mets game, a fan went to see if his tickets were still on the dashboard of his car. But he discovered that the windshield was smashed.

"Someone broke in and took our tickets?" asked his wife.

"Worse than that," the man replied. "Someone left four more."

—Quoted by JAMES DENT in the Charleston, W.Va., *Gazette*

Carl and Abe are two old baseball fanatics. They agree that whoever dies first will try to come back and tell the other one if there's baseball in heaven.

One evening Abe passes away in his sleep. A few nights later Carl hears what sounds like Abe's voice. "Abe, is that you?" he asks.

"Of course it's me," Abe replies.

"I can't believe it," Carl whispers. "So tell me, is there baseball in heaven?"

"Well, I have good news and bad news," Abe says. "The good news is, yes, there's baseball in heaven. The bad news is you're pitching tomorrow night."

—DAVID DANGLER

*"I don't know, 'fore' hardly seems adequate."*

# Chasing the Little White Ball

Jock and Angus, two craggy Scots, were sitting before the clubhouse fireplace after 18 holes on a raw, blustery day. The ice slowly melted from their beards and collected in puddles under their chairs. Outside, the wind howled off the North Sea and hail rattled against the windows.

The pair sat in silence over their whiskies. Finally Jock spoke: "Next Tuesday, same time?"

"Aye," Angus replied, "weather permittin'."

—MALCOLM MCNAIR in *Golf Illustrated*

**A**re you my caddie?" asked the golfer.

"Yes, sir," replied the boy.

"And are you any good at finding lost balls?"

"Yes, sir."

"Right, then. Find one and let's start the game."

—STAN SAACKS

**T**hree senior golfers were griping continually. "The fairways are too long," said one. "The hills are too high," said another. "The bunkers are too deep," complained the third.

Finally an 80-year-old put things into perspective. "At least," he noted, "we're on the right side of the grass."

—HAROLD L. WEAVER

**W**hen the legendary salesman was asked his secrets of success, he gave a humble shrug. "I'm sure you all know the cardinal rules: know your product; make lots of calls; never take no for an answer. But, honestly, I owe my success to consistently missing a three-foot putt by two inches."

—ASHTON APPLEWHITE, WILLIAM R. EVANS III, and ANDREW FROTHINGHAM, *And I Quote*

**Y**ou can always spot an employee who's playing golf with his boss. He's the fellow who gets a hole in one and says, "Oops!"

—BOB MONKHOUSE, *Just Say a Few Words*

**D**id you hear about the politically correct country club? They no longer refer to their golfers as having handicaps. Instead they're "stroke challenged."

—*Comedy on Call*

Husband to wife: "You're always nagging me about my golf. It's driving me mad."

Wife: "It wouldn't be a drive—just a short putt."

—Harry Leech

A married couple, both avid golfers, were discussing the future one night. "Honey," the wife said, "if I were to die and you were to remarry, would you two live in this house?"

"I suppose so—it's paid for."

"How about our car?" continued the woman. "Would the two of you keep that?"

"I suppose so—it's paid for."

"What about my golf clubs? Would you let her use them too?"

"Heck, no," the husband blurted out. "She's left-handed."

—Don Criqui on Imus in the Morning, WFAN, New York

A man played golf every Saturday and always got home around 2:00 in the afternoon. One Saturday, however, he rushed in at 7:30 pm and blurted to his wife, "I left the course at the normal time, but on the way home I stopped to change a flat tire for a young woman. She offered to buy me a drink, one thing led to another, and we spent the entire afternoon in a motel. I'm so sorry. I'll never do it again."

"Don't hand me that malarkey," the angry wife shouted. "You played 36 holes, didn't you?"

—George W. Edwards

Did you hear about Fred trying to drown himself in the water hazard on the tenth hole?" a weekend golfer asked his partner.

"No kidding!" said the other duffer. "What happened?"

"Nothing, really. He couldn't keep his head down there either."

—Quoted by Ed Baer on The Ed Baer Affair,<br>WHUD, Peekskill, N.Y.

Two male golfers were held up by two women players ahead, so one went forward to ask if they could play through.

He returned, looking embarrassed, and explained, "I couldn't speak to them—one is my wife, and the other is my mistress."

His partner then went forward, only to return muttering, "What an extraordinary coincidence!"

—L. D. TURNER

Marooned on a South Seas island, a man with a beard down to his knees is walking on the beach. Suddenly a beautiful woman emerges from the surf.

"Been here long?" she asks.

"Since 1981," he replies.

"How long has it been since you've had a cigarette?"

"Eleven years."

She unzips a pocket in the sleeve of her wet suit, pulls out a pack of Camels, lights one, and hands it to him. He inhales greedily. "How long since you've had a drink of whiskey?"

"Eleven years."

She unzips the other sleeve and offers him a flask. He takes a long pull and looks at her adoringly.

"How long," she asks coyly, "since you played around?"

"Eleven years," he says wistfully.

She starts to unzip the front of her wet suit. "Gosh," he says, "you got a set of golf clubs in there?"

—NED PARKER, quoted by ALEX THIEN
in the Milwaukee *Sentinel*

What's your handicap these days?" one golfer asked another.

"I'm a scratch golfer. . . . I write down all my good scores and scratch out all my bad ones."

—CHARLES SCHULZ, United Features Syndicate

**"I told you this was rough hole!"**

Mack the Slice, a notorious duffer, unwound on the first tee and sent a high drive far to the right. The ball sailed through an open window. Figuring that was the end of it, Mack played on.

On the eighth hole, a police officer walked up to Mack and asked, "Did you hit a ball through that window?"

"Yes, I did."

"Well, it knocked a lamp over, scaring the dog, which raced out of the house onto the highway. A driver rammed into a brick wall to avoid the dog, sending three people to the hospital. And all because you sliced the ball."

"I'm so sorry," moaned Mack. "Is there anything I can do?"

"Well," the cop replied, "try keeping your head down and close up your stance a bit."

—BILL MAJESKI in *Catholic Digest*

Golfer: "What's your handicap?"
Second golfer: "Honesty."

—*Executive Speechwriter Newsletter*

The minister was on the golf course when he heard a duffer, deep in a sand trap, let loose a stream of profanity. "I have often noticed," chided the minister, "that the best golfers are not addicted to the use of foul language."

"Of course not," screamed the man. "What do they have to swear about?"

—*Contact*

She: "How'd your doctor appointment go?"
He: "Well, there's good news and bad news. My blood pressure's high and I'm overweight. But, at the doctor's suggestion, I'm going to take up golf!"
She: "And the good news?"

—GREG EVANS, North American Syndicate

First golfer: "I have the greatest golf ball in the world. You can't lose it."

Second golfer: "How so?"

First golfer: "If you hit it into the sand, it beeps. You hit it into the water, it floats. If you want to play golf at night, it glows."

Second golfer: "Hey, sounds good. Where did you get it?"

First golfer: "Found it in the woods."

—BYRON SMIALEK in the
Washington, Pa., *Observer-Reporter*

Honey, I have a confession to make," a guy told his bride. "I'm a golf nut. You'll never see me on weekends during golf season."

"Well, dear," she murmured. "I have a confession to make too. I'm a hooker."

"No big deal," replied the groom. "Just keep your head down and your left arm straight."

—JAY TRACHMAN in *One to One*

# Fish Tales and Hunting Licenses

Question: What's the difference between a hunter and a fisherman?
Answer: A hunter lies in wait while a fisherman waits and lies.

—*One to One*

A fisherman accidentally left his day's catch under the seat of a bus. The next evening's newspaper carried an ad: "If the person who left a bucket of fish on the No. 47 bus would care to come to the garage, he can have the bus."

—Sri Lanka *Sunday Island*

*"Your father, may he rest in peace, was
considered quite a catch."*

**S**imon was an inveterate fisherman, well known for exaggerating the size of "the one that got away." But there came a day when he actually caught two enormous flounders. He immediately invited a few friends over to dine, then tried to figure out how best to serve the fish. "If I use both," he told his wife, "it will seem ostentatious."

"Why not serve a piece of each?" she suggested.

"No, if I cut them up, nobody will believe I caught two giant flounders." Simon racked his brain. Then he had an idea.

The guests were seated at the table when their host strode in with a platter, holding the biggest flounder they'd ever seen. Suddenly Simon stumbled and fell. Everyone cried out in dismay as the fish crashed to the floor, but Simon quickly brushed himself off.

"Dear," he called out to his wife, "bring in the other flounder!"

—HENRY D. SPALDING, *Jewish Laffs*

An optimist who went hunting with a pessimist wanted to show off his new dog. After the first shot, he sent his dog to fetch a duck. The dog ran across the top of the water and brought back the game. The pessimist said nothing. The dog retrieved the second and third ducks the same way—over the water. Still the pessimist did not react. Finally, the optimist could stand it no longer. "Don't you see anything unusual about my new dog?" he asked his companion.

"Yes—he can't swim."

—BOB PHILLIPS quoted by MARTHA BOLTON,
*"If Mr. Clean Calls, Tell Him I'm Not In!"*

Two would-be fishermen rented a boat, and one caught a large fish. "We should mark the spot," he said. The other man drew a large X in the bottom of the boat with a black marker.

"That's no good," said the first man. "Next time out we may not get the same boat."

—FLORENCE KILLAM

A hunting party was hopelessly lost. "I thought you said you were the best guide in Maine!" one of the hunters angrily said to their confused leader.

"I am," replied the guide. "But I think we're in Canada now."

—*Reminisce*

A New South Wales fisherman lost his dentures over the side of the boat in rough weather, so his prankster friend removed his own false teeth, tied them on his line and pretended he had caught the missing gnashers.

Unhooking the teeth, his grateful mate tried to put them into his mouth, then hurled them into the sea with the disgusted remark: "They're not mine—they don't fit!"

—"Column 8,"
*The Sydney Morning Herald*

Two Texans went up to Minnesota to go ice fishing. After setting up their tent, they started to cut a hole in the ice. As they pulled the cord on their chain saw, they heard a voice from above: "There are no fish under the ice."

When they pulled the cord again, the same voice intoned: "There are no fish under the ice."

"Is that you, God?" they asked in awe.

"No," came the reply. "I own this ice rink—and I can tell you that there are no fish under the ice."

—N. E. DUNNUCK

While hunting, Larry and Elmer got lost in the woods. Trying to reassure his friend, Larry said, "Don't worry. All we have to do is shoot into the air three times, stay where we are, and someone will find us."

They shot in the air three times, but no one came. After a while, they tried it again. Still no response. When they decided to try once more, Elmer said, "It better work this time. We're down to our last three arrows."

—ELIZABETH CLARK

The tale is told of Boudreaux, out on the bayou, fishing by dropping sticks of dynamite over the side, waiting for the "boom" and scooping the fish out with a net. After he'd done this four or five times, the game warden came out and said, "Boudreaux, you know you ain't s'posed to be fishin' that way."

Boudreaux paid him no mind. Lighting up another stick of dynamite, he handed it to the game warden and said, "You gonna talk or you gonna fish?"

—DENNIS R. EDWARDS

**"I think he's had it as a bird dog."**

A group of friends who went deer hunting separated into pairs for the day. That night, one hunter returned alone, staggering under an eight-point buck. "Where's Harry?" asked another hunter.

"He fainted a couple miles up the trail," Harry's partner answered.

"You left him lying there alone and carried the deer back?"

"A tough call," said the hunter. "But I figured no one is going to steal Harry."

*—The Jokesmith*

An American had been fishing for two weeks in Ireland without getting a bite. On the last day of his vacation, he caught a small salmon.

"Turlough," he said to his guide later, "that salmon cost me more than five hundred dollars."

"Well now, sir," Turlough comforted him, "aren't you lucky you didn't catch two!"

—IAN AITKEN

After a long day of fishing without even a nibble, a man said disgustedly to his companion, "You know the saying, 'Give a man a fish, and he'll eat for a day; teach a man to fish, and he'll eat for a lifetime'?"

"Yes?"

"Well, whoever said it wasn't a fisherman."

—DAVID SAHLIN

Irving was boasting to a fellow fisherman about a 20-pound salmon he had caught. "Twenty pounds, huh?" remarked the other guy, with skepticism. "Were there any witnesses?"

"Of course," said Irving. "Otherwise it would have weighed 30 pounds."

—JOEY ADAMS

The young boy protested vigorously when his mother asked him to take his little sister along fishing. "The last time she came," he objected, "I didn't catch a single fish."

"I'll talk to her," his mother said, "and I promise this time she won't make any noise."

"It wasn't the noise, Mom," the boy replied. "She ate all my bait."

—*The Rotarian*

Three men were sitting on a park bench. The one in the middle was reading a newspaper; the others were pretending to fish. They baited imaginary hooks, cast lines, and reeled in their catch.

A passing policeman stopped to watch the spectacle and asked the man in the middle if he knew the other two.

"Oh yes," he said. "They're my friends."

"In that case," warned the officer, "you'd better get them out of here!"

"Yes, sir," the man replied, and he began rowing furiously.

—ADAM T. RATTRAY

Said a fisherman after removing a tiny fish from his hook and throwing it back into the water: "Don't show up around here anymore without your parents!"

—*Der Stern*

The novice ice fisherman wasn't having any luck, but another man nearby was pulling up fish after fish through the ice. "What's your secret?" the newcomer asked.

"Mmnpximdafgltmm," mumbled the man.

"I'm sorry, I couldn't understand you," said the novice.

"Mmnpximdafgltmm!" the fisherman mumbled again.

The neophyte shook his head and began to turn away, when the other man held up his hand. Spitting twice into his coffee cup, he said, "You've got to keep the worms warm!"

—BRIAN D. HOXIE

Sitting in a rowboat, the novice fisherman asked his companion, "Got any more of those little plastic floats?"

"Why?"

"This one keeps sinking."

—ART SANSOM, Newspaper Enterprise Assn.

Three statisticians go deer hunting with bows and arrows. They spot a big buck and take aim. One shoots, and his arrow flies off 10 feet to the left. The second shoots, and his arrow goes 10 feet to the right. The third statistician jumps up and down yelling, "We got him! We got him!"

—BILL BUTZ, quoted by DIANA McLELLAN in *Washingtonian*

# You Must Be Jock-ing!

Before a major college basketball game between two top-20 teams, one student nudged another and said, "Look at that player. I wonder what's the matter with him. He looks so depressed."

"You haven't heard?" asked the other. "It's because his father's always writing him for money!"

—*Ideas for Better Living*

Basketball sure is an amazing game," said one fan to another. "They pay a guy $500,000 a year to shoot the ball, and then they call it a free throw."

—JAY TRACHMAN in *One to One*

He's great on the court," a sportswriter said of a college basketball player in an interview with his coach. "But how's his scholastic work?"

"Why, he makes straight A's," replied the coach.

"Wonderful!" said the sportswriter.

"Yes," agreed the coach, "but his B's are a little crooked."

—CLARENCE PETERSEN in the Jacksonville, Fla., *Times-Union*

*"He's what I call a natural."*

An avid Dallas Cowboys fan took his dog to a sports bar one Sunday afternoon to watch the game. The bartender reluctantly let the dog in, and the pooch sat quietly as the game progressed. When the Cowboys got a field goal, the dog went crazy—barking, running in circles and doing back flips. "What does he do when they score a touchdown?" the amazed bartender asked.

"I don't know," replied the owner. "I've only had him two years."

—Contributed by HOWARD R. SCHROEDER

After spending all day watching football, Harry fell asleep in front of the TV and spent the night in the chair. In the morning, his wife woke him up. "Get up, dear," she said. "It's 20 to seven."

He awoke with a start. "In whose favor?"

*—Funny, Funny World*

A college football coach had recruited a top talent, but the player couldn't pass the school's entrance exam. Needing the recruit badly, the coach went to the dean and asked if the recruit could take the test orally. The dean agreed, and the following day the recruit and the coach were seated in his office. "Okay," the dean said. "What is seven times seven?"

The recruit mulled it over for a moment, then said, "I think it's 49."

Suddenly the coach leapt to his feet. "Please, Dean," he begged, "give him another chance!"

—OSCAR ZIMMERMAN

Mort Sahl sympathized with football widows. When one woman asked him how she could get her husband's attention away from the TV set, he said, "Wear something sheer."

"What if that doesn't work?" she asked.

"Then put a number on your back," Sahl replied.

—JOEY ADAMS

What position does your brother play on the football team?" Tom was asked.

"I'm not real sure," the boy replied, "but I think he's one of the drawbacks."

—Quoted in the
Milwaukee *Journal*

P.C.VEY

**A**nthropologists have discovered a 50-million-year-old human skull with three perfectly preserved teeth intact. They're not sure, but they think it may be the remains of the very first hockey player.

—JAY LENO

**T**he 85-year-old woman decided to take up skydiving. After she attended instruction classes, the day came for her first jump. Strapping on a parachute, she stood awaiting her turn to leap out of the plane. But when she looked at the ground below, she lost her nerve.

Finally, she reached into her pocket, pulled out a small transmitter and radioed her instructor on the ground: "Help! I've gotten up, and I can't fall down!"

—KEN BEHRENS,
WJBC, Bloomington, Ill.

Young woman to boyfriend:

"Otto, you'd really rather watch soccer than me?"

"Yes," he says apologetically. "But I'd take you any day over the long jump, swimming, and the equestrian contest."

—ANDREA RATONYI

Bill and George were always competing against each other. After one argument over who was better at folding and packing parachutes, they went skydiving to settle the dispute. Bill jumped first, pulled the cord and began to float gently to earth. Then George jumped and pulled his cord, but nothing happened. Next he yanked on the safety cord, but that didn't work either. In a matter of seconds George, falling like a rock, flew past Bill. "So," Bill shouted, ripping off his harness, "you want to race!"

—MARIE THRUSH

A sky diver and his instructor peered down at the field 3,000 feet below. "There's nothing to worry about," the instructor said. "You jump, count to three and pull your rip cord. If that doesn't work, pull your reserve cord. There'll be a truck down there to pick you up."

The sky diver took a deep breath and plunged into the open air. After free-falling, he counted to three, then pulled his rip cord. Nothing happened. So he pulled his reserve. A few cobwebs drifted out.

"Darn," he said. "I'll bet that truck's not down there either."

—*Playboy*

# Horsefeathers

The cavalryman was galloping down the road, rushing to catch up with his regiment. Suddenly his horse stumbled and pitched him to the ground. In the dirt with a broken leg, terrified of the approaching enemy, the soldier called out: "All you saints in heaven, help me get up on my horse!"

Then, with superhuman effort, he leaped onto the horse's back and fell off the other side. Once again on the ground, he called to the heavens: "All right, just half of you this time!"

—MRS. JAMES LARKIN

My wife means to lose weight. That's why she rides horseback all the time."

"And what's the result?"

"The horse lost 10 kilos last week."

—M. SPIRKOV

Overheard at the track: "Horse racing is very romantic. The horse hugs the rail, the jockey puts his arms around the horse, and you kiss your money good-bye."

—SACHIN MATADE

About to take his first horseback ride, the greenhorn was checking out the horses in the stable. The old wrangler asked whether he wanted an English saddle or a Western saddle.

"What's the difference?" asked the tenderfoot.

"The English saddle is flat, while the Western has a horn in the front."

"Better give me the English saddle," the fellow replied. "I don't expect to be riding in traffic."

—R. J. LANDSEADEL JR. in *The Rotarian*

Gasping for breath and covered with sweat, a man came into a racetrack snack bar and ordered a soft drink. "What happened to you?" the waitress asked.

"I was in the paddock area," the man panted, "when I saw a $100 bill on the ground. I bent down to pick it up. While I was bent over, somebody threw a saddle on me, and a jockey jumped into the saddle. The next thing I knew, I was on the track and the jockey was whipping my flanks."

"No kidding?" said the surprised woman. "What did you do?"

"I finished third."

—Jerry H. Simpson Jr.

An elderly gentleman went to a dude ranch and asked for the rates. "Well," began the ranch director, "for people your age who can't handle horses very well, we have to charge an extra 50 dollars a day."

"Fifty dollars a day!" yelped the old-timer. "You must be putting me on!"

"No," explained the director. "That would be an additional 20 dollars."

—Ashley Cooper in Charleston, S.C., *News and Courier*

A man was walking down a country road when he heard a voice coming from behind a tree, but all he could see was a horse.

"Hello, remember me?" the voice said. "I won the Kentucky Derby two years ago."

"A talking horse!" the man exclaimed, so he rushed to a nearby field where the farmer was working and asked, "What would you take for the horse?"

"That darned horse is no good, you can have him for 20 dollars."

"Twenty dollars! I'll give you 2,000."

"Has that old haybag been giving you that baloney about winning the Kentucky Derby? Listen, I happen to know he came in last."

—*The Carpenter*

*"Mom? Dad? Who are these people?."*

# Entertainment

ROAR OF THE GREASEPAINT, SMELL OF
THE CROWD! 108

WAITER! WAITER! 114

HAPPY HOUR 119

YOU BETCHA' 123

WITH A RUB OF THE LAMP 126

# Roar of the Greasepaint, Smell of the Crowd

If he starts to cry, you'll have to leave the theater," a movie-theater usher warned a young couple with an infant, "but you can ask for your money back."

Thirty minutes into the film, the husband whispered to his wife, "What do you think?"

"This film is a waste of time."

"I agree. Why not wake the baby up?"

—CARINE SCHENKEL

Sam: "I used to be a stand-up comedian before I worked here."

Joe: "I never would have guessed that."

Sam: "Ask me why I quit."

Joe: "Why did you . . ."

Sam: "Timing!"

Joe: ". . . quit?"

—MIKE SMITH

As the man and wife returned to their seats in the dark auditorium, the husband asked a fellow seated on the aisle, "Did someone step on your feet while going out at intermission?"

"Yes, you did," he replied, expecting an apology.

"Okay, honey," the man said to his wife, "this is our row."

—DUKE LARSON, quoted by Alex Thien
in the Milwaukee *Sentinel*

In Chicago there's a new Al Capone theme park. The commercial says, "Come to the park, pay your money, and nobody gets hurt."

—JOE HOBBY

When Disneyland celebrated its 40th anniversary, Disney officials buried a time capsule," reports Jay Leno. "They say it will be dug up in 50 years—or when the last person in line at Space Mountain gets to the front, whichever comes first."

A movie producer was telling his pal about giving his fiancée a string of pearls for her birthday. "Why," asked his friend, "don't you give her something practical—like a car?"

The producer answered, "Did you ever hear of a phony automobile?"

—*Another Treasury of Clean Jokes*, edited by TAL D. BONHAM

You're blocking the way, sir," said the usher to a man sprawled in the aisle of a movie theater. "Please get up."

The man didn't move or reply. The usher called the manager over, who said, "I must ask you to move."

Still the prone man didn't reply. So the manager called the police. "Get up or I'll have to take you in," the officer said. "Where did you come from anyway?"

The man stirred finally and said, "The balcony."

—*Capper's*

Browsing at a video shop, a guy and a gal spot the last tape of a recent hit movie. He grabs it first. "Your VCR or mine?" he asks.

—BILL COPELAND in the Sarasota, Fla., *Herald-Tribune*

Hollywood is the land of make-believe. Actors pretend they're someone else, and when the movie's finished, the producers make believe it's good.

—*Current Comedy*

*"It's perfectly normal for your last film to flash before your eyes on Oscar night."*

**A** Hollywood screenwriter coming home from work spotted a police line at the end of his street. He quickly discovered the reason: His house had burned to the ground. "What happened?" he asked a cop who was posted there.

"I'm sorry," the police officer said, "but your agent came over this afternoon and kidnapped your wife and children and then torched your house."

The screenwriter looked stunned. "My agent came to my *house*?"

*—Esquire*

**T**wo Hollywood execs were overheard at a power breakfast. "You're *lying* to me!" shouted one, pounding the table.

"I know. You're right," said the other. "But hear me out."

—Quoted by JEFF GILES in *Newsweek*

**I**n a darkened theater where a suspenseful mystery story was being staged, a member of the audience suddenly stood up and cried, "Where is the murderer?"

A threatening voice behind her replied, "Right in back of you, if you don't sit down!"

—PIERRE LÉAUTÉ

**M**ovie cowboys mystify me," says Bob Hope. "How can they jump off a porch roof and onto a horse, and still sing in a normal voice?"

**W**hen I came to this country," writes comedian Yakov Smirnoff, "one of the toughest things to get used to was all the different names of rock bands like Ratt, the Grateful Dead, or Twisted Sister. Then I *saw* the people in these groups, and it began to make sense."

*—America on Six Rubles a Day*

They were watching a TV soap opera, and he became irritated by the way his wife was taking it to heart. "How can you sit there and cry about the made-up troubles of people you've never even met?" he demanded.

"The same way you can jump up and scream when some guy you've never met scores a touchdown," she replied.

—Kris Lee in *Woman's World*

You know you're getting old when you walk into a record store and everything you like has been marked down to $1.99.

—Jack Simmons, *Showtime Comedy Cable*

A quiz program contestant had to identify famous slogans. After several correct responses, he was asked, "Which company originated the phrase 'Good to the last drop'?"

He thought for a moment. "Otis Elevator?"

—Jack Tracy

Mel's son rushed in the door. "Dad! Dad!" he announced. "I got a part in the school play!"

"That's terrific," Mel said proudly. "What part is it?"

"I play the part of the dad."

Mel thought this over. "Go back tomorrow," he instructed, "and tell them you want a speaking role."

—Darleen Giannini

When a plague of flying ants caused the performance at a variety theater in the Australian outback to end prematurely, the manager cabled a message to his agent: "Show stopped by flying ants!"

"Book 'em for another week," replied the agent.

—Bob Broadfield

**A** stage mother cornered the concert violinist in his dressing room and insisted he listen to a tape of her talented son playing the violin. The man agreed to listen, and the woman switched on the tape player.

*What music*, the violinist thought. A difficult piece, but played with such genius that it brought tears to his eyes. He listened spellbound to the entire recording.

"Madam," he whispered, "is that your son?"

"No," she replied. "That's Jascha Heifetz. But my son sounds just like him."

*—The Jokesmith*

**O**verheard: "I had a disturbing discussion with my wife this morning. I said that men like Sylvester Stallone and Arnold Schwarzenegger are a dime a dozen. She said, 'Here's a nickel. Get me six!'"

*—Current Comedy*

**A** couple of extras in the play were talking backstage at the end of the performance. "What's the matter with our leading lady?" one actress asked. "She seems really mad about something."

"Oh, she's upset because she only received nine bouquets of flowers over the footlights," the other woman answered.

"Nine!" exclaimed the first actress. "That's pretty good, isn't it?"

"Yes," her friend replied, "but she paid for 10."

*—The Safe Way*

**D**id you hear about the $2.7-billion write-off Sony took on its Hollywood studio? "That was quick!" says comedy writer Michael Connor. "It took the Japanese only a couple of years to master Hollywood-style bookkeeping."

*—The Los Angeles Times*

# Waiter! Waiter!

**W**aiter," Billy roars in the restaurant. "I want a steak, but it must taste just like veal. In the soup there must be no more and no less than 16 droplets of fat, and the wine must be served at exactly 50 degrees. The crystal wineglass must sound in A-flat when I tap it."

The waiter remains stoically calm, notes down every request, and then asks: "And the toothpicks, sir? Would you like them to be Rococo, Biedermier, Jugendstil, or would you prefer something in a slightly more modern line?"

—Urbain Koopmans

**W**hen the waitress in a New York City restaurant brought him the soup du jour, the Englishman was a bit dismayed. "Good heavens," he said, "what is this?"

"Why, it's bean soup," she replied.

"I don't care what it has been," he sputtered. "What is it now?"

—Margaret Olderog

**T**he diner was furious when his steak arrived too rare. "Waiter," he barked, "didn't you hear me say 'well done'?"

"I can't thank you enough, sir," replied the waiter. "I hardly ever get a compliment."

—A. H. Berzen

**A** diner called the waiter over and asked, "What's this at the bottom of my plate?"

"It's the design," replied the waiter.

"In that case," said the diner, "it's an animated drawing—it's moving!"

—*Humor Piadas e Anedotas*

*"I realize we all look alike, sir, but I am Walter, a married man with two grown children, and an abiding interest in the theater, coin collecting, and small songbirds. Your waiter is Eddie. I'll send him over."*

In a restaurant where the service was particularly slow, a customer was fretting because the waiter had not taken his order, although he had been waiting for a quarter of an hour. When the waiter finally appeared at his table, bearing a small dish of peanuts, he found the place empty, except for a small note from the disappointed diner: "Gone out to lunch!"

—MINA and ANDRÉ GUILLOIS

The truck driver looked askance at the soup he had just been served in a backwoods eatery. It contained dark flecks of seasoning, but two of the spots were suspicious.

"Hey," he called out to the waitress, "these particles in my soup—aren't they foreign objects?"

She scrutinized his bowl. "No, sir!" she reassured him. "Those things live around here."

—DEAN MORGAN

A patron in a Montreal café turned on a tap in the washroom and got scalded. "This is an outrage," he complained. "The faucet marked C gave me boiling water."

"But, Monsieur, C stands for *chaude*—French for hot. You should know that if you live in Montreal."

"Wait a minute," roared the patron. "The other tap is also marked C."

"Of course," said the manager. "It stands for cold. After all, Montreal is a bilingual city."

—*Catholic Digest*

My family and I were eating in an expensive restaurant, when I overheard the gentleman at the next table ask the waitress to pack the leftovers for their dog. It was then that his young son exclaimed loudly, "Whoopee! We're going to get a dog."

—B. S. PRABHAKAR

How many cups of coffee will this hold?" the man asked as he placed a large thermos on the lunch-room counter.

"Six cups," advised the waitress.

"Fine," replied the man. "Give me two cups regular, two cups black, and two with extra cream."

—GEORGE E. BERGMAN

The disgruntled diner summoned his waiter to the table, complaining, "My oyster stew doesn't have any oysters in it."

"Well, if that bothers you, then you better skip dessert," replied the waiter. "It's angel food cake."

—ROBERT L. RODGERS

Ours is a good restaurant," said the manager. "If you order an egg, you get the freshest egg in the world. If you order hot coffee, you get the hottest coffee in the world, and—"

"I believe you," said the customer. "I ordered a small steak."

—JIM REED, *Treasury of Ozark Country Humor*

A man walked into a crowded New York City restaurant and caught the eye of a harried waiter. "You know," he said, "it's been 10 years since I came in here."

"Don't blame me," the waiter snapped. "I'm working as fast as I can."

—NORTON MOCKRIDGE, United Features Syndicate

Inflation is creeping up," a young man said to his friend. "Yesterday I ordered a $25 steak in a restaurant and told them to put it on my American Express card—and it fit."

—DON REBER in the Reading, Pa., *Times*

Two eggs were in a pot, being boiled. One said to the other, "It's so hot in here I don't think I can stand it much longer."

The other replied, "Don't grumble. As soon as they get you out of here, they bash your head in with a spoon."

—J. JONES

*"My, oh, my! What a fascinating guy you are, Vincent! But now, if it's not too much trouble, I'd like you to take my order."*

The big Texan, visiting New York for the first time, entered a fancy restaurant and ordered a steak. The waiter served it very rare. The Texan took one look at it and demanded that it be returned to the kitchen and cooked.

"It is cooked," snapped the waiter.

"Cooked—nothing!" shouted the Texan. "I've seen cows hurt worse than that get well."

—H. B. McClung

In a greasy spoon, a downhearted diner asked the waitress for meatloaf and some kind words. She brought the meatloaf but didn't say a thing. "Hey," he said, "what about my kind words?"

She replied, "Don't eat the meatloaf."

—*The Los Angeles Times*

# Happy Hour

While at the pub, an Englishman, an Irishman, and a Scot each found a fly swimming around in his beer. The Englishman asked the bartender for a napkin and a teaspoon. Elegantly scooping the fly out, he placed it in the napkin and delicately folded it.

The Irishman pushed his sleeve up, immersed his hand in the beer, caught the fly, threw it on the floor, and stepped on it.

The Scot silently took his jacket off, draped it neatly over the chair, folded his shirtsleeves up, and bent over his pint. Carefully he fished the fly out by picking it up by its wings. He lifted it just above the mug, shook the fly, and in a threatening voice bellowed, "Now spit it out!"

—Hans J. Gerhardt

A college professor walked into a bar and said, "Bring me a martinus." The bartender smiled and said, "You mean martini?"

"If I want more than one," snapped the professor, "I'll order them."

—Earl Wilson

A grasshopper walks into a bar. The bartender looks at him and says, "Hey, they named a drink after you!"

"Really?" replies the grasshopper. "There's a drink named Stan?"

—Faye Skulberstad

At a party the hostess served a guest a cup of punch and told him it was spiked. Next, she served some to a minister. "I would rather commit adultery than allow liquor to pass my lips!" he shouted.

Hearing this, the first man poured his punch back and said, "I didn't know we had a choice!"

—Darrell B. Thompson

Mike had stopped off at a small-town tavern and made his way to the bar when there was a commotion outside. A man at the door shouted, "Run for your lives! Big Jake's comin'!" As everyone scattered, an enormous man burst through the door, threw tables and chairs aside and strode up to the bar. "Gimme a drink!" he ordered.

Left alone at the bar, Mike quickly handed over a bottle of whiskey. The huge man downed it in one gulp, then ate the bottle. Paralyzed with fear, Mike stammered, "Can I g-get you another?"

"Nope, I gotta go," grunted the giant. "Didn't you hear? Big Jake's comin'!"

—Howard Chavez

A fellow went to a bar and ordered a drink. He gulped it down and, to the amazement of the bartender, also ate the goblet, except for the stem. He ordered another, swallowed the drink, and again ate the goblet, leaving the stem. The bartender then called in a psychiatrist, explained the man's strange behavior, and asked whether he thought the man was eccentric. "He must be," the shrink replied. "The stem's the best part."

—P. R. Engele

A man walked into a second-story bar and ordered a drink. The man next to him began a conversation about wind currents in the area. The first man said he didn't understand what was so special about the wind, so the second man said, "Let me demonstrate."

With that, he went to the window, jumped out, did a little spin in midair and came back in. "See how great the currents are? You can do the same thing."

After a few more drinks and much prodding, the first man decided to test the wind currents. He went to the window, jumped out, and fell to the ground.

The bartender looked at the other man and said, "Superman, you're really mean when you're drunk."

—Darleen Giannini

Pat Muldoon, proprietor of an Irish pub, was busy pouring for his noontime trade, while trying to keep a swarm of flies away from the buffet table. When Mike Callahan, the town drunk and biggest mooch, wandered in, Pat turned a deaf ear to his plea for a nip or two on the cuff.

But when Mike offered to kill every one of the flies circling the buffet in exchange for a short one, Pat slid a shot of whiskey across the bar. As soon as he downed it, Mike rolled up his sleeves and headed for the door. "All right, Muldoon," he said. "Send 'em out one at a time."

—GORDON H. KRUEGER

A businesswoman is sitting at a bar. A man approaches her.
"Hi, honey," he says. "Want a little company?"
"Why?" asks the woman. "Do you have one to sell?"

—Quoted by CAROLYN A. STRADLEY

Late one night, after an evening of drinking, Smitty took a shortcut through the graveyard and stumbled into a newly dug grave. He could not get out, so he lay at the bottom and fell asleep. Early next morning the old caretaker heard moans and groans coming from deep in the earth. He went over to investigate, saw the shivering figure at the bottom and demanded, "What's wrong with ya, that you're makin' all that noise?"

"Oh, I'm awful cold!" came the response.

"Well, it's no wonder," said the caretaker. "You've gone and kicked all the dirt off ya!"

—DEBBIE P. WRIGHT

Overheard: "The police in this town have a very tough sobriety test. Not only do they make you blow up a balloon, but then you have to twist it into a giraffe."

—*Current Comedy*

*"You guys know the rules! No discussing politics during happy hour."*

A bar owner locked up his place at 2 am and went home to sleep. He had been in bed only a few minutes when the phone rang. "What time do you open up in the morning?" he heard an obviously inebriated man inquire.

The owner was so furious, he slammed down the receiver and went back to bed. A few minutes later there was another call and he heard the same voice ask the same question. "Listen," the owner shouted, "there's no sense in asking me what time I open because I wouldn't let a person in your condition in—"

"I don't want to get in," the caller interjected. "I want to get out."

—*The Carpenter*

# You Betcha'

"Las Vegas is loaded with all kinds of gambling devices," says Joey Adams. "Dice tables, slot machines, and wedding chapels."

A woman in Atlantic City was losing at the roulette wheel. When she was down to her last 10 dollars, she asked the fellow next to her for a good number. "Why don't you play your age?" he suggested.

The woman agreed, and then put her money on the table. The next thing the fellow with the advice knew, the woman had fainted and fallen to the floor. He rushed right over. "Did she win?" he asked.

"No," replied the attendant. "She put 10 dollars on 29 and 41 came in."

—CHRISTINE L. CASTNER

In Las Vegas a big-time gambler dies and a friend delivers the eulogy. "Tony isn't dead," the friend says. "He only sleeps."

A mourner in the back of the room jumps up. "I got a hundred bucks says he's dead!"

—*Solutions for Seniors*

When Salley O'Malley of County Clare won the Irish Sweepstakes, she decided to treat herself to some of the finer things in life. "I've nivver had a milk bath," she told her milkman one morning. "Wouldja be bringin' me 96 quarts o'milk tomorro'?"

"Whativver ye want, mum," answered the milkman. "Will that be pasteurized?"

"No," said she. "Up to me chest will do."

—Quoted by T. D.

Sitting by the window in her convent, Sister Eulalia opened a letter from home, and found a $10 bill inside. As she read the letter, she caught sight of a shabbily dressed stranger leaning against a lamppost below. Quickly she wrote "Don't despair, Sister Eulalia" on a piece of paper, wrapped the $10 in it and dropped it out the window.

The stranger picked it up and, with a puzzled expression and a tip of his hat, went off down the street.

The next day Sister Eulalia was told that a man was at the door, insisting on seeing her. She went down and found the stranger waiting. Without a word he handed her a roll of bills. "What's this?" she asked.

"That's the 60 bucks you have coming. Don't Despair paid five to one."

—*The Joy of Words*

Bill sat at the local bar, bragging about his athletic prowess. None of the regulars challenged him, but a visitor piped up, "I'll bet you 50 bucks that I can push something in a wheelbarrow for one block and you can't wheel it back."

Bill looked over at the skinny stranger and decided it wasn't much of a challenge. "I'll take you on," he said.

The two men and a number of regulars borrowed a wheelbarrow and took it to the corner. "Now, let's see what you're made of," taunted Bill.

"Okay," said the challenger. "Get in."

—Anne Victoria Baynas, quoted in
*Old Farmer's Almanac*

I'm beginning to understand exactly how the state lottery helps education," a guy told his neighbor. "Every time I buy a losing ticket, I get a little smarter."

—*One to One*

*"I understand there are no slot machines in the original."*

**W**hat are you so happy about?" a woman asked the 98-year-old man.

"I broke a mirror," he replied.

"But that means seven years of bad luck."

"I know," he said, beaming. "Isn't it wonderful?"

—BOB MONKHOUSE, *Just Say a Few Words*

**D**id you hear about the race horse that was so late coming in, they had to pay the jockey time and a half?

*—Tom FitzGerald in the San Francisco Chronicle*

**A** confirmed horse player hadn't been to church in years even though his wife attended every week. One Sunday, however, he finally went with her.

"That wasn't so bad," he said on the way home. "The church was air-conditioned, the pews were cushioned and the singing was great. Did you notice people looking at me when I joined in with my deep baritone voice?"

"Yes, I noticed them," his wife responded. "But the next time we go to church, please try to sing 'Hallelujah, Hallelujah' and not 'Hialeah, Hialeah.'"

*—Complete Speaker's Galaxy of Funny Stories, Jokes and Anecdotes, edited by*
Winston K. Pendleton

**A**n excited woman called her husband at work. "I won the lottery!" she exclaimed. "Pack your clothes!"

"Great!" he replied. "Summer or winter clothes?"

"All of them—I want you out of the house by six!"

*—Ashley Cooper in Charleston, S.C., News and Courier*

# With a Rub of the Lamp

**E**xperimenting with a trick, a magician accidentally changed his wife into a sofa and his two children into armchairs. He called an ambulance and they were rushed to the hospital. Later, the worried sorcerer phoned to check their condition.

"Resting comfortably," said the doctor.

*—Today*

One day a man spotted a lamp by the roadside. He picked it up, rubbed it vigorously and a genie appeared.

"I'll grant you your fondest wish," the genie said.

The man thought for a moment, then said, "I want a spectacular job—a job that no man has ever succeeded at or has ever attempted to do."

"Poof!" said the genie. "You're a housewife."

—NICOLE BURKE

A despondent woman was walking along the beach when she saw a bottle on the sand. She picked it up and pulled out the cork. Whoosh! A big puff of smoke appeared.

"You have released me from my prison," the genie told her. "To show my thanks, I grant you three wishes. But take care, for with each wish, your mate will receive double of whatever you request."

"Why?" the woman asked. "That bum left me for another woman."

"That is how it is written," replied the genie.

The woman shrugged and then asked for a million dollars. There was a flash of light, and a million dollars appeared at her feet. At the same instant, in a far-off place, her wayward husband looked down to see twice that amount at his feet.

"And your second wish?"

"Genie, I want the world's most expensive diamond necklace." Another flash of light, and the woman was holding the precious treasure. And, in that distant place, her husband was looking for a gem broker to buy his latest bonanza.

"Genie, is it really true that my husband has two million dollars and more jewels than I do, and that he gets double of whatever I wish for?"

The genie said it was indeed true.

"Okay, genie, I'm ready for my last wish," the woman said. "Scare me half to death."

—TOM NEDWEK, quoted by ALEX THIEN
in the Milwaukee *Sentinel*

Overheard: "For some reason I didn't like that Disney movie. Aladdin rubbed me the wrong way."

—GARY APPLE in *Speaker's Idea File*

A man was trying to obtain a flat in Bombay. After many days of fruitless search he was returning to his slum home when he stopped to buy a tender coconut. But when he cut open the top of the coconut, smoke issued out and to the poor man's astonishment a huge genie materialized.

"Command and I will obey!" thundered the genie.

With awakening hope the man stuttered out, "I want a flat in Bombay."

"If I could get a flat for myself in Bombay," retorted the genie, "do you think I would have stayed inside a coconut?"

—RAJIV NAIR

Then there was the fellow who always had bad luck. Once he found a magic lamp, rubbed it, and a genie appeared and gave him the Midas touch. For the rest of his life, everything he touched turned into a muffler.

—*Orben's Comedy Fillers*

Arthur rubbed the old lamp he'd purchased at a flea market, and sure enough, a genie appeared. "Thanks for setting me free," said the grateful spirit.

"Aren't you going to grant me a wish?" asked Arthur.

"Are you kidding?" answered the genie. "If I could grant wishes, would I have been in that lousy lamp all this time?"

—STEVE KEUCHEL

*"I thought you had the camera."*

# Travel

# Up in the Air

It doesn't make sense," says comedian Elayne Boosler. "You're flying at 500 m.p.h., 30,000 feet in the air, and the pilot tells you to feel free to roam around the plane. But when you're on the ground taxiing to the gate at one m.p.h., he tells you to remain seated for your own safety."

Why is there mistletoe hanging over the baggage counter?" asked the airline passenger, amid the holiday rush.

The clerk replied, "It's so you can kiss your luggage good-bye."

—SEYMOUR ROSENBERG in the Spartanburg,
S.C., *Herald-Journal*

A student-pilot was making his first helicopter flight. After the takeoff, the instructor explained the instruments and, pointing to the rotor blades, said, "That's the air conditioning."

The pupil looked at him in astonishment, and the instructor said, "You don't believe me, do you? Just wait until we reach 3,000 feet and I shut it off. Then you'll see what a hot spot this can be!"

—P. VAN WINKEL

An elderly woman was nervous about making her first flight in an airplane, so before takeoff she went to speak to the captain about her fears.

"You will bring me down safely, won't you?" she anxiously inquired.

"Don't worry, madam," was his friendly reply. "I haven't left anyone up there yet."

—COLLEEN BURGER

*"I happen to be a frequent flyer, and this just doesn't feel right to me."*

**A** jet ran into some turbulent weather. To keep the passengers calm, the flight attendants brought out the beverage carts.

"I'd like a soda," said a passenger in the first row. Moving along, the attendant asked the man behind her if he would like something.

"Yes, I would," he replied. "Give me whatever the pilot is drinking!"

—MARY J. MILLER

**A** small plane with an instructor and student on board hit the runway and bounced repeatedly until it came to a stop. The instructor turned to the student and said, "That was a very bad landing you just made."

"Me?" replied the student. "I thought you were landing."

—*The Cockle Bur*

The 747 was halfway across the Atlantic when the captain got on the loudspeaker: "Attention, passengers. We have lost one of our engines, but we can certainly reach London with the three we have left. Unfortunately, we will arrive an hour late as a result."

An hour later the captain made another announcement: "Sorry, but we lost another engine. Still, we can travel on two. I'm afraid we will now arrive two hours late."

Shortly thereafter, the passengers heard the captain's voice again: "Guess what, folks. We just lost our third engine, but please be assured we can fly with only one. We will now arrive in London three hours late."

At this point, one passenger became furious. "For Pete's sake," he shouted. "If we lose another engine, we'll be up here all night!"

—Nathaniel Scott Miller

At an airline ticket counter, a small boy, with his mother, told the agent he was two years old. The man looked at him suspiciously and asked, "Do you know what happens to little boys who lie?"

"Yes. They get to fly at half-price."

—Marlene Freedman in *Chevron USA*

Pilot to airline passengers: "Ladies and gentlemen, I have some good news and some bad news. The bad news is that we have a hijacker on board. The good news is, he wants to go to the French Riviera."

—*Parts Pups*

**Q**: What's a sure sign you're flying the wrong airline?

A: The pilot has a heart attack, and the air-traffic controller talks a flight attendant through takeoff.

—PETER S. LANGSTON

The Concorde is great," says Howie Mandel. "Traveling at twice the speed of sound is fun—except you can't hear the movie till two hours after you land."

Two pilots were discussing the merits of a twin-engine, propeller-driven aircraft undergoing service trials. "How does it handle?" asked the pilot who hadn't yet flown the new plane.

"Oh, it's not bad," was the reply.

"How is it in asymmetric flight? One engine out?"

After thinking for a moment, the other pilot replied, "Ah, that's where it becomes tricky. If one engine quits, the other engine immediately takes you to the scene of the crash."

—JIM MCCORKLE

# Wheeling

Lost on back roads in Vermont, a tourist collided with a local man at an intersection. He and the local got out to examine their bent fenders.

"Well, don't look like much," observed the local. "Whyn't we just take a little pull to steady our nerves." He grabbed a jug from his battered pickup, removed the stopper and handed it to the tourist.

After taking a good slug, the tourist handed the jug back to the local, who banged in the stopper and set the jug back in his truck.

"Aren't you going to have some?" asked the tourist.

The local shook his head. "Not till after the trooper comes."

—JAMES SHANNON

Anytime you see a young man open a car door for his girlfriend, either the car is new or the girlfriend is.

—Robert E. Limbaugh II in *Boys' Life*

A juggler, driving to his next performance, is stopped by the police. "What are those machetes doing in your car?" asks the cop.

"I juggle them in my act."

"Oh, yeah?" says the doubtful cop. "Let's see you do it." The juggler gets out and starts tossing and catching the knives. Another man driving by slows down to watch.

"Wow," says the passer-by. "I'm glad I quit drinking. Look at the test they're giving now!"

—Natalie Kaplowitz

A young man was trying to park his car between two others. He put it in reverse, and bang—right into the car behind him. He then went forward and bang—right into the car in front.

A young woman watching the maneuver couldn't contain herself. "Do you always park by ear?" she asked.

—Venderci Martins Valente

A traffic cop pulled over a speeding motorist and asked, "Do you have any ID?"

The motorist replied, "About what?"

—Martha B. Roberts

After he finished his route, a bus driver had to explain to the supervisor why he was 10 minutes late: "I was stuck behind a big truck."

"But yesterday you were 10 minutes early," reminded the boss.

"Yeah," the bus driver replied. "But yesterday I was stuck behind a Porsche."

—Tim Harvey

Late for a return flight from Dublin, an American tourist in Ireland jumped into a cab. "Quick," he said, "get me to the airport as fast as you can!" The cabbie nodded and floored the gas pedal. Soon they were barreling along at more than 70 miles an hour.

Just ahead a stoplight was bright red. The cab shot through the intersection without slowing down in the slightest. "Are you blind?" shouted the tourist. "That was a red light!"

The cabbie was unfazed. "I don't believe in red lights, sir, nor do any of my five cab-driving brothers." After two more hair-raising hurtles through red lights, the tourist was relieved to see a green light. But right before the intersection, the cabbie slammed on the brakes. "Are you insane?" yelled the passenger. "That was a green light!"

"True, sir," replied the cabbie. "But you never know when one of my brothers may be coming through."

—E. H.

The truck driver stopped at a roadside diner. His waitress brought him a hamburger, a cup of coffee, and a piece of pie.

As the trucker was about to start eating, three men in leather jackets pulled up on motorcycles and came inside. One grabbed the man's hamburger, the second one drank his coffee and the other one took his pie. The truck driver didn't say a word. He got up, put on his jacket, paid the cashier and left.

One of the bikers said to the cashier, "Not much of a man, is he?"

"He's not much of a driver either," she replied. "He just ran his truck over three motorcycles."

—MICHAEL IAPOCE in *A Funny Thing Happened on the Way to the Boardroom*

Driving tip: If you rear-end a car on the freeway, your first move should be to hang up the phone.

—TOM ADAMS in *Comic Highlights*

*"Fill'er up, sir?"*

**T**he driving instructor was giving lessons to an extremely nervous student who panicked whenever another car approached on a particular two-lane road. One day, however, they got to the same stretch of road, and she remained completely calm.

"This time you're doing fine!" exclaimed the instructor.

"Yes," the novice driver agreed. "Now when I see another car coming, I shut my eyes."

—M. Herbrink

Driving back from car-repair class, John said to his buddy, Joe, "I'm going to turn now. Could you stick your head out the window to see if the blinker's working?"

"Sure," Joe replied as he peeked outside. "It is, no it isn't, yes it is, no it isn't, yes it is . . . ."

—Paulo Cesar Menegusso

The young woman sat in her stalled car, waiting for help. Finally two men walked up to her.

"I'm out of gas," she purred. "Could you push me to a service station?"

They readily put their muscles to the car and rolled it several blocks. After a while, one looked up, exhausted, to see that they had just passed a filling station.

"How come you didn't turn in?" he yelled.

"I never go there," the woman shouted back. "They don't have full service."

—*Super Automotive Service*

What an automated society we live in. Have you ever noticed that when a traffic signal turns green, it automatically activates the horn of the car behind you?

—Robert Orben in *The American Legion Magazine*

Driving down a winding country road, a man came upon a youth running hard, three huge dogs snarling at his heels. The man screeched his car to a halt and threw open the door. "Get in, get in!" he shouted.

"Thanks," gasped the youth. "You're terrific. Most people won't offer a ride when they see I have three dogs!"

—P. A. Isaacson

Wife: "There's trouble with the car. It has water in the carburetor."

Husband: "Water in the carburetor? That's ridiculous."

Wife: "I tell you the car has water in the carburetor."

Husband: "You don't even know what a carburetor is. Where's the car?"

Wife: "In the swimming pool."

*—Executive Speechwriter Newsletter*


The villager on his first trip to the city was waiting at a bus stop one morning. After some hesitation he asked a woman, "Which bus should I take for Mahim?"

"Bus Number 177," the woman replied, and caught the next bus.

The same evening, the woman got off a bus at the same stop and found the villager still waiting. "Didn't you get the bus to Mahim?" she exclaimed.

"Not yet," he said wearily. "So far 168 buses have come and gone—eight more before mine arrives."

—C. P. Murgudkar


Did you hear about the director of the Department of Motor Vehicles who resigned on Tuesday?

He tried to resign on Monday, but found he'd been standing in the wrong line.

—Dave Margolis in *The Los Angeles Times*


You know it's time to get a new car when—

The traffic reporter on the radio begins to refer to you by name.

You make a *left* turn and your date falls out.

You lose the "stoplight challenge" to a 16-year-old on a moped.

—Jay Trachman in One to One

*"North face of Everest: howling winds, sub-zero cold, insufficient oxygen, menswear."*

# Explorations

One stupid guy reads an ad about a vacation cruise that costs only $100. After he signs up and pays, the travel agent hits him with a bat, knocks him unconscious, and throws him out the back door into the river. Soon another guy comes in, pays his fee, and gets the same treatment.

Fifteen minutes later, as the two are floating down the river together, the first man says, "I wonder if they're serving any food on this cruise."

"I don't know," the second guy replies. "They didn't last year."

—MEL SMITH in *The Los Angeles Times*

An Irish lad named Sean was doing so well with his furniture business that he decided to take a trip to France. When he returned to Ireland, his friend Brendan asked him, "Why did you go to France and you not speaking a word of the language? How could you make yourself understood?"

"Let me tell you," said Sean. "I met this lass in the park. I drew a picture of plates and food, and so we went out to eat. After drawing a picture of people dancing, we went to a nightclub. At midnight, could you imagine, she took my pen and drew a picture of a bed."

"Faith 'n' begorra!" exclaimed Brendan. "How did she know you were in the furniture business?"

—Thomas R. McGuinness

Just before heading to Florida for spring break, a college student bought a skimpy bikini. She modeled it for her mother. "How do you like it?"

The parent stared in silence for a few moments, and then replied, "If I had worn a bathing suit like that when I was your age, you'd be four years older than you are right now."

—Quoted by James Dent in Charleston, W. Va., *Gazette*

Two explorers, camped in the heart of the African jungle, were discussing their expedition. "I came here," said one, "because the urge to travel was in my blood. City life bored me, and the smell of exhaust fumes on the highways made me sick. I wanted to see the sun rise over new horizons and hear the flutter of birds that never had been seen by man. I wanted to leave my footprints on sand unmarked before I came. In short, I wanted to see nature in the raw. What about you?"

"I came," the second man replied, "because my son was taking saxophone lessons."

—Al Batt in *Capper's*

Heading into the jungle on his first safari, the American visitor was confident he could handle any emergency. He sidled up to the experienced native guide and said smugly, "I know that carrying a torch will keep lions away."

"True," the guide replied. "But it depends on how fast you carry the torch."

—E. H.

From a passenger ship one can see a bearded man on a small island who is shouting and desperately waving his hands.

"Who is it?" a passenger asks the captain.

"I've no idea. Every year when we pass, he goes mad."

—*Chayan*

One day, an explorer was captured by native warriors and taken to their chieftain, a gigantic man with teeth filed to dagger-like points. Desperately, the explorer tried to think of a way to save himself. He pulled out his cigarette lighter, held it in front of the chief's face and lit it, exclaiming, "Look! *Magic!*"

The chief's eyes were huge in astonishment. "It certainly must be magic," he said. "I have never seen a lighter light on the first try!"

—*Nuggets*

One hot, dry day in the West, a traveler arrived at a small highway café. Wiping the sweat from his brow, he turned to a deeply tanned old-timer sitting at the counter and asked, "When was the last time it rained here?"

The old man looked at him. "Son, you remember in the Bible when it says it rained for 40 days and 40 nights?"

"Well, yes, I sure do."

The old man continued, "We got an inch."

—Douglas Irving in *Arizona Highways*

On our railway, children age 10 and under travel at half-price. As the conductor began checking tickets, a woman sitting next to me told her daughter, "Now remember, you are only 10." The girl nodded her head.

The conductor approached and asked the girl, "How old are you?"

"Ten, sir."

"And when will you be 11?"

"When I get off this train!"

—THEODORUS HARI WAHUANTO

Two passengers on a ship are talking. "Can you swim?" asks one. "No," says the other, "but I can shout for help in nine languages."

—MRS. ATTILANE NAGY

The sociologist on an African jungle expedition held up her camera to take pictures of the native children at play. Suddenly the youngsters began to yell in protest.

Turning red, the sociologist apologized to the chief for her insensitivity and told him she had forgotten that certain tribes believed a person lost his soul if his picture was taken. She explained to him, in long-winded detail, the operation of a camera. Several times the chief tried to get a word in, but to no avail.

Certain she had put all the chief's fears to rest, the sociologist then allowed him to speak. Smiling, he said, "The children were trying to tell you that you forgot to take off the lens cap!"

—SHARON SPENCE

**"It's faster if you use the stairs inside."**

*"No, no, not a pride. It's a bunch of tourists."*

# Tourism Department

**W**hat's this daily charge for 'fruit'?" the hotel patron asked the manager. "We didn't eat any."

"But the fruit was placed in your room every day. It isn't our fault you didn't take advantage of it."

"I see," said the man as he subtracted $150 from the bill.

"What are you doing?" sputtered the manager.

"I'm subtracting 50 dollars a day for your kissing my wife."

"*What*? I didn't kiss your wife."

"Ah," replied the man, "but she was there."

—JAMES DENT in the Charleston, W. Va., *Gazette*

Travel agent: "I can get you three days and two nights in Rome for a hundred bucks."

Customer: "How come so cheap?"

Travel agent: "The days are July 11, 12 and 13. The nights are July 21 and 22."

—BRANT PARKER & JOHNNY HART, North America Syndicate

Asia was by far my favorite destination," the woman bragged at the party, though she had never been out of the United States. "Enigmatic and magical, beautiful beyond belief. And China, of course, is the pearl of the Asian oyster."

"What about the pagodas?" a man beside her asked. "Did you see them?"

"Did I *see* them? My dear, I had *dinner* with them."

—LORD-NELSON QUIST in *Playboy*

In a panic, a traveler called down to the hotel's front desk soon after checking in. "Help!" he yelled. "I'm trapped inside my room!"

"What do you mean, trapped?"

"Well, I see three doors," the man explained. "The first opens to a closet, and the second to a bathroom. And the third door has a 'Do Not Disturb' sign hanging on it."

—PETER S. GREENBERG, Los Angeles Times Syndicate

When the fellow called a motel and asked how much they charged for a room, the clerk told him that the rates depended on room size and number of people. "Do you take children?" the man asked.

"No, sir," replied the clerk. "Only cash and credit cards."

—*Successful Meetings Magazine*

*"What do you say, honey? This looks like our kind of place."*

**A**n English traveler, asked by Australian immigration if he had a criminal record, expressed some surprise that such a qualification was still required.

—New Zealand *Herald*

**A** vacationer telephoned a seaside hotel to ask where it was. "It's only a stone's throw from the beach," he was told. "How will I recognize it?" asked the man. Back came the reply, "It's the one with all the broken windows."

—BOB STERLING

A pair of honeymooners checked into the Watergate Hotel in Washington, D.C. That night, as the husband was about to turn off the light, his bride asked, "Do you think this room is bugged?"

"That was a long time ago, sweetheart," he reassured her.

"But what if there's a microphone somewhere? I'd be so embarrassed."

So the groom searched under tables and behind pictures. Then he turned back the rug. Sure enough, there was a funny-looking gizmo in the floor. He took out the screws, got rid of the hardware, and climbed into bed.

The next morning the newlyweds were awakened by a hotel clerk who wanted to know if they had slept well.

"We did," replied the groom. "Why do you ask?"

"It's rather unusual," the clerk answered. "Last night the couple in the room below yours had a chandelier fall on them."

—HENNY YOUNGMAN, quoted by ALEX THIEN in the Milwaukee *Sentinel*

A New York retail clerk was suffering from aching feet. "It's all those years of standing," his doctor declared. "You need a vacation. Go to Miami, soak your feet in the ocean and you'll feel better."

When the man got to Florida, he went into a hardware store, bought two large buckets and headed for the beach. "How much for two buckets of that sea water?" he asked the lifeguard.

"A dollar a bucket," the fellow replied with a straight face.

The clerk paid him, filled his buckets, went to his hotel room and soaked his feet. They felt so much better he decided to repeat the treatment that afternoon. Again he handed the lifeguard two dollars. The young man took the money and said, "Help yourself."

The clerk started for the water, then stopped in amazement. The tide was out. "Wow," he said, turning to the lifeguard. "Some business you got here!"

—CARL D. KIRBY

A tourist was visiting New Mexico and was amazed at the dinosaur bones lying about.

"How old are these bones?" the tourist asked an elderly Native American, who served as a guide.

"Exactly one hundred million and three years old."

"How can you be so sure?" inquired the tourist.

"Well," replied the guide, "a geologist came by here and told me these bones were one hundred million years old, and that was exactly three years ago."

—ALLAN E. OSTAR

To celebrate their silver anniversary, a couple went to Niagara Falls and asked a motel clerk for a room. "We only have the honeymoon suite available," she told them.

"My wife and I've been married 25 years," the man said. "We don't need the honeymoon suite."

"Look, buddy," replied the clerk. "I might rent you Yankee Stadium, but you don't have to play baseball in it!"

—Parts Pups

An American couple visiting in a German village stepped into a small shop to look for souvenirs. The woman sneezed.

"*Gesundheit!*" said the clerk.

"Charles," said the American woman to her husband, "we're in luck. There's somebody here who speaks English."

—Ohio Motorist

At a swanky hotel, a guy walks up to the front desk and asks the clerk, "Do I register with you?"

"Not by any stretch of the imagination," snaps the woman.

—ASHLEY COOPER in the Charleston, S.C., *Post and Courier*

*"His majesty the Kingpin!"*

# Public Domain

### INTERNATIONAL BOUNDARIES 150

### GOVERNMENT AT ITS BIGGEST 155

### IT'S A CRIME 158

### HIGHER EDUCATION 161

# International Boundaries

Two highway workers are at a construction site when a car with diplomatic plates pulls up. *"Parlez-vous français?"* the driver asks. The two just stare.

*"Hablan ustedes español?"* the driver tries. They stare some more.

*"Sprechen Sie Deutsch?"* They continue to stare.

*"Parlate italiano?"* Nothing. Finally the man drives off in disgust.

One worker turns to the other and says, "Maybe we should learn a foreign language."

"What for?" the other replies. "That guy knew four of them, and a fat lot of good it did him."

—MAXIME COSMA, *The Best Jokes of Romania*

A minister was urged by his congregation to explain the difference between heaven and hell. "They're not as different as you might think," he said. "In heaven, the British are the policemen, the Germans are the mechanics, the Swiss run the trains, the French do the cooking, and the Italians are the lovers. In hell, only minor changes take place. The Germans are the policemen, the French are the mechanics, the Italians run the trains, the British do the cooking, and the Swiss are making love."

—JOHN MOLYNEUX in *The Bulletin*

Was Grandpa mad when they went through his luggage at the border?"

"Not in the least. They found his glasses that he'd lost two weeks earlier."

—MIKLOS MADARASZ

**"In the interests of restoring calm to world trouble spots,
UN peacekeepers invade Buckingham Palace."**

On the door: UNITED NATIONS SECURITY COUNCIL □ (WRIST-SLAPPING DIVISION)

ZIEGLER

A near-sighted diplomat attended a ball at a South American embassy. When the orchestra struck up a tune, he felt he should start the dancing. Accordingly he walked over to a figure clad in red and said, "Beautiful lady in scarlet, would you do me the honor of waltzing with me?"

"Certainly not!" came the reply. "In the first place, this is not a waltz, but a tango. And in the second place, I am not a beautiful lady in scarlet. I'm the papal nuncio."

—ROBERT L. CLARKE, quoted by WILLIAM SAFIRE and
LEONARD SAFIR in *Leadership*

Overheard: "The tragedy of Canada is that they had the opportunity to have French cuisine, British culture, and American technology, and instead they ended up with British cuisine, American culture, and French technology."

—WILL SHETTERLY

An Englishman awaiting the train to Paris at the station restaurant in Calais beckoned to the waiter and asked him in French laden with a heavy British accent, "Do you know the man smoking a pipe and reading a newspaper over by the heater?"

"No, sir. So many of our patrons are just passing through."

"Well, please call the manager for me then."

When the manager arrived, the Englishman repeated his question. The manager scrutinized the man by the heater.

"I'm sorry, sir, but I've never seen him before."

With that, the Englishman rose and walked over to the man. "Please accept my apologies, sir, for speaking to you without having been properly introduced," he said, "but your coat is on fire!"

—FRANÇOIS CHAUVIÈRE

There is a story that Soviet General Secretary Mikhail Gorbachev was late for a meeting and told his chauffeur to step on it. The chauffeur refused on the ground that it would be breaking the speeding laws. So Gorbachev ordered him into the back seat and got behind the wheel.

After a few miles, the car was stopped by a police patrol. The senior officer sent his subordinate to arrest the offender.

A moment later, the officer returned saying that the person was much too important to prosecute.

"Who is it?" demanded the police chief.

"I'm not sure, sir," replied the officer, "but Comrade Gorbachev is his chauffeur."

—"Observer" in *Financial Times*

A secret agent was sent to Ireland to pick up some sensitive information from an agent named Murphy. His instructions were to walk around town using a code phrase until he met his fellow agent.

He found himself on a desolate country road and finally ran into a farmer. "Hello," the agent said, "I'm looking for a man named Murphy."

"Well, you're in luck," said the farmer. "As it happens, there's a village right over the hill where the butcher is named Murphy, the baker is named Murphy, and three widows are named Murphy. Matter of fact, my name is Murphy."

Aha, the agent thought, here's my man. So he whispered the secret code: "The sun is shining . . . the grass is growing . . . the cows are ready for milking."

"Oh," said the farmer, "you're looking for Murphy the spy—he's in the village over in the other direction."

—RAYMOND W. SMITH in
*Vital Speeches of the Day*


On a visit to the United States, Gorbachev met a Russian who had immigrated to this country. "What do you do for a living here?" the Soviet leader asked him.

"My brother, my sister, and I work in a big factory."

"How do these capitalist bosses treat you?"

"Just fine," answered the man. "In fact, if you are walking home from work, the boss picks you up in his big car and drives you to your door. Another time, he treats you to a dinner in an expensive restaurant. Sometimes he takes you home for the weekend and buys you presents."

Gorbachev was stunned. "How often does this happen?"

"Well, to me, actually never. But to my sister, several times."

—Quoted by JAMES DENT in the
Charleston, W.Va., *Gazette*

# Government at Its Biggest

**A** young man visited his local welfare office and was asked to give his surname—all other details would be on computer. The assistant typed in his name, then read from the screen: "You are James Herbert Roberts of Oldfield Lane, London, age 22; single; unemployed for one year; now working as a plumber for Jones & Co. It's all here, every last detail. Now, what is your query?"

"Well," said the man, "it's about the widow's pension you keep sending me."

—Bill Naylor

**T**he president receives the news that his government is divided between optimists and pessimists. "Who are the optimists?" the president asks.

"They are those who believe that we will be eating grass by the end of the year," says the adviser.

"And the pessimists?"

"They are those who think that there won't be enough grass for everybody."

—*Veja*

**Q**uestion: Why wasn't Rome built in a day?
Answer: Because it was a government job.

—Glenn E. Spradlin in the Louisville *Courier-Journal*

**W**hy does the capital have so many one-way streets? So that all the civil servants coming in late won't collide with those going home early.

—Arnie Benjamin, *The Daily News*

Man to friend: "I figured out why the Postal Service raised the postage rates. The extra four cents is for storage."

—ANGIE PAPADAKIS

You don't see me at Vegas or the track throwing my money around anymore," says Bob Hope. "I've got a government to support."

A veteran congressman was asked what he had learned in the rough-and-tumble of the political arena. "Well," he said, "I found it wasn't so much whether you won or lost, but how you placed the blame."

—*American Agriculturalist Magazine*

At a Washington cocktail party, two strangers struck up a conversation. After a few minutes of small talk, one said, "Have you heard the latest White House joke?"

The second fellow held up his hand. "Wait, before you begin, I should tell you that I work in the White House."

"Oh, don't worry," the first man replied. "I'll tell it very slowly."

—T. J. McInerney in *Globe*

Overheard at the Food and Drug Administration: "If laughter is the best medicine, shouldn't we be *regulating* it?"

—BALOO in *The Wall Street Journal*

Highway sign: "SPEED LIMIT 65 for most cars and some trucks under 8,000 pounds—only if they're empty, unless you weigh over 300 pounds—then divide by six. For additional information call the IRS, which helped write this."

—MIKE PETERS, Tribune Media Services

**"Ladies and gentlemen, I believe I can announce that at long last we've isolated the gene that determines political affiliation."**

Four friends met at a restaurant for lunch. For quite a while, no one said a word. Finally the first man mumbled, "Oh, boy!" To which the next one said, "It's awful." The third then muttered, "What are ya gonna do?"

"Listen," exclaimed the last friend, "if you guys don't stop talking politics, I'm leaving!"

—*The Big Book of Jewish Humor,* edited by
WILLIAM NOVAK and MOSHE WALDOKS

# It's a Crime

**D**id you hear about the desperado who tried to hijack a bus full of Japanese tourists? Fortunately, police had 5,000 photographs of the suspect.

—BARRY CRYER on *American Radio Theater*

**C**an you describe your assailant?" asked the officer as he helped the bruised and battered man get up.

"Sure," the man replied. "That's what I was doing when he hit me."

—ALAN THOMAS in *Quote*

**A** man was applying for a job as a prison guard. The warden said, "Now these are real tough guys in here. Do you think you can handle it?"

"No problem," the applicant replied. "If they don't behave, out they go!"

—JOEY ADAMS

**W**hen a Colorado mine operator found that his office safe had jammed, he called the nearby state prison and asked whether any of the inmates might know how to open it. Soon, a convict and a prison guard showed up at the office. The inmate spun the dials, listened intently and calmly opened the safe door.

"I'm much obliged," said the mine operator. "How much do you figure I owe you?"

"Well," said the prisoner, "the last time I opened a safe I got $25,000."

—W. T. LITTLE

Two prisoners were making their escape over the jailhouse roof when one of them dislodged a tile. "Who's there?" shouted a guard.

The first prisoner replied with a convincing imitation of a cat's meow. Reassured, the guard went back to his rounds.

But then the second prisoner dislodged another tile. The guard repeated, "Who's there?"

"The other cat," answered the prisoner.

—LAURENT GREBERT

Sent to prison as a first offender, a student of English was told by a longtime inmate that if he made amorous advances to the warden's wife, she'd get him released quickly.

"But I can't do that," he protested. "It's wrong to end a sentence with a proposition."

—*Financial Times*

Comedy writer Paul Ryan tells of the cable TV repairman who was charged with faking his own kidnapping. Police became suspicious when they had to wait at home with the ransom from 9 am to 5 pm.

—*The Los Angeles Times*

Outside city hall, a boy selling newspapers bellowed, "Extra! Extra! Read all about it! Two men swindled!" A man walked up to the boy, bought a paper, and sat down to read it. "Hey, kid," he protested a few moments later, "there's nothing in here about two men being cheated."

"Extra! Extra!" shouted the boy. "Three men swindled!"

—MIKE LESSITER in *Country Chuckles, Cracks & Knee-Slappers*

**"Mr. Cosgrove has stepped away from his desk.
May I take a message?"**

Three friends who always argued about who was the smartest are sitting on death row. The first one's number comes up, but when he sits down in the electric chair, nothing happens. The warden commutes his sentence on the spot and releases him.

Same thing happens with the second friend and he's let go. Then the third guy steps up to the platform and sits down.

The switch is pulled and again there's no charge. But before the warden can say anything, the prisoner starts pointing excitedly. "You know," he says, "if you'd just cross that black wire with the yellow one. . . ."

—Quoted on *The Gary McKee Hometown Radio Show*,
WSB-AM, Atlanta

People say New Yorkers can't get along. Not true. I saw two New Yorkers, complete strangers, sharing a cab. One guy took the tires and the radio; the other guy took the engine.

*—Late Show with David Letterman*

The inmate was aware that all prison mail passes through censors. When he got a letter from his wife asking about the family garden— "Honey, when do I plant potatoes?"—he wrote back, "Do not, under any circumstances, dig up our old garden spot. That's where I buried all my guns."

Within days his wife wrote back, "Six investigators came to the house. They dug up every square inch of the back yard."

By return mail she got his answer: "Now is the time to plant potatoes."

—REV. ROBERT MOORE JR., quoted by CHARLES ALLBRIGHT
in the *Arkansas Democrat Gazette*

# Higher Education

During a college examination, the professor found a student peeking at a classmate's answers.

"How can you cheat so blatantly?" the professor shouted. "You have already stolen more than one look at your classmate's paper!"

"Don't blame me, sir," replied the student. "If his handwriting weren't so bad, I could have got it all at one glance."

—SHIH YU HSIEH

Q: What's the difference between ignorance and apathy?
A: I don't know and I don't care.

*—Daily Telegraph*

**A** young man hired by a supermarket reported for his first day of work. The manager greeted him with a warm handshake and a smile, gave him a broom and said, "Your first job will be to sweep out the store."

"But I'm a college graduate," the young man replied indignantly.

"Oh, I'm sorry. I didn't know that," said the manager. "Here, give me the broom—I'll show you how."

—Richard L. Weaver II in *Vital Speeches of the Day*


**D**uring a lecture for medical students, the professor listed as the two best qualities of a doctor the ability to conquer revulsion and the need for keen powers of observation. He illustrated this by stirring a messy substance with his finger and then licking his finger clean. Then he called a student to the front and made him do the same.

Afterward the professor remarked, "You conquered your revulsion, but your powers of observation are not very good. I stirred with my forefinger, but I licked my middle finger."

—S.K.D.


**O**ur son came home from college for the weekend and I asked him, "How are things going?"

He said, "Good."

I said, "And the dormitory?"

He said, "Good."

I said, "They've always had a strong football team. How do you think they'll do this year?"

He said, "Good."

I said, "Have you decided on your major yet?"

He said, "Yes."

I said, "What is it?"

He said, "Communications."

—*Orben's Current Comedy*

**"Is this any way to treat a dissident?"**

"Our economics professor talks to himself. Does yours?"
"Yes, but he doesn't realize it. He thinks we're listening!"

—CHARISMA B. RAMOS

During class, the chemistry professor was demonstrating the properties of various acids. "Now I'm dropping this silver coin into this glass of acid. Will it dissolve?"

"No, sir," a student called out.

"No?" queried the professor. "Perhaps you can explain why the silver coin won't dissolve."

"Because if it would, you wouldn't have dropped it in."

—HERBERT V. PROCHNOW, *Speaker's and Toastmaster's Handbook*

I'd like to donate a million dollars, tax-free, to this institution," a Texan announced to the president of a small college. "But there's a condition. I would like an honorary degree for my horse."

"Horse?" stammered the president.

"Yes, for my mare, Betsy. She's carried me faithfully for many years, and I think she deserves a doctorate in transportation."

"But we can't give a degree to a horse!"

"Sorry, then you don't get the million dollars."

The board of trustees was hastily convened and each member in turn condemned the idea as a disgrace. Finally the oldest trustee spoke. "Let's take the money," he said. "It's about time we gave a degree to a *whole* horse!"

—Isaac Asimov, *Asimov Laughs Again*


An engineer, a mathematician, and a physicist were standing around the university flagpole when an English professor wandered by. "What are you doing?" he asked.

"We need to know the height of the flagpole," answered one, "and we're discussing the formulas we might use to calculate it."

"Watch!" said the English professor. He pulled the pole from its fitting, laid it on the grass, borrowed a tape measure and said, "Exactly 24 feet." Then he replaced the pole and walked away.

"English professor!" sneered the mathematician. "We ask him for the height, and he gives us the length."

—*The Jokesmith*

*"We super-rich are few in number. People should value us instead of always picking on us!"*

# Money Matters

# The Rich and the Foolish

A tightwad was convinced by a friend to buy a couple of tickets in the state lottery. But after he won the big prize, he didn't seem happy. "What's wrong?" the friend asked. "You just became a millionaire!"

"I know," he groaned. "But I can't imagine why I bought that second ticket!"

—Ohio Motorist

A stockbroker had made millions of dollars for an Arabian oil sheik. The sheik was so pleased he offered her rubies, gold, and a silver-plated Rolls-Royce. She declined the gifts, telling him she had merely done her job. But the sheik insisted.

"Well," the woman said, "I've recently taken up golf. A set of golf clubs would be a fine gift."

Weeks went by. One morning the stockbroker received a letter from him.

"So far I have bought you three golf clubs," it said, "but I hope you will not be disappointed because only two of them have swimming pools."

—Alex Thien in the Milwaukee *Sentinel*

Selling at an auction was halted when the auctioneer announced, "Someone in the room has just lost his wallet containing $1,000. He is offering a reward of $250 for its immediate return." After a moment of silence, there was a call from the back of the room, "$255."

—Rotary Down Under

An MG Midget pulled alongside a Rolls-Royce at a traffic light. "Do you have a car phone?" its driver asked the guy in the Rolls. "Of course I do," replied the haughty deluxe-car driver.

"Well, do you have a fax machine?"

The driver in the Rolls sighed. "I have that too."

"Then do you have a double bed in the back?" the Midget driver wanted to know.

Ashen-faced, the Rolls driver sped off. That afternoon, he had a mechanic install a double bed in his auto.

A week later, the Rolls driver passes the same MG Midget, which is parked on the side of the road—back windows fogged up and steam pouring out. The arrogant driver pulls over, gets out of the Rolls and bangs on the Midget's back window until the driver sticks his head out. "I want you to know that I had a double bed installed," brags the Rolls driver.

The Midget driver is unimpressed. "You got me out of the shower to tell me that?"

—Quoted by David Greason, New York Times News Service

A 70-year-old millionaire had just married a beautiful 20-year-old.

"You crafty old codger," said his friend. "How did you get such a lovely young wife?"

"Easy," the millionaire replied. "I told her I was 95."

—Fiona Golding

The miserly millionaire called a family conference. "I'm placing a box of money in the attic," he said. "When I die, I intend to grab it on my way up to heaven. See to it that no one touches it until it's my time to go."

The family respected his wishes. After his death the millionaire's wife looked in the attic. The box was still there. "The fool!" she said. "I told him he should have put it in the basement."

—Gene Jennings

A yuppie was driving his new BMW convertible. He had the top-down, his right hand on the wheel, and his left arm hanging over the door. With the tape deck going full blast, he didn't notice the rust bucket that pulled around to pass until it sideswiped him. The yuppie pulled to a stop.

"My car!" he cried. "My beautiful car!"

When a policeman came by, the yuppie told him about the accident. His car was a wreck, and it didn't even have 50 miles on it.

"You've got more to worry about than your car," the officer replied. "You need an ambulance. Your arm is badly injured."

The yuppie looked at his arm and cried, "My Rolex watch—my beautiful Rolex!"

—ALEX THIEN in the Milwaukee *Sentinel*

When the preacher's car broke down on a country road, he walked to a nearby roadhouse to use the phone. After calling for a tow truck, he spotted his old friend, Frank, drunk and shabbily dressed at the bar. "What happened to you, Frank?" asked the good reverend. "You used to be rich."

Frank told a sad tale of bad investments that had led to his downfall. "Go home," the preacher said. "Open your Bible at random, stick your finger on the page and there will be God's answer."

Some time later, the preacher bumped into Frank, who was wearing Gucci shoes, sporting a Rolex watch, and had just stepped out of a Mercedes. "Frank," said the preacher, "I am glad to see things really turned around for you."

"Yes, preacher, and I owe it all to you," said Frank. "I opened my Bible, put my finger down on the page and there was the answer—Chapter 11."

—PATRICK DIXON

*"I don't think you're trying very hard to look at things from a royal perspective."*

And then there's the shop-a-holic whose friend complimented her on her new car. "Oh, thanks," the woman replied. "I'm getting about 20 malls per gallon!"

—Nuggets

Only the billionaire and his friend remained after all the guests at his weekend ranch party scurried off for the afternoon's entertainment. The host answered the phone and slammed down the receiver in disgust. "I have to go to Dallas, and I've no way to get there!"

"Sure you do," his friend reassured him. "Isn't that a Cadillac convertible with the keys in it?"

"Yes, but that's my wife's car."

"So why can't you use it?"

"Are you kidding? The windshield's ground to her prescription."

—David Cox

Having purchased a new car, my friend was chary of hiring a new chauffeur because he had been warned that most chauffeurs exchanged new car parts for old and made some money on the sly. However, since my friend did not know how to drive, he had to engage a chauffeur, but he questioned every movement of the driver.

Once when we were riding together, the car slowed, then picked up speed.

"What happened?" my friend asked the driver.

"I just changed the gear, sir," the driver replied.

Turning to me, my friend whispered, "I have to fire this fellow. He not only changed the gear but has the audacity to admit it!"

—M. L. Bhagat

A guy walks up to the owner of a store and says, "You probably don't remember me, but about five years ago I was broke. I came in here and asked you for $10, and you gave it to me."

The store owner smiles and replies, "Yes, I remember."

The guy says, "Are you still game?"

—Ron Dentinger in the Dodgeville, Wis., *Chronicle*

A farmer who was notoriously miserly called a doctor to attend his sick wife.

"They say you're a skinflint," said the doctor. "Can I be sure of my fee?"

"Whether you kill my wife or cure her, you'll get your money without having to sue," said the farmer.

But the woman died, despite all the doctor's efforts to save her. He duly asked for his payment.

"Did you cure my wife?" asked the man.

"No," admitted the doctor.

"Did you kill her?"

"Certainly not!" the doctor said indignantly.

"Well, then, I owe you nothing."

—MICHELE VACQUIER

Mrs. Flinders decided to have her portrait painted. She told the artist, "Paint me with diamond earrings, a diamond necklace, emerald bracelets, and a ruby pendant."

"But you're not wearing any of those things."

"I know," said Mrs. Flinders. "It's in case I should die before my husband. I'm sure he'd remarry right away, and I want her to go nuts looking for the jewelry."

—MAE MORRISON

Take a pencil and paper," the teacher said, "and write an essay with the title 'If I Were a Millionaire.'"

Everyone but Philip, who leaned back with arms folded, began to write furiously.

"What's the matter," the teacher asked. "Why don't you begin?"

"I'm waiting for my secretary," he replied.

—BERNADETTE NAGY

*"I like to think of myself as an artist, and money is the medium in which I work best."*

# High Finance

Houston stockbroker to client: "If you put one hundred thousand dollars in a certificate of deposit at the bank, you get either a toaster or an offshore drilling rig. But hurry. The toasters are going fast."

—BILL SHEPHERD, quoted by PAUL HARASIM
in the Houston *Post*

Chicken Little on Wall Street: "The sky is making a technical correction!"

—*Current Comedy*

A pair of economists went to a restaurant for lunch. "Never mind the food," one said to the waitress. "Just bring us the bill so we can argue about it."

—Carol Simpson in *Funny Times*

I'm thinking of leaving my husband," complained the economist's wife. "All he ever does is stand at the end of the bed and tell me how good things are going to be."

—Jay Trachman in *One to One*

The sales manager was complaining to a colleague about one of his salesmen. "George is so forgetful that it's a wonder he can sell anything. I asked him to pick up some sandwiches on his way back from lunch, but I'm not sure he'll even remember to come back."

Just then, the door flew open and in came George. "You'll never guess what happened!" he shouted. "At lunch, I met Fred Brown, the president of a Fortune 500 company. He hadn't bought anything from us in 10 years. Well, we got to talking, and he gave me an order worth 15 million dollars!"

"See?" said the sales manager. "I told you he'd forget the sandwiches."

—*Executive Speechwriter Newsletter*

The economy is weird," remarked one worker to another. "My bank failed before the toaster did."

—*Coffee Break*

*"A monster called the commodities market tried to eat me today."*

A bank in New York City is now making it possible to buy and sell stock using their ATM machines. This is great—it gives muggers a chance to diversify their portfolios.

—*Late Show with David Letterman*

A man was forever writing to his bank asking for his overdraft limit to be increased. The bank had always obliged, but when things eventually started to get critical, he received a letter from the manager that began: "Dear Sir. We are concerned about three overdrawn accounts at this bank, your own, Mexico's and Brazil's—in that order."

—Vincent Murphy

Question: What do you need to make a small fortune on Wall Street?

Answer: A large fortune.

*—Country*

Overheard: "Things are still bad in the banking industry. The other day, a friend of mine went to the bank and asked the teller to check her balance. The guy leaned over and pushed her!"

*—TOM BLAIR in the San Diego* Union-Tribune

A woman visited the bank to close her account because she was convinced the institution was going under.

Asked by a startled manager why she thought so, she produced one of her checks, endorsed by the bank, "Insufficient funds."

*—Financial Mail*

Loan Officer: "Based on your credit history, it seems the only kind of loan you qualify for is an auto loan."

Customer: "You mean money to buy a car?"

Loan Officer: "I mean money you lend yourself."

*—J. C. DUFFY, Universal Press Syndicate*

At a testimonial dinner in his honor, a wealthy businessman gave an emotional speech. "When I came to this city 50 years ago," he said, "I had no car, my only suit was on my back, the soles of my shoes were thin, and I carried all my possessions in a paper bag."

After dinner, a young man nervously approached. "Sir, I really admire your accomplishments. Tell me, after all these years, do you still remember what you carried in that brown paper bag?"

"Sure, son," he said. "I had $300,000 in cash and $500,000 in negotiable securities."

*—The Lion*

T. Boone Pickens told this joke to a group of bankers:

A banker calls in an oilman to review his loans. "We loaned you a million to revive your old wells, and they went dry," says the banker.

"Coulda been worse," the oilman replies.

"Then we loaned you a million to drill new wells, and they were dry."

"Coulda been worse."

"Then we loaned you another million for new drilling equipment, and it broke down."

"Coulda been worse."

"I'm getting tired of hearing that!" snaps the banker. "How could it have been worse?"

"Coulda been my money," says the oilman.

An accountant answered an advertisement for a top job with a large firm. At the end of the interview, the chairman said, "One last question—what is three times seven?"

The accountant thought for a moment and replied, "Twenty-two."

Outside he checked himself on his calculator and concluded he had lost the job. But two weeks later he was offered the post. He asked the chairman why he had been appointed when he had given the wrong answer.

"You were the closest," the chairman replied.

—S. NETTLE

I think my wages are frozen," one worker said to another. "When I opened my pay envelope, a little light went on."

—ROGER DEVLIN in the Tulsa *Tribune*

Answer: Rugs, fish batter, and savings and loan executives.
Question: List three things that should be beaten every Friday.

—JOHNNY CARSON on *The Tonight Show*

Edith and Norbert had a knock-down, drag-out battle over his inability to earn a better living. She told him he wasn't forceful enough in asking the boss for a raise.

"Tell him," she yelled, "that you have seven children. You also have a sick mother, you have to sit up many nights, and you have to clean the house because you can't afford a maid."

Several days later, Norbert came home from work, stood before his wife and calmly announced that the boss had fired him. "Why?" asked Edith.

"He says I have too many outside activities."

*—The Larry Wilde Treasury of Laughter*

Dialogue between a sharp-tongued boss and a dissatisfied employee seeking a raise: "I know perfectly well you aren't being paid what you're worth!"

"So . . ." asked the employee, his hope returning.

"But I can't allow you to starve to death, can I?"

—Madame B. Legé

# Buyers Beware

Said a skeptical customer to a used-car dealer: "And how is your customer service?"

"Oh, that's first class. Anybody who buys a car from us gets a free copy of the latest railroad train schedules!"

*—Der Stern*

Sign in store window: "Any faulty merchandise will be cheerfully replaced with merchandise of equal quality."

—Martha Jane B. Catlett

In Jaipur, India, a man broke his own world record for tiny writing. He squeezed 1,314 characters onto a single grain of rice. When he finished, he went back to his old job of printing rental-car contracts.

—JOHNNY CARSON on *The Tonight Show*

Husband, holding mail-order catalog, to wife: "It says on the cover that if we don't buy $10 worth of merchandise, they'll send our name to every catalog in the country!"

—SCHOCHET in *The Wall Street Journal*

When he found a six-year-old shoe-repair ticket in the pocket of an old suit, Brown called the shop to see if the shoes were still around.
"Were they black wingtips needing half soles?" asked a clerk.
"Yes," said Brown.
"We'll have them ready in a week."

—Quoted in *Lutheran Digest*

An optometrist was instructing a new employee on how to charge a customer. "As you are fitting his glasses, if he asks how much they cost, say '$75.' If his eyes don't flutter, say 'For the frames. The lenses will be $50.' If his eyes still don't flutter, you add 'Each.' "

—MAMIE BROWN

A gentleman entered a busy florist shop that displayed a large sign that read "Say It with Flowers."
"Wrap up one rose," he told the florist.
"Only one?" the florist asked.
"Just one," the customer replied. "I'm a man of few words."

—*Domenica del Corriere*

*"You call that the trappings of wealth?"*

**O**verheard: "I think our bank is in trouble. I was about to complete a withdrawal at the ATM and the machine asked me if I wanted to go double or nothing."

—*The Rotarian*

**T**hese yuppies are really getting to me," a man complained to his friend. "Have you seen the new funeral home in New York? It's called 'Death 'n' Things.' "

—JIM KERR, WWPR, New York

**I** think it's wrong," says comedian Steven Wright, "that only one company makes the game Monopoly."

I went to a bookstore today," says comic Brian Kiley, "and I asked the manager where the self-help section was. She said, 'If I told you, that would defeat the whole purpose.' "

I can't believe what's happened to gas prices! The other day I handed the kid at the pump a $20 bill, and he used it to wipe the dipstick!

—Quoted by PETE SUMMERS, WLAD, Danbury, Conn.

As the cashier totaled the man's purchases, she asked, "Do you wish to charge?"
Looking at the amount, he answered, "No. I think I'll surrender."

—GEORGE E. BERGMAN

# If It Isn't Death, It's Taxes

Once, a man with an alligator walked into a pub and asked the bartender, "Do you serve IRS agents here?"
"Sure do," the barkeep replied.
"Good, give me a beer," said the man. "And my gator'll have an IRS agent."

—*Farmer's Digest*

Discussing the environment with his friend, one man asked,
"Which of our natural resources do you think will become exhausted first?"
"The taxpayer," answered the other.

—WINSTON K. PENDLETON, *Complete Speaker's Galaxy of Funny Stories, Jokes and Anecdotes*

Two IRS agents were traveling through a rural area when their car broke down. They walked to a nearby mansion and knocked on the door. A beautiful widow answered and said they were welcome to spend the night while her hired hands worked on the car.

Months later one of the agents received a package of legal documents. After surveying the contents, he quickly called the other agent.

"When we were up in the country," the first agent asked, "did you slip away in the night and go to that widow's bedroom?"

"Yes," the second agent admitted.

"Did you use my name?"

"Why, yes, but how'd you find out?"

"She died and left me her estate."

—GAYLEN K. BUNKER

A grieving widow was discussing her late husband with a friend. "My Albert was such a good man, and I miss him so. He provided well for me with that fifty-thousand-dollar insurance policy—but I would give a thousand of it just to have him back."

—*Farmer's Digest*

Mrs. Willencot was very frugal. When her husband died, she asked the newspaper how much it would cost for a death notice.

"Two dollars for five words."

"Can I pay for just two words?" she asked. "Willencot dead."

"No, two dollars is the minimum. You still have three words."

Mrs. Willencot thought a moment. "Cadillac for sale."

—PATRICIA SCHULTZ

My tax man is so considerate and compassionate," says Joey Adams. "He's the only accountant I know with a recovery room."

*"Look, I know it's not fair, but taking everyone at the flat age of 37 greatly simplifies the system."*

On her eightieth birthday, a woman from Brooklyn decides to prepare her last will and testament. She goes to her rabbi to make two final requests. First, she insists on cremation.

"What is your second request?" the rabbi asks.

"I want my ashes scattered over Bloomingdale's."

"Why Bloomingdale's?"

"Then I'll be sure that my daughters visit me twice a week."

—*The Big Book of Jewish Humor*, edited by
WILLIAM NOVAK and MOSHE WALDOKS

The couple had reached an age where the wife thought it was time to start considering wills and funeral arrangements rather than be caught unprepared. Her husband, however, wasn't too interested in the topic. "Would you rather be buried or cremated?" she asked him.

There was a pause, then he replied from behind his paper, "Surprise me."

—JIM GIBSON in the Victoria, B.C., *Times-Colonist*

A guy walked into the tax collector's office with a huge bandage on his nose. "Had an accident?" asked the tax agent.

"No," answered the man. "I've been paying through it for so long, it gave way under the strain."

—RALPH GOLDSMITH in the Boscobel, Wis., *Dial*

Fire swept the plains and burned down the farmer's barn. While he surveyed the wreckage, his wife called their insurance company and asked them to send a check for $50,000, the amount of insurance on the barn.

"We don't give you the money," a company official explained. "We replace the barn and all the equipment in it."

"In that case," replied the wife, "cancel the policy I have on my husband."

NAOMI WILKINS in *Woman's World*

President Clinton says he looks forward to the day a citizen can call the IRS and get the right answer to a question," says Jay Leno. "I look forward to the day I can call the IRS and get a voice that says, 'Sorry, that number has been disconnected.'"

*"I suppose it's inevitable that we occasionally lose someone to a better mousetrap!"*

# Technology

# Gadgets and Gizmos

Frank was setting up a sundial in his yard when a neighbor asked, "What's that for?"

Frank stopped to explain, "The sun hits that small triangular spike and casts a shadow on the face of the sundial. Then, as the sun moves across the sky, the shadow also moves across the calibrated dial, enabling a person to determine the correct time."

The neighbor shook his head. "What will they think of next?"

—RON DENTINGER in the
Dodgeville, Wis., *Chronicle*

Son to his father as they watch television: "Dad, tell me again how when you were a kid you had to walk all the way across the room to change the channel."

—BUCELLA in *VFW*

Overheard: "I hate talking cars. A voice out of nowhere says things like, 'Your door is ajar.' Why don't they say something really useful, like 'There's a state trooper hiding behind that bush.'"

—*Current Comedy*

And then there's the fellow who's sorry he ever installed a car telephone. He finds it such a nuisance having to run to the garage every time it rings.

—*The Rotarian*

One hypochondriac to another: "My doctor is on the cutting edge of technology. He told me to take two aspirin and fax him in the morning."

—*Current Comedy*

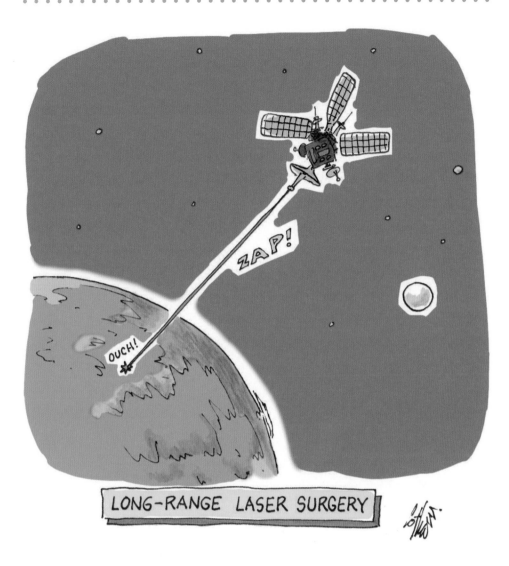

LONG-RANGE LASER SURGERY

*Dragnet's* Sgt. Joe Friday decided to upgrade the office communication system, so he went to an electronics store to see what was available. A saleswoman showed Friday the latest in cellular phones, intercoms, facsimile machines, and two-way radios. "Are you interested in purchasing a new telephone system?" she asked.

"No," replied Friday. "Just the fax, ma'am."

—Tim Moore

Clem decided it was time to purchase a new saw to help clear his heavily timbered property. A salesman showed him the latest model chain saw and assured him that he could easily cut three or four cords of wood per day with it.

But the first day Clem barely cut one cord of wood. The second morning he arose an hour earlier and managed to cut a little over one cord. The third day he got up even earlier but only managed to achieve a total of 1 1/2 cords of wood.

Clem returned the saw to the store the next day and explained the situation. "Well," said the salesman, "let's see what's the matter." He then pulled the cable and the chain saw sprang into action.

Leaping back, Clem exclaimed, "What the heck is that noise?"

—GREGORY POTTER

Overheard: "Even my mother is getting caught up in our high-tech environment. Just the other day she was complaining, 'You don't write, you don't call, you don't fax.' "

—*Current Comedy for Speakers*

Did you hear about the high-tech ventriloquist?
He can throw his voice mail.

—GARY APPLE in *Speaker's Idea File*

And what would you like for Christmas this year?" a department store Santa asked the cute kid sitting on his lap.
The little girl was indignant. "Didn't you get the fax I sent you?"

—Quoted by ELSTON BROOKS in the Fort Worth *Star-Telegram*

There's a new telephone service that lets you test your IQ over the phone," says Jay Leno. "It costs $3.95 a minute. If you make the call at all, you're a moron. If you're on the line for three minutes, you're a complete idiot."

Overheard: "Yesterday I got my tie stuck in the fax machine. Next thing I knew, I was in Los Angeles."

—STEVE HAUPT

When I was a youngster," complained the frustrated father, "I was disciplined by being sent to my room without supper. But my son has his own color TV, phone, computer, and CD player."

"So what do you do?" asked his friend.

"I send him to my room!"

—*Capper's*

They say by the year 2000, video cameras will be the size of postage stamps and will cost 50 dollars. Of course by then postage stamps will cost 60 dollars. . . .

—WAYNE COTTER, *Comic Strip Live*, FOX TV

Satan agreed to be interviewed on the Larry King show. Asked what he thought were his greatest accomplishments, the devil thought for a minute.

"I always look back with a smile on the sinking of the *Titanic*," he mused. "But there are so many fond memories of wars, disasters, and cities laid waste, it's hard to pick out a favorite."

"Come on," pressed King. "There must be one foul deed you consider your crowning achievement."

"Well, yes," admitted Satan. "I invented Call Waiting."

—ARGUS HAMILTON in Oklahoma City *Daily Oklahoman*

My sister gave birth in a state-of-the-art delivery room," said one man to another. "It was so high-tech that the baby came out cordless."

—*Current Comedy*

Department store automatic answering machine:
"If you are calling to order or send money, press 5.
"If you are calling to register a complaint, press 6 4 5 9 8 3 4 8 2 2 9 5 5 3 9 2.
"Have a good day."

—HAL THUROW

Patron: "What time do you have?"
Bartender: "I don't have a watch anymore. I bought one that was waterproof, dustproof, and shockproof."
Patron: "Well, where is it?"
Bartender: "It caught fire."

—YOUNG and DRAKE, King Features Syndicate

Phone-answering machines for the rich and famous:
- Sylvester Stallone—"Yo. You. Message. Now."
- Sally Field—"If you like me—if you really *like* me—leave your name and number after the beep."
- Clint Eastwood—"Go ahead, leave a message. Make my day."
- Shirley MacLaine—"I already know who you are and what you're calling about. Simply leave a brief description of your present incarnation."

—Maureen Larkin in *Ladies' Home Journal*

Did you hear about the robot that was so ugly it had a face only a motor could love?

—Shelby Friedman

Two executives in expensive suits stopped off at a small country bar. As the bartender served them, he heard a muffled *beep beep* sound and watched as one of the men calmly removed a pen from his inside coat pocket and began carrying on a conversation. When he was done talking, the exec noticed the bartender and other customers giving him puzzled looks. "I was just answering a call on my state-of-the-art cellular pen," he explained.

A short while later another odd tone was heard. This time the second executive picked up his fancy hat, fiddled with the lining and started talking into it. After a few minutes he put the hat back on the bar. "That was just a call on my state-of-the-art cellular hat," he said matter-of-factly.

A few stools down one of the locals suddenly let out a loud burp. "Quick!" he exclaimed. "Anybody got a piece of paper? I have a fax comin' in!"

—*John Boy & Billy,* Radio Network

While Milgrom waited at the airport to board his plane, he noticed a computer scale that would give your weight and a fortune. He dropped a quarter in the slot, and the computer screen displayed: "You weigh 195 pounds, you're married, and you're on your way to San Diego." Milgrom stood there dumbfounded.

Another man put in a quarter and the computer read: "You weigh 184 pounds, you're divorced, and you're on your way to Chicago."

Milgrom said to the man, "Are you divorced and on your way to Chicago?"

"Yes," came the reply.

Milgrom was amazed. Then he rushed to the men's room, changed his clothes and put on dark glasses. He went to the machine again. The computer read: "You still weigh 195 pounds, you're still married, and you just missed your plane to San Diego!"

—STEVE WOZNIAK and LARRY WILDE,
*The Official Computer Freaks Joke Book*

# Bright Ideas

**Q**: How many car salesmen does it take to change a light bulb?
A: I'm just going to work this out on my calculator, and I think you're going to be pleasantly surprised.

—ROBERT WILBURN, quoted by
MARY ANN MADDEN in *New York*

How many politicians does it take to change a light bulb?
A. Five—one to change it and four to deny it.

—TINA FRENCH

**Q**: How many bullies does it take to change a light bulb?
A: Four. Do you have a problem with that?

—DENNIS LEEKE

**Q**: "How many bureaucrats does it take to change a light bulb?"
A: "Two. One to assure us that everything possible is being done while the other screws the bulb into a water faucet."

*—Voice for Health*

**Q**: How many unemployed actors does it take to change a light bulb?
A: 100. One to change it, and 99 to stand around and say, "Hey, I could've done that!"

*—One to One*

**Q**: How many economists does it take to change a light bulb?
A: How many did it take this time last year?

*—The Jokesmith*

**Q**: How many real-estate agents does it take to change a light bulb?
A: Ten. But we'll accept eight.

*—*BILL HOMISAK, quoted by
MARY ANN MADDEN in *New York*

**Q**: How many liberated women does it take to change a light bulb?
A: Five! One to turn it, and four to form a support group.

*—*JAY TRACHMAN in *One to One*

**Q**: How many surrealist painters does it take to change a light bulb?
A: A fish.

*—*HORACE DAVIES, quoted by
MARY ANN MADDEN in *New York*

*"I'll make a deal with you. I'll tell you the secret of life if you'll tell me how to program my VCR."*

**Q**: How many feminists does it take to change a light bulb?
A: That's not funny.

—CHRISTINA HOFF SOMMERS,
*Who Stole Feminism?*

**T**homas Edison spent years trying to invent the electric light, testing and retesting. Finally, late one night, he got the bulb to glow. He ran out of his laboratory, through the house, up the stairs to his bedroom. "Honey," Edison called to his wife, "I've done it!"

She rolled over and said, "Will you turn off that light and come to bed!"

—RON DENTINGER in
*Work Sheet*

**Q**: How many country-western singers does it take to change a light bulb?

A: Five. One to put in the new bulb, and four to sing about how much they long for the old one.

—Leslie R. Tanner

# :) \&/HA HA!

Delbert and Fletch, two industrial robots, escaped from the engineering lab one Saturday night. They decided to separate, pick up some dates and meet later.

A few hours passed and Delbert arrived at the meeting place. He found Fletch standing in front of a mailbox and a fire alarm. "Who are your two friends?" asked Delbert.

"Forget them," sighed Fletch. "The short, fat one with the big mouth just stands there, and if you touch the redhead she screams her lungs out."

—Ed McManus, quoted by Steve Wozniak and Larry Wilde in *The Official Computer Freaks Joke Book*

Mrs. B: "Why are you laughing?"
Mrs. D: "A salesman tried to sell my husband a lap-top computer."
Mrs. B: "What's so funny about that?"
Mrs. D: "My husband hasn't had a lap in 20 years!"

—Young and Drake, King Features Syndicate

Did you hear about the new computer Apple has developed, small enough to be carried in a fanny pack? It will be called the Macintush.

—Tom Cloud, quoted by Abigail Van Buren, Universal Press Syndicate

A computer salesman dies and meets St. Peter at the Pearly Gates. St. Peter tells the salesman that he can choose between heaven and hell. First he shows the man heaven, where people in white robes play harps and float around. "Dull," says the salesman.

Next, St. Peter shows him hell: toga parties, good food and wine, and people looking as though they're having a fine time. "I'll take hell," he says.

He enters the gates of hell and is immediately set upon by a dozen demons, who poke him with pitchforks. "Hey," the salesman demands as Satan walks past, "what happened to the party I saw going on?"

"Ah," Satan replies. "You must have seen our demo."

*—Digital Review*

Chip Ahoy
I bought the latest computer;
It came completely loaded.
It was guaranteed for 90 days,
But in 30 was outmoded.

—BILL IHLENFELDT in *The Wall Street Journal*

That computer you sold me is no good," complained the customer. "It keeps flashing insulting messages, like 'Look it up yourself, stupid.'"

"Oh," replied the store clerk, "you must have one of our new 'User Surly' models."

—JOHNNY HART, Creators Syndicate

The computer programmer, it seems, had allowed for every contingency. One day the operator became frustrated with her work and punched in a highly unladylike message. On the console a response immediately flashed up: "Tut, tut, improper expression."

—JANE ROUX

**Q**: Why is a modem better than a woman?

A: A modem doesn't complain if you sit and play at the computer all night. A modem doesn't mind if you talk to other modems. A modem will sit patiently and wait by the phone. A modem comes with an instruction manual.

—JAY TRACHMAN in *One to One*

The exec was making a presentation to the company board. "Computers have allowed us to cut costs," he explained. "We expect even more dramatic improvements as computers become increasingly self-sufficient." He unveiled a large chart showing a man, a dog, and a computer. "Here is our organization plan of the future."

"What kind of plan is that?" demanded a board member.

"It's simple," replied the exec. "The man's job is to feed the dog. The dog's job is to bite the man if he touches the computer."

—LOUIS A. MAMAKOS

# Space Invaders

Upon their return from an excursion to our planet, two Martians presented their chief with a television set. "We couldn't manage to capture any Earthlings," they explained, "but we did get our hands on one of their gods."

—MINA and ANDRÉ GUILLOIS

A pair of Martians landed on a country road on Earth in the middle of the night. "Where are we?" one asked.

"I think we're in a cemetery," his companion answered. "Look at the gravestone over there—that man lived to be 108."

"What was his name?"

"Miles to Omaha."

"Take me to your remote control."

**A** service station attendant watching a Martian put gas into its spacecraft noticed that "UFO" was printed on the spaceship's side. "Does that stand for 'Unidentified Flying Object'?" he asked the Martian.

"No," the creature replied. " 'Unleaded Fuel Only.' "

—DELFORT D. MINOR

**T**he White House is proposing we collaborate with Russia to build a new space station," says Jay Leno. "Know what that means? We're going to wind up with a space station that has a $30-million-dollar toilet—and no toilet paper."

**T**he week before a space launch, an astronaut tries to relax at an out-of-the-way pub. But the bartender recognizes him and says, "You fellows at NASA think you're something, going to the moon. But we've got a couple of guys here who've been building their own spaceship out back."

Reluctantly, the astronaut goes outside to look—the spaceship is a mess of beer bottles, cans and junk. "We're planning to go to the sun," boasts one guy.

"This thing will be incinerated before you can get close to the sun," the astronaut warns.

"We got that all figured out—we're going at night!"

—HERMAN GOLLOB in *Texas Monthly*

**I**t's the year 2210, and the planets have long been colonized. Interplanetary flight is as everyday as transcontinental flight, and on one of these interplanetary liners a Martian colonist strikes up a conversation with the passenger next to him. "Where are you from?" he asks.

"Earth," is the reply.

"Oh, really? By any chance do you know . . .?"

—MARK S. ZUELKE

*"See you, Roger. I'm returning to the private sector."*

# Talking Animals

## PET PEEVES 202

## WILD THINGS 210

# Pet Peeves

Is our parrot a daddy or a mommy?" asked the young boy of his mother on a crowded bus.

"She is a mommy parrot," the mother replied.

"How do we know?" the boy asked.

A hush fell over the passengers as they listened for how the mother would cope with this one. But she was ready for the challenge and replied, "She has lipstick on, hasn't she?"

—R. SARANGAPANI

The neighbor's young son came knocking at the housewife's door every day to ask if he could take her dog for a walk. Her husband, who was a carpenter, almost always took the animal with him to his jobs, so she told the child, "I'm sorry, but the dog is at work with my husband." Because the boy kept coming over every day with the same request, she always gave him the same response.

The youngster met the woman on the street one day, stopped and eyed her suspiciously. "Say," he asked, "what does your dog do for a living?"

—METTE R. NYHUS

John, teaching his parrot to talk: "Repeat after me, 'I can walk.'"
Parrot: "I can walk."
John: "I can talk."
Parrot: "I can talk."
John: "I can fly."
Parrot: "That's a lie."

—FATEH ZUNG SINGH

Overheard: "My neighbor's dog is taking the advanced course at obedience school. He knows how to fetch, heel and beg—now he's learning to fax."

—JAY TRACHMAN in *One to One*

When the farmer arrived at the obedience school to pick up his newly trained bird dog, he asked the instructor for a demonstration. The two men and the dog went to a nearby field, where the dog immediately pointed to a clump of brush, then rolled over twice.

"There are two birds in there," the instructor said, and sure enough, two birds were flushed. A minute later, the dog pointed to another bunch of bushes, and then rolled over five times.

"There are five birds in there," the instructor noted, and indeed five birds were driven from the brush. Then the dog pointed to a third clump. He began to whine and run in circles until he found a stick, which he shook mightily and dropped at the men's feet.

"And in that clump of brush there," the proud instructor concluded, "there are more birds than you can shake a stick at!"

—*Country*

Sign seen in a veterinarian's office: The doctor is in. Sit. Stay.

—GALE SHIPLEY

An agent arranged an audition with a TV producer for his client, a talking dog that told jokes and sang songs. The amazed producer was about to sign a contract when suddenly a much larger dog burst into the room, grabbed the talking pooch by the neck and bounded back out.

"What happened?" demanded the producer.

"That's his mother," said the agent. "She wants him to be a doctor."

—*Cheer*

**O**verheard at the veterinarian's: "I had my cat neutered. He's still out all night with the other cats, but now it's in the role of consultant."

—*Current Comedy*

**W**alking down the street, a dog saw a sign in an office window. "Help wanted. Must type 70 words a minute. Must be computer literate. Must be bilingual. An equal-opportunity employer."

The dog applied for the position, but he was quickly rebuffed. "I can't hire a dog for this job," the office manager said. But when the dog pointed to the line that read "An equal-opportunity employer," the office manager sighed and asked, "Can you type?" Silently, the dog walked over to a typewriter and flawlessly banged out a letter. "Can you operate a computer?" the manager inquired. The dog then sat down at a terminal, wrote a program and ran it perfectly.

"Look, I still can't hire a dog for this position," said the exasperated office manager. "You have fine skills, but I need someone who's bilingual. It says so right in the ad."

The dog looked up at the manager and said, "Meow."

—DONALD WEINSTEIN, quoted by LAWRENCE VAN GELDER
in *The New York Times*

**A** dog goes into the unemployment office and asks for help finding a job. "With your rare talent," says the clerk, "I'm sure we can get you something at the circus."

"The circus?" echoes the dog. "What would a circus want with a plumber?"

—JAY TRACHMAN in *One to One*

**D**id you hear about the cat that gave birth in a Singapore street? It got fined for littering.

—DAWN FUNG

*"Have you noticed how Ed has changed since he started going to law school?"*

Please keep your dog beside you, sir," a woman said crossly to the man sitting opposite her on the bus. "I can feel a flea in my shoe."

"Bello, come here," replied the man. "That woman has fleas."

—J. G.

Mrs. Klapisch brought her cat to the veterinarian. The doctor had her hold the animal on the examining table as he touched and gently squeezed it. He then walked slowly around the table, all the while looking back and forth, back and forth. When he was done, he gave out some medication and presented Mrs. Klapisch with the bill.

"What?" she cried. "One hundred fifty dollars for two pills?"

"Not just for pills," said the vet. "I gave her a cat scan too."

—David W. Fleeton

Henry's new job had him spending a lot of time on the road, and out of concern for his wife's safety he visited a pet shop to look at watchdogs.

"I have just the dog for you," said the salesman, showing him a miniature Pekingese.

"Come on," Henry protested, "that little thing couldn't hurt a flea."

"Ah, but he knows karate," the salesman replied. "Here, let me show you." He pointed to a cardboard box and ordered, "Karate the box!" Immediately the dog shredded it. The salesman then pointed to an old wooden chair and instructed, "Karate the chair!" The dog reduced the chair to matchsticks. Astounded, Henry bought the dog.

When he got home, Henry announced that he had purchased a watchdog, but his wife took one look at the Pekingese and was unimpressed. "That scrawny thing couldn't fight his way out of a paper bag!" she said.

"But this Pekingese is special," Henry insisted. "He's a karate expert."

"Now I've heard everything," Helen replied. "Karate my foot!"

—Jim Ellsworth

Several racehorses are in a stable. One of them starts boasting about his track record.

"Of my last 15 races," he says, "I've won eight."

Another horse breaks in, "Well, I've won 19 of my last 27!"

"That's good, but I've taken 28 of 36," says another, flicking his tail.

At this point a greyhound who's been sitting nearby pipes up. "I don't mean to boast," he says, "but of my last 90 races, I've won 88."

The horses are clearly amazed. "Wow," says one after a prolonged silence, "a talking dog!"

—Peter S. Langston

I'm really worried about my dog," Ralph said to the veterinarian. "I dropped some coins on the floor and before I could pick them up, he ate them." The vet advised Ralph to leave his dog at the vet's office overnight.

The next morning, Ralph called to see how his pet was doing. The vet replied, "No change yet."

—MIKE WALT, SR.

The pet-shop customer couldn't believe his good fortune. The parrot he had just bought could recite Shakespeare's sonnets, imitate opera stars and intone Homer's epic poems in Greek. And he cost only $600.

Once the man got the bird home, however, not another word passed his beak. After three weeks the disconsolate customer returned to the shop and asked for his money back. "When we had this bird," said the proprietor, "he could recite poetry and sing like an angel. Now you want me to take him back when he's no longer himself? Well, all right. Out of the goodness of my heart I'll give you $100."

Reluctantly the man accepted his loss. Just as the door shut behind him he heard the parrot say to the shop owner, "Don't forget—my share is $250."

—C. A. HENDERSON

A man answered his doorbell, and a friend walked in, followed by a very large dog. As they began talking, the dog knocked over a lamp, jumped on the sofa with his muddy paws and began chewing a pillow. The outraged householder, unable to contain himself any longer, burst out, "Can't you control your dog better?"

"*My* dog!" exclaimed the friend. "I thought it was *your* dog."

—*The Great Clean Jokes Calendar*

*"I'm sick and tired of begging."*

**A** man trained his dog to go around the corner to Bud's Lounge every day with two dollar bills under his collar to get a pack of cigarettes. Once the man only had a five, so he put it under the collar and sent the dog on his way.

An hour passed and the pooch still hadn't returned. So the man went to Bud's and found his dog sitting on a bar stool, drinking a beer. He said, "You've never done this before."

Replied the dog, "I never had the money before."

—GARRISON KEILLOR, *We Are Still Married*

**A** guy walks into a bar and orders a beer. "Listen," he says to the bartender. "If I show you the most amazing thing you've ever seen, is my beer on the house?"

"We'll see," says the bartender. So the guy pulls a hamster and a tiny piano out of a bag, puts them on the bar, and the hamster begins to play. "Impressive," says the bartender, "but I'll need to see more."

"Hold on," says the man. He then pulls out a bullfrog, and it sings "Old Man River." A patron jumps up from his table and shouts, "That's absolutely incredible! I'll give you $100 right now for the frog."

"Sold," says the guy. The other patron takes the bullfrog and leaves.

"It's none of my business," says the bartender, "but you just gave away a fortune."

"Not really," says the guy. "The hamster is also a ventriloquist."

—ANDY BALE, WHUD, Peekskill, N.Y.


**A** man went to the movies and was surprised to find a woman with a big collie sitting in front of him. Even more amazing was the fact that the dog always laughed in the right places through the comedy.

"Excuse me," the man said to the woman, "but I think it's astounding that your dog enjoys the movie so much."

"I'm surprised myself," she replied. "He hated the book."

—GRAHAM FOSTER in Tomahawk, Wis., *Leader,*
quoted by DEBBIE CHRISTIAN in the Milwaukee *Journal*


**K**erry the tomcat was scampering all over the neighborhood—down alleys, up fire escapes, into cellars. A disturbed neighbor knocked on the owner's door and said, "Your cat is rushing about like mad."

"I know," the man conceded. "Kerry's just been neutered, and he's running around canceling engagements."

—LARRY WILDE, *Library of Laughter*

# Wild Things

**A** forest ranger, trekking through a remote campground area, caught a whiff of something burning in the distance. Farther along the trail he found an old hermit making his evening meal.

"What are you cooking?" the ranger asked.

"Peregrine falcon," answered the hermit.

"*Peregrine falcon!*" the conservationist said, shocked. "You can't cook that! It's on the endangered species list."

"How was I to know?" the hermit questioned. "I haven't had contact with the outside world in ages."

The ranger told the recluse he wouldn't report him this time, but he wasn't to cook peregrine falcon ever again. "By the way," he asked, "what does it taste like?"

"Well," replied the hermit, "I'd say it's somewhere between a dodo bird and a whooping crane."

—RICHARD SCHULDt, quoted by Alex Thien
in the Milwaukee *Sentinel*

**A** father took his children to the zoo. All were looking forward to seeing the monkeys. Unfortunately, it was mating time and, the attendant explained, the monkeys had gone inside their little sanctuary for some togetherness. "Would they come out for some peanuts?" asked the father.

"Would you?" responded the attendant.

—CHARLEY MANOS in *The Detroit News*

**W**hen a snail crossed the road, he was run over by a turtle. Regaining consciousness in the emergency room, he was asked what caused the accident.

"I really can't remember," the snail replied. "You see, it all happened so fast."

—CHARLES MCMANIS

*"I don't know why I even made this trip—I'm not even sexually active."*

The photographer had been trying for hours to get some action shots of a bear that preferred to sleep in its cage. "What kind of bear is that?" he finally asked the zoo keeper.

"Himalayan," was the reply.

"I know that," snarled the photographer. "What I want to know is when him a getting up."

—RICHARD A. UECKER

The zoo built a special eight-foot-high enclosure for its newly acquired kangaroo, but the next morning the animal was found hopping around outside. The height of the fence was increased to 15 feet, but the kangaroo got out again. Exasperated, the zoo director had the height increased to 30 feet, but the kangaroo still escaped. A giraffe asked the kangaroo, "How high do you think they'll build the fence?"

"I don't know," said the kangaroo. "Maybe a thousand feet if they keep leaving the gate unlocked."

—JERRY H. SIMPSON, JR.

A woman lion tamer had the big cats under such control they took a lump of sugar from her lips on command. "Anyone can do that!" a skeptic yelled.

The ringmaster came over and asked, "Would you like to try it?"

"Sure," replied the man, "but first get those crazy lions out of there!"

—*Healthwise*

A rooster was strutting around the henhouse one Easter morning and came across a nest of eggs dyed every color of the rainbow. The rooster took one look at the colorful display, ran outside and beat the heck out of the resident peacock.

—SEYMOUR ROSENBERG in the
Spartanburg, S.C., *Herald-Journal*

As spring migration approached, two elderly vultures doubted they could make the trip north, so they decided to go by airplane.

When they checked their baggage, the attendant noticed that they were carrying two dead armadillos. "Do you wish to check the armadillos through as luggage?" she asked.

"No, thanks," replied the vultures. "They're carrion."

—FRED BRICE

The old big-game hunter is recounting his adventures to his grandson:

"I remember, I once had to brave eight ferocious lions with no gun, nothing but a knife to defend me. My life was at stake. . . ."

"Granddad, the last time you told this story, there were only three lions!"

"Yes, but then you were too young to hear the terrible truth."

—ADAM WOLFART

Did you hear about the scientist who crossed a carrier pigeon with a woodpecker?

He got a bird that not only delivers messages to their destination but knocks on the door when it gets there.

—JOHN R. FOX

An antelope and a lion entered a diner and took a booth near the window. When the waiter approached, the antelope said, "I'll have a bowl of hay and a side order of radishes."

"And what will your friend have?"

"Nothing," replied the antelope.

The waiter persisted. "Isn't he hungry?"

"Hey, if he were hungry," said the antelope, "would I be sitting here?"

—*Current Comedy*

An expert on whales was telling friends about some of the unusual findings he had made. "For instance," he said, "some whales can communicate at a distance of 300 miles."

"What on earth would one whale say to another 300 miles away?" asked an astounded member of the group.

"I'm not absolutely sure," answered the expert, "but it sounds something like 'Can you still hear me?'"

—STEVE KEUCHEL

TALKING ANIMALS

*"Forgive me? It must have been the beast in me talking."*

We have a skunk in the basement," shrieked the caller to the police dispatcher. "How can we get it out?"

"Take some bread crumbs," said the dispatcher, "and put down a trail from the basement out to the backyard. Then leave the cellar door open."

Sometime later the resident called back. "Did you get rid of it?" asked the dispatcher.

"No," replied the caller. "Now I have two skunks in there!"

—*Ohio Motorist*

And then there was the male spotted owl who told his wife, "What do you mean you have a headache? We're an endangered species!"

—John Bunzel, quoted by Herb Caen
in the San Francisco *Chronicle*

While drinking at the lake, a young bear admires its reflection and growls, "I am the king of beasts!"

Along comes a lion and roars, "What was that I just heard?"

"Oh, dear," says the bear, "you say strange things when you've had too much to drink."

—Lea Berner

Dad," a polar bear cub asked his father, "am I 100 percent polar bear?"

"Of course you are," answered the elder bear. "My parents are 100 percent polar bear, which makes me 100 percent polar bear. Your mother's parents are all polar bear, so she's 100 percent polar bear. Yep, that makes you 100 percent polar bear too. Why do you want to know?"

Replied the cub, " 'Cause I'm freezing!"

—"T & T," KCYY, San Antonio

A male crab met a female crab and asked her to marry him. She noticed that he was walking straight instead of sideways. *Wow*, she thought, *this crab is really special. I can't let him get away.* So they got married immediately.

The next day she noticed her new husband walking sideways like all the other crabs, and got upset. "What happened?" she asked. "You used to walk straight before we were married."

"Oh, honey," he replied, "I can't drink that much every day."

—Gity Kazemian

# LAUGHTER
## REALLY IS
## THE BEST MEDICINE

Reader's
Digest's
Funniest Jokes,
Quotes, and
Cartoons

# Contents

# A Note from the Editors

"You grow up the day you have the first real laugh—at yourself."

Those words from Ethel Barrymore couldn't be more true. Something we all have in common is the ability to laugh at ourselves and the comical situations life brings to us. The comedian Rodney Dangerfield may have joked about not getting any respect, but in reality his talent for tickling our funny bones earned him many guffaws and fans. Moments of laughter take us to another place—one filled with much-needed comic relief.

Inside this collection of jokes, one-liners, cartoons, and quotable quotes from the popular Reader's Digest column "Laughter, the Best Medicine®," you'll find Dangerfield, Barrymore, and hundreds more celebrities, professional comedians, joke writers, as well as everyday folks, who poke fun at the facts and foibles of daily life. And you'll find that no subject is sacred. From politics, religion, technology, doctors, and lawyers to sports, pets, children, and relationships—our day-to-day experiences provide all we need for this unbeatable collection.

So take a break and get ready to laugh. We think that these lighthearted glimpses of life are just what the doctor ordered!

# @Work

Some laughs to make the 9-to-5 grind a little less bumpy

# In the Office

My friend had been pounding the pavement in search of a job with no luck. Frustrated, she asked her dad to look at her résumé. He didn't get much further than the first line of her cover letter before spotting the problem.

"Is it too generic?" she asked.

"I doubt it," said her father.

"Especially since it's addressed 'Dear Sir or Madman.'"

—GISELLE MELANSON

My friend's hour-and-a-half commute to work got old quickly—the time spent stuck in traffic was sending him over the edge. So I was happy for him when he found a new job closer to home.

"That's great," I said. "What are you doing now?"

"I'm a bus driver."

—ELYSA STANTON

My secretary liked to yammer on the phone with friends. One day I was about to interrupt her chat to tell her to get back to work, when she looked up at the clock and put an end to the conversation. "Sorry, I have to hang up now," she said. "It's time for my break."

—JAMES R. MAXWELL

Applicants for jobs at the company where my friend Diana works are asked to fill out a questionnaire. Among the things candidates list is their high school and when they attended. One prospective employee dutifully wrote the name of his high school, followed by the dates attended: "Monday, Tuesday, Wednesday, Thursday and Friday."

—JENNIFER CARUANA

**"What did you take away from the meeting?"**

My coworker Sarah was annoyed that our company's automated telephone directory had mangled her last name. She called the person in charge and asked that he fix it.

"Sorry," he said. "All requests must be made via e-mail."

"Okay," said Sarah, "just tell me how to e-mail the correct pronunciation for Zuckschwerdt."

—REBECCA COLE

**"Tech support was no help.
Now I'm on hold for dialect support."**

**W**inding his way through the office cubicles, my son Mike spotted one of his employees playing a video game on the computer.

"Why aren't you working?" Mike asked him.

The employee had an excellent excuse: "I didn't see you coming."

—ROSEMARY SIEVE

"Good morning," I said to a coworker in the parking lot. She mumbled something back and continued to the front door, distracted. As we walked, I couldn't help but notice that she was muttering to herself: "It pays the bills, it pays the bills, it pays the bills . . ."

—LINDA TILLMAN

Our office manager is a tyrant when it comes to keeping the printer area clean. Recently, a coworker printed something, but when he went to pick up the document, it was gone.

"You know I throw out everything that's more than 24 hours old," the manager told him.

"But I just printed it," my friend insisted.

"Sorry," she said. "But I'm not in tomorrow."

—NOEL ROWLAND

As a business-writing instructor, I read lots of résumés. Inevitably, I run across some students with skills no employer could pass up, such as:

- The young paramedic who "makes life-threatening decisions on a daily basis."
- A child-care worker who can "overlook up to 35 children at one time."
- An enterprising young woman who is "flexible enough to perform in all manner of positions if the situation gets desperate."

—AUTUMN CAMPBELL

**?** **So how do you make a computer your best bud?**

Buy it a nice bunch of software and get it loaded.

DAVID E. BOELTER

**B**efore leaving my assistant job for greener pastures, I was asked to reply to applicants hoping to replace me. "Very smart and intelligent," my boss had written on one of the applications. "Too good for this job."

—VI BRIERLEY

**A**fter my wife landed a coveted job offer from DHL, we went out of town to celebrate. While on our trip, she was contacted by the company's human resources department with an urgent request to complete and send back her tax forms.

"No problem," she said. "I'll FedEx them right over."

—ROSS MCCOY

**T**he average insurance agent's workday can be pretty mundane—except when he gets to read claim forms like these from actual auto accidents.

- The pedestrian had no idea which way to go, so I ran over him.
- I had been driving my car for 40 years when I fell asleep at the wheel and had an accident.
- I was on the way to the doctor's with rear-end trouble when my universal joint gave way, causing me to have an accident.
- An invisible car came out of nowhere, struck my vehicle and vanished.

**W**hen I phoned my employee to find out why she hadn't come to the office, I expected to hear a sob story about how sick she was, blah, blah, blah. Instead, her excuse was pretty plausible.

"When I was driving to work, I took a wrong turn," she explained. "And then I just decided to keep going."

—JUDIE SHEWELL

I've heard every excuse from coworkers for missing a day of work. But this one actually sounded legit.

"What's wrong?" I asked a woman who called in. "Are you sick?"

"No," she said. "I can't find a cute pair of shoes to wear."

—JOSHUA DONALDSON

**"Here you go, Fenniman. This is where the budget meets the road."**

Asked about the kind of job he wanted, an applicant at our tax management company stated, "I seek full authority but limited responsibility."

—MIKE WILKERSON

"What starting salary are you looking for?" the head of human resources asks the newly graduated engineer at the end of a job interview.

Going for it, the guy says, "Well, sir, I was thinking about $125,000, depending on the benefits package."

"Okay," the HR director says. "How about five weeks' vacation, 14 paid holidays, full medical and dental, 100% company match for your 401(k) and a Porsche for your company car?"

The engineer gasps and says, "Wow! Are you kidding?"

"Yeah," he replies. "But you started it."

Many senior executives find talking with management consultants invaluable. My friend, a no-nonsense businessman who works for a large firm, is not one of them. Halfway through their meeting, and noting my friend's terse answers, the consultant asked, "How do you cope with managerial stress?"

"I don't," came the gruff reply. "I cause it."

—CLIVE ATTWATERS

"That's a great place to work!" shouted my 16-year-old brother after coming home from the first day at his first job. "I get two weeks' paid vacation."

"I'm so glad," said my mother.

"Yeah," added John. "I can't wait to find out where they send me."

—STEPHANIE DIOCEDO

**"W**hy did you leave your last job?"
**"I**t was something my boss said."
**"W**hat did he say?"

**"'You're fired!'"**

—HEIDI GORDON

**W**hen asked her opinion on punctuality, an applicant for an office job assured me she thought it was extremely important. "I use periods, commas, and question marks all the time," she said.

—MEL ROBERTS

**I** work for a chartered bank in Ottawa, but my support unit is in Toronto. A colleague from the support unit e-mailed me to say she was missing a report due from one of my clients. I e-mailed back that I had faxed it to her earlier that morning and to check another file because the two reports were faxed at the same time.

"Thanks," she replied when she found it, "but please don't staple files together when you are faxing them to us."

—DENISE LOSIER

**D**ave irritated everyone in our office. Whether it was the tone of his voice or his condescending attitude, we all steered clear. He must have suspected he was annoying because he asked a coworker, "Why does everybody take an instant dislike to me?"

Larry responded, "It saves time."

—DAVID GOEHRING

**A** job interviewer asked me where I wanted to be in five years. I said, "Ideally, suspended with pay."

—COMIC ANDREA HENRY

PLEASE PICK UP GPS SYSTEM BEFORE ENTERING.

**R**ob and Tom apply for the same job. They take a written test. "You both got the same number of questions wrong," the HR person tells them, "but Rob gets the job."

"If we both got the same number of questions wrong, how come he gets the job?" Tom asks indignantly.

"Well," says the HR person, "one of his incorrect answers was better than yours."

"Whoa, how can that be?"

"For problem No. 46, Rob wrote, 'I don't know.' You wrote, 'Me neither.'"

—SAQIB AHMAD

In the human resources department in the large corporation where I work, I receive absentee slips for all of the employees. Over the years I've heard every excuse, ranging from the reasonable ("I had no hot water") to the questionable ("My dog might have rabies"). But the other day I found one in my voice mail that I'd never heard before.

"I won't be in today," said my absent coworker. "I'll call back later with an excuse."

—KATHY PRICE

A junior manager, senior manager and their boss were on their way to a lunch meeting. In the cab they found a lamp. The boss rubbed it, and a genie appeared. "I'll grant you one wish each," the genie said.

Grabbing the lamp from his boss, the eager senior manager shouted, "I want to be on a fast boat in the Bahamas with no worries." And *poof*, he was gone.

The junior manager couldn't keep quiet. He shouted, "I want to be in Miami, with beautiful girls, food and cocktails." And *poof*, he was gone.

Finally, it was the boss's turn. "I want those idiots back in the office after lunch."

—ASHFAQ AHMED

Having looked the other way for weeks, the boss finally called Smith into his office for a sit-down.

"You know, Smith," he said, "I've noticed that every time you have to take your dear old aunt to her doctor's appointments, there's a home game over at the stadium."

"Wow, sir. I guess you're right," Smith answered.

"I didn't realize it. You don't think she's faking it, do you?"

—SHARON KANSAS

Percentage of the workweek that a typical worker spends in meetings: 25. **Odds that a person at a meeting doesn't know why he's there: 1 in 3.**

—FROM *FIRED!* BY ANNABELLE GURWITCH (TOUCHSTONE)

When a woman applies for a job at a citrus grove, the foreman asks, "Do you have any experience picking lemons?"

"Well," she answers, "I've been divorced three times."

—MARILYN ADKINS

A friend had a waitressing position open at his diner and asked job seekers to fill out an application. Under "Salary Expected," a woman wrote, "Friday."

—MARSHA MARINO

During a company-held workshop on emergencies, our instructor asked, "What would you do if you received a letter bomb?" One guy knew: "Write 'Return to Sender.'"

—KERVYN DIMNEY

I input a junior manager's self-evaluation, which said in part, "I have been on the job for three months, and I finally feel as if I've accomplished something." I made one mistake, however. I replaced the word *job* with *John*.

—JANE FOX

Because finding the proper work-life balance is crucial, our company scheduled a meeting on the subject for all employees. To make sure no one fell behind on their work, the conference was held from 5 p.m. to 8 p.m. on a Friday night.

—MARCO RONO

Although desperate to find work, I passed on a job I found on an employment website. It was for a wastewater plant operator. Among the job requirements: "Must be able to swim."

—MICHAEL LEAMONS

Someone advertising on Craigslist said she was well suited for child care. After all, she had plenty of experience in "CPR and Choking Children."

—ANN BOBBE

The businessman was self-conscious because he had no ears. So when he hired a manager, he asked each candidate, "Notice anything unusual about me?"

The first replied, "You have no ears." He was shown the door. When the second candidate's response was the same, he was also tossed out. But the third guy had a different answer.

"You're wearing contact lenses," he said.

The businessman was flabbergasted. "How did you know?"

"Because people who don't have ears have to wear contacts."

Who says companies only care about the bottom line? Ours is socially conscious and offers employees fun outdoor activities throughout the complex.

Both of these admirable elements were driven home one day when a voice over the loudspeaker boomed, "Everyone who signed up to donate blood, please report to the rifle range!"

—LISA CARNES

I once had a boss tell me, "Don't dress for the job you have; dress for the job you want." I showed up the next day in a Cubs uniform.

—ROB PARAVONIAN

After giving birth, I quit my job. The exit questionnaire asked, "What steps would have prevented you from leaving?" My answer: "Birth control."

—MELISSA EGGERTSEN

I used to work at the unemployment office. I hated it because when they fired me, I had to show up at work anyway.

—WALLY WANG

My very busy boss placed this want ad in the newspaper: "Local photocopy shop looking for employee who has reproductive experience."

—BRANDON JOHNSON

After interviewing a potential employee, I walked him to the door. We shook hands, and he left me with this parting thought: "Don't work too hard!"

—DAVE ZEDAKER

I was furiously cranking out reports recently when my office mate got a phone call. I did my best to ignore what I heard him tell the person on the other end: "No, I'm not busy. I'm just at work."

—LAURA SWANSSON

How not to become a member of senior management:
During a meeting, our bosses held a contest to name a new project. As members of the management team read through the entries, our CEO picked one out and asked, "Who knows what a phoenix is?"
A junior manager answered, "It's a bird in *Harry Potter*."

—MARIE ALCAREZ

Conversation at our business lunch turned to illegal immigration. "I read an article that said 60 percent of Americans are immigrants," commented one of my colleagues.

"That can't be true," another said.

"No," agreed a Native American coworker. "There's a lot more of you than that."

—DANIELLE PRIMAS

**"I'm pulling up your account information now and —YIPES! Sorry, I clicked on your Facebook photos by mistake."**

The other day, a manager sent me a form letting me know that one of his staff was no longer employed here. In the "Reason for separation" field, he wrote, "Employee deceased." Under "Recommended for rehire?" he wrote, "Yes."

—JEFF ZEILMANN

My real name is Wilton, but everyone at the plastics factory calls me Dub. And that's where the confusion began. A woman from the front office came by with a form to fill out. But when she asked for my name, I wasn't sure which one to give.

Waiting patiently for me to make up my mind, she said, "I don't have any easier questions."

—WILTON ROSE

Our friend worked in an office where an e-mail flame war erupted. Coworkers were blasting outraged notes back and forth. Finally, their boss stepped in. The e-mails stopped, and everyone got back to work. Then the boss sent one more e-mail.

"Thank goodness that's solved. Does anyone have any questions?"

The flame war was rekindled when a woman, forgetting an important comma, responded, "No thanks to you."

—*SEND: THE ESSENTIAL GUIDE TO EMAIL FOR OFFICE AND HOME* (KNOPF)

After months of fruitless searching, I ran across a job in the want ads that I knew I was qualified for. The posting read: **"Position may be filled by male or female only."**

—RACHAEL DANIELS

A woman looking for a data-processing job at our company was nothing if not eager to please. When I asked, "Can you type?" she answered excitedly, "No, but my sister can."

—MARCELLA THOMPSON

The best you could say about one job candidate was that she was honest. Her résumé stated, "I was entrusted to ruin our office in our partner's absence."

—JOANNA STOCK

I work at a store manned by grumpy old men. One day a ray of light showed up in the form of a cheerful young customer. She was chatty and charming and left the store gushing. "How lucky we are to be alive!" she announced before the door closed.

"Wow! She was certainly jovial," I remarked to a coworker.

"Yeah," he agreed. "I didn't like her either."

—DUANE BOEVE

With a pile of 300 résumés on his desk and a need to pick someone quickly, my boss told me to make calls on the bottom 50 and toss the rest.

"Throw away 250 résumés?" I asked, shocked. "What if the best candidates are in there?"

"You have a point," he said. "But then again, I don't need people with bad luck around here."

—BECKY HOROWITZ

I was checking out a job website when I found a gig that left me wondering, How tough can it be? "Morgue assistant. Job requirements: Excellent customer-service skills."

—DENISE DANIGELIS

CUTBACKS

**A** few weeks after our office purchased expensive handheld organizers for everyone, our director asked an assistant at a staff meeting for the date of an upcoming event. Proudly flipping open her new PDA, she announced the date, then flipped it closed again.

"Are you sure about that?" he said.

"Of course," she said. And with that, she reopened her PDA and handed the director the sticky note she had affixed to the screen with all the upcoming meetings listed on it.

—CHRISTOPHER DERAPS

Jake is struggling with two huge suitcases when a stranger asks, "Got the time?"

Jake glances at his wrist. "A quarter to six."

"Nice watch," the stranger says.

"Thanks," Jake says.

"I built it. It can speak the time aloud for any city, in any language. Plus, it's got GPS and an MP3 player."

"Wow!" the man says. "How much?"

"This is my prototype. It's not for sale."

"I'll give you $1,000."

"Can't," Jake says. "It's not ready."

"$5,000!"

"Well, okay, but . . ."

The man slaps a wad of cash into Jake's hand, grabs the watch and starts to walk away.

"Wait," Jake yells, running toward him with the suitcases. "Don't forget your batteries."

—MICHAEL & EDITH MILLER


A waitress at our restaurant had a change of clothes stolen from the break room. Making matters worse, she'd planned on wearing them to the Christmas party.

As a brand-new employee, I didn't know any of this backstory, so I was a bit surprised to find this indignant note posted on the community board: "It has been two weeks since the Christmas party, and I still have not found my clothes."

—DAVID BUTTS


Customer: "Can I please get your name and position with the company?"

Employee: "This is Ryan, and I am sitting down."

—MELANIE LOEB

Johnson, who always shows up for work on time, comes in an hour late, his face scratched and bruised, his glasses bent.

"What happened to you?" his boss asks.

"I fell down two flights of stairs," Johnson answers.

"That took you a whole hour?"

—ETHAN PATTON

Computers are great for modernizing the world, putting information at our fingertips, and keeping techies busy answering silly customer questions like these.

Tech Support: "Click on the My Computer icon to the left of the screen."

Customer: "Do you mean your left or mine?"

—ANNA HANSEN

Everyone knows I'm a stickler for good spelling. So when an associate e-mailed technical documents asking me to "decifer" them, I had to set him straight.

"Decipher is spelled with a ph, not an f," I wrote. "In case you've forgotten, spell-checker comes free with your Microsoft program."

A minute later came his reply: "Must be dephective."

—TERESA FISHER

During a job interview at my granddaughter's pharmacy, an applicant was asked, "Have you ever been convicted of a felony?"

"No," he answered. **"My hearing is scheduled for next week."**

—SHIRLEY ELLIOTT

# QUOTABLE QUOTES

"When in doubt, look intelligent."

—GARRISON KEILLOR IN *PREMIERE*

**"Stress is your body's way of saying you haven't worked enough unpaid overtime."**

—SCOTT ADAMS,
*DON'T STEP IN THE LEADERSHIP:
A DILBERT BOOK*

**"You'll never achieve 100 percent if 99 percent is okay."**

—WILL SMITH IN *PREMIERE*

"Hard work spotlights the character of people:
Some turn up their sleeves, some turn up their noses,
and some don't turn up at all."

—SAM EWING, RADIO ANNOUNCER

"Somebody once said that in looking for people to hire, you look for three qualities: integrity, intelligence, and energy. But if they don't have the first, the other two will kill you."

—WARREN BUFFETT

**"Work is a slice of your life. It's not the entire pizza."**

—JACQUELYN MITCHARD

**"Doing nothing is very hard to do—you never know when you're finished."**

—LESLIE NIELSEN

"We live in a society exquisitely dependent on science and technology, in which hardly anyone knows anything about science and technology."

—CARL SAGAN

**"The key to success? Work hard, stay focused, and marry a Kennedy."**

—ARNOLD SCHWARZENNEGER

"No, giving your computer steroids will not add oomph to your PowerPoint presentations."

I'd recently started my new job at an insurance company when I noticed something peculiar—six employees had daughters who also worked there.

"That's incredible," I remarked.

My boss nodded.

"We ask a lot of our employees," he said, "including their firstborn."

—SUSAN PIELASA

Voice mail is my sworn enemy—I have never understood how it works. Finally, I broke down and called the office operator to walk me through it.

"I can send you an instruction sheet," she said.

"Great, fax it over."

"Sure," she said. "But fax it right back. It's my only copy."

—ROBERT BALK

I work in the library's Local Studies section. Recently, my colleagues and I received invitations to attend a presentation at the town hall. The invites were computer-generated and used abbreviations for job titles.

So, the Reference Librarian became Ref Lib and so on.

I'm not sure whether my coworkers were impressed or amused when my invitation arrived—addressed to "Local Stud."

—ALAN DUCKWORTH

I spent 20 minutes explaining life insurance options to one of our employees. After reviewing the different plans and monthly deductions, he decided to max out, choosing $100,000 worth of life insurance. But he had one last question.

"Now," he said, "what do I have to do to collect the money?"

—MICHELE CUNKO

A computer-illiterate client called the help desk asking how to change her password.

"Okay," I said, after punching in a few keys. "Log in using the password 123456."

"Is that all in caps?" she asked.

—SUSAN KESSLER

My laptop was driving me crazy. "The A, E, and I keys always stick," I complained to a friend.

She quickly diagnosed the problem. "Your computer is suffering from irritable vowel syndrome."

—ANGIE BULAKITES

My friend was job hunting with little luck. "Maybe I've set my sights too high," she said. "I'm looking for a position that's mentally challenging but not intellectually challenging."

—CHRISTOPHER BREEN

When hiring new staff at her public library, my daughter always asks applicants what sort of supervision they'd be most comfortable with.

One genius answered, "I've always thought Superman's X-ray vision would be cool."

—DAVE GLAUSER

? Tech Support: "What does the screen say now?"
Customer: "It says 'Hit Enter when ready.'"
Tech Support: "Well?"
Customer: **"How do I know when it's ready?"**

BECQUET.COM

# Customer Service

A customer in our pharmacy yelled at one of the technicians before storming out. Another customer asked if everything was all right.

"Sure," said the tech. "You have to understand, most of our customers are on drugs."

—MINERVA REYES

It was the usual busy day at our bank. A woman came up to customer service and demanded, "What do I have to do to change the address on my account?"

Without looking up, I replied, "Move."

—CAROL GOODWIN

A customer brought her car into our Saturn dealership complaining of rattling noises. Later the technician said the problem was no big deal. "Just a case of CTIP: Customer Thinks It's a Porsche."

—ERIK DAVISON

Even though a patient owed our medical office $95, when I contacted him, I was told in no uncertain terms that he didn't appreciate our calls or the bills stamped "Past due."

"I want to be removed from the mailing list," he insisted.

"No problem," I assured him. "Just one thing: There's a $95 processing fee."

—MEGHAN COCHRAN

You didn't have to be a brain surgeon to figure out that a customer at our post office was an off-duty mail clerk from another plant. He'd written on his package, "Fragile: Toss Underhand."

—DENISE MARTIN

On her first full day working at a discount store, my niece encountered her first cranky customer. The man had brought over mouse poison and demanded to know why it cost so much. "What's in there?" he said sarcastically. "Steak?"

"Well, sir," said my niece, "it is their last meal."

—BELINDA ANDERSON

The phone rang. It was a salesman from a mortgage refinance company. "Do you have a second mortgage on your home?"

"No," I replied.

"Would you like to consolidate all your debts?"

"I really don't have any," I said.

"How about freeing up cash for home improvements?" he tried.

"I don't need any. I just recently had some done and paid cash," I parried.

There was a brief silence, and then he asked, "Are you looking for a husband?"

—NANCY JORDAN

When you've got a long list of things to buy at a department store, you tend to tune out announcements like "All cashiers to the front register" or "Associate, pick up line three." But one did catch my attention: "Customer service needed in men's boxers."

—PAT ROMANO

Our routine was always the same when unloading the delivery truck for our department store: clothes in the morning and special orders in the afternoon. That wasn't good enough for one antsy customer. He wanted his special-ordered pool table that morning.

"Okay," I reassured him. "Just as soon as we take off our clothes."

—KEITH BARRY

The dynamic young saleswoman was offering a lot of unsolicited advice as my mother was trying on pants. Each time Mom came out of the dressing room, it was "Too short" or "Too baggy" or "No, no, no. Wrong color."

It ended when my mother stepped out and heard, "Those are the worst yet."

"These," Mom said, "are mine."

—STACY BAUGH

"I would like to return this mirror. Its reflection doesn't look anything like me."

**"We call it the 'don't ask, don't tell' aisle."**

**W**hen I overheard one of my cashiers tell a customer, "We haven't had it for a while, and I doubt we'll be getting it soon," I quickly assured the customer that we would have whatever it was she wanted by next week. After she left, I read the cashier the riot act.

"Never tell the customer that we're out of anything. Tell them we'll have it next week," I instructed her. "Now, what did she want?"

"Rain."

—MARGARET ARTHURS

For the umpteenth time in one shift, my coworker at the grocery store somehow managed to offend a customer.

"Do you ever think about the things you say before you say them?" I asked.

"No," he admitted.

"I like to hear them for the first time along with everybody else."

—PATRICK CHENOWETH

My brother delivered prescriptions to people too ill to go out. Since the neighborhoods he visited were often unsafe, he decided to get some protection.

"Why do you need a pistol?" asked the clerk at the gun shop.

My brother had to explain, "I deliver drugs at night and carry a lot of money."

—LAURA LOFTIS

It seems the manager of the vegetable department at my grocery store doesn't tolerate picky customers. He posted this sign: "Notice! Take lettuce from top of stack, or heads will roll!"

—RICK PARKER

One afternoon the manager of our grocery store saw a somewhat bewildered man staring at his shopping list. When the manager approached, he noticed these words printed in large capital letters at the bottom of the page: "YOU ARE NOW DONE SHOPPING—COME HOME!"

—BECQUET.COM

**?** **Where does a one-armed man shop?**
At a secondhand store.

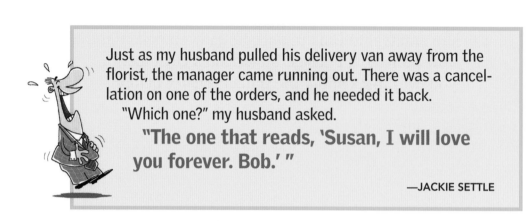

Just as my husband pulled his delivery van away from the florist, the manager came running out. There was a cancellation on one of the orders, and he needed it back.

"Which one?" my husband asked.

**"The one that reads, 'Susan, I will love you forever. Bob.' "**

—JACKIE SETTLE

My wife and I were living in Cambridge, Massachusetts—the quintessential college town. Rushing through the supermarket checkout, we didn't notice we were in a 12-item line and what we had was way over the limit.

The weary cashier looked at all our groceries. "Are you from Harvard and can't count or from MIT and can't read?"

—BRADFORD CRAIN

Watching us fill balloons with helium at our gift shop, a customer asked the price.

"It's a quarter per balloon," a coworker said.

"It used to be ten cents," she complained.

Another customer concluded, "Well, that's inflation."

—MELISSA BURNS

Being very organized came in handy when I put an extension on my house. I made sure all my bills were paid promptly. So I was mortified when I received a letter from an electrician that stated in bold letters, "Second and Final Notice!"

"I'm sorry," I said when I called him. "I never saw the first notice."

"I didn't send one," he told me. "I find second notices are much more effective."

—JEREMY K., FROM *THE CLASSIFIED GUYS*

Our coworker Patrick shared his worst workday ever. He was at an appliance store and the delivery truck had broken down, which meant he was flooded with angry phone calls from customers. One irate caller canceled the delivery and told Patrick what he could do with it.

"I'm sorry," said Patrick. "That's impossible. I already have a stove, a vacuum cleaner, and a microwave up there."

—JANE BENOIST

My husband uses scraps of wood, called "shorts," for carving. In a lumber store, he saw some lovely pieces in a bin behind the counter. But he had a lot of explaining to do after he asked the clerk, "Do you mind if I come around and poke through your shorts?"

—CATHY GROVES

Practically bounding into the advertising department of his newspaper, my husband announced the great news: "We've reached our ad sales target! I just sold the last spot."

"July?" another rep asked excitedly.

"No," my husband gloated. "I didn't have to."

—CELIA NOTLEY

I learned a lesson in marketing from a man who bought a trailer, an old boat, and a motor from me. "Thanks," he said as he loaded them up. "I'm planning to resell them." Good luck, I thought. I had been trying to get rid of them for months. But when I ran into him weeks later, he'd sold everything.

"How did you do that?" I marveled.

"I took out an ad: 'Heavy-duty boat trailer with free boat.' When the buyer came to get it, I asked if he had a motor. He said no. I told him I happened to have one in my garage. Bought that too."

—PAT MCCLAIN

Working on a computer all day has definitely messed with my girlfriend's view of reality. We had just placed our lunch order, and as our waitress walked away, she slipped on a wet spot on the floor.

"How about that?" Amy observed dryly. "Our server is down."

—JOSEPH LASSEGARD

A restaurant posts a sign that says, "$500 if we fail to fill your order." A customer decides to put it to the test by ordering "elephant ears on rye." The waitress writes down his order and walks to the kitchen. Seconds later, the chef storms out of the kitchen, goes to the customer's table, and slams down five hundred-dollar bills.

"You got me," he tells the customer. "But I want you to know that this is the first time in 10 years we've been out of rye bread."

—BOB BRITTAIN

A couple's meal had just arrived in a cast-iron pot when the top lifted. Spotting two beady little eyes, the woman gasped and the lid slammed down.

"Did you see that?" she asked her husband.

"See what?"

Just then, the top rose, again revealing two eyes. "Waiter!" the man called. "There's something strange in that pot."

"What did you order?"

"The chicken surprise," the man said.

"Oh, I apologize, sir," the waiter replied. "This is the peeking duck."

—MIKE PILOTTI

A shopper at my in-laws' clothing store couldn't understand why she had to pay so much for her purchase. "I got this from the '15% to 35% Off' rack," she complained. "And I pick 35%."

—KATY GIBBS

Spotting one of his customers wandering the aisles of his specialty food shop, my boss approached.

"We're having a sale on tongue," he said. "Would you like some?"

*"Eeww!"* shuddered the woman. "I would never eat anything from an animal's mouth!"

"In that case," my boss said, "how about a dozen eggs?"

—TERRY STROBAUGH

**"He just filed for bankrupcy online, and he says now he doesn't have to pay for his lunch!"**

Sliding the loan agreement across the desk for my psychologist husband to review, the bank officer apologized, "I ran out of room here." She pointed to the space for "occupation."

It read, "Licensed psycho."

—MARION WHITLEY

Our salesman at the electronics store was pitching a high-definition television. A fellow shopper, overhearing the spiel, mentioned that he'd upgraded his regular TV to high-def.

"How'd you do that?" my husband asked.

"I dusted the screen."

—JENNIFER NEELY

I was in a crowded pub one night when a large man sat down next to me and began pounding on the bar. The waitress was juggling three mugs of beer in each hand and said she'd be right back. But that wasn't soon enough for him, and he again pounded away. Going to the cash register, the waitress wrote the number "567" on a piece of paper and laid it in front of the man.

"You'll have to wait until your number is called," she said. Then, turning to the other patrons, she called out, "Who has number one?"

—BECQUET.COM

Since my purchases came to $19.06, I handed the cashier a twenty.

"Do you have six cents?" she asked.

"Sorry," I said after fishing around in my pockets, "I have no cents."

"Finally," she muttered, "a man who can admit it."

—KELLY SMITH

At the salon, I overheard the receptionist admit to another customer, "I haven't taken my vitamins today. I'm walking around unprotected."

The customer commiserated with her. "I haven't taken my Prozac today—everyone's walking around unprotected."

—DEBRA HAIR

Days after buying a thriving rosebush, I returned it to the store. "Is something the matter?" the clerk asked. I handed her a brown mass of sticks and said, "It's dead."

She examined the former flora thoroughly, then smiled pleasantly before asking, "And is there anything else wrong with it?"

—ELIZABETH TORHAN

Returning home from dinner out one night, I started feeling sick. Suspecting food poisoning, I called the restaurant's manager.

"I cannot believe that happened," the woman said. She sounded genuinely shocked. "What did you order?"

"I had the stuffing."

"That's weird," she observed. "Usually it's the meat loaf."

—JANCY QUINN

The halls of the shopping mall that I manage were cluttered with boxes. So I had the maintenance staff check the labels and place the packages in front of the stores they belonged to. The next day I got a call from the manager of a furniture store wondering why there were so many boxes piled up outside his door.

"What's the name of your store?" I asked him.

**"This End Up."**

—MIKE DEMARCO

# Law and Order

With a young child on the stand, the district attorney knew he needed to start with some simple questions.

"If I were to tell you that this pen was red, would that be the truth or a lie?" he asked.

"The truth," said the child.

"Very good!" said the D.A. "And if I were to say that dogs could talk, would that be the truth or a lie?"

"The truth," said the child again.

"Really?" asked the D.A. "Dogs can talk? What do they say?"

"I don't know," the child answered. "I don't talk dog."

—LOS ANGELES COUNTY SUPERIOR COURT COMMISSIONER
MICHAEL A. COWELL IN *LOS ANGELES DAILY JOURNAL*

Being a bailiff, I've heard it all. One woman asked to get off jury duty, insisting that side effects from her medication could interfere with her ability to concentrate.

"What are you taking?" the judge asked her.

"A fertility drug," she answered. "I'm trying to get pregnant."

"And what are the side effects?"

"It gives me a headache," she said.

—BECQUET.COM

The guest speaker at our training sessions for correctional officers was a leading psychologist. We appreciated the fact that he was able to answer in plain English a question many of us had: What is the difference between someone who is delusional and someone who is schizophrenic?

"Delusional people build castles in the air," he explained. "Schizophrenics move in and live there."

—REBECCA LEWIS

**"Couldn't you have found another shirt to wear?"**

As I pulled into a crowded parking lot, I asked the cop standing there, "Is it all right to park here?"

"No," he said. "Can't you see that No Parking sign?"

"What about all those other cars in there?"

He shrugged. "They didn't ask."

—ARTHUR CLUM

Two requirements for a security position advertised online raise the question: Why the latter if you have the former? "Must be able to carry a weapon and have excellent customer-service skills."

—KRISTIN PAWLIK

When I taught in a prison, one of my students kept missing classes. First it was because he had a tooth pulled; then his tonsils were removed. Finally, he chopped off the tip of his finger in work-shop. All of this led one guard to comment, "We better keep an eye on this guy. He seems to be trying to escape one piece at a time."

—LUCY GRACE

When a car blew past a stop sign at a busy intersection, my uncle, a Mississippi state trooper, gave chase and pulled the driver over.

"Didn't you see that Stop sign back there?" my uncle asked.

"Yeah, I saw it," admitted the driver. "The problem is, I didn't see you."

—MICHAEL HAMILTON

"Does anyone in this room need to be dismissed from jury duty?" my father, a judge, asked a roomful of prospective jurors.

A nervous young man stood up. "I'd like to be dismissed," he said.

"And why is that?"

"My wife is about to conceive."

Slightly taken aback, Dad responded, "I believe, sir, you mean 'deliver.' But either way, I agree. You should be there."

—BETH DUNCAN

I teach inmates at a correctional facility. Recently I was asking another staffer who teaches anger management about some of the books on his shelf, which covered topics such as stress and aggression. "Those," he answered, "are the tools of my tirade."

—CHRIS WITTEK

The stressed-out store clerk quits and becomes a cop.
"How's the new gig?" his friend asks.
"The pay is bad and the hours are awful, but I love that the customer is always wrong."

—ROBERT FLEMING

"Hurry up!" I yelled to my niece. We were running late for the movies, and she hadn't even gotten in the car.
"It's better to get there late than not at all," she chimed.
"That's great advice. Did your mother teach you that?"
"No," she said. "That's what the cop told Mommy last week when he pulled us over."

—PATRICIA STILES

My brother was alarmingly at ease speeding through a red light. I, on the other hand . . .
"What if traffic cameras are watching?" I shrieked.
"Stop worrying. Besides, it doesn't matter even if they are," he assured me. "I don't have license plates yet."

—ANDREW BENSON

**?** **What do you call twin policemen?**
Copies.

TYLER MEASOM

My mom drove cross-country to visit me in college. Heading south from Tucson, we were on our way to spend the day in Mexico when a state trooper pulled us over. "What seems to be the problem?" Mom asked.

"Drug smugglers use this road a lot," he explained, "and a suspicious-acting Buick with Pennsylvania plates has been spotted going up and down it."

"I just got in yesterday," Mom said. "And I'm hardly a smuggler. Just a teacher on sabbatical."

The patrolman eyed her suspiciously. "Do you have a prescription for that?"

—JOSEPH BLUMBERG

"Of course you're a flight risk! We're all flight risks!"

Shortly after the sheriff announced he would not seek reelection, the prisoners in the jail began razzing my husband, Joe, a deputy sheriff.

"You oughta run," said one prisoner, as he was led back to his cell. "I'd vote for you."

"Maybe," said Joe, as he slammed the cell door shut. "After all, it looks like I've got the inmate vote all locked up."

—CAROL WARD

Arrested on a robbery charge, our law firm's client denied the allegations. So when the victim pointed him out in a lineup as one of four men who had attacked him, our client reacted vociferously.

"He's lying!" he yelled. "There were only three of us."

—KATHRYN ENSLOW

My brother was having dinner with his girlfriend, Colleen, and her family, when her brother, an RCMP officer, stretched across the table for the butter dish. Colleen's mother admonished, "Watch that boardinghouse reach!"

"That's not a boardinghouse reach," he corrected. "It's the long arm of the law."

—KATHLEEN SUTCLIFFE

At the end of the day, I parked my police van in front of the station house. My K-9 partner, Jake, was in the back barking, which caught the attention of a boy who was passing by.

"Is that a dog you have back there?" he asked.

"It sure is," I said.

"What did he do?"

—CLINT FORWARD

Lots of people get hurt in Napa Valley, and after reading a recruiting ad for hotline volunteers in *The Register,* I think I know why. It said: "Over 300 people in Napa Valley are assaulted each year. Volunteer to help."

—MIKE REEVES

Just out of law school and dressed in a conservative white shirt, gray pants and tie, I was rushing off to court when I was stopped by an elderly woman.

"Are you one of those Latter-day Saints boys on a mission?" she asked politely.

"No, ma'am," I said. "I'm an attorney."

"Oh," she said. "You're playing for the other team."

—KEITH POGUE

Caught up running errands, my mom's friend forgot where she'd parked. A police officer, noticing her agitation, asked, "Is something wrong?"

"I can't find my car," she explained.

"What kind is it?"

She gave him a quizzical look. "Name some."

—LILA DRYER

A cop was rushed into the OR for an emergency appendectomy. The surgery went well, but afterward he felt a weird pulling sensation on his chest. Worried that something else might be wrong, he lifted his hospital gown to take a look.

Attached firmly to his chest hairs was a wide strip of tape. "Get well soon" was written on it, and it was signed, "The nurse you gave a ticket to this morning."

—JACKSON HALL

When the driver in front of my police cruiser began weaving in and out of his lane, I quickly hit the sirens and pulled him over. As I approached his window, I was hit with the stench of alcohol.

"Sir," I said, "can you tell me when you started drinking and how much you've had?"

"Well, Officer, I can't tell you how much I've had," he slurred. "But I started drinking in 1967."

—ROBERT W. MILLER

From the *Westfield* (Massachusetts) *Evening News* police log: "A caller reports that her neighbors are having another argument. The responding officer reports the resident was alone and not intoxicated but was having a disagreement with his Christmas tree, which was giving him trouble as he was taking it down."

—DOROTHY CUSSON

Our barbershop quartet—an all-girl group—was invited to perform at the Utah State Prison. We never had a better audience. The inmates called for encore after encore.

Finally our director announced, "This next number is a little long. How much time do you have?"

Someone shouted, "Five to ten years."

—LENORE SPENCER

An inmate at our prison asked to go to the infirmary.

"It's acne," he said.

"I get it whenever I come to jail."

"Let me get this straight," I said. "Every time you come to jail, you break out?"

—KENNETH SHAFFER

A fellow cop from our precinct had only a few months left on the job, and he could always be heard ticking off the weeks, days, hours, and minutes. Our chief was not amused.

"I've been on the job for 43 years, and I've never counted off the days until I'm outta here," he said.

I couldn't help agreeing with him. "That's because everyone else is counting for you."

—JESSE THATCHER

My father-in-law, a retired detective, told me about the time he arrested a mobster who ran a gambling ring. Once in custody, the guy began spilling names.

"I'm surprised how easily these tough guys break down," I said.

Bill shrugged. "Sometimes that's just the way the bookie crumbles."

—JOHN MASTERSON

A Jacksonville, Florida, man was so upset when a sandwich shop left the special sauce off his hero that he called 911 . . . twice. The first time was to ask if officers could make sure his sandwich was made properly. The second time, to complain that the cops weren't responding fast enough to the first call.

—USA TODAY

A man is on trial for armed robbery. The jury comes back with the verdict. The foreman stands, clears his throat, and announces, "Not guilty."

The defendant leaps to his feet. "Awesome!" he shouts. "Does that mean I get to keep the money?"

—LAWRENCE ADELSON

My father was a guard at San Quentin, and we lived on the prison grounds. Occasionally, inmates came by and helped with yard work. One day Mom lost the keys to the shed. A man who was mowing the lawn offered to help. Picking up a hammer, he gave the lock two sharp taps, and it magically opened. "Wow," said Mom. "How did you do that so quickly?"

Handing back the hammer, the prisoner said, "Ma'am, I'm not in this place for nothing."

—LANE BECKER

**"Don't tell anyone, but I'm actually wearing a *Snuggie*."**

**A** murder has been committed. Police are called to an apartment and find a man holding a 5-iron in his hands, looking at the lifeless body of a woman on the floor. The detective asks, "Sir, did you kill her with that golf club?"

"Yes. Yes, I did," says the man, stifling a sob.

"How many times did you hit her?"

"I don't know. Five . . . maybe six . . . Put me down for a five."

—BRIAN HANSEN

**A** small town's sheriff was also its lone veterinarian. One night the phone rang and his wife answered.

"Let me speak to your husband!" a voice demanded.

"Do you require his services as a sheriff or a vet?" the wife asked.

"Both," cried the caller. "We can't get our dog's mouth open, and there's a burglar in it."

**"I had a terrible lawyer.**
**She ended up getting the kids and the house."**

**?** A survey sent out to our contractors posed the question, "What motivates you to come to work every day?"

**One guy answered, "Probation officer."**

— E. HEWITT

---

**S**uspicious person: Officer made contact with a man walking backward down a street. When asked, the man told the officer he did not want anyone sneaking up on him.

—FROM THE (SEARCY, ARKANSAS) *DAILY CITIZEN*; LINDA WALLER

**A**n attorney I worked with at a personal-injury law firm deeply resented the term *ambulance chaser*.

"It's not right to call us that," he told me. "Besides, we usually get there before the ambulances do."

—BRIAN MAYER

**S**tanley R. Zegel was rear-ended while stopped for a red light.

Police were told by the driver of the offending car that he had been distracted looking at a paper for the address of the nearby court-ordered driving-improvement course he was on his way to attend.

—FROM *THE WINFIELD* (ILLINOIS) *REGISTER*; JOANNE AHER

**G**oing with a prisoner to the local hospital to have blood work done was too much for me: I fainted as the needle was inserted into his arm. I was out for only a second, but it was long enough for the inmate to become concerned for my well-being.

"You know," he said, "if you take these cuffs off me, I can drive us back to prison."

—JOY DAY

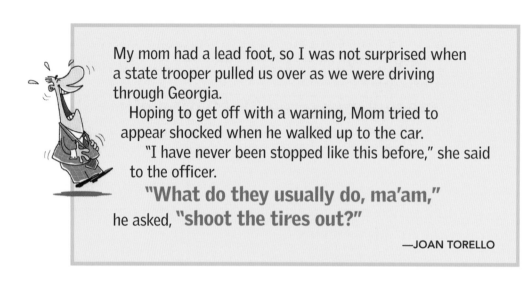

My mom had a lead foot, so I was not surprised when a state trooper pulled us over as we were driving through Georgia.

Hoping to get off with a warning, Mom tried to appear shocked when he walked up to the car.

"I have never been stopped like this before," she said to the officer.

**"What do they usually do, ma'am,"** he asked, **"shoot the tires out?"**

—JOAN TORELLO

Inmates at our Ohio prison are allowed to shine shoes in order to make a few extra bucks. One day I was having my shoes shined when the prisoner began to complain.

"Here I am with a degree, and I have to resort to shining shoes," he grumbled.

"What kind of degree do you have?" I asked.

Without looking up: "First degree."

—STEVEN RAY

A lawyer was playing golf when he got hit by a ball. When the player came over looking for the ball, the lawyer said, "I'm a lawyer, and this will cost you $5,000."

"I'm sorry," said the golfer. "But I did say 'fore.'"

"I'll take it," said the lawyer.

Our waitress's favorite customers are cops. "When they're done," she says, "I get to give them their ticket and they have to pay it before they can leave."

—PHILLIP TILLEY

A police officer arrives at the scene of an accident to find a car smashed into a tree. The officer rushes over to the vehicle and asks the driver, "Are you seriously hurt?"

"How should I know?" the driver responds. "I'm not a lawyer!"

—MICHAEL KNIGGE

Part of my job at the district attorney's office is to send letters to people accused of crimes, informing them when a court date is scheduled. One such notice was returned, clearly by a criminal mastermind, with this jotted on the envelope: "I DO NOT LIVE HERE."

—CASSIE GALINDO

A friend was reading the front page of the newspaper when she asked, "What part of the body is the melee?"

"A melee isn't a part of the body," I said.

"I didn't think so, but it's right here in the paper."

"How's it used?"

"It says, 'A police officer was injured in the melee.' "

—JASON CORNWELL

When a seven-year-old girl called 911 and then hung up, the Burnett, Wisconsin, police were dispatched to her home. When they arrived, they discovered the problem—the girl's grandfather was cheating in a game of cards.

—ANANOVA NEWS

I was the court stenographer the day a teenager, who'd been in drug rehab, came before the judge. He told the court how he was gradually overcoming his addiction. The judge was impressed. "Well done," he said. "Let's hope you end the year on a high."

—PHILIP HORTON

Did you hear they arrested the devil?
Yeah, they got him on possession.

—GREGG SIEGEL

**A**n old-school cop and I were leaving the precinct when a couple of teens flashed peace signs at us. "Great," he muttered. "Now they're giving us *two* fingers."

—CAROLYN ANDREWS

**W**hile prosecuting a robbery case, I conducted an interview with the arresting officer. My first question: "Did you see the defendant at the scene?"

"Yes, from a block away," the officer answered.

"Was the area well lit?"

"No. It was pretty dark."

"Then how could you identify the defendant?" I asked, concerned.

Looking at me as if I were nuts, he answered, "I'd recognize my cousin anywhere."

—MORRISON LEWIS, JR.

**L**ike many attorneys, I have handwriting that's barely legible. After I scribbled instructions for one of my clients, he spent a minute trying to decipher what I'd written before declaring, "If I took this to a pharmacy, I bet I could have a prescription filled."

—DARRELL F. SMITH

**A**n attorney specializing in personal injury decided to branch out, so he added libel claims to his practice. He wanted to add insult to injury.

—SHARON BERKEY

**"Hello, Tech Support?—
I hit 'Escape' and I'm still here."**

Potential jurors know that much of their time is spent simply cooling their heels. As the court attendant, I was doing my best to keep a jury pool of 75 happy while they waited to be called. After a full morning of doing nothing, however, one man suggested this:

"Open the blinds," he commented, "and we could watch the seasons go by."

—CAROL BECKLEY

I was at my desk in the station house writing up a report on a drunk driver when our police chief yelled over, "Is your squad car running?" Budget cuts made him watch every penny, and he didn't want us wasting gas.

"The engine's off," I assured him.

"You on overtime doing reports?" he persisted. "We're not paying officers to sit around doing reports."

That's when the drunk offered his assistance. "Hey, Chief," he slurred, "if it would help the department, I could drive myself to jail."

—JED SEIDL

So what did the cop have to say to his stomach?
Nothing. He's always been one to listen to his gut.

—A. J. GIORDANO

Alabama state troopers were closing in on a speeding car when it crossed into Georgia. Suddenly the officer behind the wheel slowed to a stop.

"What are you doing?" his partner asked. "We almost had him!"

"He just crossed over into the eastern time zone," he said. "Now he's a full hour ahead of us."

—SCOTTIE BARRON

# Family
## and Friends

Through thick and thin,
these folks bring some
humor to our days

# Family Fun

Joe figured out a way to remember his wife's birthday and their wedding anniversary. He opened an account with a florist and told him to send flowers to his wife on those dates, along with a note signed, "Your loving husband." His wife was thrilled by the attention, and all was great until one anniversary. Joe came home, saw the bouquet, kissed his wife, and said, "Nice flowers. Where'd you get them?"

Jeff's blind date with Suzanne was bad from the start—in short, they loathed each other. Fortunately, Jeff had asked his friend to call him so he'd have an excuse to leave if the date wasn't going well.

When his friend called, Jeff pretended to be in shock. "I have to leave," Jeff said to Suzanne. "My aunt just died."

"Thank God," Suzanne replied. "If yours hadn't, mine would've had to."

—FROM *LAUGH OFF* BY BOB FENSTER (ANDREWS MCMEEL)

A woman rubbed a lamp and out popped a genie. "Do I get three wishes?" she asked.

"Nope, I'm a one-wish genie. What will it be?"

"See this map? I want these countries to stop fighting so we can have world peace."

"They've been at war thousands of years. I'm not that good," he said. "What else do you have?"

"Well, I'd love a good man. One who's considerate, loves kids, likes to cook, and doesn't watch sports all day."

"Okay," the genie said with a sigh. "Let me see that map again."

—D. RICHARDS

**"We're in the tub together, but not like it used to be."**

My sister-in-law phoned to ask my opinion about a special pecan dish she had served at her daughter's wedding reception. "What was that all about?" my husband asked after I hung up.

"It was just a recipe question," I replied. "Do you remember the nuts they had at Arrah's reception?"

He furrowed his brow for a moment, then said, "I don't recall all their names."

—DEBBIE STEPHENS

My husband is a car nut. That's why I could appreciate the card he gave me on our fifth wedding anniversary. It read, "The last 72,000 miles of my life have been the best ever!"

—CYNTHIA ADCOCK

**W**atching a TV show on couples prompted me to ask my wife of 60 years, "If you had it to do over again, would you marry me?"

"You've asked me that before," she answered.

"What'd you reply?"

She said, "I don't remember."

—MILTON LIBMAN

**O**ur agency helps people figure out their marital woes. One man who came to us seemed to have solved his own problems even before he chatted with anyone. On the registration form, under marital status, he wrote, "Devoiced."

—PATRICIA LANGFORD

**"The wedding's off. You'd understand if you kept up with my blog."**

**A** drunk walked into a lounge. After staring at a beautiful woman who was sitting at the bar for 10 minutes, he sauntered over and kissed her. She jumped up and slapped him silly.

"I'm sorry," he said. "I thought you were my wife. You look just like her."

"Ugh. Get away from me, you worthless, insufferable, no-good drunk!" she yelled.

"Wow," he said. "You even sound like her."

—NICK MCCONNACHIE

**A**fter listening to her complain about her boyfriend, I tried steering my friend toward the positive side of their relationship. But she was having none of it.

"I was just trying to offer some perspective," I said.

"I have perspective," she snapped. "That's what I was just sharing with you."

—MARY ODBERT

**I** was thrilled to see a beautiful bouquet of flowers awaiting me at the teachers lounge. But I was mystified by the card, which read, "With love from A. C. Credmire."

That evening I told my husband about A. C. Credmire.

"That's me," he said, laughing. "When I called it in, I'd asked the florist to sign it, 'With love from a secret admirer.'"

—GERI WILLES

**S**urfing the Net, I came across a movie poster of a man and woman kissing passionately in the pouring rain. I called my husband over. "How come you never kiss me like that?"

He studied the sodden couple. "Because we haven't had that much rain."

—SERENA S.

I asked my husband if he wanted to renew our vows.

## He got so excited— he thought they had expired.

—RITA RUDNER ON *COMIC RELIEF 2006* (HBO)

"Honey, I have good news and bad news," a man tells his wife.
"What is it?" she asks.
"First, I think I'm losing my voice," he croaks.
"So," his wife says, "what's the bad news?"

—MINNIE MORETZ

When we finished a personality assessment at work, I asked my friend Dan if he would share the results with his wife. "That would require me to go home and say, 'Hi, honey. I just paid someone $400 to tell me what's wrong with me,' " he said. "And based on that, considering we've been married 23 years, she'd hand me a bill for $798,000."

—RON JAMES

When a friend's marriage began to unravel, my 12-year-old son offered, "I think the problem is largely psychological."
"How so?" I asked.
"He's psycho and she's logical."

—DEBORAH MOLER

Fresh out of gift ideas, a man buys his mother-in-law a large plot in an expensive cemetery. On her next birthday he buys her nothing, so she lets him have it.
"What are you complaining about?" he fires back.
"You still haven't used the present I gave you last year."

—L. B. WEINSTEIN

I was passing a couple in the produce aisle and noticed the man fastening a twist tie on a bag of oranges. "Those are gorgeous," I said. "Did you pick them out?"

"I don't pick," he replied. "I just hold the bag open." As his wife stepped away, he muttered, "And sometimes I don't even do that right."

—DALE BOOTH

Randy Pausch was a renowned computer science professor, but that didn't carry much weight with his mother. After he got his PhD, she introduced him to friends by saying, "This is my son. He's a doctor, but not the kind who helps people."

Servers at Disney World's Cinderella Castle treat you like royalty—literally. After lunch our waiter asked, "Is there anything else My Lord wishes?"

"Yes," I joked. "I'd like my wife to treat me like this at home."

He bowed to my wife, Donna. "My Lord desires to be treated like a king in his castle. May I suggest a reply?"

"Sure," my wife said. "Tell him he's spent a little too much time in Fantasyland."

—TERRY GRAY

I suppose it speaks volumes about the state of my marriage when I admit to nodding knowingly at a remark made by a colleague. She was telling me about the death of another coworker's spouse, when she commented,

**"How sad. They'd been married only five years, so I imagine she still loved him."**

—JANET IVES

I had obviously crossed some line while talking with my wife because suddenly she was steaming mad. Without coming right out and asking what I'd said wrong, I tried a Dr. Phil trick: "How could this conversation have gone better?"

She replied, "I could have had it with a different person."

—ALAN SCHORY

Purely by coincidence, I ran into my husband in our local grocery store on Valentine's Day. Tom was carrying a beautiful pink azalea, and I joked, "That better be for me."

From behind, a woman's voice: "It is now."

—PATRICIA RUT

My ex-wife was deaf. She left me for a deaf friend. To be honest, I should have seen the signs.

—TERRY SANGSTER

A man walks into the street and hails a passing taxi.

"Perfect timing," he tells the driver. "You're just like Frank."

"Who?" asks the cabbie.

"Frank Fielding. He did everything right. Great tennis player, wonderful golfer, sang like Pavarotti."

"Sounds like quite a guy."

"Not only that, he remembered everyone's birthday, was a wine connoisseur, and could fix anything. And his wardrobe? Immaculate. He was the perfect man. No one could ever measure up to Frank."

"Amazing. How'd you meet him?"

"Oh, I never met Frank."

"How do you know so much about him?"

"I married his widow."

—STEPHANIE CAPLEN

Steve, my accountant husband, and I both suffer from insomnia. One night I suggested we try a relaxation technique. Lying with my eyes closed, I described a calming scene: "We're in a beautiful bungalow on a tropical island. A gentle breeze comes through the French doors that lead to our private beach . . ."

A wide-awake voice startled me. "How much is this vacation costing us?" Steve asked.

—BRANDY DELVES

> Halfway through a romantic dinner, my husband smiled and said, "You look so beautiful under these lights." I was falling in love all over again when he added, **"We gotta get some of these lights."**
>
> —SHAWNNA COFFEY

**M**y pregnant daughter and her husband were checking out a new birth facility that was more like a spa. The birthing room had a hot tub, soft music, and candlelight.

"What do you think?" she asked.

He looked around. "Isn't this how we got here in the first place?"

—STEVE SANDERSON, GCFL.NET

**O**n the last night of our childbirth classes, our teacher took us to see the maternity center. We were gathered by the door when a mom, clearly in labor, and her nervous husband came rushing down the hall.

When he saw our group of pregnant women, he screamed, "Oh, my God. Look at the size of that line!"

—RACHEL ZEBOSKI

**W**e had been trying for a child for years, so I was ecstatic when I got up at five one morning, took a home pregnancy test, and found I was expecting.

"Richard," I yelled to my husband, "we're going to have a baby!"

"Great," he said, and rolled over.

"How can you go back to sleep?"

Muttering into his pillow, he said, "I'm stocking up."

—JUDITH FRIEDMAN

"**F**or sale," read the ad in our hospital's weekly newsletter, "sleeveless wedding gown, white, size 8, veil included. Worn once, by mistake."

—ELIZABETH EVANS

**M**y wife's doctor wanted to wean her off antidepressants. "What would happen if you stopped taking them?" he asked.

"To me? Nothing," she said.

"But all of a sudden, my husband becomes a real jerk."

—D. D.

**W**hen my husband pointed out my tendency to retell the same stories over and over, I reminded him that he was just as guilty.

"Allow me to clarify," he said in response. "I review. You repeat."

—JACQUELINE COOLEY

**A**fter my second year of medical school, I moved back home. One night I was up late studying for my clinical exam. Because my father woke me every morning at seven, I put a note on my door: "DO NOT DISTURB. Studying until 3 a.m."

This got me no sympathy from my dad, who is himself a doctor. He left a note attached to mine: "The hotel management hopes you're enjoying your stay. We'd like to remind you that checkout was at noon—approximately six years ago."

—VARGHESE ABRAHAM

**?** **What's the difference between an outlaw and an in-law?**

Outlaws are wanted.

**"Mom, how old was I when Dad first hired you to do all this stuff around the house?"**

I was sprawled on the living-room couch watching my favorite show on the Food Network when my husband walked in.

"Why do you watch those food shows?" he asked. "You don't even cook."

Glaring back at him, I asked, "Then why do you watch football?"

—LINDSAY WRIGHT

Leaving the party late, two friends compare notes. "I can never fool my wife," the first says. "I turn off the car engine, coast into the garage, sneak upstairs and undress in the bathroom. But she always hears me. And she wakes up and yells at me for being out late."

"You should do what I do," says his buddy. "I roar into the garage, stomp up the steps, throw open the door, and start kissing my wife. And she pretends to be asleep."

Our family took hours to set up camp on a recent outing. But the couple and three kids who pulled up next to us did it in mere minutes.

"How did you manage that?" I asked the father.

"I have a system," he said. "No one goes to the bathroom until everything is set up."

—ARI ROSNER

Leave it to my husband to make me feel good about my body. He was marveling about some football player who was five feet nine inches tall and weighed 250 pounds when I commented, "That'll be me if I keep eating like I've been eating."

"No, not you," my beloved assured me. "You'll never be five foot nine."

—ELLEN BREUNIG

I was cleaning a hotel room when the previous occupant came in, looking for her husband's keys. We searched high and low without luck. I finally peeked underneath the bed closest to the wall.

"Don't bother—that was my bed," she said. "He wouldn't have gone anywhere near it."

—SHARON GARDNER

Marry an orphan: **You'll never have to spend boring holidays with the in-laws.**

—GEORGE CARLIN

For our first Thanksgiving my wife's parents came over for dinner. My bride roasted a beautiful turkey, which she brought to the table on a silver tray. With a very sharp knife I carved it into lovely piles of thinly sliced white and dark meat. I smiled at my father-in-law, a well-known surgeon, and said, "How was that for a stunning bit of surgery?"

He laughed and replied, "Not bad. Now let's see you put it back together."

—CARL ROSS

When I asked a friend the secret to his 52 years of marriage, he replied, "We never go to sleep angry."

"That's a great philosophy," I noted.

"Yes. And the longest we've been awake so far is five days."

—DON BOLDEN

Considering divorce, I was feeling pretty blue. "It's not just me," I whined to my mother. "Do you know anyone who is happily married?" Mom nodded. "Your father."

—C. HEINECKE

My wife's first husband passed away at a young age, and she didn't want that to be my fate. After watching me laze around all day, she said, "You need a hobby."

"I have one—I collect rich widows," I said, lying on the couch.

"Well, isn't that a coincidence?" she replied. "I collect dead husbands."

—GERIG HUGGINS

En route to Atlanta, my stepfather spotted some mules by the side of the road. "Relatives?" he asked my mother.

Not taking the bait, she responded, "Yeah, through marriage."

—ERICA VANNOY

Before going out to a movie, my husband and I stopped at the town dump to drop off some garbage. As I waited for him in our pickup truck, a man walked by. Glancing at my dress and jewelry, he said, "I certainly hope this isn't your first date."

—VIDA MCHOES PICKETT

I felt like my boyfriend, Brian, was taking me for granted. "You're never home," I complained. "All you want to do is hang out with your buddies. We only go out if they're not available."

"That's not true," Brian protested. "You know I'd rather be with you than have fun."

—LISA SIMONS

"I had to stop seeing my girlfriend, the biologist," a guy told his friend.

"Why?"

"I couldn't take it anymore," he said. "She kept trying to expose me to different cultures."

—ROBERT HANSHEW

I pointed to the young couple in the car ahead of us. The woman had her head on the man's shoulder. "Look," I said to my husband. "We used to ride like that. What changed?"

Staring straight ahead, he replied, **"I didn't move."**

—BOBBIE MOONEY

On my parents' 50th anniversary, I remarked to my father that he and Mom never seemed to fight.

"We battled," he said, "but it never amounted to much. After a while one of us always realized that I was wrong."

—GARY MARKMAN

A group of guys are in the locker room when a cell phone rings. One of them picks it up.

Man: "Hello."

Woman: "Honey, it's me. Are you at the club?"

Man: "Yes."

Woman: "Well, I have news. The house we wanted is back on the market. They're asking $950,000."

Man: "Well then, go ahead and make an offer, but make it $1.2 million so we'll be sure to get it."

Woman: "Okay. I'll see you later. I love you!"

Man: "Bye. I love you too."

The man hangs up. Then he asks, "Anyone know whose phone this is?"

—DENISE STEWART

Whack! Right on the head with a rolled-up magazine! "What was that for?" the husband shouts.

"That," his wife says, "was for the piece of paper I found—with the name Laurie Sue on it."

"But dear," he says, "that was just the name of a horse I bet on when I went to the track."

"Okay," she says. "I'll let it go . . . this time."

Two weeks later—whack!

"Now what?" he wails.

"Your horse called."

—JODY L. ROHLENA

## Mom's Voice Mail

**O**ne thing I've learned from my last relationship is that if an argument starts with, "What did you mean by that?" it's not going to end with, "Now I know what you mean by that."

—COMIC DONALD GLOVER

**T**he downside to retirement, I told my daughter, a stay-at-home mom with three young girls, is that you no longer feel euphoric about Fridays. "When you're retired, every day is Friday."

"I know what you mean," my daughter replied. "When you're a stay-at-home mom, every day is Monday."

—BRENDA JOULLIAN

Chris was assigned a paper on childbirth and asked his parents, "How was I born?"

"Well, honey," his mother said, "the stork brought you to us."

"Oh," he said. "So how were you and Daddy born?"

"The stork brought us."

"What about Grandpa and Grandma?" Chris persisted.

"The stork brought them too!" Mom replied, squirming in her recliner.

A few days later Chris handed his paper to the teacher with an opening sentence that read, "This report has been very difficult to write due to the fact that there hasn't been a natural childbirth in my family for three generations."

Lying on her deathbed, a woman tells her husband of 60 years that he can finally open the chest at the foot of the bed, which had been off-limits to him throughout their marriage. Much to his surprise, he finds three ears of corn and $100,000 inside. "Why are there three ears of corn in here?" he asks.

"Every time I cheated on you, I put an ear of corn in the chest."

"I forgive you," said the husband. "But what about the $100,000?"

"Every time I got a bushel of corn, I sold it."

We bought my mother a shelf for Christmas, and I asked my husband if he'd hang it as part of her gift.

"Sure," he agreed. "Just remind me to take my tools."

I scribbled a note and stuck it on the gift.

"Holidays getting you down, Mom?" my daughter said. She pointed to my Post-it: **"Take items to hang self."**

—BEVERLY WOLF

"What's a couple?" I asked my mother. She said, "Two or three." **Which probably explains why her marriage collapsed.**

—JOSIE LONG, ON *COMEDY SMACK*

**E**ven with a thousand games, dolls, and crafts to choose from, my customer at the toy store still couldn't find a thing for her grandson.

"Maybe a video or something educational?" I asked.

"No, that's not it," she said.

We wandered the aisles until something caught her eye: a laser gun with flashing lights and 15 different high-pitched sounds. "This is perfect," she said, beaming. "My daughter-in-law will hate it."

—MICHAEL TURNER

**R**eturning home early from a business trip, a man finds his wife in the bedroom. She isn't wearing a stitch of clothing.

Surprised, he says, "It's the middle of the afternoon. Why aren't you dressed?"

"I have nothing to wear," his wife answers.

"Nonsense," he says, throwing open her closet. "You have a red dress, a green dress . . . Hi, Harry . . . a purple dress . . ."

**"I**f I were to die first, would you remarry?" the wife asks.

"Well," says the husband, "I'm in good health, so why not?"

"Would she live in my house?"

"It's all paid up, so yes."

"Would she drive my car?"

"It's new, so yes."

"Would she use my golf clubs?"

"No. She's left-handed."

—HAROLD HESS

**"Seriously, how well do we really know Mom?"**

Abe, an old penny-pincher from way back, was dying. On his deathbed, peering up through his cataracts, he asked, "Is my wife here?"

"Yes, I'm here next to you," she answered.

"And the kids?"

"We're here, Daddy," the youngest answered.

"Is the rest of the family here too?"

"Around your bed," his wife assured him.

At that, Abe sits up and yells, "So why is the kitchen light on?"

Scene: The Garden of Eden. Eve to Adam: "Do you love me?"
Adam to Eve: "Do I have a choice?"

—MASOUD SHIEHMORTEZA

**B**oth of my parents work and lead hectic lives. So my father was bound to forget their wedding anniversary.

Remembering at the last minute, he sped to the stationery store, flew through the door, and breathlessly asked the salesclerk, "Where are the anniversary cards?"

To his surprise he heard my mother call out, "Over here, Bill."

—ELIZABETH RANSOM

**I** was pregnant with our eighth child and couldn't visit my mom in the hospital, so my husband went instead.

"There's a risk of sterility if you get that close to someone who's having radiation treatments," a nurse warned.

My husband smiled and said, "I know."

—ARLENE CALDWELL

**M**y wife wanted to play the violin at our wedding reception, but right before, a string snapped. Her mother made the announcement to our guests: "I'm sorry to say that Amy cannot perform today. Her G string broke."

—BRET WALKER

**T**he topic in the office break room was the high price of divorce.

"I should've taken out a home-improvement loan to pay for my attorney," said one disgusted woman.

"Can you do that?" I wondered.

"She got her bum husband out of the house, didn't she?" said a friend. "I'd call that a home improvement."

—MARTI MCDANIEL

I was presiding over a wedding when the best man asked if I wouldn't mind also keeping an eye on the gift table. "There are a few people here the newlyweds don't trust around all that money," he confided.

"Then why on earth were they invited?" I asked.

Looking at me as if I were nuts, he said, "They're family."

—DAVID GILBERT

The new bride wanted everything to be perfect for the Thanksgiving dinner she was hosting for her in-laws. So she called the turkey hotline and said, "I bought a 12-pound bird. How long does it need to cook?"

"Just a minute," said the hotline operator, paging through her reference book.

"Thanks!" said the bride as she hung up.

—MICHAEL DEMERS

I'm not much of a gift wrapper, especially compared with the women who work at our shop. But I was the only one available the day a customer wanted a gift wrapped for his mother.

"Sorry," I said, handing back a box covered with wrinkled, oddly taped paper. "It's wrapped, but it sure looks like a guy did it."

"Great," he said happily. "Now my mom will think I did it myself."

—ANDREW BRANNON

My girlfriend broke up with me. She said it's because I was always correcting her. She came over to my house and said, "Eddie, we need to talk."

I said, "My name is Eric."

She said, "See! I can't say anything right around you."

—ERIC HUNTER, AS HEARD AT PUNCHLINE COMEDY CLUB IN ATLANTA

# "QUOTABLE QUOTES

"Friends are God's way of apologizing
to us for our families."
—ANONYMOUS

"Being a good husband is like
being a stand-up comic.
You need 10 years before you
can even call yourself
a beginner."
—JERRY SEINFELD IN *O*

"When you're in love, it's the
most glorious two-and-a-half
minutes of your life."
—RICHARD LEWIS

"When my daughter was born, we videotaped
the birth. Now when she makes me angry, I just
hit Rewind and put her back in."
—COMIC GRACE WHITE

"My mother used to say that there are no strangers, only
friends you haven't met yet. She's now in a maximum-security
twilight home in Australia."
—DAME EDNA EVERAGE

"The formula for a happy
marriage? It's the same as
the one for living in California:
When you find a fault, don't
dwell on it."
—JAY TRACHMAN, HUMORIST

"Families are about
love overcoming
emotional torture."
—MATT GROENING,
*THE SIMPSONS* CREATOR

"Friendship will not stand the strain of very
much good advice for very long."
—ROBERT LYND, *THE PEAL OF BELLS*

# Kids' Play

My oldest sister had made a salad for dinner and served it on everyone's plate before we sat down. Coming to the table, Dad caught my four-year-old sister, Amy, poking his salad and told her to stop.

Amy was very quiet all through dinner. Finally, when the meal was over, Dad asked her, "Amy, why were you playing with my food?"

"I was trying to get the moth out," she replied.

—ANNA WOZNIAK

I was going over a basic math concept with my Grade 1 students, but they were having a great deal of difficulty. After the umpteenth attempt, I was running out of patience—apparently, this was evident to my students. I had to chuckle when one of the girls proclaimed to the class, "Uh-oh! That's the same look my mom gets before she tells me I'm driving her up the wall."

—ALLISON ANSORGER

Our five-year-old twins had been squabbling all day, and I'd finally had enough. Pulling them apart, I said, "How would you feel if Daddy and I argued like that?"

My son replied, "But you and Daddy chose each other. We had no choice."

—JANE LIVINGSTON

My young daughter loves to go to performances at the local high school, so when her brother was in a spelling bee, she happily came along. But halfway through, she lost interest. Leaning in to me, she whispered, "This is the most boring play I have ever seen."

—ANGIE AIKEN

My Grade 2 class was doing a special project in which they raised butterflies from caterpillars. The students and I watched the insects in our classroom aquarium as they attached themselves to the lid, each forming a chrysalis. Within a week they began to emerge, wet and crumpled. The kids watched in fascination as the wings began to straighten, and with careful fanning, the butterflies dried themselves.

About three days after hatching, the insects began to fly. One little boy in particular, who had been watching carefully each day, saw this and excitedly announced, "They're flying!"

"Of course they're flying!" a little girl in the class replied, rolling her eyes. "They're called 'butterflies.' If they didn't fly, they'd just be butter!"

—DIANE R. MARTIN

"No one squealed on you. I saw your prank on YouTube."

When he received a journal as a gift, my eight-year-old son was mystified. "Mom, what am I supposed to do with this? The pages are blank."

"You write down interesting stuff that happens to you," I said. "So it's like a blog . . . on paper."

—BEVERLY TAYLOR

The night we took our three young sons to an upscale restaurant for the first time, my husband ordered a bottle of wine. The server brought it over, began the ritual uncorking, and poured a small amount for me to taste. My six-year-old piped up, "Mom usually drinks a lot more than that."

—T. ELLSWORTH, ON GCFL.NET

"How about if I meet you halfway? I'll sit up straight, but I won't eat my vegetables."

While leading a tour of kindergarten students through our hospital, I overheard a conversation between one little girl and an X-ray technician.

"Have you ever broken a bone?" he asked.

"Yes," the girl replied.

"Did it hurt?"

"No."

"Really? Which bone did you break?"

"My sister's arm."

—A. L. GRABER

Thanks to reruns, my kids discovered the old *Ozzie & Harriet* TV shows. My 11-year-old son was especially taken with Ricky Nelson. He wanted a guitar like his, wanted to sing like him, and decided to hunt down some of his old recordings.

After a long search he came home and announced, "I couldn't find any Ricky Nelson albums, so I got some made by his brother."

"David?" I asked, not recalling that he had much of a musical career.

"No. Willie."

—WENDY SILVEY

I have always tried to be conscientious about teaching my children respect by example, keeping an even tone when speaking to my boys, and reserving my "big voice" for serious, repeated offences. I found myself reflecting on this one morning after waking up with laryngitis.

I croaked out an explanation in a barely audible whisper to my eight-year-old son who turned to his five-year-old brother and said excitedly, "Matt! Mom can't yell at us! What do you want to do?"

—TRACY COSTA

The first time my son was on a bike with training wheels, I shouted, "Step back on the pedals, and the bike will brake!"

He nodded but still rode straight into a bush.

"Why didn't you push back on the pedals?" I asked, helping him up.

"You said if I did, the bike would break."

—WILLIAM B. FROM *THE CLASSIFIED GUYS*

I was on the computer in my home office when my eight-year-old son asked what I did for a living.

"I'm a consultant," I said.

"What's a consultant?"

"It's someone who watches people work and then tells them how they could do it better."

"We have people like that in my class," he said, "but we call them pests."

—KATIE ADAMS

After passing his driver's test, my grandson was asked to sign up to be an organ donor. Unsure, he turned to his father and asked, "Will it affect my football playing?"

—JANET RANNALS

I was standing at a crosswalk when a group of students marched by. "Okay, children, why do we all need to stay on the sidewalk?" the teacher asked.

I expected to hear something about the dangers of traffic. Instead I heard, **"Because if we don't, our health insurance won't cover us."**

—SANDRA JERGENSEN

For Christmas I gave my kid a BB gun.
**He gave me a sweater with a bull's-eye on the back.**

—RODNEY DANGERFIELD

**A**nyone with toddlers knows that trying to control them is like herding cats. So I was impressed by a parenting trick of my husband's.

Our two-year-old bolted out of our van in a busy parking lot, but my husband, Bill, got him to stay put by shouting, "Hands on the van."

"Where'd you learn that?" I asked.

"From that TV show."

"*Supernanny? Nanny 911?*"

"No," he said. "*Cops.*"

—CHERI DRAPER

**T**hree boys are bragging about their fathers.

"My dad can shoot an arrow and reach the target before the arrow does."

"Well, my dad's a hunter, and he can fire his gun and be there before the bullet."

"That's nothing," the third boy says. "My dad works for the city. He stops working at 4:30 and gets home by 3:45."

**T**o commemorate his first visit to our library, I gave a six-year-old boy a bookmark. More familiar with electronic gadgets than old-school tools, he had no clue how it worked. So I demonstrated by placing it between two pages, then closing the book. "When you start reading again, *voilà!*" I said, opening the book to my bookmarked page.

"Wow!" he said. "That's cool!"

—CARRIE MULLER

During Sunday school the substitute teacher asked my four-year-old what his name was. "Spider-Man," said my son.

"No, I mean your real name," pressed the teacher.

My son apologized. "Oh, I'm sorry. It's Peter Parker."

—JENNIFER NORTON

A little boy went to the library to check out a book titled *Comprehensive Guide for Mothers.*

"Is this for your mother?" the librarian asked.

"No," said the boy.

"So why are you checking it out?"

"Because I started collecting moths last week."

—L. B. WEINSTEIN

Just before a boy enters the barbershop, the barber tells his customer, "This is the dumbest kid in the world. Watch." The barber puts a dollar in one open palm and two quarters in the other and asks the kid, "Which do you want?" The boy takes the quarters and leaves.

"See?" says the barber, laughing.

Later, the customer passes the boy, who is standing outside a candy store. "Why'd you take the quarters and not the dollar?" he asks.

"Because," says the boy, "the day I take the dollar, the game's over."

—CONNIE BEHENSKY

My sister explained to my nephew how his voice would eventually change as he grew up. Tyler was exuberant at the prospect. "Cool!" he said. "I hope I get a German accent."

—STACI BAILEY

"No, the cat isn't my science project. The cat **ATE** my science project."

**M**y bargain-happy brother took his eight-year-old son to the pizzeria to pick up their order. Corey wanted to get the pizza himself, so my brother handed him a $20 bill and a $2 coupon and waited in the car. A few minutes later Corey appeared with the pizza, change, and the coupon.

"Wouldn't they take the coupon?" my brother asked.

"Oh, sure, but we didn't need it," said Corey. "We had enough money."

—ALAN ZOLDAN

Teacher: "George Washington not only chopped down his father's cherry tree but also admitted it. Now, Joey, do you know why his father didn't punish him?"

Joey: "Because George still had the axe in his hand?"

**W**hen our son, Joe, turned six, my husband and I decided it was high time for him to ditch the Winnie the Pooh underwear for something a bit more studly. So I bought him some Incredible Hulk briefs. When Joe got home, he found the package lying on his bed.

"Finally!" he exulted. "Adult underwear!"

—NORA DORSO

**K**eith, a coworker, was driving his family to a campsite when an SUV towing a beautiful vintage Airstream trailer pulled up beside them. Keith was salivating at the thought of owning one when his three-year-old daughter weighed in.

"Look at that," she said. "I guess they can't afford a tent."

—KARIN HORLINGS

**I** love making clothes for my five-year-old granddaughter. And she, in turn, always seems happy to accept them. The other day I asked if she would like me to make her a skirt.

"Yes," she said. "But this time, could you make it look like it came from a store?"

—BONNIE LOGAN

**A** fellow teacher assigned his fourth-grade student to write a topic sentence for the following phrases: "Sam always works quietly. Sam is polite to the teacher. Sam always does his homework."

The student's topic sentence? "I hate Sam."

—JEREMY BULLINGER

When a nosy fourth-grade student wanted the scoop on what another teacher and I were discussing in private, I decided it was time for an impromptu lesson in manners.

"Do you know what 'minding your own business' means?" I asked pointedly.

He didn't, but a student clear across the room shouted, "I do!"

—CARLEE NEWTON

One day my three-year-old daughter asked when her birthday was. Knowing that the date, April 14, would mean nothing to her, I said, "It's either just before or just after Easter."

"Great," she said.

"You don't know when my birthday is either."

—MARTHA HYNSON

My friend Susan was helping her five-year-old son review his math while her teenager was in the kitchen making a snack.

"You have seven dollars and seven friends," Susan said. "You give a dollar each to two of them but none to the others. What do you have left?"

From the next room she heard her teenager call out, "Two friends."

—DIANE KOH

We rushed our four-year-old son, Ben, to the emergency room with a terrible cough, high fever, and vomiting. The doctor did an exam, then asked Ben what bothered him the most.

After thinking it over, Ben said hoarsely, **"I would have to say my little sister."**

—ANGELA SCHMID

**"But Mom, why can't I just stay home and telecommute?"**

In the last two years our Micmac family, living in northern Ontario, has begun to find our roots. In doing this, one of the most important things for me is to share everything I am learning with my children.

I had explained to my eight-year-old daughter, Emma, that Columbus had mistakenly named us Indians, but that we called ourselves native or Anishinabe. I realized the impact my words were having when one day I was looking through Emma's school agenda. There, on a map of the world, the words "Indian Ocean" had been neatly scratched out, and it now read proudly in bright red pen, "Native Ocean."

—THERESA EAGLES

Concerned when one of his most reliable workers doesn't show up, the boss calls the employee's home. The phone is answered by a giggling child.

"Is your dad home?" the boss asks.

"Yes."

"May I speak to him?"

"No."

"Well, can I speak to your mom?"

"No. She's with the policeman."

Alarmed, the boss says, "Gosh. Well then, may I speak with the policeman?"

"No. He's busy talking to the man in the helicopter that's bringing in the search team."

"My Lord!" says the boss, now really worried. "What are they searching for?"

"Me," the kid chortles.

—DENISE STEWART

Last Christmas morning, after all the presents were opened, it was clear that my five-year-old son wasn't thrilled with the ratio of toys to clothes he'd received. As he trudged slowly up the stairs, I called out, "Hey, where are you going?"

"To my room," he said, "to play with my new socks."

—RICK BURNS

This teenager was in my boutique for at least an hour choosing the perfect dress for a party. But the next day she was back with the outfit.

"Can I exchange this for something else?" she asked.

I was surprised, but I couldn't argue with her explanation: "My parents like it."

—SALI THOMAS

On the way back from a Cub Scout meeting, my grandson asked my son *the* question. "Dad, I know that babies come from mommies' tummies, but how do they get there in the first place?" he asked innocently. After my son hemmed and hawed awhile, my grandson finally spoke up in disgust. **"You don't have to make something up, Dad. It's okay if you don't know the answer."**

—HARRY NEIDIG

Every morning I do a mad dash to drop off my son Tyler at day care so I can get to work on time. My impatience hit home one morning when he piped up from the back of the car, "Our car is really fast, and everyone else's is slow because they're all idiots, right, Mom?"

—RHONDA ROBERTS

Scene: the bookstore where I work.
*Dramatis personae:* a father and his son.
Son: "Dad, does it really tell you how?"
Father: "How to what, Son?"
Son: "How to kill a mockingbird?"

—THERESA FINE-PAWSEY

When our last child moved out, my wife encouraged me to join Big Brothers. I was matched with a 13-year-old named Alex. Our first outing was to the library, where we ran into his friend.

"Who's he?" the friend asked Alex, pointing to me.

"My Big Brother, Randall."

The boy looked at me, then back at Alex. "Dude, how old is your mother?"

—RANDALL MARTIN

A teenager brings her new boyfriend home to meet her parents. They're appalled by his haircut, his tattoos, his piercings.

Later, the girl's mom says, "Dear, he doesn't seem to be a very nice boy."

"Oh, please, Mom!" says the daughter. "If he wasn't nice, would he be doing 500 hours of community service?"

—MARIA SALMON

Last June my friend told me about her plans for our upcoming prom. "I'm renting a stretch limo and spending $1,000 on a new dress, and I've reserved a table at the most expensive restaurant in town," she said.

Our teacher overheard her and shook her head. "I didn't spend that much on my wedding."

My friend answered, "I can have three or four weddings. But a prom you do only once."

—STEPHEN BIDDLE

The pregnant guppy in the science-room fish tank fascinated my seventh-grade class. We all anxiously awaited the arrival of her babies. But a lesson on human growth and development raised a question for one student.

"Mrs. Townsend," she called out, "how will we know when the fish's water breaks?"

—DANA TOWNSEND

In lectures on human genetics, I explained to my college students that males determine the sex of the offspring by contributing either an X or a Y chromosome. So at the end of the year, I put it on the final exam: "How is the sex of the child determined?"

One student wrote, "By examining it at birth."

—PATRICIA S. GINDHART

A Cherokee Indian was a special guest at my sister's elementary school. He talked to the children about his tribe and its traditions, then shared with them this fun fact: "There are no swear words in the Cherokee language."

One boy raised his hand. "But what if you're hammering a nail and accidentally smash your thumb?"

"That," the fellow answered, "is when we use your language."

—ANGELA CHIANG

Teacher: "There are two words I don't allow in my class. One is gross, and the other is cool."

Johnny: "So, what are the words?"

"Boys just like one thing," my ten-year-old told a friend. Oh no, the end of her innocence, I thought. Then she announced her finding: "PlayStations."

—ALAN ZOLDAN

Flummoxed by his true-false final exam, a student decides to toss a coin up in the air. Heads means true; tails, false. Thirty minutes later he's done, well before the rest of the class. But then the student starts flipping the coin again. And soon he's swearing and sweating over each question.

"What's wrong?" asks the concerned teacher.

"I'm rechecking my answers," says the student.

One of my Grade 3 pupils came to my desk one morning, sporting a bandaged finger. When I asked her what had happened, she replied, "Well, you know those things you sharpen carrots with?"

—NANCY PERRY

Shortly after becoming landed immigrants in Canada, our family was returning to Montreal after a vacation in the United States. As we neared the Canadian border, we asked our five children to settle down and be quiet.

At the border the customs officer asked my husband, "What is your status in Canada?"

Before he could answer, our nine-year-old daughter piped up with, "We are all landed hypocrites!"

—JANE B. GLOWKA

**A** student tore into our school office. "My iPod was stolen!" she cried. I handed her a form, and she filled it out, answering everything, even those questions intended for the principal. Under "Disposition," she wrote, "I'm really ticked off."

—DEBORAH MILES

**I**nterviewing a college applicant, the dean of admissions asks, "If you could have a conversation with someone, living or dead, who would it be?"

The student thinks it over, then answers, "The living one."

—DAVE GAU

**M**ystery writer P. D. James told a college audience that her career path was laid out early in life. "My parents had an inkling of what I might become when I was five years old. When they read me 'Humpty Dumpty,' I asked, 'Was he pushed?' "

—SHIRLEY SAYRE

**D**riving my three-year-old daughter to day care before work, I noticed a family of dead raccoons on the road. I quickly sped past, hoping she wouldn't spot them. No such luck.

"Mommy, what was that?"

"Some wood must have fallen from a truck," I fibbed.

"Oh," she said. "Is that what killed all those raccoons?"

—TAMMY MAAS

**I** see a sign that says "Caution, Small Children Playing." I slow down, and then it occurs to me: I'm not afraid of small children.

—JONATHAN KATZ

# Beware of Pets

**M**y mother-in-law's dog was overweight, so the vet gave her some diet pills for the dog. On the return visit the dog's weight was unchanged. The vet asked if she was having trouble getting the dog to take the pills. "Oh no," my mother-in-law answered. "I hide them in her ice cream!"

—VI KNUTSON

**M**y sight-impaired friend was in a grocery store with her guide dog when the manager asked, "Is that a blind dog?" My friend said, "I hope not, or we're both in trouble."

—SUE YOUNG

**I** heard the dog barking before he and his owner actually barreled into our vet practice. Spotting a training video we sell, the owner wisely decided to buy one.

"How does this work?" she asked, handing me a check. "Do I just have him watch this?"

—BRANDI CHYTKA

**T**ourists come to Yellowstone National Park armed with a lot of questions. As someone who works nearby, I don't always have answers. Like the time one earnest woman wanted to know, "At what elevation do deer turn into elk?"

—AMY BUCKLES

A marine biologist was telling his friends about some of his most recent research findings.

"Some whales can communicate at a distance of 300 miles," he said.

"What the hell would one whale say to another 300 miles away?" asked his sarcastic friend.

"I'm not absolutely sure," the expert said, "but it sounds something like, 'Can you hear me now?'"

While staring at a monkey in the zoo, one of my preschool students had a question: "What does he eat?"

The zookeeper rattled off a long list of foods that the monkeys were fed.

"Where does he get his food from?" asked the student.

"Oh, just the regular supermarket," answered the zookeeper.

My student wasn't finished. "Well, who drives him?"

—MICHELLE MUELLER

A farmer pulls a prank on Easter Sunday. After the egg hunt he sneaks into the chicken coop and replaces every white egg with a brightly colored one.

Minutes later the rooster walks in. He spots the colored eggs, then storms out and beats up the peacock.

—ADAM JOSHUA SMARGON

There was no way we were giving up the stray kitten that adopted us. We called her Princess.

When we took her to the animal hospital to get her checked out, the vet had news: She was actually a He. "So what's the new name going to be?" he asked. "The Cat Formerly Known as Princess?"

—JEANETTE ANDERSON

I dressed my dog up as a cat for Halloween.
Now he won't come when I call him.

—REID FAYLOR, HEARD AT THE ROOFTOP COMEDY TALENT INSTITUTE

**A** zookeeper spotted a visitor throwing $10 bills into the elephant exhibit.

"Why are you doing that?" asked the keeper.

"The sign says it's okay," replied the visitor.

"No, it doesn't."

"Yes, it does. It says, 'Do not feed. $10 fine.'"

**A** woman walked into my aunt's animal shelter wanting to have her cat and six kittens spayed and neutered.

"Is the mother friendly?" my aunt asked.

"Very," said the woman, casting an eye on all the pet carriers. "That's how we got into this mess in the first place."

—SARAH MITCHELL

**T**he week we got our puppy, I caught a stomach bug and stayed home from work one day. That afternoon my wife called to check up on me.

"I'm okay," I said. "But guess who pooped in the dining room." My wife's response: "Who?"

—RUSSELL MOORE

**"W**hat should I do?" yelled a panicked client to the receptionist at our veterinarian's office. "My dog just ate two bags of unpopped popcorn!"

Clearly not as alarmed as the worried pet owner, the receptionist responded coolly, "Well, the first thing I would do is keep him out of the sun."

—BRENDA SHIPLEY

The injury to our piglet wasn't serious, but it did require stitches. So I sent my teenage daughter back into the farmhouse to get needle and thread and bring it to me, while I looked after the squealing animal.

Ten minutes later she still hadn't returned.

"What are you doing?" I called out.

She yelled back, "Looking for the pink thread."

—JUNE HALEY

I was shopping in the pet section of my local supermarket when I overheard a woman singing the praises of a particular water bowl to her husband.

"Look, it even has a water filter!" she concluded, holding the doggie dish out for her husband's inspection.

He had a slightly different take on things: "Dear, he drinks out of the toilet."

—JAMES JENKINS

A lonely woman buys a parrot for companionship. After a week the parrot hasn't uttered a word, so the woman goes back to the pet store and buys it a mirror. Nothing. The next week, she brings home a little ladder. Polly is still incommunicado, so the week after that, she gives it a swing, which elicits not a peep. A week later she finds the parrot on the floor of its cage, dying. Summoning up its last breath, the bird whispers, "Don't they have any food at that pet store?"

—LUCILLE ARNELL

**? Why do black widow spiders kill their mates after mating?**

To stop the snoring before it starts.

———————————————————————— ARLANA LOCKETT

**A** fellow salesperson, an animal lover, was suddenly overcome by allergies at one of our company meetings. Coughing, sniffling, watery eyes . . . she was a mess.

"If you have such terrible allergies, why do you keep so many pets?" asked a friend.

"Because"—sneeze, cough, hack—"if I'm going to be sick, I might as well have company."

—JOHN CALDWELL

**I** was admiring a picture on my design client's wall when she came up from behind and mentioned, "That's my mother and her dog."

"She's very attractive," I said.

"She was more like a friend, really. I miss her."

"She's no longer alive?" I asked.

"No. But my mother is."

—SANDRA BOLETCHEK

**A** man and his dog go to a movie. During the funny scenes the dog laughs. When there's a sad part, the dog cries. This goes on for the entire film: laughing and crying in all the right places.

After the show a man who was sitting in the row behind them comes up and says, "That was truly amazing!"

"It sure was," the dog owner replies. "He hated the book."

—DONALD GEISER

**T**here, in the reptiles section of our zoo, a male turtle was on top of a female behaving very, um, affectionately. My daughter was transfixed. She asked, "Mommy?"

Uh-oh, I thought. Here comes The Question. "Yes?" I said.

"Why doesn't he go around?"

—DAWN HOISINGTON

A guy drives into a ditch, but luckily, a farmer is there to help. He hitches his horse, Buddy, up to the car and yells, "Pull, Nellie, pull!" Buddy doesn't move.

"Pull, Buster, pull!" Buddy doesn't budge.

"Pull, Coco, pull!" Nothing.

Then the farmer says, "Pull, Buddy, pull!" And the horse drags the car out of the ditch.

Curious, the motorist asks the farmer why he kept calling his horse by the wrong name.

"Buddy's blind," said the farmer. "And if he thought he was the only one pulling, he wouldn't even try."

**A** talking horse shows up at Dodger Stadium and persuades the manager to let him try out for the team.

In his first at bat, the horse rips the ball deep into right field—then just stands there.

"Run! Run!" the manager screams.

"Run?" says the horse. "If I could run, I'd be in the Kentucky Derby."

—CHARLES LEERHSEN

**A** guy finds a sheep wandering in his neighborhood and takes it to the police station. The desk sergeant says, "Why don't you just take it to the zoo?"

The next day, the sergeant spots the same guy walking down the street—with the sheep.

"I thought I told you to take that sheep to the zoo," the sergeant says.

"I know what you told me," the guy responds. "Yesterday I took him to the zoo. Today I'm taking him to the movies."

—TAMARA CUMMINGS

**A**n orangutan in the zoo has two books—the Bible and Darwin's *Origin of Species.* He's trying to figure out if he's his brother's keeper—or his keeper's brother.

—SAMUEL J. STANNARD

The first thing I noticed about the pickup truck passing by the grocery store was the goofy-looking pooch sitting in the passenger seat wearing goggles.

The second thing was the rear bumper sticker, which read, **"Dog is my copilot."**

—ANNA COOPER

**?** **A rabbit and a duck went to dinner. Who paid?**
The duck—he had the bill.

---

**C**arrying two dead raccoons, a buzzard tries to check in at LAX for the red-eye to New York. "Sorry, sir," says the ticket agent. "We allow only one item of carrion."

—JANET HUGHES

**S**taring at an empty cage, a zoo visitor asks, "Where are all the monkeys?"

"It's mating season," the keeper replies. "They're inside."

"Do you think they'd come out for peanuts?"

"Would you?"

—DENNIS RICKMAN

**T**wo men went bear hunting. While one stayed in the cabin, the other went looking for a grizzly. He soon found one. Taking aim, he fired his rifle, nicking the bear. Enraged, it charged the hunter, chasing him back to the cabin. As the hunter reached the open cabin door, he slipped and fell. The bear tripped over him and rolled into the cabin. The man leaped up, slammed the cabin door shut, and yelled to his friend inside, "You skin this one while I go get another!"

**"C**an I purchase frogs for my new pond here?" a customer asked at our garden center.

"You don't buy frogs," I explained. "They just sort of choose where they live, then turn up."

"Right . . ." agreed the gentleman. "And is the same true with fish?"

—SAMANTHA DAVIS

**A** garden center customer picks up a container of insecticide and asks the salesperson, "Is this good for red ants?"

"No," says the salesperson. "It'll kill 'em!"

—DONALD CLEMENTS

**A** kangaroo orders a beer. He puts down a $20 bill.

The bartender gives him $1 in change and says, "Don't see a lot of kangaroos in here."

"At these prices," says the kangaroo, "I'm not surprised."

—CHARLES LEERHSEN

Just as I was finishing my hike at Carl Sandburg National Historic Site in North Carolina, I heard a group of campers discussing recent bear sightings.

"If you meet a bear, don't run," one person said.

His friend seemed surprised. "Really? Why?"

"Because," I interjected, "bears like fast food."

—DENISE EDEN

"What is that sound?" a woman visiting our nature center asked.

"It's the frogs trilling for a mate," Patti, the naturalist, explained. "We have a pair in the science room. But since they've been together for so long, they no longer sing to each other."

The woman nodded sympathetically. "The trill is gone."

—KATHYJO TOWNSON

When a lonely frog consults a fortune-teller, he's told not to worry. "You are going to meet a beautiful young girl," she says, "and she will want to know everything about you."

"That's great!" says the excited frog. "When will I meet her?"

"Next semester," says the psychic, "in biology class."

—ZHANG WENYI

During a trip to the zoo, we saw a sign posted next to the empty polar bear exhibit stating that the bear had died after eating a glove.

"The poor polar bear," remarked the woman standing next to us.

Her husband's slightly different reaction: "The poor guy wearing the glove."

—MELINDA ERICKSON

Spotted outside a veterinary hospital in Clinton, Utah:
"Happy Father's Day! Neutering Special."

—SHARON NAUTA STEELE

The highlight of our zoo trip was a peacock showing off its plumage. My four-year-old son was particularly taken with it. That evening he couldn't wait to tell his father: "Dad, guess what! I saw a Christmas tree come out of a chicken!"

—CAROL HOWARD

Buffalo were roaming the range when a tourist passed by.

"Those are the mangiest-looking beasts I've ever seen!" he exclaimed.

One buffalo turned to another and said, "I think I just heard a discouraging word."

—JONATHAN BELL

It's really humid in the woods, so the two hiking buddies remove their shirts and shoes. But when they spot a sign saying "Beware of bears," one of them stops to put his shoes back on.

"What's the point?" the other says. "You can't outrun a bear."

"Actually," says his friend, "all I have to do is outrun you."

—DON PAQUETTE

A farmer wonders how many sheep he has in his field, so he asks his sheepdog to count.

"So what's the verdict?" the farmer asks when the dog is done.

"Forty."

"Huh?" the farmer says, puzzled. "I only had 38."

"I know," the dog says. "But I rounded them up."

# Life and Death

Even with its ups and downs, life can be pretty funny at times

# Life in These Times

**B**efore I could enroll in my company's medical insurance plan, I needed to fill out a questionnaire. As expected, the form was very thorough, leaving nothing to chance. One question asked, "Do you think you may need to go to the emergency room within the next three months?"

—HAIFENG JI

**A** hot-air balloonist had drifted off course. He saw a man on the ground and yelled, "Excuse me, can you tell me where I am?"

"Yes," the guy said. "You're in a balloon."

"You must work in I.T.," the balloonist said.

"How did you know?"

"What you told me is technically correct but of no use to anyone."

"And you must work in management," the man on the ground retorted.

"Yup."

"Figures. You don't know where you are or where you're going, but you expect me to help. And you're in the same position you were in before we met, but now it's my fault."

—MICHAEL & EDITH MILLER

**M**oving back to Austin, Texas, after 10 years, I was surprised at how much the city had grown. I asked my real estate agent about the commute. She said, "On Mondays, rush hour starts at 5. On Tuesdays and Wednesdays, it starts around 4:30. On Thursdays, it starts at 4."

"When does it begin on Fridays?" I asked.

"On Thursday."

—KRISTIN HOLDGRAFER

In a recent poll one in four people said they'd donate a kidney to a complete stranger. Yeah, sure. Ninety percent won't even let a stranger merge in traffic.

—JAY LENO, THE *TONIGHT* SHOW (NBC)

His new hybrid car was my friend's pride and joy. He was always bragging about it and boring his buddies to death.

As he was giving us a ride one day, he pontificated, "They should have a special lane for people who care about the environment."

"They already do," came a voice from the backseat. "It's called a sidewalk."

—JAMES SEWELL

Three contractors bid on a minor fence-repair job at the White House.

The first contractor, from Florida, comes in with a bid of $1,000: $400 for material, $400 for labor and $200 profit.

The second contractor, from Tennessee, says he'll do the job for $800: $300 for material, $300 for labor, and $200 profit.

Then comes the contractor from New Jersey, who submits a bid of $100,800.

"Why so much?" asks the startled government official.

"Well," says the contractor, "I figure, $50,000 for me, $50,000 for you, and $800 for the guy from Tennessee to fix the fence."

As I wandered down an aisle of my local warehouse store, I overheard the man next to me talking on his cell phone.

"Now is just not a good time for me. I need to concentrate on this," he said, exasperated. "I'll call you back when I get to the car."

—MARTHA STEVENS

New York city straphangers were told over the subway PA to expect the expected: "Because of construction, this train will be making express stops. The MTA reminds all passengers that to better serve our customers, construction will be going on for the rest of your lives."

—OVERHEARD IN NEW YORK

My husband placed a perfectly good set of used tires outside his garage with a sign that read "Free." After a few weeks with no takers, he changed the sign to "$20."
**The next day they were stolen.**

—JEANNIE CABIGTING

I figured out how to cure the high divorce rate in this country. Have cell phone companies write the marriage contracts—you'll never get out of them.

—BUZZ NUTLEY

I just got a GPS for my car, and my first trip with it was to a drugstore. Since the manual said not to leave it in the car unattended, I brought it with me into the store. While there, the GPS came alive, and a voice stated, "Lost satellite contact."

I wasn't embarrassed until a woman turned to me and said, "Your ankle bracelet monitor is talking to you."

—DAVID MCAFEE

Normal is getting dressed in clothes that you buy for work and driving through traffic in a car that you are still paying for, in order to get to the job you need to pay for the clothes and the car and the house you leave vacant all day so you can afford to live in it.

—ELLEN GOODMAN IN *THE BOSTON GLOBE*

We got a registered letter from the city clerk saying we were in arrears on property taxes. I rushed to our town hall to settle the matter. It turned out we had paid our taxes a day late and there was a fine. "How much?" I asked the clerk.

She checked her computer. "Eight cents. Anything else?"

"Yes," I said, counting out the pennies. "Just for the record, you spent 70 cents in postage to tell us this."

—SARAH SAPORT

Did you hear that General Motors is coming out with a new car? It's called the Filibuster, and it's supposed to run forever.

—BUZZ NUTLEY

One day at a local café, a woman suddenly called out, "My daughter's choking! She swallowed a nickel! Please, anyone, help!"

Immediately a man at a nearby table rushed up to her and said he was experienced in these situations. He calmly stepped over to the girl, then with no look of concern, wrapped his arms around her and squeezed. Out popped the nickel.

The man returned to his table as if nothing had happened.

"Thank you!" the mother cried. "Tell me, are you a doctor?"

"No," the man replied. "I work for the IRS."

—MIKE THOMAS

"It's saved us from having to get real lives."

The opposite of talking isn't listening. **The opposite of talking is waiting.**

—FRAN LEBOWITZ

Since he runs a pawnshop, I decided to ask a friend of mine to appraise my grandfather's violin. "Old fiddles aren't worth much, I'm afraid," he explained.

"What makes it a fiddle and not a violin?" I asked.

"If you're buying it from me, it's a violin. If I'm buying it from you, it's a fiddle."

—LARRY BICKEL

The plumber fixes a leak in the doctor's house—then bills him for $1,000.

"This is ridiculous!" the doctor says. "I don't even charge that much."

The plumber says, "Neither did I when I was a doctor."

—JEFFREY RAIFFE

"Read all about it!" yelled the newsboy, hawking his papers on the corner. "Fifty people swindled! Fifty people swindled!"

Curious, a businessman bought a paper. "Hey," he said, "there's nothing in here about 50 people being swindled."

"Read all about it!" yelled the newsboy again. "Fifty-one people swindled!"

The deafening car alarm outside the supermarket got everyone's attention. So by the time I entered the store, this announcement was coming over the PA system: "Would the owner of a silver PT Cruiser please return to the parking lot? Your car is crying."

—BOB NEWTON

Well, at least there's one good thing about high gas prices:
**Whenever I fill the tank, I double the value of my car.**

—ELIZABETH HAMILTON

So there I was, tearing my hair out trying to sign up for an online basketball pool. For my username, I offered terms like Hoops and Hangtime, only to be told, "That user ID is taken. Please select another."

I realized I wasn't the only frustrated one when I saw my last two entries were also taken: ForPetesSake and ThisIsInsane.

—GAIL WORKMAN

I think Ford names trucks by how many times you cuss when you fill them up: F-150, F-250 . . .

—BUZZ NUTLEY

As a stockbroker gets out of his BMW, a car slams into the door, shearing it off. When the police arrive, the stockbroker is apoplectic.

"See what that idiot did to my beautiful Bimmer?" he shouts. "Do you know what this car cost?"

"Sir," says the officer, "you're so worried about your car that you haven't even noticed that your left arm was ripped off."

The stockbroker takes a look at where his arm once was and screams, "Where's my Rolex?"

My youngest son was in Montreal getting ready to leave for Australia. I spoke to him the night before he left and suggested he write me a letter once he was settled.

"You mean," Todd said, "with a pen and paper?"

—JANET BINGLEY

# QUOTABLE QUOTES

"Life is too short to drink the house wine."

—HELEN THOMAS

"You have to remember one thing about the will of the people. It wasn't that long ago that we were swept away by the Macarena."

—JON STEWART

"People often overestimate what will happen in the next two years and underestimate what will happen in 10."

—BILL GATES, *THE ROAD AHEAD*

"If people concentrated on the really important things in life, there'd be a shortage of fishing poles."

—DOUG LARSON

"Most of my life, if a man did something totally other than the way I thought it should be done, I would try to correct him. Now I say, 'Oh, isn't that interesting?'"

—ELLEN BURSTYN IN *O*

"Think of life as a terminal illness, because if you do, you will live it with joy and passion, as it ought to be lived."

—ANNA QUINDLEN IN *A SHORT GUIDE TO A HAPPY LIFE*

"The way I see it, if you want the rainbow, you gotta put up with the rain."

—DOLLY PARTON

"The one thing that unites all human beings, regardless of age, gender, religion or ethnic background, is that we all believe we are above-average drivers."

—DAVE BARRY

"Money isn't everything, but it sure keeps you in touch with your children."

—J. P. GETTY

Scientists now say that people should not use their cell phones outdoors during thunderstorms because of the risk of being struck by lightning.

You should also avoid using them in movie theaters because of the risk of being strangled.

—BEN WALSH

Our town tends to be politically active, so as the editor of the local newspaper, I'm used to getting phone calls about all sorts of important issues. That includes this message left on my voice mail after a recent election: "Would you give me a call and explain to me what we were voting on? I'd like to see if I voted the way I wanted to."

—MATT LUBICH

When my friend phoned the IRS recently, he prefaced his comments by stating, "I'm calling with the stupid question of the day."

The tired-sounding agent replied, "Too late."

—CINDY MOORHEAD

I was at a local festival and noticed a guy in bad circus make-up doing intricate balloon animals.

He was twisting something together when a little girl asked, "What are you making?"

He sighed, "Minimum wage."

—EMILY SHULTZ

**?** ## What's the difference between a pigeon and an investment banker?

The pigeon can still make a deposit on a BMW.

PAUL STRAMBERG

## Funny Thing about Aging

For her 40th birthday, my wife said, "I'd love to be 10 again." So that Saturday, we had a heaping stack of chocolate-chip pancakes, her favorite childhood breakfast. Then we hit the playground and a merry-go-round. We finished the day with a banana split.

"So how did you enjoy being a kid for a day?" I asked.

"Great," she said. "But when I said I wanted to be 10 again, I meant my dress size."

—SEBASTIAN E., ON *CLASSIFIED GUYS*

**"I look forward to growing old with you. It's the maintenance I hate."**

"Tell you what . . . I'll explain the birds and bees to you, if you explain tweeting to me."

I'm not keen on taking pills, so when my doctor gave me a prescription to lower my blood pressure, I asked him if there were any side effects.

"Yes," he said. "Longevity."

—BELLA KELLY

Though I often pride myself on appearing younger than my 59 years, I had a reality check when I brought my mother back to the nursing home after a visit with us. As I struggled with her suitcases, two elderly gentlemen held the door open for me.

"We hope you will be very happy here," one of them said to me.

—MARION CLOUSE

I was feeling pretty creaky after hearing the TV reporter say, "To contact me, go to my Facebook page, follow me on Twitter, or try me the old-fashioned way—e-mail."

—LEE EVANS

To celebrate my retirement, my wife and I dined with a friend we hadn't seen in years. The next day he sent us an e-mail that included—I hope—an honest mistake: "How wonderful it was to see you both aging."

—LAWRENCE DUNHAM

We had a satellite dish installed on our roof, and my 22-year-old son was trying to teach me how to operate the remote. Since I am not the most technologically savvy person, it was not going well.

After repeating the instructions for the umpteenth time, he sighed, "This would be a lot easier if you were 12."

—PAULA MAHARREY

Here's one way of making sure a sales promotion won't bankrupt your business. A sign in a local barbershop read "We offer senior-citizen discounts. Must be at least 80 years old and accompanied by a parent."

—ROBERT MCGRORY

Not long after my grandfather bought my grandmother a pair of powerful—and expensive—hearing aids, Grandma accidentally washed her hair with them in.

"Oh, great," she said to me. "If your grandfather finds out that I damaged these hearing aids, I'll never hear the end of it."

—JERE SANDBERG

I recently ran into the woman who used to clean our house and was surprised to hear that she was still at it despite her advanced age.

"How do you manage it?" I asked.

She explained her secret: "I just keep clients who can't see the dirt any better than I can."

—MALCOLM CAMPBELL

No generation gap between me and my younger college classmates, I thought. Wrong. When a teacher used the expression "broken record," a young man next to me asked, "What's that mean?"

"Endless repetition," I explained. "If a record were scratched, the needle would skip and play the same piece of music over and over."

His face brightened. "Like a corrupted MP3 file?"

—CHRISTINA LINDSEY

Teaching is not for sensitive souls. While reviewing future, past and present tenses with my ninth-grade English class, I posed the question, " 'I am beautiful' is what tense?"

**One student raised her hand. "Past tense."**

—REEMA RAHAT

## ? How can you tell you're getting old?

You go to an antiques auction and three people bid on you.

A couple are getting ready for bed after a long day's work.

"I look in the mirror, and I see an old lady," the woman says to her husband. "My face is all wrinkled, and I'm sagging and bagging all over. And look at this flab on my arms."

Her husband is silent.

"Hey!" she says, turning to him. "Tell me something positive to make me feel better about myself."

"Well," he says, "your eyesight is still great."

—JEFFREY RAIFFE

For my 75th birthday my son gave me a beautiful purse and filled it with 75 one-dollar bills. The next day I went shopping and pulled out my fat wad of singles.

The cashier's eyes bugged out of her head. "Are you a cocktail waitress?" she asked.

"No," I replied, counting out my money. "An exotic dancer."

—HELEN KLEIN

Feeling listless, I bought some expensive "brain-stimulating" pills at the health-food store. But it wasn't until I got home that I read the label.

"This is just rosemary extract," I complained to my husband. "I can't believe I spent all that money for something that I have growing like wild in the yard!"

"See?" he said. "You're smarter already."

—SUSANNE HIGBEE

The antiaging ad that I'd like to see is a baby covered in cream, saying, **"Ah! I've used too much!"**

—COMIC ANDREW BIRD

A nurse friend of mine took a 104-year-old patient for a walk in the hospital corridor. When she got him back to his room and sat him down, he took a deep breath and announced, "That was great! I don't feel a day over 100!"

—MARY CIPOLLONE

My friend's grandmother was in the hospital and was fading fast. When he visited her the next day, he was delighted to find her alert and on the mend. "You really gave us a scare," he said. "We thought you were going to buy the farm."

"I'm fine," she reassured him. "I was just checking out the property."

—RICK HOSMER

When I checked into a motel, I noticed a card in our room indicating that guests 55 or older received a seniors' discount. As a newly minted 55-year-old, I returned to the front desk armed with photo ID. Imagine my chagrin when the clerk told me he had already given me the discount!

—JACKIE GREENHALGH

My friend was looking at home-gym equipment with her husband. She stepped on a treadmill and said, "Honey, if you buy this for me, I will look like I did in high school."

"Sweetheart," he said gently, "it's a treadmill, not a time machine."

—LORETTA NISSEN

**"You can try, but once they're past 40, you can't teach them new tricks."**

Even though she's been teaching English for 25 years, my mother never felt her age was an issue, until the day she helped a student with a report on the Vietnam War. Mom recognized the name of a war correspondent mentioned in the textbook and blurted, "I used to go out with him!"

Peering up from his work, another wide-eyed student asked, "You dated someone from our history book?"

—SHANA GREEN

A neighborhood photography studio offered a special that few could resist. The sign read:

## Now shooting seniors for free.

—LINDA CANTRELL

Inspirational speaker Dr. Wayne Dyer still remembers the card his kids gave him for his 64th birthday. The front said, "Inside is a message from God."

Pleased they finally appreciated his work, he opened it to read, "See you soon!"

—CHRISTINE KITTO

Sadly, in the nightclub world, bald singers don't fare well—hence my reason for buying a hairpiece. When I asked my accountant if I could write off the toupee as an expense, he hesitated. Then he changed his mind.

"All right," he said finally, "I'll put it down as an overhead."

—GEORGE SIMPKIN

We invite grandparents to a special day at our school, culminating in a photo op with grandparent and grandchild posing in front of a colorful display from a history class.

Only after the last shot was snapped did we notice what appeared above each grandparent's head: a banner screaming, "Discover the Ancient World."

—DEBBIE WOOSTER MILLER

I heard an older woman complain about her aches. But her friend one-upped her: "I woke up this morning and thought I was dead because nothing hurt."

—NANCY KUNKEL

I walked into the music store to buy a CD of Rachmaninoff's Second Piano Concerto. I found the hip-hop, R&B, country, and jazz sections, but no area where I might look for Rachmaninoff.

"Excuse me," I said to a young store clerk. "Do you have a classical section?"

After a brief hesitation she asked, "You mean . . . like Elvis?"

—TOM LISKER

Man, times have officially changed since I was a kid. I was at the mall with my daughter when we saw a man with a patch over his eye. My daughter said to me, "What is he trying to quit?"

—BUZZ NUTLEY

There was no way I was going to allow myself to go gray while only in my 30s. So I dyed my hair. Later, I modeled the new look for my husband. "Well, do I look five years younger?" I asked.

"No," he said. "But your hair does."

—STACY OATES

A guy sees a beautiful woman at the other end of the bar. He walks up to her and says, "Where have you been all my life?"

"Well," she says, "for the first half of it, I wasn't even born."

—ROBERT GABBITAS

Even at age 88, my mother was vain about her looks. At a party an old friend exclaimed, "Edith, you haven't changed in 20 years!"

**"Oh," said Mom, horrified. "I hope I didn't look like this 20 years ago."**

—JIM BRADING

I'm bald—well, balding. I like to say "balding" because it sounds more productive. And I don't like to say I'm losing my hair, because that makes it sound like had I been more responsible, this wouldn't have happened. "Where's your hair?" "I lost it. You know me. Where are my keys?"

—ISAAC WITTY, AS HEARD ON ROOFTOPCOMEDY.COM

The woman in front of me at the motor vehicles office was taking the eye test, first with her glasses on, then off. "Here's your license," the examiner said when she was done. "But there's a restriction. You need to wear glasses to drive your car."

"Honey," the woman declared, "I need them to *find* my car."

—NICOLE HAAKE

Some of us took our friend, an older woman, out to lunch to celebrate her birthday. When the waitress came to take our order, one of the women told her, "This is a special occasion. Elsie is 92 today."

The waitress made seven instant enemies and one friend by asking, "Which one is Elsie?"

—ANONYMOUS

Two neighbors appeared in court, each woman accusing the other of causing trouble in their building.

"Let's get to the evidence," the judge said in an effort to end their bickering. "I'll hear the oldest woman first."

The case was dismissed for lack of testimony.

The thing you need to focus on in your 20s is not getting a bad tattoo. You don't want to be 40 and going, "No, dude, it was different back then—everyone loved SpongeBob."

—TOM PAPA IN *TIME OUT NEW YORK*

An elderly couple with memory problems are advised by their doctor to write notes to help them remember things.

One evening, while watching TV, the wife asks her husband to get her a bowl of ice cream. "Sure," he says.

"Write it down," she suggests.

"No," he says. "I can remember a simple thing like that."

"I also want strawberries and whipped cream," she says. "Write it down."

"I don't need to write it down," he insists, heading to the kitchen.

Twenty minutes later he returns, bearing a plate of bacon and scrambled eggs. "I told you to write it down!" his wife says. "I wanted fried eggs!"

—WENDY LEVINE

"You know when you're getting old," my friend said, "when you tell your best friend you're having an affair and she asks, **'Is it catered?'"**

The kids in my third-grade class were struggling with the day's lesson on homonyms. I'd said the word I and wanted them to guess the soundalike word eye, but they just couldn't.

Finally, I pointed to my eye. Bingo! One boy got it. He shouted out, "Crow's-feet!"

—JANE RAY

The remote for our television broke, so my son went to get a new one at the electronics store. Later he called. "Mom, I forgot to bring it with me. What's the brand?"

I glanced at it. "It's a Volch."

"A what?"

"V-o-l-c-h," I spelled.

"Mom," he sighed, "that's short for Volume and Channel."

—JOAN WHITE

When a storm blew in around our cruise ship, an older woman on deck struggled to hang on to her hat and keep her skirt from flaring up at the same time. My wife ran over to help. "Should I hold your skirt down?" she asked.

"Forget about that," the woman yelled. "I've got an 85-year-old body. This hat is brand-new."

—MIKE DREA

**346** LAUGHTER REALLY IS THE BEST MEDICINE

# Dying to Laugh

Most businesses like that our credit card machines automatically print, "Thank you, please come again," at the bottom of receipts. Though one guy called to ask if I could take it off.

"Sure," I said. "But do you mind my asking why?"

"It just seems inappropriate," he answered. "We're a funeral home."

—MICHELLE BALLARD

During my uncle's wake I saw two of his friends peer into the open casket. "Doesn't Stanley look good?" said one.

"He should," said the other. "He just got out of the hospital."

—MARY KINNEY

Lying on his deathbed, the rich, miserly old man calls to his long-suffering wife. "I want to take all my money with me," he tells her. "So promise me you'll put it in the casket."

After the man dies, his widow attends the memorial service with her best friend. Just before the undertaker closes the coffin, she places a small metal box inside.

Her friend looks at her in horror. "Surely," she says, "you didn't put the money in there."

"I did promise him I would," the widow answers. "So I got it all together, deposited every penny in my account, and wrote him a check. If he can cash it, he can spend it."

Junk mail for my father-in-law clogged our mailbox months after he passed away. Usually I tossed the stuff, but one envelope made me hesitate. In bold letters it promised, "Here's that second chance you hoped for!"

—ERREN KNIGHT

An acquaintance of ours was—how do I put this delicately?—
not well loved. So when he died, I was amazed to see how many
people showed up for his funeral.

"I'm not surprised," said my husband. "As P. T. Barnum said,
'Give the people what they want, and they'll show up.'"

—JOYCE FITZSIMMONS

My father, a gravedigger, was told to prepare for a funeral.
But on the day of the service, it was discovered that he had dug up
the wrong plot. Luckily for him, the deceased's daughter was very
understanding.

"Poor Dad," she lamented. "He always complained he could
never find a parking space."

—EMILY WILLMOT

Pillsbury spokesman Pop N. Fresh died yesterday, at 71. In attendance at the funeral were Mrs. Butterworth, the California Raisins, Hungry Jack, Betty Crocker and the Hostess Twinkies.

Fresh rose quickly in show business, but his career was filled with many turnovers. He was not considered a smart cookie, wasting much of his dough on half-baked schemes. Still, even as a crusty old man, he was a roll model for millions.

Fresh is survived by his second wife. They have two children and one in the oven.

The funeral was held at 3:50 for about 20 minutes.

—CHARLES SULLIVAN

A customer named Willie Smith called our dry cleaners looking for his suit.

"We have a William Smith," I told him.

"No, Willie Smith," he insisted. I looked in our logbook and discovered that the suit had been picked up by the sister of William Smith. I phoned her, then got back to Willie.

"You're not going to believe this," I said. "But William died and was buried in your suit."

"Well, you're not going to believe this," he said. "I was at that funeral. And I remember thinking, What a nice suit William's wearing."

—CARL POWALIE

It was my four-year-old's first time at a funeral, and I wanted to make sure he behaved at the cemetery. "What is the most important rule to remember?" I asked. He thought for a while, then answered, **"Don't dig up the bodies?"**

—STACIE TERREAULT

Leaving a funeral, my 13-year-old son dropped a heavy question on me: "What will happen to us if you and Dad die?" My young daughter knew: **"We'd go in the limo."**

—CHERYL ROBERTS

As I shampooed his carpet, an elderly client began to tell me what a wonderful woman his recently deceased wife was.

"Bless her soul, we had 35 happy years together," he said, pausing to reminisce. Looking up, he added, "That ain't too bad outta 50."

—STEPHEN PRYJDA

Before he made the big time, actor Ray Liotta held a less glamorous job working in a cemetery. Though some might have been put off by it, Liotta told the women on *The View* that he didn't mind the gig.

"I had a hundred people under me, and it was quiet," he said.

—JOSEPH BLUDIS

A lawyer dies and goes to heaven. "This must be a mistake," he says to Saint Peter at the golden gates. "I'm too young to die. I'm only 50."

"Fifty?" says Saint Peter. "According to our calculations, you're 82."

"How'd you get that?"

"We added up your billable hours."

The burial service for the elderly woman climaxed with a massive clap of thunder, followed by a bolt of lightning, accompanied by even more thunder. "Well," said her husband to the shaken pastor when it ended, "she's there."

—NORM SCHMITZ

During a funeral the organist played a beautiful rendition of Bach's "Sheep May Safely Graze" as the casket was carried out of the church. After the service the minister complimented him on his performance. "Oh, by the way," the minister asked, "do you know what the deceased did for a living?"

"No idea," said the organist as he began packing up.

The minister smiled. "He was a butcher."

—PETER LUNN

When Luciano Pavarotti died, the TV newscaster insisted that the tenor's funeral would not be a sad affair but rather a celebration of his life, featuring the opera world's greatest stars. "With so many celebrities and dignitaries in attendance, who wouldn't want to be at the funeral?" the reporter asked.

My daughter knew: "Pavarotti."

—HOLLY HASSELBARATH

Following a funeral service, the pallbearers are carrying the casket out of the church when they accidentally bump into a wall. From inside the coffin they hear a faint moan. Opening the lid, they find the man inside alive! He leaps out, performs a little jig, and lives another 10 years before eventually keeling over.

Once again, a ceremony is conducted, and at the end the pallbearers carry out the casket. As they head toward the doors of the church, the wife of the deceased leaps to her feet and shouts, "Watch the wall!"

—DORIS POOLE

"As another year rolls in," read an ad in our paper, "we'd like to offer our best wishes to all of you who have given us reason to celebrate." It was signed, "Gunter's Funeral Homes."

—JAN ASLIN

# Humor in Medicine

The teenage boy seemed placid as I approached his hospital bed to give him a psychiatric evaluation. His mother was seated nearby, immersed in her knitting.

I walked over and introduced myself to the boy. He looked right through me and started screaming: "I can't see! I can't see!"

I had never witnessed such a dramatic example of hysterical blindness. "How long has this been going on?" I asked his mother.

Without looking up, she replied, "Ever since you stepped in front of his television."

—ISAAC STEVEN HERSCHKOPF, MD, IN *THE NEW YORK TIMES*

My patient in the hospital had led a tough life, and it showed—he was disheveled and unkempt. Recently, while he was in a particularly somber mood, I was combing his hair when he mumbled, "It's hopeless."

"Don't say that," I insisted. "It's not hopeless. You just need to make a decision to change your life and seek help. You'll see, things will start looking up!"

Turning around, he said, "I was talking about my hair."

—NADINE GINTHER

A psychiatrist gets a frantic call. "You've got to help me, Doctor," a woman says. "My husband thinks he's a big opera star. He sings every night at the top of his lungs! *Aida! Rigoletto! Traviata!*"

"Send him to me," the shrink says. "I'll see what I can do."

A week later the woman calls again. "Doc, I don't know how you did it! He's not singing nearly as much. Did you cure his delusion?"

"No," says the psychiatrist. "I just gave him a smaller part."

—MARY LODGE

"This is about all I have in your price range . . ."

One of our patients wasn't taking any chances. Prior to her operation, she taped notes all over her body for the surgeon: "Take your time," "Don't cut yourself," "No need to rush," "Wash your hands," etc.

After surgery, as I helped her back into her bed, we discovered a new note taped to her, this one from the doctor: "Has anyone seen my watch?"

—ALBERTA ALLEN

Part of my job on the hospital's cardiac floor was shaving patients from chin to toe in preparation for bypass surgery. The women tended to be fine with this procedure, but not the men. One guy in particular gave me a rough time, refusing to let me come near him. Finally, I made a suggestion that helped him overcome his shyness.

"If you like," I told him, "I can do this with my eyes closed."

—MARSHEA LEWIS

After transporting hospital patients from one floor to the next, I stopped to chat with a new volunteer. "I work in patient transfer," I told him. "I push people around."

Not the type to be one-upped, he countered, "I work at the information desk. I tell them where to go."

—RALPH JOHNSON

"Hello, nurse," said a rabbi, phoning me at our hospital nurses station. "I got a call that a patient wanted to see me, but I'm not sure which one it was."

Clueless myself, I took a wild stab. I walked into a room, woke the patient, and asked, "Did you request a rabbi?"

"No," she said sleepily, "I ordered the chef's salad."

—MARGARET KRAFT

Before writing a prescription for my young daughter, the pediatrician asked her if she was allergic to anything. Erica whispered something in his ear.

That night, before giving her the medicine, I read the directions on the bottle. The doctor had warned,

**"Do not take with broccoli."**

—JOHN JOHNSTON

I was on line in the cafeteria of the hospital where I work when I overheard a doctor ask an anesthesiologist how his day was.

**"Good," came the response. "Everyone's woken up so far."**

—JENNA GALAZEN

Whatever happened to "First do no harm"? While I was paying my bill at my doctor's office, I noticed blood trickling down my leg. The Band-Aid they had put on me after a procedure had come loose.

"I'm bleeding all over your floor," I said to the receptionist.

She looked up immediately, alarmed. "Thanks for telling me. I'll call housekeeping."

—TRACY KRAFT-THARP

Visiting the psych ward, a man asked how doctors decide to institutionalize a patient.

"Well," the director said, "we fill a bathtub, then offer a teaspoon, a teacup and a bucket to the patient, and ask him to empty the tub."

"I get it," the visitor said. "A normal person would use the bucket because it's the biggest."

"No," the director said.

"A normal person would pull the plug."

—JOSH ROBERTS

A woman called our hospital switchboard requesting an ambulance. "You need to dial 911," I said.

"Okay," she answered. "And they'll have the phone number for the ambulance?"

—SONYA SQUIRRELL

"I hate taking my allergy medicine," my friend Mikayla complained. "The stuff makes me groggy."

"Why not stop?" I asked.

"Well, it does work. So I guess that means I'd rather be dopey or sleepy than sneezy."

—SARAH POLEYNARD

Say what? I was phoning a specialist to make an appointment. A woman picked up and announced, "Urology. Can you please hold?"

—FREDERICK KOENIG

"But why should I explain in layman's terms something that you will never understand?"

Sitting in the orthopedic surgeon's office cradling my broken hand, I racked my brains but couldn't come up with the medical term for my scheduled procedure. "Excuse me," I said to the physician's assistant. "What's the term doctors use for setting a broken bone?"

He grinned. "Billable procedure."

—PAUL SMITH

A man goes to his doctor and hands him a note that says, "I can't talk! Please help me!"

"Okay," says the doctor. "Put your thumb on the table."

The man doesn't understand how that will help, but he does what he's told. The doctor picks up a huge book and drops it on the man's thumb.

"AAAAAAAA!" the man yells.

"Good," says the doctor. "Come back tomorrow, and we'll work on B."

—L. B. WEINSTEIN

In order to process a medical claim, I asked a patient's mother to send details of her son's accident to me at our hospital's business office. The boy had suffered a broken arm, so the file was coded "Treatment of limb." Aptly so, I thought, after reading her description of the accident: "My son was running through the yard and turned into a tree."

—KIMBERLY SHERRELL

A patient at my daughter's medical clinic filled out a form. After "Name" and "Address," the next question was "Nearest Relative." She wrote, "Walking distance."

—GIA SPOOR

## Patients, beware: Doctors and nurses are writing things on your charts behind your back.

- "Hourly observations should be taken every half-hour."
- "At the beginning of treatment, the patient should be taken into the treatment room, where a member of the nursing staff will get familiar with him."
- "Encourage the patient to eat; if he does not, supplement the diet with smacks."
- "I calmed the patient down by calling her names quietly."
- "The patient has been depressed since I started nursing her."

—JOHN WIGHTMAN

One crazy day in our pediatric clinic saw me hand a young patient a urine-sample container and tell him to fill it up in the bathroom.

A few minutes later he returned to me at my nurses station, holding the empty cup in his hand. "I didn't need this, after all," he said. "There was a toilet in there."

—LINDA FEIKLE

My doctor swore that my colonoscopy would be painless, but the nurse made it seem otherwise. "The lab," she said, "will call to set a date for your screaming."

—DEBBIE MASTERSON

At the dentist's office for oral surgery, I was handed a couple of forms to fill out. As I signed the first one, I joked with the receptionist: "Does this say that even if you pull my head completely off, I can't sue you?"

"No, that's the next sheet," she said. "This one says you still have to pay us."

—LAWRENCE MARQ GOLDBERG

Three psychiatrists agree that people always come to them with their problems, but they have no one to go to with theirs, so they decide to listen to one another's deepest, darkest secrets.

The first confesses, "I'm a compulsive shopper, deeply in debt. So I always overbill patients."

The second admits, "I have a drug problem, and I pressure my patients into buying drugs for me."

The third says, "I know it's wrong, but no matter how hard I try, I just can't keep a secret."

—L. B. WEINSTEIN

When my mother hit her head at work, she suffered a nasty gash and bled all over her blouse. It was bad enough that the hospital gave her a donated T-shirt. Imagine my surprise, then, when I got to the ER and found the woman who raised me with two black eyes and stitches on her forehead, wearing a T-shirt that read, "I Survived the Grand Rapids Pub Crawl."

—SEAN PARKER

Mary decides to consult a diet doctor. "What's the most you've ever weighed?" he asks her.

"One hundred fifty-nine pounds."

"And the least?"

"Six pounds, four ounces."

—SYBIL CARR

Prior to his biopsy, a patient confessed to a fellow nurse just how nervous he was. "Don't worry," the nurse assured him. **"You're just having a little autopsy."**

—ANNE SANTORO

You can't blame the woman for being upset. After all, she was delivering her baby in our hospital elevator.

"This is nothing," said my fellow nurse, trying to console the new mother. "Last year a friend of mine helped a woman deliver her baby on the front lawn of the hospital."

The patient began to wail. "That was me!"

—STEPHANIE NIEDERBERGER

Proofreading an instruction manual for a hospital ventilator, I did a double-take when I came across this questionable troubleshooting tip: "If the problem persists, replace patient immediately."

—ADRIAN URIAS

On my first day working at a psychiatric hospital, I met a friendly man who assured me that the staff was great. "You'll like it here," he said.

"Good to know," I said. "Thanks."

That afternoon, we assembled for a round of meetings with our patients. Standing among them was my new friend.

"Psst, get over here," he whispered, giggling.

"What's so funny?" I asked.

"You were standing in the staff's section."

—KEVIN SU

Maybe I was overreacting, but I couldn't help worrying about the quality of care at the local hospital. On a form titled, "Some Questions for Our Pregnant Patients," the very first item was:

"1. Gender? (check one) M__ F __."

JENNIEY TALLMAN

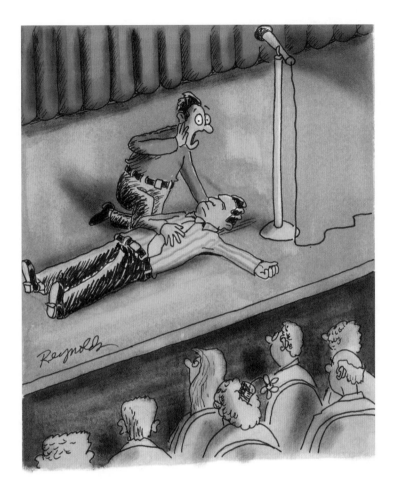

"Is there a healh-care representative in the house?"

When my wife gave birth to our son, she shared a room with a woman whose last name was Pope. One day their doctor came in and asked me how things were going.

"Fine," I answered. "How are you?"

"Great!" he said. "So far this morning, I've circumcised a Bishop and a Pope."

—JOE BISHOP

**"Pick something you can tolerate from this list of side effects, and I'll prescribe something appropriate."**

"I'm afraid you've only got three weeks to live," the doctor told his patient.

"Then I'll take the last two weeks of July and the week between Christmas and New Year's."

—GEORGE NORDHAM

When the patient was wheeled into the emergency room, I could tell he was out of it. I asked if he knew the date. He didn't.

"Do you know what season it is?"

He thought a moment. "Baseball?"

—A. H.

ONe diagnostic-imaging center claims that its high-tech medical procedures are second to none. The center's newspaper advertisement proclaimed, CT Colonoscopy:

## No Scope, No Sedation, No Recovery.

—FLORENCE CRUMLEY

Our friend Kathy, a school nurse, took one look at the emergency card filled out by a student's mother and knew she had to give the woman a call. "It says here that your son's allergic to Sicilians," Kathy said.

"He is," came the reply. "He's allergic to all of the Sicilians. You know, penicillin, amoxicillin . . ."

—RUTH PERSON

The pharmacist arrives at work to find a frightened-looking man leaning against the wall.

"What's wrong with him?" the pharmacist asks his clerk.

"He wanted cough medicine, but I couldn't find any, so I gave him a laxative."

"Laxatives won't cure a cough," yells the owner.

"Sure they will. Look at him. He's afraid to cough."

An elderly woman is being examined by a young physician. After about four minutes in the examination room, she bursts out of the door. Spotting an older doctor, she tells him what happened.

Astounded, he marches down the hallway toward his young colleague.

"What's the matter with you?" he demands. "That woman is 74! Why would you tell her she's pregnant?"

The young doc asks, "Well, does she still have the hiccups?"

—GINGER SIMPSON

Following my husband's physical exam, the doctor delivered some bad news. "Your white blood cells are elevated," he said.

"What does that mean?" I asked.

Looking concerned, the doctor explained, "Up."

—MERNA JOHANNESSEN

As I was admitted to the hospital prior to a procedure, the clerk asked for my wrist, saying, "I'm going to give you a bracelet."

"Has it got rubies and diamonds?" I asked coyly.

"No," he said. "But it costs just as much."

—EILENE COOK

A man walks into a bar and orders six whiskeys. Putting them in a row, he downs the first glass, then the third and finally the fifth.

"Excuse me," the bartender says as the man turns to leave. "But you left three glasses untouched."

"I know," the man says. "My doctor says it's okay to have the odd drink."

—JEE WAN YAU

My husband, an auto mechanic, was on the kidney transplant list, and as you can imagine, it was a tense time for our family. But one day the phone rang, and our teenage son answered. It was the hospital with good news. "Dad," he yelled excitedly. "Your parts are in!"

—BETTE LARSEN

When I was at the hospital being prepared for surgery, the floor nurse asked, "Which eye is to be operated on?"

I answered, "The left eye is the right eye. The right eye is the wrong eye."

—WILLIAM SHANK, IN *THE NEW YORK TIMES*

# Holy Jokes

A famous director goes to heaven.

"Boy, are we glad to see you," Saint Peter says. "God has the perfect project for you."

"I'm done making movies," the director says. "I just want to rest."

"But you'd have a dream crew. Mozart has signed on to write the score, Michelangelo will design the sets, and Shakespeare is hard at work on the screenplay."

"Wow! How can I say no to that? I'm in."

"Fabulous. There's just one thing," Saint Peter says. "God has this buddy who thinks he can act . . ."

The bishop spoke to the congregation about the priest and nun shortage.

"Too many of you are only having one child and letting them go off into other professions. I propose that each family should have three children: one for the father, one for the mother and one for the church."

A few days later the bishop was out grocery shopping when he saw a pregnant woman from his parish. But before he could say hello, she shouted above the crowd, "This one is yours, Bishop!"

—EDWIN KLINE

Two kids are on their way to Sunday school when one says to the other, "What do you think about this Satan stuff?"

**"Well, you remember Santa? This could turn out to be your dad, too."**

—PAT RUZSBATZKY

A banker approaches the Pearly Gates sweating and struggling with a heavy suitcase. Saint Peter greets him and says, "Set the suitcase down and come in."

"No way!" barks the banker. "I have to bring it in."

"What could possibly be in there that's so important?" asks Saint Peter.

The banker opens the suitcase to reveal 50 gold bricks. Saint Peter's jaw drops: "You brought pavement?"

—JIMMY HOLMES

The pastor asks his flock, "What would you like people to say when you're in your casket?"

One congregant says, "I'd like them to say I was a fine family man."

Another says, "I'd like them to say I helped people."

The third responds, "I'd like them to say, 'Look! I think he's moving!'"

—L. B. WEINSTEIN

"Hello, Reverend Smith? This is the Internal Revenue Service. Is Samuel Jones a member of your congregation?"

"He is."

"Did he donate $10,000 to the church?"

"He will."

—HUGH NEELD

During a church meeting on family, the instructor asked, "When we reach the end of our mortal existence, will we say, 'I wish I'd spent more time on the job'?" He persisted, "Has anyone ever wondered that?"

"Yes," said one man. "Right after I got fired."

—FRANK MILLWARD

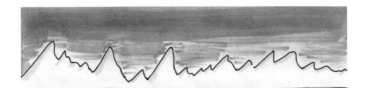

**"What am I missing here? We walk on water all the time."**

My brother-in-law was a lay minister, so when his sister wanted a small, casual wedding, she asked him to officiate. He had never performed a marriage ceremony before, so he decided to ask his pastor for advice.

"My sister has asked me to marry her," he began, "and I'm not sure what to do."

The minister answered, "Try telling her you just want to be friends."

—HEIDI MORTON

"**Well, yes, I am happy, but I could be happier.**"

An atheist is walking through the forest when Big Foot jumps out at him. As he approaches menacingly, the atheist yells, "Lord, save me!"

Seconds later a voice rumbles from heaven, "I thought you didn't believe in me."

"Well," the man says, "until a minute ago, I didn't believe in Big Foot either."

—GREGG PICILLO

The Earth is wicked again. I'm going to flood it and start over," God told Noah. "Build another ark and save two of every living thing."

Six months later the Lord looked down and saw Noah weeping in his yard—but no boat. "Where's the ark?" he roared. "I'm about to start the rain."

"Well, things have changed," Noah said. "First, I needed a building permit. Then some group said it was inhumane to put the animals in such a close space. Then the government halted construction to conduct an environmental-impact study on the flood."

Suddenly the clouds cleared, and a rainbow stretched across the sky.

"You mean, you're not going to destroy the world?" Noah asked.

"What's the point?" God said. "Looks like someone beat me to it."

—E. T. THOMPSON


Al's assets are going down the drain as the market takes a nosedive. Depressed, he goes to church.

"Grab your Bible and drive to the ocean," the minister advises. "Sit at the water's edge, and open the Bible. The wind will riffle the pages, but eventually it'll stay open. Read the first words your eyes fall on, and they will tell you what to do."

Al does as he is told. When the pages stop moving, his eyes fall on the words that are meant for him.

A year later Al, wearing a $1,000 suit and driving a new Jag, returns to see the minister. He hands the minister a thick envelope. "Please accept this donation for the church," he says. "Thanks for your advice."

"What words did you see that brought you such fortune?" the minister asks.

"Chapter 11."

Every day a woman stood on her porch and shouted, "Praise the Lord!"

And every day the atheist next door yelled back, "There is no Lord!"

One day she prayed, "Lord, I'm hungry. Please send me groceries."

The next morning she found a big bag of food on the stairs. "Praise the Lord," she shouted.

"I told you there was no Lord," her neighbor said, jumping from behind a bush. "I bought those groceries."

"Praise the Lord," the woman said. "He not only sent me groceries, but he made the devil pay for them."

The new monk is assigned to copy the old texts by hand. Noticing that he'll be copying from copies and not from the original manuscripts, he tells an elderly monk, "If there was an error in the first copy, that error would be continued in all the subsequent copies."

The elderly monk agrees and goes to the cellar with a copy to check it against the original. Hours go by and nobody sees him. Concerned, the new monk searches for him in the cellar. Hearing wailing, he finds the old monk leaning over one of the original books. Looking up, he sobs, "The word is celebrate."

The rabbi and the priest met at the town's annual picnic. Old friends, they began their usual banter.

"This ham is really delicious," the priest teased the rabbi. "You really ought to try it. I know it's against your religion, but you just haven't lived until you've tried Mrs. Hall's prized Virginia Baked Ham. Tell me, when are you going to break down and have some?"

The rabbi looked at his friend with a big grin and said, "At your wedding."

—ANDREA GERAGHTY

**"We especialy like your sermons on the website because we can scroll through them quickly."**

Johnny's mother stops to watch her son read the Bible to their cat. "Isn't that sweet?" she says. But an hour later she hears a terrible racket. Running out the door, she finds Johnny stuffing the cat into a bucket of water.

"Johnny, what are you doing?"

"I'm baptizing Muffin," he replies.

"But cats don't like to be in water."

"Well then, he shouldn't have joined my church."

Just as I began my Christmas Eve service, the electricity in the church failed. The ushers and I found some candles and placed them around the sanctuary. Then I reentered the pulpit, shuffled my notes, and muttered, "Now, where was I?"

A tired voice called out, **"Right near the end!"**

—REV. DOUGLAS C. WOODS

A man was driving down the street in a lather because he had an important meeting and couldn't find a parking space. Looking up to heaven, he said, "Lord, take pity on me. If you find me a parking space, I promise to go to church every Sunday for the rest of my life and give up swearing."

Miraculously, a spot opened right in front of the building.

The man looked up and said, "Never mind. I found one."

Our Sunday school speaker had riveting stories to share with the kids: He was working near Mount St. Helens when it erupted. He was in Florida when Hurricane Andrew hit and was visiting friends in New Orleans as Katrina struck.

One child raised his hand. "Staying long in Tucson?"

—MARGIE DORAME

One Sunday a minister played hooky from church so he could shoot a round of golf. Saint Peter, looking down from Heaven, seethed. "You're going to let him get away with this, God?"

The Lord shook his head.

The minister took his first shot. The ball soared through the air 420 yards and dropped into the cup for a hole in one. Saint Peter was outraged. "I thought you were going to punish him!"

The Lord shrugged. "Who's he going to tell?"

Moses and Jesus are playing golf. Moses selects a five iron and tees off. His ball lands in the lake.

It's Jesus' turn. "Tiger Woods would use this," he says, grabbing a five iron.

"But my shot ended up in the lake!" Moses protests. "You should use a four iron."

"Nope. Tiger would use a five."

So Jesus swings hard—and hits the ball into the lake. He's walking on the water looking for it when a man approaches.

"Who does he think he is, Jesus Christ?" the man asks.

"No," Moses explains. "He *is* Jesus. He thinks he's Tiger Woods."

An engineer is standing outside the Pearly Gates.

"Sorry," Saint Peter tells him, "but you're in the wrong place." He snaps his fingers, and the engineer finds himself in hell.

Dissatisfied with the level of comfort there, the engineer starts making improvements.

One day God phones Satan to ask how things are going.

"Great," he answers. "We've got central air and escalators now. There's no telling what that engineer will come up with next."

"You've got an engineer?" God says. "There's been a mistake. Send him back up here, or I'll sue."

"Yeah, right." Satan chuckles. "Where are you going to find a lawyer?"

—VICKY BULLETT

## ? Who's the patron saint of e-mail?
Saint Francis of a CC.

———————————————————————— TERRY SANGSTER

**"Turns out you can take it with you. You just can't change the ring tone."**

Three buildings in town were overrun by squirrels—the town hall, the hardware store, and the church. The town hall brought in some cats. But after they tore up all the files, the mayor got rid of the predators, and soon the squirrels were back.

The hardware store humanely trapped the squirrels and set them free outside town. But three days later the squirrels climbed back in.

Only the church came up with an effective solution. They baptized the squirrels and made them members. Now they see them only on Christmas and Easter.

Adam bit the apple and, feeling great shame, covered himself with a fig leaf. Eve, too, felt shame and covered herself with a fig leaf. Then she went behind the bush to try on a maple leaf, a sycamore, and an oak.

—TERRY SANGSTER

Three guys are fishing on a lake when an angel appears in the boat with them. The first guy gets over his shock and humbly says to the angel, "I've suffered from back pain for years. Is it too much to ask that you help me?" The angel touches the man's back, and he feels instant relief.

The second guy points to his Coke-bottle glasses and asks if the angel could cure his poor eyesight. The angel tosses the man's glasses into the lake. When they hit the water, the man's vision clears and he can see everything distinctly.

The angel now turns to the third guy, who throws up his hands in fear. "Don't touch me!" he cries.

"I'm on disability!"

After my fire crew put out a fire in a barn, the monks who owned it invited us in for some tea and lighthearted conversation—or so we thought. But as we entered the monastery, one fireman was reminded of a particularly rude joke. And worse yet, repeated it.

A monk responded, "My son, you are fighting fires in this life, and you will surely be fighting them in the next."

—MICHAEL TOWNSEND

I accompanied one of my congregants to court to settle some legal affairs. As I waited, a man took note of my clerical collar. "So," he said, "prayer didn't help you either, huh?"

—REV. F. WILLIAM HODGE

The sign by the minister's parking spot at a church in Senath, Missouri, cleverly kept parishioners moving: **"You Park, You Preach."**

—PATSY HANNERS

After examining the paltry tips left by a church group, our waitress was not pleased. Looking toward my table, she grumbled, "These people come in with the Ten Commandments and a ten-dollar bill, and they don't break any of them!"

—ELZENA ARGUELLO

My father, a pastor, met with a couple who wanted to marry in his church. When he raised the subject of premarital counseling, the two were quick to nix it.

"We don't need counseling," the bride-to-be assured him. "We've both been married several times before."

—MICHELLE PATTERSON

When my back seized up, I called my doctor's office, explaining that I was a minister and was in too much pain to deliver my sermon. Could they help?

The woman on the other end asked me to hold. The next thing I heard was a loud voice announcing, "I have a minister on the phone who can't stand to preach!"

—GILBERT VIEIRA

Our professor assigned a two-page paper on one of the seven deadly sins. On the due date I heard a student tell his buddy, "That was so easy. All I did was write one page and double-space it."

"Which sin did you pick?" his friend asked.

"Sloth."

—JASON O'SHEA

# Last
## Laughs

Laugh-out-loud jokes
we couldn't resist

# Dumb and Dumber

Larry wins the lottery and dashes downtown to claim his prize. "Give me my $20 million," he tells the man in charge.

"Sorry, but it doesn't work that way," the man says. "You'll get a million today, and then the rest will be spread out over the next 19 years."

Larry is furious. "Look, I want my money! And if you're not going to give me my $20 million right now, then I want my dollar back!"

After my speech at a tech conference on "Tips for Going Paperless," I opened the floor to questions. "I have one," said a man. "Where are the handouts?"

—MIKE BROWNING

Two snowmen are standing in a field when one says to the other, "Do you smell carrots?"

—PATRICK HIGGINS

Jim arrives home to find his wife lying on the floor in a pool of sweat. He rushes over and rouses her. It's then that he notices that she's wearing a parka and a mink.

"Are you okay? What are you doing?" he asks.

"You've been promising to paint the living room for months now," she explains groggily. "I wanted to prove that I could do just as good a job as you, and faster too."

"Well, it does look like you did a good job," Jim says, looking around. "But why are you all bundled up?"

"I know how to read," she snaps. "The can said, 'For best results put on two coats.'"

—CORA M. BOGGS

**"No, he's not stuffed. He just has a weird sense of humor."**

**F**rantic while getting ready for a party at home, I asked my husband to run out for a quart of milk. When he returned empty-handed, I asked, "Where's the milk?"

"All out," he said. "They only had pints."

Did I mention that he has a PhD? In statistics?

—LOUISE WEISS

**A** customer at our bookstore asked me, "Do you have the original book *Romeo and Juliet*? My daughter needs it for school, and all I can find is the play."

—AUDRIE WESTON

Posted on the elevator at work is the usual warning sign: "In case of fire, do not use elevator." Scrawled in pen beneath it is this addendum: **"Use water."**

—DAVID MOORE

With talk of downsizing the U.S. Postal Service always in the air, our union steward passed the word to all the letter carriers that we needed to be proactive.

"Save our jobs," he urged. "E-mail your Congressman."

—SUSAN KEMP

"You have to explain this to me," I told the chef at our restaurant. The chalkboard read, "Today's Special: Broiled Snaper with 2 Peas."

The chef laughed. "Yeah, I saw that the hostess had misspelled snapper too," he said. "But she misunderstood me when I said, 'The special has two p's.'"

—CANDICE WOHLFIEL

Recently, one of the guys at the warehouse called my husband, the general manager, to tell him that he wouldn't be in that day.

"I'm having my autopsy," he said. "But with any luck I'll be in tomorrow."

—TERRI RITTER

As manager of an electronics shop, I ordered a part, number 669, from the factory. When it arrived, I noticed they'd sent me part 699 instead. I fired off an angry letter and sent it back. A few days later I got the replacement. It was the same part, along with a note containing these four words: "Turn the box over."

—BECQUET.COM

Heading down the interstate, our car passed through a huge swarm of gnats so dense that their bodies made popping noises as they hit the windshield. "I can't get over how loud they are," my wife said.

"Well, we are hitting them at 65 miles an hour," I pointed out.

Her reply left me speechless. "I didn't know bugs could fly that fast."

—JOHN SHINDLEBOWER

I answer a lot of questions at the information desk at Olympic National Park, in Washington State. But one visitor stumped me: "Do you have any trails that just go downhill?"

—MIKE PERZEL

A woman walked into our thrift shop and deposited a lamp on our counter.

"I'd like to donate this," she said. "I know you don't take electrical equipment, so I've cut the plug off."

—DEBORAH SUTTON

After my business conference ended for the day, I headed back to my hotel. The lobby and the elevators were packed. I went up to the front-desk clerk. "Can you direct me to the stairs? It'll probably be faster to walk up to my floor."

"I'm afraid that's not possible," she said, completely seriously. "Our stairs only go down."

—ABBY CONLEY

**?** **How did the blonde die raking leaves?**
She fell out of the tree!

Try as I might, I just couldn't get in sync with my insurance customer. When I asked if he lived in the eastern or central time zone, he answered, "We're normal time."

Not sure what that meant, I continued. "Let me put it this way: Is it 10:45 where you are?"

"No," he said. "It's 10:46."

—CHERYL KOCHANEK

When my friend Rachel said she was expecting, I asked, "Do you know the baby's sex?"

"Yes," she replied, "but we've decided not to announce it."

"Can I take a guess?"

"Sure, go ahead."

"Is it a girl?"

"Oh, no," she replied. "You're way off."

—NAFTALI DOMBROFF

In our storeroom we use a stepladder to get items from the top shelf. But it's always in the way, and after banging my shin on it for the umpteenth time, I asked the staff to please keep it somewhere safe.

The next day I found the ladder neatly collapsed and placed where it couldn't hurt anyone: on the top shelf.

—NEIL HUDSON

On his way home from work recently, my husband came upon a "Road Closed" sign. Undeterred, he maneuvered his truck around it and continued on. But he didn't get very far. The pavement ended, giving way to another, larger sign: "What Part of 'Road Closed' Didn't You Understand?"

—TERI KERSCHEN

After hearing stories about radioactivity in granite countertops, my wife became alarmed.

"I have granite in my kitchen," she told a friend.

"Maybe you should get a Geiger counter," her friend suggested.

My wife was intrigued. "Are those the granite imitations they sell at Costco?"

—DANIEL OSTER

I was leading a tour through Carlsbad Caverns in New Mexico when a woman asked, "How many miles of undiscovered passageways are there in this cave?"

—JIM DAVIS

A customer walked into our auto-parts store looking for a flat washer. "That'll be 15 cents," I said.

"Fifteen cents for a washer? Are you crazy?" he yelled. "I'll drill a hole in a quarter and make my own."

—JACK REEVES

After weighing a woman's letter on our post office scale, I told her the envelope was too heavy and would require another stamp. Confused, she asked, "But won't another stamp make it heavier?"

—CYNTHIA FRANKLIN

Seen on a marquee outside the Clinton Correctional Facility, a maximum security prison in Dannemora, New York: "The Dannemora Fire Department reminds you it's fire prevention week. Practice your escape plan."

—DICK BECKER

My wife, a professor of medicine, has published five books. After she'd written her latest one, I stopped at a market to buy some chocolate and champagne.

"Are you celebrating something?" asked the clerk as he bagged my items.

"Yes," I replied proudly. "My wife just finished a book."

He paused a moment. "Slow reader?"

—DENNIS DOOK

The instructor of our paramedic certification class taught us to keep performing chest compressions until backup arrived. "But what if we can't keep going?" a fellow student wanted to know. "Should we call 911?"

**"Son," said our instructor, "you are 911."**

—CRISTY FIGUEROA

A colleague at the nursing home was excited about the English literature class he was taking at night school.

"We're reading Shakespeare," he said.

"Great," I replied. "Which one?"

"William."

—PENNY BOWDEN

After browsing the restaurant menu, I had a question for the waitress. "About the salmon entrée, is that a steak or a fillet?"

"Neither," she said. "It's a fish."

—ROBERT PETRIN

While I was making a huge batch of snickerdoodle cookies, I asked my ten-year-old to read the recipe and ingredients off the box to me, doubling them as he went along. He did as he was told. His first instruction: "Preheat the oven to 700 degrees."

—DEBBIE DEERWESTER

After a day full of accidents and mistakes, my coworker had had it. "Why," she cried out in exasperation, "do things that happen to stupid people keep happening to me?"

—ADAM FRICKE

My cousin's not bright. She got an AM radio—
**took her a month to realize she could use it at night.**

—FROM *LAUGH OFF* BY BOB FENSTER (ANDREWS MCMEEL)

Anyone traveling on business for our company must fill out an expense report. A field on the form asks for "name on credit card." One Einstein entered "MasterCard."

—PAM THOMPSON

"What's the quickest way from here to Philadelphia?"
"Are you walking or driving?"
"I'm driving."
"That's definitely the quickest way."

After a tourist parked herself on our Washington Island, Wisconsin, trolley, she wanted to know if we had any beaches.
"Yes," I assured her. "Four of them."
"Great!" she exclaimed. "Which one's closest to the water?"

—TERRI MOORE

This report from an agent landed on my desk in the auto claims division of our insurance company: "Driver encountered a large deer that jumped out from the woods to challenge his vehicle. The deer attacked his vehicle without having any insurance."

—BROOK ROBINSO

Three dolts are in the forest when they spot a set of tracks.
Dolt No. 1 says, "Hey, deer tracks!"
Dolt No. 2 says, "No, dog tracks!"
Dolt No. 3 says, "You're both crazy—they're cow tracks!"
They were still arguing when the train hit them.

A dull-witted king is losing a territorial dispute with a neighboring monarch.

As the fight wears on, he gets more and more frustrated until finally he roars, "Where are my two court jesters?"

In seconds two jesters appear at his side.

"Okay, let's continue," he says, "now that I have my wits about me."

—RICHARD MARINO

My niece was thrilled to hear that a new car wash was opening up in her neighborhood.

"How convenient," she said. "I can walk to it."

—CATHY MCCOURT

Driving along a country road, I ignored a Bridge Out sign and continued on. But in a few miles I came to a stop: The road was completely barricaded. So I turned around and retraced my route. That's when I saw this sign on the back of the first: "It was, wasn't it?"

—THOMAS ROY

As a retired chemist, I was interested in some unusual chemical towers at a factory. Curious, I asked a guard, "What do they make there?" He replied, "$8.35 an hour."

—ROBERT JOSLIN

Family members came down from Fairbanks, Alaska, to visit us in Anchorage just as the thermometer dropped to zero. I was freezing, but not them. "We're used to cold weather," my brother-in-law said.

"Sure," I replied. "To you folks, zero is nothing."

—WALT ARDEN

On the first day of our marriage retreat, the instructor talked about the importance of knowing what matters to each other.

"For example," he began, pointing to my husband, David, "do you know your wife's favorite flower?"

David answered, "Pillsbury All Purpose."

—ANNEMARIE WOODS

A customer called our florist shop to order a bouquet. "Make it bright and festive looking," she said. **"I want it to cheer up a friend. She just lost her Seeing Eye dog."**

—KATHY BRENING

A woman came to our bank to cash a check.
"Do you have identification?" I asked.

**"Yes," she said. "A strawberry mark on my left knee."**

—HARRY CHALKLY

Trying to do my share to help the environment, I set up a trash basket at my church and posted above it this suggestion: "Empty water bottles here."

I should have been a little more specific, because when I went to check it later, I didn't find any bottles in it. But it was full of water.

—MAHMOOD JAWAID

Our client sought short-term disability insurance after injuring a knee. In order to process his claim, I had to ask the obvious: "And which knee is it?"

He replied, "Mine."

—CAROLYN PETERSON

Some people just don't have a green thumb. When my son Bill learned his friend was going to The Home Depot, he asked, "Would you pick up some tulip bulbs? I need to get some for my mom."

"Sure," his pal responded. "How many watts?"

—BEATRIX NOVAK

Shopping for deodorant, my daughter picked one up and read the label: "Dermatologist Tested."

"Good," she said. "They're no longer testing it on rabbits."

—LYNN CARROLL

I had just eaten the worst meal in my life and had to say something.

"Is everything okay?" the waitress asked.

"No," I replied. "The chicken is so tough, you can't cut it with a knife."

"I'm so sorry," she said. "Can I bring you a different knife?"

—JOHN CARLSON

I walked into the lobby of my apartment building recently and was greeted by this notice: "To whoever is watering these plants, please stop. They are the property of the building, and our maintenance staff will take care of them. They may have already been watered, in which case you will be overwatering them. Besides, these plants are fake."

—PAUL ROGERS

Waiting my turn to enter a rotary intersection, I noticed a guy drive around twice, then leave by the same road he'd entered. **His vanity license plate read "GENIUS."**

—KATHLEEN GOWDY

A pirate walks into a bar with a paper towel on his head. The bartender says, "What's with the paper towel?" The pirate says, "Arrr! I've got a Bounty on me head!"

My sister, Sandy, was driving in Vancouver when she was rear-ended by a car driven by a younger woman. Sandy had seen in her rearview mirror that the woman appeared to be on her cell phone and was not slowing down, so Sandy braced herself for the inevitable impact.

"If you can't drive and talk at the same time, you shouldn't be on a cell phone!" Sandy said to the woman.

"I'll have you know," the woman replied, "I was not on my cell; I was putting on makeup!"

—SHIRLEY LADRET

I work for an office equipment company. One day Dave, a coworker of mine, received a phone call from a customer who was having trouble changing the toner in a photocopier.

"What seems to be the problem?" Dave asked.

"Well," the customer said, "it's telling me to change toner. But every time I open the door to do it, it tells me to 'please close front door.' What do I do?"

—ROBERT FEDORUK

I used to drive an Eclipse. I think it was a nice car, but I couldn't look directly at it.

—BUZZ NUTLEY

# Just for Laughs

Lost in the desert for three days, a man suddenly hears, "Mush!"

Looking up, he sees what he thinks is a mirage: an Eskimo on a sled, driving a team of huskies. To his surprise, the sled comes to a stop at his feet seconds later.

"I don't know why you're here, but thank goodness," the man says. "I've been lost for days."

Panting, the Eskimo replies, "You think *you're* lost?"

—ROBERT LUTZ

On a trip together, a Hindu, a rabbi, and a lawyer stop at a farmhouse and ask to stay the night. There's space for two, but one will have to sleep in the barn.

"I'll go," the Hindu volunteers. A few minutes later, the lawyer and the rabbi hear a knock.

"There's a cow in the barn," the Hindu says. "A cow is sacred, and I cannot sleep with a sacred beast."

"No problem, I can do it," the rabbi says, grabbing his pillow. But minutes later, the rabbi knocks.

"There's a pig in the barn. It's an unclean animal—my belief forbids me to be near such a creature."

With a tired sigh, the lawyer heads out. Almost immediately, there's a third knock at the door.

It's the cow and the pig.

Back when I was working as a graphic designer, I often grabbed lunch at a Chinese restaurant. I'll never forget a bit of wisdom from a fortune cookie I received one day: "In case of fire, keep calm, pay bill, then run!"

—BORYS PATCHOWSKY, IN *THE NEW YORK TIMES*

"**Getting water from a cactus? I know I have an APP for that.**"

**A**fter a fruitless year of entering the Publishers Clearing House Sweepstakes online, I suddenly drew a blank on my password. I chose the new-password option on the website and waited for the company to e-mail it to me. An hour later, I got it. The password they gave me: loser61.

—KATHLEEN SLACK

**T**here's a lunch wagon offering "Filly Cheese Steaks" I see almost every day. Each time I pass it, I chant to myself: "Please let it be a misspelling. . . . Please let it be a misspelling."

—CINDY GREATREX, IN *THE NEW YORK TIMES*

Looking down the stairs at a football game, a fan spots an open seat on the 50-yard line. He asks the man sitting next to it if the seat is taken.

"No," he replies. "I used to take my wife to all the games, but ever since she passed away, I've gone alone."

"Why don't you invite a friend?"

"I can't. They're all at the funeral."

—JOEL BRANSCOME

Our old house needed constant TLC. Fortunately my dad is handy and can do most of the work himself. One day he crawled under the foundation to prop up some sagging floorboards. Suddenly we heard a muffled yell, and Dad crawled out on his hands and knees at a speed I hadn't thought possible.

"What's wrong?" my mother asked.

"I reached to pick up the crowbar," Dad gasped, "and it slithered out of my hand."

—ROBERT SHELLEY

"It's crucial that we stay together on this field trip, kids."

Days after gorging myself at an Easter dinner, I did penance by going to the gym across the street from work. The first thing I noticed as I signed in was a bowl of Easter candy sitting on the counter, calling to me.

"That doesn't seem fair," I joked to the trainer.

Patting the bowl, she smiled. "Job security."

—JULIE BLACKWOOD

Two American tourists are driving through Wales. They decide to stop for a bite to eat in the village of Llanfairpwllgwyngyllgogerychwyrndrobwllllantysiliogogogoch.

Baffled by the name, one of them turns to a local and asks, "Would you please say where we are—very slowly?"

The Welshman leans over and says, very slowly, "Burrr-gerrr Kinngg."

—DENISE STEWART

Dad's a safety-first kind of guy. But while vacationing with some buddies, he was talked into going parasailing. He was on the back of the boat getting hooked into the parachute when he nervously asked the pilot, "How often do you replace the rope?"

The pilot replied, "Every time it breaks."

—MICHAEL WASSMER

My husband's expanding waistline was a sore subject, but I could no longer ignore it, especially since he's still young and handsome.

"Honey," I said, using my seductive voice, "if you lose 20 pounds, I promise to dance for you."

Using his sarcastic voice, he shot back, "Lose 10 pounds, and I'll watch."

—EMILY GURLEY

"A hamburger and fries," a man orders.

"Me too," says the ostrich, sitting beside him.

"That's $9.40," the waitress says. The man reaches into his pocket and hands her the exact change.

They return the next day. Both order a steak and potato, and again the man pays with exact change.

"How do you do that?" the waitress asks.

"A genie granted me two wishes," explains the man. "My first was that I'd always have the right amount of money to pay for anything."

"Brilliant! But what's with the ostrich?"

"My second wish was for an exotic chick with long legs who agrees with everything I say."

—EDWARD M. JEAN

I was in the back of our ambulance tending to a patient when we slowed to a crawl. Just ahead of us, a huge semi was hauling a house.

"Don't you hate that?" said our driver. "When people are simply too lazy to pack."

—ANTHONY ADKINS

I had an inauspicious start as a dog groomer when one of my first clients bit me. Noticing my pain, my boss voiced her concern.

"Whatever you do," she said, "don't bleed on the white dogs."

—JAN VIRGO

Johnny swallowed a quarter. A man walking by turned Johnny upside down and patted his back with great precision. The quarter popped out.

"You must be a quarterback. Thank you!" said Johnny's mom.

—STEVEN SHWE

I was talking to my doctor about a weight-loss patch I had seen advertised. Supposedly you stick it on, and the pounds melt away. "Does it work?" I asked.

"Sure," he said. "If you put it over your mouth."

—MARY KAAPKE

A man staggered up to the pharmacy counter.

"Would you give me something for my head?" the man asked.

"Why?" the pharmacist said, looking up. "What would I do with it?"

"Excuse me, what are those women dressed in white doing?" a tourist asked his guide.

"Oh, well, it's custom for brides in Jerusalem to pray at the Wailing Wall on the day of their wedding," he replied.

"Why?"

**"So they can get used to talking to a wall."**

—RACHEL BERMAN

Three rough-looking bikers stomp into a truck stop where a grizzled old-timer is having breakfast.

One of the bikers extinguishes his cigarette in the old guy's pancakes. The second biker spits a wad of chewing tobacco into his coffee. The third biker dumps the whole plate on the floor.

Without a word of protest, the old guy pays his bill and leaves.

"Not much of a man, was he?" says one of the bikers.

"Not much of a driver either," says the waitress. "He just backed his truck over three motorcycles."

I love playing Santa at the mall. But parents often have trouble getting young children to sit on my knee. It took a lot of coaxing for one little girl to perch there, so I got straight to the point.

"What do you want most of all for Christmas?" I asked.

She answered, "Down!"

—MORLEY LESSARD

On the first day of her vacation, my coworker fell and broke her leg. As the doctor examined her, she moaned, "Why couldn't this have happened on my last day of skiing?"

He looked up. "This is your last day of skiing."

—EDNA KITCHEN

I live for baseball. But I had to go to work during an important game, so I asked my wife to tape it for me. After I left the office, I flew through our front door, bursting with anticipation.

"Don't tell me the score!" I yelled to her.

"I don't know the score," she assured me. "All I know is that your team lost."

—MICHAEL BOGGESS

Three guys were fishing when one of them hooked a mermaid. She promised to grant each of them a wish if they'd let her go.

"Deal," the first fisherman said. "I'd like you to double my intelligence." Immediately, he began to recite Shakespeare's *Macbeth*.

"Wow!" the second guy exclaimed. "Could you triple my intelligence?" He'd no sooner made the request than he started spouting Einstein's equations on the theory of relativity.

"That's amazing!" the third fisherman yelled. "Quintuple my intelligence."

"Are you sure?" the mermaid asked. "You might not like the outcome."

"I'm sure. Just do it," the guy said.

He closed his eyes to wait for the wish to be granted and—*poof!*—he became a woman.

—DANNY HOCHSTETLER

## ? So what has six eyes but can't see?

A: Three men in a house with dirty dishes in the sink, laundry that needs to be folded, and kids that need a bath.

DARREN BAKER

While visiting his wife's cousin's farm in Manitoba for the first time, our Icelandic friend Gunnar was warned about the big, blood-sucking mosquitoes. Gunnar was out in a field one day, driving a tractor, when he suddenly screeched to a halt, ran pell-mell through the field, and burst through the farmhouse door and into the kitchen. "I just saw a MOSQUITO!" Gunnar gasped.

Turns out it was actually a dragonfly!

—AMANDA DINSDALE

While taking down the vitals for a soon-to-be mom, I asked how much she weighed.

"I really don't know," she said in response.

"More or less," I prompted.

"More, I guess."

—AGNES HALVERSON

"They make it look so easy."

Sitting in a hospital waiting room, I watched a woman helping her son finish a crossword puzzle. "Mom," he asked, "what fits here?"

"It's man's best friend," she hinted.

The boy thought for a second then guessed, "Duct tape?"

—CAEL JACOBS

A Dutchwoman explains her nation's flag to an American friend. "It symbolizes our taxes," she jokes. "We get red when we talk about them, white when we get our bill, and blue after we pay."

"Same with us," says the American. "Only we see stars, too."

Did you hear about the man who spent his life collecting memorabilia of Wonder Woman, Joan of Arc, and Florence Nightingale? Apparently, he was a heroine addict.

Teeing off on the 12th hole at a golf resort, we stopped to buy cold drinks from the young woman driving the beverage cart. As my buddy reached for his wallet, he said to her, "You're in great shape. You must work out a lot."

Flattered, she gave him a big smile. "Thank you."

The next day a different young woman was driving the cart. "Watch this," I whispered. I walked up to her and said, "Wow, you must work out a lot."

"Yeah," she replied. "You should try it."

—THOMAS OSBORNE

After my wife and I had navigated through a website for 20 minutes, a talking image of a woman popped up to offer help. "At last," my wife said, "a real person."

—VINCENT PELOZA

Why do mermaids wear seashells?
**Because B-shells are too small and D-shells are too big.**

—ADAM RUDEBUSCH

Two buddies were watching the game when one turned to his friend and said, "You won't believe it. All last night I kept dreaming of a horse and the number five. So I went to the track, put $500 on the fifth horse in the fifth race, and you won't believe what happened."

"Did he win?"

"Nah," the guy said. "He came in fifth."

—LUIS ANDRE

The knit cap my friend sent me from England was a bit small. But it was lovely, so I wore it to church that Sunday. Afterward, I e-mailed her to say how nice it looked on me. She shot me back a note saying how glad she was. "Especially," she wrote, "since it's a tea cozy."

—JAMIE CARLSON

The gunslinger swaggered into the saloon. He looked to his left. "Everybody on that side of the room is a lily-livered, yellow-bellied coward," he shouted.

He looked to his right. "Everybody on this side is a flabby, dim-witted saddle tramp." No one dared challenge him.

Satisfied, he was ordering his drink at the bar when he heard the sound of hurried footsteps.

"Where do you think you're going?" he yelled at the little guy who'd stopped in his tracks.

"Sorry," the man said. "I was on the wrong side of the room."

—GEORGE MORRIS

# "QUOTABLE QUOTES

**"The only nice thing about being imperfect is the joy it brings to others."**

—DOUG LARSON

"The only time to eat diet food is while you're waiting for the steak to cook."

—JULIA CHILD

**"I always cook with wine. Sometimes I even add it to the food."**

—W. C. FIELDS

"Airplane travel is nature's way of making you look like your passport photo."

—AL GORE

**"A man has to be Joe McCarthy to be called ruthless. All a woman has to do is put you on hold."**

—MARLO THOMAS

"The word aerobics came about when the gym instructors got together and said, 'If we're going to charge $10 an hour, we can't call it jumping up and down.'"

—RITA RUNDER

**"You grow up the day you have the first real laugh—at yourself."**

—ETHEL BARRYMORE

**"If you don't have enemies, you don't have character."**

—PAUL NEWMAN

"Anyone who believes the competitive spirit in America is dead has never been in a supermarket when the cashier opens another checkout line."

—ANN LANDERS

**"At the Sharper Image store, I saw a body fat analyzer. Didn't that used to be called a mirror?"**

—JAY LENO

Did you hear about the mermaid and the fisherman?
**They met online.**

One year my father was in and out of the hospital. Each time, his tireless neighbors stepped in—mowing the lawn, shoveling the driveway, taking Mom to the hospital, picking up prescriptions.

After Dad recovered, my mother said, "I'd like to thank the neighbors for all they did. What would be something they'd appreciate?"

Dad suggested, "Tell them we're moving."

—MARK REILLEY

My son, a used-car dealer, showed his customer a 2005 Chevy in great condition. "And it's only $7,000," he told the man.

"I'm willing to give you $3,500," said the customer.

My son feigned disappointment. "If at all possible," he responded, "I'd like to sell you the whole car."

—LIZ BROOKER

Bob: Al, when did you get a trombone?
Al: I borrowed it from my neighbor's kid.
Bob: I didn't know you could play the trombone.
Al: I can't. And now, neither can he.

—CAPERS SIMMONS

When his house went up in flames, my brother-in-law watched firemen fight a losing battle to save the greenhouse. One firefighter tried to console him: "We couldn't get the plants out, but we did water them."

—ROBERTA HUNT

Some New Yorkers were on a safari in the jungles of a little-explored faraway country when they were captured by cannibals.

"Oh, yes!" the chief of the tribe exclaimed. "We're going to put you all into big pots of water, cook you, and eat you."

"You can't do that to me," the tour leader said. "I'm the editor of *The New Yorker!*"

"Well," he responded, "tonight you will be editor-in-chief!"

—HERM LONDON

Every year, my father visits a friend in Tennessee. During one stay his buddy teased, "You should move down here. Of course, then you wouldn't be a Yankee anymore."

"I've always wondered about something," Dad said. "What's the difference between a Yankee and a damn Yankee?"

"A Yankee," his friend replied with a smile, "only comes to visit."

—CRESAYA WINCHELL

"First you're ice cream, then you're steak."

For a story about safe driving, a BBC anchorwoman had this revelation: **"Most cars have only one occupant, usually the driver."**

—ALEX CHERN

At the DMV to renew her license, my mother had her photo taken and waited for her new card. Finally her name was called, and she went to the counter to pick it up.

"Good grief," she said. "My picture's hideous. It looks nothing like me."

The woman in line behind her plucked it out of her hand. "That's because it's mine."

—CLARE SPAULDING

Our surname, Stead, rhymes with bed, but people often say steed, like the horse. One day a business associate of mine came over to the house and was greeted by my mother.

"Is Mr. Steed in?" the woman asked.

"He's Stead," my mother snapped.

"Oh, no," the woman gasped. "I was talking to him only yesterday."

—J. STEAD

You don't just see the sights when you work at the San Diego Convention & Visitors Bureau—you see and hear it all, as these queries can attest:

• "How many oceans does San Diego have?"

• "Why is your office called the International Visitor Info Center if you don't have information on Oklahoma?"

• "I'm calling from Canada. Is it acceptable to wear navy blue in November?"

—*THE SAN DIEGO UNION-TRIBUNE*, C. TUCKER

I was working as a lab instructor at Stadacona's Naval Combat Systems Engineering School in Halifax when I overheard two students having an animated discussion. One of them was explaining a concept using technical terms like "pulse modulation" and "plasma-based." I was impressed by their scholastic enthusiasm, but was quickly brought back down to earth when the second student replied, "Yeah, that's great against the Romulans, but don't forget that the Klingons use . . ."

—JOHN C. ARKSEY

A young American tourist goes on a guided tour of a creepy old castle in England. "How did you enjoy it?" the guide asked when it was over.

"It was great," the girl replied, "but I was afraid I was going to see a ghost in some of those dark passageways."

"No need to worry," said the guide. "I've never seen a ghost in all the time I've been here."

"How long is that?" she asked.

"Oh, about 300 years."

—DONALD GEISER

I helped a lost little girl by taking her to the store's service counter and having them page her mother. I saw this as a chance to teach my 12-year-old daughter, Kylie, a safety lesson.

"That girl did the right thing," I said. "Do you know why? Because she asked a woman for help, not a man."

Kylie looked at me, mystified.

**"Why on earth would I ask a man for help if I was already lost?"**

—STEPHANIE TAIT

"**It's an old family recipe, googled down from generation to generation.**"

hree days of suffering through a nasty virus left me wiped out. But I found a silver lining the very first day I could crawl out of bed. Throwing on a pair of pants, I called out to my husband, "Look! These jeans fit—they finally fit!"

"Great," he said. "But they're mine."

—ANN DWYER

friend and I were listing all the disgusting foods we like to eat. I guess I won the contest because when I told her how much I enjoyed tongue, she shuddered.

"*Ewww,*" she said. "Why would you want to taste something that tastes you back?"

—DONNA EIDINGER

Freelance newspaper writers don't get nearly as much attention as writers with regular bylines. So I was delighted when I finally got some notice. It was at the bank, and I was depositing a stack of checks.

"Wow," said the teller, reading off the names of publishers from the tops of the checks. "You must deliver a lot of papers."

—MEAGAN FRANCIS

Traveling through Spain, my friend Amy and I soaked in the culture, gorged ourselves on excellent food, and basically, indulged our every whim. One day we walked into a shop that had the most gorgeous coats. As we tried a few on, we noticed the odd looks we were getting from the shopkeepers. We didn't know why until one kind English-speaking patron took pity on us.

"Excuse me," she said. "This is a dry cleaners."

—ROSIE SPIEGEL

The escalator was broken, and the only way out of the airport was up a flight of stairs. I had a big suitcase and a sore knee.

I began dragging my bag and was making a loud thud on every step when a man behind me grabbed the suitcase and carried it to the top.

"That was so chivalrous," I gushed, thanking him.

"Chivalry had nothing to do with it," he said. "I've got a splitting headache."

—MEGAN SICLARI

Our friend hates to work out, which means the treadmill in her bedroom barely gets used. Nevertheless, she swears by it.

"It really works," she told me.

"I throw my jeans over it, and they get smaller."

—SHEILA TARNER

After standing in line at the DMV for what felt like eons, my brother finally got to the counter. As the clerk typed his name into the computer, she said, "That's odd."

"What's wrong?" James asked.

"My computer says you're deceased."

Surveying his surroundings, James muttered, "Great. I died and went to hell."

—FAE BUNDERSON

When I arrived at my mother's apartment complex, I was greeted by the disconcerting sight of a fire truck parked outside. There was no sign of smoke, and the firefighters didn't seem worried. Still, I asked one, "Is it safe to go inside? I'm a little wary of entering a building when the fire truck's lights are on."

"Don't worry about it," he said. "We do it all the time."

—NANCY DOANE

After a severe storm walloped Kentucky, our utility company sent us to the hardest-hit area to get power restored. I was picking up fallen wires when a car horn blared at me.

"Hey!" I yelled at the driver.

"Didn't you see all those red flags, signs, and barriers back there?"

"Oh, yes," he replied. "I got by them all right. It's your truck that's in the way now."

—GLEN STAUFFER

An amateur pilot wannabe, I knew I'd finally made progress with my flight training the day my instructor turned to me and said, **"You know, you're not as much fun since you stopped screaming."**

—BARBARA MACLEAN

## ? How come married women are heavier than single women?

A single woman goes home, sees what's in the fridge, and goes to bed. A married woman sees what's in bed and goes to the fridge.

At Air Canada Jazz, we have four different paint schemes on our aircraft. The most prominent feature is a maple leaf on the tail. The fleet features either a green, yellow, red, or orange leaf, symbolizing the four seasons.

Upon arriving at Harrisburg, Pennsylvania, on a sunny but cool fall morning, the air-traffic controller asked why, yesterday, our plane had a yellow tail, but today's was orange. Without any hesitation my first officer replied, "It is autumn now, you know."

—MIKE CHUTSKOFF

Saving for a new car on a teacher's salary takes a while. So in the meantime, a mechanic friend loaned me an old junker so beat up, even its dents had dents. I came out of school one day to find a police officer and a woman examining it. "What's going on?" I asked.

"I saw her hit your car," the cop explained. "But I can't figure out where."

—YEFIM A. BRODD

I took a real estate client to a handyman special. The place was great, and we couldn't understand why it was so cheap, until we turned on the water main and water gushed from the ceiling. Dripping wet, my client put a positive spin on the showing: "Nice house," he said. "It's even self-cleaning."

—TIFFANY J. IN *THE CLASSIFIED GUYS*

When my luggage didn't make the flight home with me, I stormed over to the airport's customer-service counter.

"Can you describe your suitcase?" the clerk asked.

"It's a navy-blue duffel bag, 24 inches long, 18 inches wide, and 20 inches high," I said. "It has red piping around the edges, three big stars on one side, and the words Atlanta Olympics in big letters on the other side."

"Okay," she said. "And is there anything distinctive about your bag?"

—KRIS MUCKERHEIDE

A mobster discovers that his deaf accountant has cheated him out of 10 million bucks. He confronts him, bringing along an interpreter. "Ask him where the money is," the mobster says.

The interpreter does so, and the accountant signs back, "What are you talking about?"

The interpreter tells the godfather, "He says he doesn't know what you're talking about."

The mobster puts a pistol to the bookkeeper's head. "Ask him again!"

The interpreter signs, "He'll kill you if you don't tell him!"

"Okay, okay!" the bookkeeper signs back. "The money is buried behind the shed in my cousin Enzo's backyard!"

"What'd he say?" asks the don.

"He says you don't have the guts to pull the trigger."

My son's first job took him to Shenzhen, China. During the Chinese New Year I asked Todd why it was called the Year of the Pig.

"I'm not sure," he wrote back. "A few months ago it was the Year of the Dog, and I'm still writing *Dog* on all my checks."

—PHAMA WOODYARD

One morning, my mom went out to the freezer to get some meat to thaw. When she returned, my 15-year-old sister, Rebekah, looked up from the computer and exclaimed: "You've got enough meat to feed an army!"

She added, on second thought, "Well, maybe the Canadian army."

—ABIGAIL WHEALE

**My wife loves sales. She'll buy anything that's marked down. Yesterday she came home with an escalator.**

—JOHN SFORZA

A teetotaler is seated next to a rock star on a flight to Texas. After the plane takes off, the musician orders a whiskey and soda.

"And the same for you?" the flight attendant asks the teetotaler.

"I'd rather be tied up and ravaged by crazed women than let liquor touch my lips," he snorts.

"Here," says the rocker, handing back his drink. "I didn't know we had a choice."

—JOHN BOWMAN

One of the youth league soccer coaches didn't care much for my refereeing and had no problem letting me know it. Fed up, I threatened him with a penalty if he didn't can it. He calmed down, but an older woman took up where he'd left off.

"You'd better control your sideline," I warned the coach.

The coach turned to the woman and barked, "Knock it off, Mom!"

—JOSEPH WHEELER

Dad's satellite dish conked out. When I walked into his living room, I found my father talking on the phone with the help desk. The TV set was pulled away from the wall, and he was staring at the mass of tangled wires spilling out from the back of it. He looked completely overwhelmed.

"Tell you what I'm going to do," Dad said to the technician. "I'm going to hang up now, go to college for a couple of years, then call you back."

—DANA MARISCA

You can take the man out of the auto business . . .

I was walking through the door after a morning of appointments—I'd gone to the beauty salon to have my hair colored and then to the chiropractor—when I heard my husband talking on the phone with my son.

"She's not in," he said. "She's gone out for a paint job and a realignment."

—ARLENE SHOVALD

After giving birth, I couldn't lose the 40 pounds I'd gained. So I dragged my husband to the mall in search of more flattering clothes. We were encouraged by a sign over a rack of suits: "Instantly hides 10 pounds!"

"Look," he said. "You just need to buy four of these."

—CINDY DAYE

"Purpose of visit?" asked the customs agent as we approached a checkpoint at the Canada-U.S. border.

"We're going to a wedding," my wife said.

"Are you carrying any weapons—knives, guns?" he asked.

"No," she said. "It's not that kind of wedding."

—MARTIN JAGODZINSKI

Traveling is a major part of my wife's job as a saleswoman, and it's not unheard-of for her to visit four or five cities in one week. I hadn't thought too much of it until she returned wiped out from her last long business trip.

As her head hit the pillow, she sighed, **"It's so nice to be sleeping in my own bed, with my own husband."**

—DAVID HARRISON

The manager of a jewelry store nabs a shoplifter trying to steal a necklace. "Listen," the crook says, "you don't want any trouble, and neither do I. What do you say I just buy the necklace and we forget this ever happened?"

The manager agrees and writes up a sales slip.

"You know," says the crook, "this is more than I wanted to spend. Got anything less expensive?"

—ROSEMARY COVERT

My brother and I were stopped at a red light when a landscaping truck drove past, its entire back laden with fresh green sod.

"Wow," he deadpanned. "I wish I had enough money to send my lawn out to get cut."

—MICHAEL VONDRAK

The barber's client looked depressed, so the barber told him, "Cheer up. I knew a guy who owed $5,000 he couldn't pay. He drove his vehicle to the edge of a cliff, where he sat for over an hour. A group of concerned citizens heard about his problem and passed a hat around. Relieved, the man pulled back from the cliff's edge."

"Incredible," said the client. "Who were these kind people?"

"The passengers on the bus."

—PATRICK BROOME

After my four-year-old and I turned the department store upside down looking for a bathing suit for me, we finally found a black-and-white one-piece that we both liked. I tried on the suit and modeled it for her. It was a hit.

"Mommy, you look so pretty!" she squealed. "You look just like Shamu the whale."

—LORI RHODES

During my physical fitness class, I had everyone lie on their backs with their legs up as if pedaling a bike. After several minutes one man suddenly stopped.

"Why did you stop pedaling?" I shouted.

"I didn't stop," he said, wheezing. "I'm coasting."

—HENRY BOTWINICK

"I'll never find the right guy," I heard the young guest at the wedding shower sigh.

"Don't give up," urged an older woman. "Every pot has a lid."

"Or," a cynical voice behind her offered, "you could just be a skillet."

—GEORGIANNA GUTHRIE

"Let me do the talking."

My sister and I decided to reframe a favorite photograph of our mother and father from when they were dating, some 60 years ago. After removing the picture from the frame, I turned it over, hoping to find a date. I didn't. Instead, my mother had written, "128 lbs."

—JEAN TATE

While stationed in Germany in the mid-'70s, I was the driver for Canada's Chief of Defence while he attended a conference in Belgium. After the conference, I drove the general back to Germany.

At the border, German Customs asked for our passports. The officer took them and sat in his booth, staring at us for 15 minutes. The general was about to make inquiries when the customs officer finally nodded at me to drive on.

When I got home, my wife asked if there had been any problems on the trip. I started to tell her about the incident at the border when she interrupted, asking if I'd looked at my passport lately.

"Uh, no," I answered.

If I had, I would have noticed my wife's picture staring back at me: I'd accidentally grabbed her passport before leaving.

—JOE WALSH

My wife left the car unattended for only a minute, but it was long enough for our two-year-old to climb in, throw the car into reverse and crash into a lamppost. He was fine, but the car wasn't, and I had a hard time explaining who was behind the wheel to the insurance company.

After a pause, the adjuster asked,

**"Do you let him drive often?"**

—DON LEE

Our lease on our house was coming to an end and I was trying to decide where we should move. Since my three kids are teens, I felt they should have a say in the decision, so, over the course of a few months, I bombarded them with questions as to where they wanted to live. It became apparent that I had caused some confusion when I noticed a box I'd packed and left in the dining room. On the box I had marked CHINA in large bold letters.

Someone had scribbled a note to the side—"NOT moving there!"

—KAREN BIRCH, CALGARY

As a flight attendant, I always give this advice: "Folks, make up your mind about what you're going to do before entering the lavatory, because once you close that door, there's no turning around."

—JULIE ELROD

With the crowded quarters in coach, I can't blame airplane passengers for asking flight attendants for free upgrades to first class. On a recent fully booked flight, a passenger stopped me with hat in hand.

"Is there any way I can get bumped up to first class?" he pleaded.

I shook my head. "Not unless we hit turbulence."

—SUZANNE RICKABAUGH

A new study says there is no connection between breathing recirculated airplane air and catching colds. There is, however, a strong connection between breathing recirculated airplane air and losing your luggage.

—GREGG SIEGEL

Did you hear that the world's biggest optimist fell out a window on the 79th floor? As he sailed past the 20th floor, he was overheard saying, "Doing okay so far!"

—DANIEL KING

I doubt if there's a state where my friend's parents, Bud and Beth, haven't traveled in their camper. They bought a new RV, and to celebrate, their son-in-law gave them a plaque to hang on the outside.

It reads "Bud, Beth and Beyond."

—KAREN MANSOR

I recently called the library to ask what research material they had on the Renaissance artist Donatello. After giving me some book and Web titles, the librarian sheepishly added another bit of interesting information.

"I have to confess, I couldn't remember how to spell Donatello," she said. "So I went into our search engine and typed in Ninja Turtles."

—RYAN JUGUETA

The biggest loser at my weight-loss club was an elderly woman. "How'd you do it?" we asked. "Easy," she said. "Every night I take my teeth out at six o'clock."

—CATHY J. SCHREIMA

A bicyclist came whizzing down a steep hill and smashed into a car as I stood there watching in horror. I ran over to see if I could help and discovered the wild rider was a friend of mine, an attorney.

I knew he was going to be just fine when the first words out of his mouth were, "Did the driver admit he was at fault?"

—GRETCHEN HUMPHREY

Unlike many other professionals, my parents, both mathematics professors, can't seem to leave their work in the classroom. Recently I witnessed the following conversation.

Mom: Has my midsection gotten larger?
Dad: Yes.
Mom: Since exactly when?
Dad: I don't know. It's a continuous function. But it became statistically significant about six months ago.

—PRIYANKA BASAK

Scary business headline:
## "Air Traffic Controllers Can Apply for Job in Braille"

—THISISPLYMOUTH.CO.UK

Fred comes home from his usual Saturday golf game. "What a terrible day," he tells his wife. "Harry dropped dead on the tenth tee."

"Oh, that's awful!" she says.

"You're not kidding," says Fred. "For the whole back nine, it was hit the ball, drag Harry, hit the ball, drag Harry . . ."

—CRAIG CHEEK

The flight I was piloting to Cleveland was overbooked. So the gate agent came aboard with an offer. In exchange for deplaning, two volunteers would get free hotel rooms, meal vouchers and tickets on the next morning's flight. When nobody volunteered, I decided to try a little levity.

"Ladies and gentlemen," I said over the PA, "if it helps, I'm not a very good pilot."

A loud voice from the back yelled, "Then YOU get off!"

—QUINCY NELSON

Harry asks his friend Larry to help him with something. "I think the blinker signal on my car is broken," he says. "Stand behind the car. When I turn it on, tell me if the blinker's working."

Larry situates himself behind the car while Harry gets in the driver's seat and hits the blinker.

"Is it working?" he yells back.

"Yes!" says Larry. "No! Yes! No! Yes! No . . ."

"I am a Yankees fan," a first-grade teacher explains to her class. "Who likes the Yankees?"

Everyone raises a hand except one little girl. "Janie," the teacher says, surprised. "Why didn't you raise your hand?"

"I'm not a Yankees fan."

"Well, if you are not a Yankees fan, then what team do you like?"

"The Red Sox," Janie answers.

"Why in the world are you a Red Sox fan?"

"Because my mom and dad are Red Sox fans."

"That's no reason to be a Red Sox fan," the teacher replies, annoyed. "You don't always have to be just like your parents. What if your mom and dad were morons? What would you be then?"

"A Yankees fan."

—TOM ZAHN

Grandpa is a late convert to the technological age. The other day, he called my father to complain that he couldn't use his printer: "The screen says 'Warming Up.'"

Dad ran over there, only to find half the printer melted. "What happened?" he asked.

"I don't know," said Grandpa. "But even the space heater didn't help."

—AARON ATHERTON

As the teleconference with our London branch concluded, my British colleague suggested that we continue our meeting the next day.

"Sorry," I said. "Tomorrow's July 4th, and the office will be closed."

"Ah, yes, Independence Day," he said. "Or as we refer to it over here, Thanksgiving."

—DALE JENKINS

I had to voice my concern when a coworker said she found dates using the Internet.

"Don't worry about me," she said. "I always insist we meet at a miniature golf course."

"Why there?" I asked.

"First, it's a public spot," she said. "Second, it's in broad daylight. And third, I have a club in my hand."

—LINDA AKINS

## ? Why is Cinderella bad at sports?

Because she has a pumpkin for a coach, and she runs away from the ball.

SEAN MCELWEE

Following his motivational talk at a Weight Watchers meeting, my father noticed one client's small son climbing onto a scale.

"Don't go on that, Joey," warned the boy's slightly older brother.

**"It makes people cry."**

—CARTER DICKERSON

My husband was booking a business flight when the reservation clerk gave him a choice of seats: behind the bulkhead or in Shakespeare's chair.

A seasoned traveler, my husband was confused. "Shakespeare's chair? What's that?"

"You know," said the operator. "2B."

—HOLLY RIDLEY

My mother lacks a green thumb, but she keeps at it. Pointing one day to a line of new plants by the kitchen window, my sister whispered to me, "Look—death row."

—MICHAEL KNIGGE

As a new member of the Royal Canadian Mounted Police, I attended a ceremony where a light lunch was served. Ready to leave, I walked towards the garbage can to throw out my plate and some leftover turkey. Our commanding officer happened to be standing near the garbage can and jokingly said to me, "Eat your meat; it's good for you."

I took a few steps backward to figure out what to do when the member standing next to him said, "Sir, she only has two months service. If you told her to, she would eat her plate!"

—DIANE MACDONALD

Canada Post has just issued a stamp to commemorate jury duty. **It's being sold in packs of 12 with two alternates.**

—BEN WALSH

During the January playoffs, my husband lapses into a football-fan coma. Once, I left him to watch our 13-month-old daughter. "Honey, put Izabelle down for her nap," I said. "But not for more than an hour."

When I got back, he was watching a game and the baby was napping. "When did she go to sleep?" I asked.

Still staring at the screen, he mumbled, "Halfway through the third quarter."

—NORA BRYSON

Everyone in our neck of the woods knows that trailer parks and tornadoes are not a good mix. So my brother-in-law wasn't the least bit surprised when the lead story on our local news was about a tornado wiping out a mobile-home factory.

"Look at that," he said. "Got them in the larval stage."

—PETE MAY

One of the players on our junior high football team never saw action in a game. But my brother, the assistant coach, liked the kid and always gave him pep talks.

"Remember, Ben," he told him, "everyone on this team has an important role. There is no *I* in *team*."

"True," said the boy. "But there is a *Ben* in *bench*."

—ALICIA ELLEY

I'm not into exercising. Yesterday my wife said, "Let's walk around the block." I said, "Why? We're already here."

—COMIC WENDELL POTTER

My grandfather hates television. Ask him and he'll tell you that the tube is stultifying and addictive. The plug-in drug, he calls it.

Not long ago, Grandpa discovered my five-year-old brother, Frankie, watching TV with his nose practically on the screen. Appalled, he called me over.

"Look!" he shouted, pointing to Frankie. "Now he's snorting it."

—WENDY DAVIS

# LAUGHTER
## Still Is
# THE BEST MEDICINE

More than
**1,000**
**ALL-NEW**
**LAUGHS**

# CONTENTS

# A Note from the Editors

Have you ever stopped to consider just how unattractive laughter is? People are rarely at their best when caught mid-guffaw. Here, try this experiment. Walk over to someone and tell them a funny joke, say, the one on page 86. Now sit back and watch. Their eyes crinkle and their wrinkles become really pronounced. Their nostrils flare. Strange animal-like sounds escape from their mouths. Sometimes out of their noses. Occasionally out of their ears. They show a lot of teeth and gums. Sometimes they laugh so hard they spit out food or their eyes water. Who would enable such conduct?

We would!

We're not particularly attractive people here at *Reader's Digest,* so we consider humor the great equalizer. Besides, laughter is what we do best. We've been sharing jokes ever since the Goths invaded the Red Sox, or whoever they went after. We have a library full of hilarious jokes, cartoons, and one-liners, not to mention anecdotes about family, friends, work, and even military life. And this volume is filled with the best of them. So go ahead, take a read. But whatever you do, please don't laugh.

# VENUS and MARS

"To be happy with a man you must understand him a lot and love him a little. To be happy with a woman you must love her a lot and not try to understand her at all."

—HELEN ROWLAND

# COURTSHIP QUIPS

Ole and Inge were in their car heading for Minneapolis when Ole put his hand on Inge's knee.

"Ole," she murmured softly, "you can go further if you want."

And so he drove to Duluth.

—DICK FLOERSHEIMER

*Dating is complicated. You don't believe us?*
*Here are some examples:*

- Right after we broke up, my ex-girlfriend called to ask how to change her relationship status on Facebook.

- I got into a 90-minute argument with my girlfriend because she was adamant that *Moby-Dick* was a true story. I finally let her win so I could go to sleep.

- My now ex-girlfriend and I were in my room one day, and the Internet was particularly slow. After I complained, she suggested that I untangle my Ethernet cord so that more Internet could get through.

- I recently joined an online dating site, and one of my matches was my first cousin.

An enormously wealthy 65-year-old man falls in love with a young woman in her 20s and is contemplating a proposal. "Do you think she'd marry me if I tell her I'm 45?" he asked his friend.

**"Your chances are better," said the friend, "if you tell her you're 90."**

—PROSANTA CHAKRABARTY

"If he likes *you* better, how come he always buys *me* perfume?!"

**My girlfriend and I worry about different things. One day, I was like, "What do you fear the most?" And she was like, "I fear you'll meet someone else, and you'll leave me, and I'll be all alone." And she was like, "What do you fear the most?" And I was like, "Bears."**

—COMEDIAN MIKE BIRBIGLIA

"Why doesn't your mother like me?" a woman asks her boyfriend.

"Don't take it personally," he assures her. "She's never liked anyone I've dated. I once dated someone exactly like her, and that didn't work out at all."

"What happened?"

"My father couldn't stand her."

—JAMES RICHENS

Driving my friend Steve and his girlfriend to the airport, we passed a billboard showing a bikini-clad beauty holding a can of beer. Steve's girlfriend glanced up at it and announced, "I suppose if I drank a six-pack of that brand, I'd look like her."

"No," Steve corrected. "If *I* drank a six-pack, you'd look like her."

—JOHN D. BOYD

Visiting the *Musée Marmottan Monet* in Paris, I was awestruck by one of Monet's water lily paintings. I whispered to my boyfriend that I would happily give everything I owned for the huge, stunning painting. Ever practical, he whispered, "And it still wouldn't be enough."

—REBECCA TRUMAN

**L**ast winter I was laid up at home with the flu. My fiancée called and volunteered to come over, fix dinner and play nursemaid to me. I declined, not wanting to pass on the flu to her.

"Okay, honey," she told me. "We'll wait till after we get married. Then we'll spend the rest of our lives making each other sick!"

—STEVE POMERANTZ

**A** couple is lying in bed one night when the woman turns to the man, smiles and says, "I'm going to make you the happiest man in the world."

The man replies, "I'll miss you."

## BLISSFUL BANTER

**W**hen I ran out of shampoo, I borrowed some from my wife. Later, I complained that the scent was too feminine for my taste.

"No problem," she said. "Just dab a little gasoline behind each ear. You'll smell fine."

—PIERRE LAPLANTE

**A** married couple has been out shopping for hours when the wife realizes that her husband has disappeared. So she calls his cell phone.

"Where are you?!" she yells.

"Darling," he says, "do you remember that jewelry shop, the one where you saw that diamond necklace you loved? But I didn't have enough money at the time, so I said, 'Baby, it'll be yours one day'?"

"Yes!" she shouts excitedly.

"Well, I'm in the bar next door."

—BONNIE TOWNSEND

**"** I guess you have another excuse not to take out the garbage. **"**

**O**n a business trip to New Orleans, my son-in-law Mike bought a set of expensive kitchen knives for his wife. His coworker was surprised.

"You shouldn't buy such an expensive gift for your wife on a business trip," he said. "She'll think you've been up to something."

"If I'd been up to something," Mike replied, "I wouldn't be bringing her knives."

—LINDA BRUMLEY

**M**y wife got pulled over for making an "S" turn. She started to make a "U," then changed her mind.

—COMEDIAN GABE ABELSON

Overheard at my garden-club meeting: **"I never knew what compost was until I met my husband."**

—MARY HALLER

I was nervous the first time my husband and I were hired to photograph a wedding. Making matters worse, we arrived at the wrong venue. In a panic, we bolted out of the building—my husband in the lead and me trailing behind, in tears. As we fled, I heard a security guard remark, "That ceremony didn't go too well."

—JOANNE CAMPBELL

After learning that her parents were in a minor car accident, my wife called her mother.

"What happened?" she asked.

"I was driving and fell asleep," said her mother, irritated. "And of course, your father wasn't paying attention!"

—GUY LAMBERT

For some reason the bookstore clerk couldn't get the computer to recognize my preferred customer card. Peering over her shoulder at the screen, I said, "There's part of the problem. It shows my birth date as 12/31/1899."

"That's right," my husband chimed in. "She was born in June, not December."

—M. PATRICIA CAPIN

My grandmother figured that breakfast time was as good a time as any to get something off her chest. So over morning coffee, she turned to my grandfather and said, "We've been married 56 years, and it still seems that you are always correcting me."

Grandpa replied, "We've been married 58 years."

—CALEB ZELLERS

Leena was tired of her husband coming home drunk and decided to scare him straight. One night, she put on a devil costume and hid behind a tree to intercept him on the way home. When her husband walked by, she jumped out and stood before him with her red horns, long tail, and pitchfork.

"Who are you?" he slurred.

"I'm the devil," she answered.

"Well, come on home with me," he said. "I married your sister."

My dapper 51-year-old husband supervises scads of attractive younger women at his law firm. After friends divorced, I had to ask. "Honey, have you ever been tempted by the idea of a May-December romance?"

"Not really," he replied. "I don't see myself dating older women."

—SUSAN FERGUSON

Suspecting he had a serious medical condition, I nagged my husband until he agreed to see a doctor. Once there, he was handed a mountain of forms to fill out. Next to "Reason for visit?" he wrote, "My wife made me."

—SUSAN HUTTON

I came down with the flu and wanted my husband to do some of the housecleaning. I wasn't sure how to tell him, so I tried reverse psychology.

"Honey, I'm sorry I'm leaving you with such a mess," I said between sniffles. "The laundry needs to be done, the dishes washed, the floors cleaned."

"Don't you worry," he said sympathetically. "It can all wait until you feel up to it."

—GAIL WHITE

One friend complained to another, "All my husband and I do anymore is fight. I've been so upset, I've lost 20 pounds."

"If it's that bad, why don't you just leave him?" asked the second friend.

"I'd like to lose another 15 pounds first."

—MARY BUOYE

In the natural childbirth classes my wife and I took, the birthing process was represented by a hand puppet being pushed through a sock. So at the actual birth, I was shocked to see all this blood. The thing I had prepared myself for was a lot of lint.

—COMEDIAN STEVE SCROVAN

My husband will not be confused for Jamie Oliver anytime soon. Before I ran off to work, I gave him detailed instructions on how to cook dinner. That evening, I returned home to find a dry chicken roasting in the oven next to a Pyrex measuring cup full of water.

"What's that doing in there?" I asked.

Clearly offended, he sputtered, "You told me to put the chicken in the oven with a cup of water!"

—PAM BRENNAN

The garage called to say that the car we had taken in to be serviced was ready.

"Great," I said. "My wife's in the bathroom 'getting beautiful,' and we'll be over as soon as she's finished."

The voice on the other end asked, **"Will that be today?"**

—NORMAN JANSSEN

At the end of a crazy day, my husband and I collapsed on our bed and watched TV. As I made myself comfortable in the crook of his arm, I said, "Know what's comforting? When I'm old and gray, I can lean on you, and you'll still feel young and strong. Isn't that wonderful?"

"For you, maybe," he said. "I get the old, shriveled lady."

—LISA LIPMAN

While standing on an eight-foot ladder, trimming a bush that grew across the top of our garage door, I realized that if my wife entered the garage from the house and pushed the opener, it might spell doom for me. So I climbed down and, unable to find her, scribbled a note and stuck it to the opener: "Push Button and Kill Tom."

I finished my pruning job and went about my yard work. Later I went into the house, and my wife said, "I don't understand your note in the garage. I pushed the button, and the only thing that happened was that the garage door opened."

—TOM BROWN

My friend's wife came home to find her husband entrenched in front of the TV set, switching between a fishing show and an erotic movie. After a few minutes of back-and-forth, she offered this suggestion: "Honey, you might as well just watch the erotic movie. You already know how to fish."

—MARJORIE LONG

In the doghouse with my wife, I ordered her some flowers and told the florist that the card should read, "I'm sorry, I love you."

Unfortunately, my instructions must not have been clear enough. When the flowers arrived, the card read, "I'm sorry I love you."

—MARK S. MAURER

"It wasn't his fortune. I married him for his mind, but then that went too."

My husband has always been disdainful of people who, in his estimation, talk too much. Recently he proudly told me he'd heard that men use 2200 words a day, while women use 4400.

I pondered that a moment, then concluded, "That's because women have to repeat everything they say to their husbands."

He looked up and asked, **"Come again?"**

—DARLENE KELLY

During birth-preparation class, we were learning relaxation techniques, and the instructor asked us to come up with ideas to lower stress levels. Silence pervaded the room, but one dad, a slight fellow with round glasses and a religious T-shirt, finally offered: "Prayer?"

"Good," the instructor replied. "Anything else?"

"How about sex?" suggested another father-to-be.

Once again, silence followed. Then the devout dad-to-be muttered under his breath, "What do you think I've been praying for?"

—TRACY AND SCOTT YANCEY

I was dining in our Georgia town, when a tourist stopped by my table.

"Excuse me," he said. "But my wife loves your sandals. Did you buy them locally?"

"Yes, just down the street," I said.

"May I ask how much they cost?"

"They were $77."

"Thank you." He then hollered to his wife, "Honey, she got them in Florida."

—REBA CRISP

During a recent vacation in Las Vegas, I went to see a popular magic show. After one especially amazing feat, a man from the back of the theater yelled, "How'd you do that?"

"I could tell you, sir," the magician answered. "But then I'd have to kill you."

After a short pause, the man yelled back, "Okay, then—just tell my wife!"

—SUZANNE OLIVER

My wife and I were going through a rough patch financially, but we kept ourselves sane by repeating, "As long as we have each other, we don't need anything else." But when the television and radio in our bedroom broke within a few days of each other, my wife lost it.

"That's just great!" she shouted. "Now there's no entertainment in our bedroom at all!"

—VINCENT DAY

While working for the Social Security Administration, I helped an elderly woman—who was no longer married—fill out her claim form.

Reading off a question, I asked, "How did your marriage end?"

"Just fine," she said, grinning a little too broadly. "He died."

—WILLIS BIRD

My husband and I were driving past our neighbors' home when I noticed a decorative wooden stork in their driveway.

"Did they have a baby?" I asked.

"I don't know," he said. "Why?"

"There's a stork in their yard."

"Dear," he said, "that's not the way it happens."

—JENNIFER WALKER

My husband asked me to dress up as a nurse tonight to fulfill his fantasy . . . **that we have health insurance.**

—COMEDIAN WENDY LIEBMAN

My wife and I were at the circus watching a shapely young woman dangling from a trapeze. The woman appeared to be wearing a very revealing costume, and my wife exclaimed, "There's nothing underneath!"

At first I agreed, but studying the woman closely, I saw there was flesh-colored material under her costume. So I said, "Yes, there's flesh-colored material underneath."

My wife replied, "I meant there is no net underneath the trapeze. What were you referring to?"

—THANE LAFOLLETTE

My wife asked me if I thought she looked fat in her new dress. Pointing to what I was wearing, I replied, "Do I look stupid in this shirt?"

—BRIAN RICE

A woman was having a passionate affair with an exterminator when her husband arrived home unexpectedly.

"Quick," she said to her lover, "into the closet!" And she pushed him into the closet, stark naked.

The husband, however, became suspicious. And after looking high and low, he discovered the man in the closet.

"Who are you?" he demanded.

"I'm an exterminator," said the man.

"What are you doing in there?"

"I'm investigating a complaint about an infestation of moths."

"And where are your clothes?"

The man looked down at himself and cried, "Those little bums!"

# QUOTABLE QUOTES

**"AS SOON AS WOMEN START REGISTERING A COMPLAINT, MEN CALL IT NAGGING."**

—STEVE HARVEY

"I have bad luck with women. A woman I was dating told me on the phone, 'I have to go. There's a telemarketer on the other line.'"

—ZACH GALIFIANAKIS

**"IF LOVE IS THE ANSWER, COULD YOU REPHRASE THE QUESTION?"**

—LILY TOMLIN

"We all want to be in love and find that person who is going to love us no matter how our feet smell, no matter how angry we get one day, no matter the things we say that we don't mean."

—WILL SMITH

"I love being married. It's so great to find that one special person you want to annoy for the rest of your life."

—RITA RUDNER

**"A MARRIED MAN SHOULD FORGET HIS MISTAKES; NO USE TWO PEOPLE REMEMBERING THE SAME THING."**

—DUANE DEWEL

"Marriage has no guarantees. If that's what you're looking for, go live with a car battery."

—ERMA BOMBECK

"If there hadn't been women, we'd still be squatting in a cave eating raw meat, because we made civilization in order to impress our girlfriends."

—ORSON WELLES

"I've been told that when you meet the right person, you know immediately. How come when you meet the wrong person, it takes a year and a half?"

—COMEDIAN PHIL HANLEY

"I can handle my wife's *Honey-Do* list.
It's her *Honey-Don't* list that just about kills me."

My ex-husband was both difficult and prescient. Before our wedding, I declared in a fit of pique, "John, I don't know if I should marry you or leave you."

John replied, "Well, baby, you'll probably do both."

—JANET STREET

Bob went over to his friend Joe's house and was amazed at how well Joe treated his wife. He often told her how attractive she was, complimented her on her cooking and showered her with hugs and kisses.

"Geez," Bob remarked later, "you really make a big fuss over your wife."

"I started to appreciate her more about six months ago," Joe said. "It has revived our marriage, and we couldn't be happier."

Inspired, Bob hurried home, hugged his wife, told her how much he loved her and said he wanted to hear all about her day. But she burst into tears. "Honey," Bob said, "what's the matter?"

"This has been the worst day," she replied. "This morning Billy fell off his bike and hurt his ankle, then the washing machine broke. Now, to top it off, you come home drunk!"

—LYNDELL LEATHERMAN

My parents divorced when I was two but remained friends. So much so that on my wedding day, Dad toasted my husband and me by saying, "I hope y'all are as happy together as your mother and I are apart."

—MELANIE FRANKLIN

## ? How many divorced men does it take to change a lightbulb?

Who cares? They never get the house anyway.

— ELSPETH MCVIE

During a heartfelt chat with her friend about relationships, my wife sighed and said, "You know, if something happened to Lloyd, I don't think I could ever marry again."

Her friend nodded sympathetically.

**"I know what you mean," she said. "Once is enough."**

—LLOYD G. YOUNG

With a new baby and a new car, my husband and I realized that we wouldn't have any extra money to buy each other gifts for our first anniversary. We decided to wait a few months and buy gifts on the anniversary of the day we met.

My husband seemed pleased with the idea. He then pulled a piece of paper out of his pocket. "The first anniversary is supposed to be paper," he confessed, "but I didn't think you'd be too happy with this."

I unfolded the paper. Inside he had scribbled a little heart with the letters I.O.U.

—TIFFANY BEHRENS

Because my husband and I were having trouble conceiving, we paid regular visits to a fertility clinic. One day, Andy's parents were over. The clinic called while I was out and left detailed instructions on our answering machine for what to do in bed later that night. I relayed the message to Andy.

"Yeah, I know," he said. "I had the messages playing and went to the bathroom. When I came out, Dad told me."

—CRYSTAL HOUGHTON

Shortly after I married, my parents came to visit. To please my father I made a buttermilk pie, a treat I know he liked but rarely got to eat.

After everyone proclaimed it delicious, my father smiled nostalgically and said, "Susan, do you know you're only the second person ever to make buttermilk pie for me?"

Because my mother is not known for her baking, I was surprised by this comment. "Mom," I asked, "did you make him a buttermilk pie?"

"Of course!" she replied.

Dad thought for a second and said, "Then I guess you're the third."

—SUSAN E. ANDREWS

A friend parked his car at the supermarket and was walking past an empty cart when a woman asked, "Excuse me, sir, did you want that shopping cart?"

"No, I don't," he answered. "I'm only after one thing."

As he walked toward the store, he heard her murmur, "Typical male."

—ABBY MECHLING

While I was attending church, someone yelled out my husband's name. It was his long-lost cousin, whom he hadn't seen in 40 years.

"It's amazing that you could recognize him after all this time," I marveled.

"Yes," said his wife. **"He was always good at remembering useless things."**

—MARGARET BOWMAN

# WRINKLE CREAM

After one glance at my updated driver's license photo, I said the first thing that came to mind: "Ugghhh!"

"What's wrong?" the DMV clerk asked.

"I look ancient in this picture."

"Well, look at the bright side: In five years, you'll love it."

—ANDREA RAITER

When you're young and you get to choose between sleep and sex, you take sex every time. You start getting older, you get to choose between sleep and sex, you choose sleep and just hope you have a dream about sex.

—JEFF FOXWORTHY

We'd finally built our dream home, but the contractor had a concern: the placement of an atrium window for our walk-in shower. "I'm afraid your neighbors might have a good view of you au naturel," he said.

My middle-aged wife put him at ease. "Don't worry," she said. "They'll only look once."

—GREGG BARNER

At a senior citizens' function, I watched an older fellow ease his wife ahead of him in line. "You ask for the tickets, dear," he told her. "You look older than I do."

Seeming to ignore his uncomplimentary remark, she stepped up to the counter. "I'd like two tickets, please," she said loudly. **"One for me, and one for my father."**

—JEAN L. SCHAUER

I knew I was going bald **because it was taking longer and longer to wash my face.**

—COMEDIAN HARRY HILL

On my 40th birthday, I waltzed out of my bedroom dressed in an old outfit.

"I wore this on my 30th birthday. I guess that means my wardrobe is ten years old," I said to my husband, hoping he'd take the hint and buy me some clothes as a present.

"Or," he offered instead, "it means when you were 30, you had the body of a 40-year-old."

—BETH GEFFERS

I was taking my 50th birthday pretty well until I went to visit my family. I have two aunts living in different nursing homes.

When I visited Aunt Alice, she blurted out, "Jennifer, you are getting gray."

"Well, yes," I admitted. "But I still feel young."

I put the thought aside until I drove over to see my other aunt. "You look so young and healthy," my aunt Bernice gushed. "How do you do it? You have a youthful glow."

I thanked her for the compliment but couldn't resist telling her about Aunt Alice's comment on my gray hair.

"Well, yes, it's true," Aunt Bernice acknowledged. "Alice was always blessed with better eyesight than I."

—JENNIFER CUMMINGS

My grandma always says that she never gets any phone calls. So for her birthday, I put one of those "How's my driving?" bumper stickers on her car. The phone's pretty much ringing off the hook now.

—COMEDIAN CHRIS HOBBS

While visiting a retirement community, my wife and I decided to do some shopping and soon became separated. "Excuse me," I said, approaching a clerk. "I'm looking for my wife. She has white hair and is wearing white shoes." Gesturing around the store, the clerk responded, "Take your pick."

—ALBERT CUTINI

Three old friends are taking a memory test. The doctor asks the first, "What's three times three?"

"Two hundred seventy-four," he answers.

"Hm." The doctor turns to the second man. "What's three times three?"

"Tuesday," he replies.

"What's three times three?" the doc asks the last man.

"Nine," he answers.

"Great," the doctor says. "How did you get that?"

"Simple. I subtracted 274 from Tuesday."

—AMIT RASTOGI

No longer relishing my reputation as a technophobe, I bought an iPhone and peppered the young salesman with a ton of questions.

"Please excuse my ignorance," I said. "I'm from the Smith-Corona generation." He had no clue what I was talking about, so I asked, "Do you know what a Smith-Corona is?"

He replied tentatively, "A drink?"

—VICTORIA GEIBEL

After imbibing at her young son's birthday party, an angry Tina Gonzales bit her Naples, Florida, neighbor. Cops pinned the crime on her by counting tooth marks on the victim. Gonzales was the only adult present with all her teeth.

**"I'm middle-aged, thirty pounds overweight and balding. Quite frankly, I couldn't think of anything scarier than that."**

When my husband returned from a jog, I joked, "What are you running from?"

"Old age," he said.

"Oh, yeah? Then what are those gray hairs on your head?"

"Camouflage."

—ANN HANSEN

An old man was rowing a boat on a lake when a frog swam up to him and yelled, "Mister! Mister! I'm really a beautiful princess. Kiss me and we'll live happily ever after!" The man put the frog in his pocket and rowed to shore. The frog called out again, "Hey, mister! I'm really a gorgeous princess. Kiss me, and we'll live happily ever after!"

Still the man said nothing and walked down the road toward town. The frog was getting angry at being ignored. "Why don't you kiss me? I told you I'm really a beautiful princess."

"Listen, lady," the man replied. "I'm 90 years old. At this point in my life I'd rather have a talking frog."

—CHANTELL WILLIAMS

**Two guys are sitting in a bar when one of them casually points to a couple of old drunks sitting across from them and says, "That's us in ten years."**

**His friend disagrees. "That's a mirror."**

—TESS ELLIOTT

As my dad approached his 40th birthday, he visited the Department of Motor Vehicles to renew his driver's license. A lifeguard in his youth, Dad is particularly proud of his once-blond hair, which has darkened considerably over the years. Still, under "hair color" on the application, he wrote "blond."

As the DMV clerk reviewed the form, she muttered to herself, "Eyes: blue; Hair: brown," at which point Dad interrupted politely with, "Excuse me, my hair is blond."

The woman looked up and, without skipping a beat, told him, "Yes, sir. But here we call that shade of blond brown."

—BETH VAN BRUSSEL

I overheard two EMT volunteers talking about the time they went to the aid of an elderly man. As one took down his information, the other opened his shirt to attach EKG cables. "Any history of heart trouble?" asked the first volunteer. "None," said the patient. Looking at the telltale scars of bypass surgery, the second volunteer wasn't so sure. "In that case," he said, "do you remember when the lion attacked you?"

—MONICA GILLIGAN

Our group was third in line behind two other foursomes at the golf course. A young man in the first group walloped his tee shot straight down the middle of the 410-yard fairway to within a few yards of the green.

"Wow," said an older man in the second foursome, "I don't even go that far on vacation."

—RICHARD C. PETERS

I called a patient to confirm an appointment with the doctor I work for, and her husband answered.

"Hello, may I speak with Anna?"

"Who?" he said.

"Anna."

"Santa?"

"No, Anna."

"Who is this?"

"This is the doctor's office calling for Anna."

"Who?"

"The doctor's office calling for Anna!"

"Oh, Anna," he said. "You better talk to me; Anna's hard of hearing."

—D.P.

My college roommate and I have remained good friends, and now that we're hitting middle age, I never miss a chance to kid him about being older than I am—even if it's only by one month. So for his 40th birthday I gave him a not-so-subtle jab by gift-wrapping a CD by the British reggae group UB40.

A month later, he sent me my own birthday gift—the latest release from the Irish rock band U2.

—JOHN DAVIS

My nine-year-old daughter walked in while I was getting ready for work.

"What are you doing?" she asked.

"Putting on my wrinkle cream," I answered.

"Oh," she said, walking away. "I thought they were natural."

—DEB FILLMAN

You could have knocked me over with a feather when my two older daughters, both in their 50s, announced they were marrying their long-time boyfriends.

"Well, no one can accuse them of having a shotgun wedding," I joked when I shared the good news with their younger sister.

"You got that right," Lori agreed. "More like a stun gun wedding."

—DOROTHY AMATO

Recently I sat in a restaurant watching two older men go at it. It quickly grew heated as one of them declared, "I'm so mad, I'm taking you off my pallbearer list!"

—TOM CALVERT

After church one Sunday, my wife, Norma, and I went out for lunch. Outside the restaurant, a schoolmate I hadn't seen for 50 years recognized me, and we stopped to chat while my wife went ahead into the restaurant.

"Wow!" I said when I joined Norma, "that guy told me I haven't changed since Grade 9."

Norma laughed. "You mean," she said, "you looked that old when you were in Grade 9?"

—WOLF MAYDELL

*You know you are no longer a kid when:*

- Driving a car doesn't always sound like fun.
- You laugh at your parents' jokes.
- You don't buy a new sports car because of the insurance premiums.
- You actually buy scarves, gloves and sunscreen.
- You leave ballgames early to beat the crowd.
- The only thing in your cereal box is cereal.
- You look into the surveillance-camera monitor at a convenience store and wonder who the overweight guy with the bald spot is, then realize that it's a shot of you from behind.

—LYNDELL LEATHERMAN

A woman walked up to a little old man rocking in a chair on his porch. "I couldn't help notice how happy you look," she said. "What's your secret for a long and happy life?"

"I smoke three packs of cigarettes a day," he said. "I also drink a case of whiskey a week, eat fatty foods and never exercise."

"That's amazing," the woman said. "How old are you?"

"Twenty-six."

Our family was at an outdoor fair watching a caricature artist at work, when a 50-something woman stopped to watch as well. When she saw that the artist charged $15 for a color caricature, she gasped, "Fifteen dollars—just to have someone draw my wrinkles!"

The artist turned slowly and studied her face for a moment before replying, "I don't see any wrinkles."

She immediately sat down and had her portrait drawn.

—MARGARET WELLS

A new patient reported to his doctor and asked: "Doctor, do you think I'll live to be a ripe old age?"

The doctor asked: "Are you married?"

The patient said he wasn't.

"Do you smoke?"

"No."

"Do you drink?"

Again the patient answered in the negative.

"Do you follow a healthy diet?"

"Very healthy, Doctor."

"Have you ever been in hospital for treatment?" continued the doctor.

"Never."

"Do you ever go out on the town and not get home until dawn?"

"Never. I wouldn't do anything like that."

"Are there many women in your life?" asked the doctor.

"Not a one," admitted the patient.

"Well," concluded the doctor, "you probably will live to be a ripe old age. But I wonder if it'll be worth it."

—MARTIEN STASSEN

# BATTLE OF THE BULGE

**N**eeding to shed a few pounds, my husband and I went on a diet that had specific recipes for each meal of the day. I followed the recipes closely, dividing each in half for our individual plates. We felt terrific and thought the diet was wonderful—we never felt hungry!

But then we realized we were gaining weight, not losing it, and I checked the recipes again. There, in fine print, was: "Serves 6."

—BARBARA CURRIE

**A**fter peering at myself in the mirror, I looked dolefully at my husband and complained, "I'm fat."

Responding with the tact, sympathy, and carefully chosen words that I've come to expect, he said, "I'm fat too."

—BETH HARTZELL

**M**y friend Kimberly announced that she had started a diet to lose some pounds she had put on recently.

"Good!" I exclaimed. "I'm ready to start a diet too. We can be dieting buddies and help each other out. When I feel the urge to drive out and get a burger and fries, I'll call you first."

"Great!" she replied. "I'll ride with you."

—KATINA FISHER

**D**uring a trip to the mall, my wife noticed the video store was having a clearance sale. Thinking she might find an exercise tape, she searched and searched but found nothing. Finally she asked a clerk where they might be.

"Exercise videos? They're located between Science Fiction and Horror," he said with a completely straight face.

—DALE MATSUDA

As I quizzed my driver's-education students about road signs, the one for Slow Moving Vehicle stumped them. So I offered them a hint by lifting the sign above my head and slowly parading up and down the room.

One student thought he had it: "Wide load!" he called out.

—VERN PINNT

The trouble with jogging is that by the time you realize you're not in shape for it, it's too far to walk back.

—FRANKLIN P. JONES

I was walking to lunch with my friend Tristan and discussing the need to start an exercise program. A mutual friend Chris joined us on the walk, and after listening to Tristan and I talk about fitness, Chris said, "I'm exercising every day."

"You're exercising?" we asked. "Daily?"

"Yeah!" he replied. "I swim after work on Mondays, Wednesdays and Fridays. And I run on Tuesdays and Thursdays."

We stopped walking, and I asked Chris, "How long have you been doing this?"

"Oh, I don't start until next week!" he replied.

—JAKE PEDROSA

The professor's last patient for the day asks: "Tell me, doctor, what is the best exercise to lose weight?"

"I advise you to move your head first to the right, then to the left.

And how many times?"

**"Every time someone offers you something to eat."**

—KOMSOMOLSKAYA PRAVDA

Everyone is on this low-fat craze now. **The Mayo Clinic just changed its name to the Balsamic Vinaigrette Clinic.**

—BUZZ NUTLEY

Recently, I bought a step counter for my evening walks and soon began wearing it everywhere. While visiting my parents, I went for a walk with my mother, who noticed the counter on my belt.

"What's that?" she asked.

"An exercise tool," I replied. "It keeps track of your steps. It's to help you stay healthy and lose weight."

She gave me a quizzical look and said, "Don't you think it would work better if it counted your bites?"

—ANGELA GIACCI

An elderly patient paid me a wonderful compliment. "You're beautiful," she said.

I must have looked skeptical because she was quick to assure me that she was sincere. "It's just that I rarely hear flattering comments about my looks," I explained.

She smiled understandingly. "That's because you're fat. But it doesn't mean you aren't pretty."

—AMY MOTZ

My parents had one of those old-time rotary telephones. This drove my brother crazy. Once, he misdialed a long-distance number and had to do it all over again.

"Mom," he asked in frustration, "why don't you replace this thing with a touch-tone phone?"

"If we did," my mother said, "your father would never get any exercise."

—DEBRA COPELAND

" If I get dizzy and pass out, there's a cherry danish in my lunch box. "

I was reading the nutrition labels on some cans of food when something caught my eye.

"What's saturated fat?" I asked my mother.

She answered, "Your father taking a shower."

—TOSHIA MITCHELL

The woman sashays out of the bedroom modeling a lovely garment.

"Look at this!" she says to her husband. "I've had it for 20 years, and it still fits."

Her husband nods. **"It's a scarf."**

—D. GOLIGHTLY

My husband was going on a diet, but when we pulled into a fast-food restaurant he ordered a milkshake. I pointed out that a shake isn't exactly the best snack for someone who wants to lose weight. He agreed but didn't change his order.

The long line must have given him time to make the connection between his order and his waistline. As the woman handed him his shake, she said, "Sorry about the wait."

"That's okay," he replied self-consciously. "I'm going to lose it."

—KAREN NAZARENUS

With fire alarms blaring at my mom's apartment complex, she grabbed her favorite bathing suit and ran out.

"A bathing suit?" I said later. "Of all the priceless things in that apartment, that's what you chose to save?"

"Material things come and go," she said. "But a one-piece suit that doesn't make you look fat is impossible to replace."

—CATHY PEACOCK

We put our old NordicTrack on the curb with a sign that read "Free: Fun exercise machine!" By that afternoon, it was gone. But the next day, it reappeared with this note attached: "Define fun."

A woman in our diet club was lamenting that she had gained weight. She'd made her family's favorite cake over the weekend, she reported, and they'd eaten half of it at dinner.

The next day, she said, she kept staring at the other half, until finally she cut a thin slice for herself. One slice led to another, and soon the whole cake was gone. The woman went on to tell us how upset she was with her lack of willpower and how she knew her husband would be disappointed.

Everyone commiserated, until someone asked what her husband said when he found out. She smiled. "He never found out. I made another cake and ate half!"

—BARBARA A. JOSLIN

**My sister's dieting stint ended the day her eight-year-old saw the price tag on her weight-loss shake. "Whoa!" he yelled out.**

## "Eight bucks for this, and it doesn't even work."

—D.W.

On my husband's second visit to the exercise class he enrolled in, he used the rowing machines, rode a stationary bicycle and did leg exercises with one-kilo weights attached to each ankle. When he finished, he walked ten minutes to the garage where he had parked his car, then picked me up.

"I'm exhausted," he complained. "I wonder if I should continue this program."

When we got home, he trudged into the house and finally sat down to rest his tired legs. He eased his shoes off—and discovered the weights still strapped to his ankles.

—RENATE HUXTABLE

**F**or several years, I had been trying to convince my husband that he should do more cardiovascular exercise. One day, he announced that he was going golfing at our local course and that he was going to walk instead of riding in a cart.

I thought this was a good start to getting in shape and that my nagging was finally paying off. When he came back, he walked into the house moaning and groaning over how much his back and his legs hurt.

"What does that tell you?" I asked.

He replied, "It tells me I should have taken the cart!"

—MAGGIE WHEELER

**"I've lost 80 pounds, and nobody notices it."**

Scientists are now saying that obesity can be caused by viruses. **I guess you have to eat a lot of them.**

—GREGG SIEGEL

The teacher in our Bible class asked a woman to read from the Book of Numbers about the Israelites wandering in the desert.

"The Lord heard you when you wailed, 'If only we had meat to eat!'" she began. "Now the Lord will give you meat. You will not eat it for just one day, or two days, or five, or ten or twenty days, but for a month—until you loathe it."

When the woman finished, she paused, looked up and said, "Hey, isn't that the Atkins diet?"

—DAVID MARTINO

Clearly I was not going to win the battle of the bulge on my own, so I decided to join a gym.

"Before you start working out, we like to do a health assessment," explained the gym representative. "When you come in, wear loose-fitting clothing."

"If I had loose-fitting clothing, we wouldn't be having this conversation."

—KELLY BLACKWELL

My friend's husband asked her what she'd like for her 40th birthday.

"Oh, something that will make me look beautiful and feel good," she said.

Hoping for an expensive new outfit or a trip to a spa, she was surprised but excited on her birthday morning when he left a large box waiting for her in the hallway.

Inside it was an exercise bike.

—JENNY GRAHAM

## ? Did you hear about the sword-swallower who was on a diet?

He was on pins and needles for six weeks.

— TODD S. HARRIS

A note on the soda machine in our break room warned, "Diet cola isn't working."

Beneath that, someone else had written, "Try exercise and a low-carb diet."

—PAUL COOPER

Early one Saturday, I checked out a local yard sale and came across some exercise equipment I had been looking for. As I paid the owner for her Thighmaster and aerobic step, I inquired if she also had a Buttmaster.

"No," she replied quickly, "but I should have it in time for my next yard sale."

—MELODY LEAR

My husband and I were standing in line at the Pittsburgh airport ticket counter. The wait got the best of me, and I left him holding our place while I looked for a seat. There were no chairs around, so I settled on a substitute—an opening in the counter where suitcases are pushed through to the ticket agents.

As I sat there, I noticed several people smiling at me. I became a little self-conscious when I saw a few of them nudge others to look in my direction. I squirmed around uncomfortably—and that's when I noticed the screen above my head flashing my weight in green lights every time I wiggled.

—JAN LARKEY

# FAMILY FUN

"I never met anyone who didn't have a very smart child. What happens to these children, you wonder, when they reach adulthood?"

—FRAN LEBOWITZ

"Oh my god, we forgot the kids."

# PARENTING PRIDE

At the airport, Sylvia was anxiously waiting for her daughter's plane. After graduating from college, Ashley had been gone a year, adventuring in faraway places. Sylvia's heart raced when she saw her lovely child step out of the Jetway. Then she noticed a tall man directly behind Ashley, dressed in feathers and beads, with exotic markings all over his body. Ashley greeted her mother and introduced the man as her husband. Sylvia felt faint. She screamed, "I said you should marry a rich doctor! A rich doctor!"

—CHRIS PARKE

Having found her daughter playing doctor with the neighbor's son, the irate mother marched across the street to confront his parents.

"Oh, don't take it so seriously," the kid's mother said. "It's only natural for children their age to want to satisfy their curiosity."

"Curiosity? Curiosity?" the girl's mother said, fuming. "He removed her appendix!"

I realized my family didn't get out enough when we went to a restaurant recently: We had just finished eating when my five-year-old brother got up from the table and headed for the kitchen, dishes in hand.

—ANTHONY PRYOR

As a new parent, I've come to appreciate the sacrifices my mother and father made for me. For example, not long ago, I thanked my mother for all the time and money that was spent on me for orthodontics.

"We had to," she said, "or you would still be living at home."

—KRIS BOEDIGHEIMER

## Overheard:

**Mom:** You're 18. You can do what you want.
**Daughter:** So I can run away!?
**Mom:** No. You're 18. You would just be leaving.
**Daughter:** Oh.

—LAURA MORRISON

**O**n his 18th birthday, my son announced that he was no longer obligated to observe the curfew we'd imposed on him.

"I'm 18," he announced. "And you can't stop me from leaving the house if and when I want to."

"You're right," I said. "I can't stop you from leaving. But I can stop you from coming back."

—PAUL ENNIS

**W**hen I took my ten-year-old grandson to his first flea market, I taught him the fine art of haggling.

"Say someone's selling a hunting knife for $20. Offer him $15," I instructed. He got the concept, and when he spotted a ring he wanted that was selling for $5, he went into action.

"I only have $3," he told the woman at the booth.

She smiled. "Then $3 it is."

With that, he pulled out a $5 bill and waited for change.

—CINDY COLEMAN

My parents, married 45 years, raised a brood of 11 children. Now they enjoy 22 grandchildren. When asked the secret for staying together all that time, my mother replies, "Many years ago we made a promise to each other: **The first one to pack up and leave has to take all the kids.**"

—BETTY STUMPF

At the supermarket, a rambunctious child stopped moving long enough to stare at my neck brace.

"What happened to her?" he asked his mother.

Seeing a great teaching opportunity, she replied, "Maybe she wasn't sitting down in her grocery cart!"

—HARRYL HOLLINGSWORTH

During a church social activity, I had to say a few words about myself. I mentioned that I was born in Quebec, that the first Côté had immigrated in 1635, and that I was a tenth-generation Canadian.

"I doubt anybody in this room can beat that," I boasted.

"I can!" came a voice from the back. Everyone turned around. It was my daughter.

—ALAIN CÔTÉ

To celebrate her parents' Golden Wedding anniversary, their daughter gave them two tickets to a lavish performance of classical ballet. It was the first time they had been to the opera. The next day, the daughter asked them for their impressions.

"Oh! It was wonderful," her father replied. "They were so graceful and kind. When they saw your mother asleep in her seat, they danced on tip-toe not to wake her up."

—EVELYN KATZ

I was thrilled to be moving into my own house, even though it was only a block away from my parents'. The first morning on my own I relaxed on the porch and listened to some music, enjoying my new independence.

Then the phone rang. It was my father telling me to turn the sound system down.

—ELI STICKLER

Spotted on a bumper sticker:
**"I'm not a brat. Am not, am not, am not!"**

—JACQUELINE PORTER

After discussing my dating life—or lack thereof—with my mother, I told her about a friend of mine who had been in a terrible car accident, broken both her legs, and wound up marrying her orthopedic surgeon. My mother sighed: "Why can't anything like that ever happen to you?"

—BARBARA ALBRIGHT

I had never been so zonked in my life. After my first child, Amanda, was born, my mother came to stay with me for a few weeks to help out, but I still woke up whenever the baby made the slightest sound during the night. One morning, I groggily asked my mom, "How long before I stop hearing every noise Amanda makes?"

Mom was obviously only half-listening. "Honey, are you coming down with something?" she asked. "You were coughing in your sleep."

—CAROL HERLONG

A mother is waiting for her son excitedly on the last day of term.

"At last you're home. Where's your report?"

"I haven't got it."

"How come?"

"I lent it to Béla."

"And why does he need it?"

"He wants to scare his parents with it."

—GYULA MECSÉRI

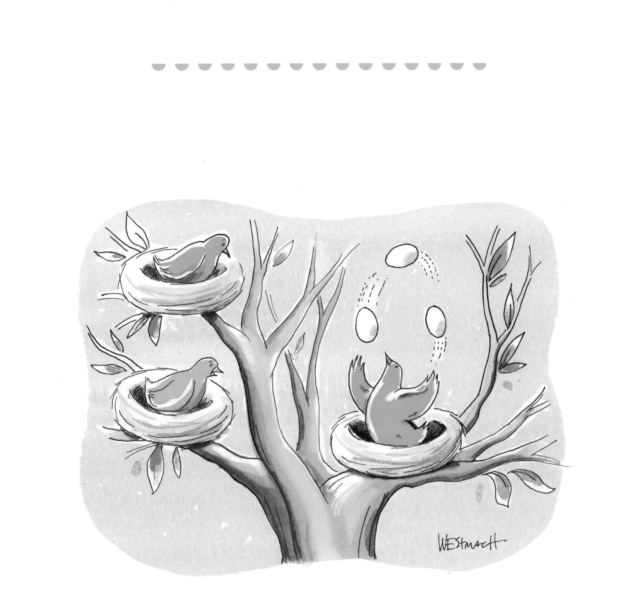

"I'm not sure Mary's ready for motherhood."

One day the four-year-old boy I babysit told me he was going to have a baby sister. Knowing that his parents wanted more children, I asked, "So when are you going to get this baby?"

"Daddy says as soon as I start sleeping in my own bed," was his innocent reply.

—HILLARY GEORGE

As my mother headed out her office door last election day, she announced, "Well, I'm off to the polls to cancel my daughter's vote."

"You know," replied a colleague, "it doesn't matter how old they get. You still have to clean up behind them, don't you?"

—LAYNA REED

My husband and I drove a thousand miles with our three young children to visit my parents. The reunion included my two brothers' bustling families, plus other friends and relatives. As we were piling into our van for the return trip, my father offered us a fistful of bills "to help with gas."

"You don't have to pay us to come see you!" my husband said.

"We're not paying you to come," my mother quickly replied. "We're paying you to leave!"

—LYNDA SHENEFIELD

I am an anesthesiologist who frequently takes emergency calls. Late one evening, a teenage boy arrived in the operating room for an appendectomy, accompanied by his mother. He wore jeans and a T-shirt and had long, flowing hair. Prior to surgery, I asked if they had any questions.

Immediately the mother leaned over toward me. "Doctor," she whispered, "while you have him asleep, could you give him a haircut?"

—ERNST HEILBRUNN

I'd been secretly dating for several months, and it was time to break the news to my very protective father. My mother thought he'd take it better if she explained to him that my boyfriend was a marine who had just returned from Iraq. This pleased Dad immensely. **"A marine? Good!" he said. "That means he can take orders."**

—MELISSA ESMILLA

Listening to a speaker in church, I was impressed that he still recalled his father telling him to "remember who you are" before he left the house. I leaned over to my 18-year-old son and whispered, "Is there anything that I used to say to you that stands out in your mind?"

He pondered, then leaned over and whispered, "Bring back the change."

—LAURA CRAPO

While my parents were painting their bedroom, my five-year-old sister walked in and asked, "What the hell are you doing?" Not realizing what she had said, she casually walked out.

After she left, my stunned dad then turned to my mother and asked, "Where the hell did she learn to talk like that?"

—MARJORIE ERICKSON

My two daughters were discussing the less than desirable physical attributes they had inherited from their father.

The older one: "I hate my freckles from Dad."

Her unsympathetic younger sister: "At least you got his freckles. I got his eyebrow."

—TAMMY RIDDLE

While watching the Olympics, my mother turned to my sister and said, "You just know the athletes' mothers are so proud of them. I'm proud of you girls, and you're nothing."

—LESLIE MCCLURG

A woman calls her husband to tell him that their
two sons want to go to the zoo, then a movie.
"That's too expensive," he says. "It's one or the other."
"Okay, which one do you prefer?"

"Mikey."

Two little boys, ages eight and ten, were always getting into trouble. The boys' mother heard that a preacher in town had been successful in disciplining children, so she asked if he would speak to them. The preacher agreed, but asked to see them individually.

The mother sent the eight-year-old in the morning. The preacher, a huge man with a deep booming voice, sat the younger boy down and asked him sternly, "Do you know where God is, son?"

The boy's mouth dropped open, but he made no response, sitting there wide-eyed with his mouth hanging open.

So the preacher repeated the question in an even sterner tone, "Where is God?!"

Again, the boy made no attempt to answer.

The preacher raised his voice even more and shook his finger in the boy's face and bellowed, "WHERE IS GOD?!"

The boy screamed and bolted out of the room, ran directly home and dove into his closet, slamming the door behind him.

When his older brother found him in the closet, he asked, "What happened?"

The younger brother, gasping for breath, replied, "We are in BIG trouble this time! GOD is missing, and they think WE did it!"

—M & M TEE

**"How many times do I have to tell you to slouch?"**

Out shopping, my friend Darin noticed a mother with three little girls and a baby. The woman's patience was wearing thin as all the girls called "Mama" while she tried to shop.

Finally, Darin heard her say, "I don't want to hear the word "Mama" for at least five minutes."

A few seconds went by, then one girl tugged on her mom's skirt and said, "Excuse me, miss."

—MARIEL RAECHAL

Upset over a newlywed squabble with my husband, I went to my parents' house to complain. Trying to console me, my dad said that men aren't like this all the time.

"Baloney," I said. "Men are good for only one thing!"

"Yes," my mother interjected, "but how often do you have to parallel park?"

—JENNIFER L. LEE

On his birthday, my husband was stuck driving our six rambunctious children around. As usual, they were yelling, punching and annoying one another. Joel finally had had enough. "Kids," he said over the din, "if you would behave and be kind to each other, that would be a very nice birthday present for me."

Our six-year-old shot back: "Too late, I already got you another present."

—GAYLE TROTTER

Even though I'm in my 30s, I still stop by my parents' house to mow their lawn. One afternoon, the kid next door was cutting his grass at the same time.

"It's punishment for skipping a day of school," he explained. "Why are you still doing your folks' yard?"

"Because I cut a class when I was your age," I said with a straight face.

I'm told he's had perfect attendance ever since.

—ROBERT THOMPSON

I knew my kids watched too much TV when my seven-year-old asked me to pick him up from school at 3 p.m./2 p.m. Central.

—JOANNE LEVI

# QUOTABLE QUOTES

**"BECAUSE OF THEIR SIZE, PARENTS MAY BE DIFFICULT TO DISCIPLINE PROPERLY."**

—P. J. O'ROURKE

"It's great to be a godmother. She calls me 'god' for short."

—ELLEN DEGENERES

"Don't bother discussing sex with small children. They rarely have anything to add."

—FRAN LEBOWITZ

"My mom buys paper plates, 300 in a big plastic bag. We can take one, but the rule is that we have to put the twist tie back on the bag. I guess it's to keep them fresh. Nothing ruins my lunch more than a stale plate."

—COMEDIAN JORDAN BRADY

**"WHEN I WAS A KID, WE HAD A QUICKSAND BOX IN OUR BACKYARD. I WAS AN ONLY CHILD, EVENTUALLY."**

—STEVEN WRIGHT

"The other night I ate at a real nice family restaurant. Every table had an argument going."

—GEORGE CARLIN

**"MY MOTHER COULD MAKE ANYBODY FEEL GUILTY. SHE USED TO GET LETTERS OF APOLOGY FROM PEOPLE SHE DIDN'T EVEN KNOW."**

—JOAN RIVERS

"A Harvard Medical School study has determined that rectal thermometers are still the best way to tell a baby's temperature. Plus, it really teaches the baby who's boss."

—TINA FEY

# KIDS SAY THE DARNDEST THINGS

When my husband was away at basic training, my four-year-old daughter and I stayed with my sister. Since my daughter already called me Mommy, she started calling her aunt Mom—the way her six-year-old cousin did. One day, someone called. I picked up the extension and overheard the person ask my daughter if her daddy was home.

She said, "No, he's in the army."

"Is your mom home?" he asked.

"Yes, but she's asleep with Uncle Danny."

—TONYA ALEISAWI

"Now, who can spell the word straight?" the third-grade teacher asked her students.

"S-T-R-A-I-G-H-T," answered a boy seated in the front row.

"Great job. And do you know what it means?"

"Without ice."

—VICTOR CONWAY

My five-year-old son was badgering us to get him an iPad. "My friend brought his to school, and I want one too," he insisted.

"Absolutely not," said my husband. "They're expensive and fragile. Besides, what would you even do with an iPad?"

Our son replied, "I'd put it over my eye and play pirates with my friends."

—JULIE R.

On the day of my father-in-law's funeral, our two-year-old son was appropriately somber—until he spied the coffin. "Oooh, Mama!" he shouted. "Look at that big suitcase!"

—HELEN BALDWIN

"I have to go directly to the corner? I thought there would be an appeals process."

After downing half a glass of milk, my ten-year-old son declared, "I am an optimist: The glass is half-empty!"

"Looking at the glass as half-empty is a sign of pessimism," I said.

He corrected me: **"Not if you don't like what's in it."**

—PRATIK PANDYA

My three-year-old daughter, Chantelle, begged me for a story about when she was born.

"Daddy brought Mommy to the hospital, and the doctor helped you to be born," I began. "When you came out, we both said, 'What is it?' And the doctor said, 'It's a girl!' "

"How did the doctor know I was a girl?" asked Chantelle.

"Well, when you were born, you came to us with no clothes on."

"Ahh," said Chantelle. "And boys have clothes on."

—ANNETTE CAMPBELL

Usually, the secretary at my son's elementary school answers when I call, but on one occasion, I spoke to an unfamiliar voice.

"Do you know who it might have been?" I asked my son.

"It could have been Mrs. Campbell," he said thoughtfully. "Did it sound like she was wearing a blue coat?"

—MANDY WILLIAMS

My grandson is making great strides with his potty training, but every now and then, he waits too long before going. Once, sensing an emergency, he rushed into the bathroom—which was occupied by his mother—and shouted, "Scoot over!"

—CAROLYN WHITAKER

My six-year-old grandson watches a lot of TV. This became apparent the day he asked his father, "Am I healthy enough for sexual activity?"

—JOHN BALL

For our 20-year-old daughter's birthday, my wife gave her a laptop computer. When Lorena opened her gift and saw what it was, she reached for a tissue, saying, "Wait, I have something in my eye."

We all burst out laughing when her ten-year-old sister said, "It's called a tear."

—CLAUDE BÉCHARD

My two daughters were having a discussion about family resemblance. "I look like Mom," said my nine-year-old, "but I have Dad's eyes and Dad's lips."

The six-year-old said, "And I look just like Dad, but I have light hair." Then she turned to me. "Mom," she asked, "what does Dad have to do with us being born anyway?"

Her older sister jumped right in. "Don't be stupid, Christina. Dad is the one who drove Mom to the hospital."

—KATHLEEN O'NEILL

### Scene: My son speaking to his three-year-old son.

**Dad:** Do you want to know a secret?
**Son:** Uh huh.
**Dad:** I love you.
**Son:** Do you want to know a secret?
**Dad:** Uh huh.
**Son:** I'm Batman.

—GARY PANKOW

"My dad said I should get the best education money
can buy, so how much for an A?"

Three boys are boasting about their grandfathers.

"My grandpa is a great swimmer," says the first. "He can swim for hours!"

"That's nothing," says the second. "My grandpa goes swimming at six in the morning every day and doesn't get out till six at night."

"Big deal!" smirks the third boy. "My grandpa started swimming in this pond 20 years ago, and he still hasn't come out!"

While reviewing math symbols with my students, I drew a greater-than (>) and a less-than (<) sign on the whiteboard.

"Does anyone know what these mean?" I asked.

A boy raised his hand: "One means fast-forward, and the other means rewind."

—PEGGY HORACHEK

Our tour guide at historical Arlington National Cemetery thought he had an answer for everything . . . until he met our students.

"Excuse me," said one kid. "Are the graves in alphabetical order?"

—WILLIAM CULLEM

My six-year-old son, Michael, was so afraid of monsters lurking in his closet that he refused to go to bed. So I devised a plan to put his mind at ease: I filled a spray bottle with scented water and glued on a label that read "Creature Repellent."

This worked great . . . for a week.

"Monsters aren't real," I said, frustrated. "They're imaginary."

"Oh, yeah?" he shot back. "So how come they sell creature repellent?"

—ANNE-MARIE GIONET

An hour after I'd put my seven-year-old son to bed, I heard him cry out. I ran to his room, where I found him sobbing. "Mommy, I had a bad nightmare about a big monster," he said.

"And he had a face just like yours."

—DOROTHY AMARAL

**T**wo letters arrived from my nine-year-old daughter, who was away at camp. One was addressed to Mom, the other to Dad. The sweet, short note to me said, "Dear Mom, I am having a lot of fun at camp. Tell Eddie [our cat] I miss him. I miss you. Love, Kenna." The even shorter note she sent to her father: "Dear Dad, Read Mom's note. Love, Kenna."

—ROBIN HOLT

**W**hen a teacher asked my six-year-old nephew why his handwriting wasn't as neat as usual, he responded, "I'm trying a new font."

—JUDITH FISHER

**I** asked my eighth graders, "Why are you looking forward to becoming a teenager?"

A student answered, "You're treated more like an adult because you are getting closer to adultery."

—KELLY THOMPSON

**I** gave an apple to a girl in our after-school program. It must have been very fresh, because she declared, "Mmm, I must get the recipe for this."

—LAURA MELVILLE

My young children had plenty of questions after witnessing a cat give birth. But I was ready. I grabbed a book off the shelf that explained in terms kids could understand how mommies and daddies have babies, one that I'd bought for this very occasion. But after I read it aloud, my four-year-old still wasn't satisfied.

"I don't want to know how people have babies," he said. "I want to know how cats have babies."

—FLORENCE MARCUS

During a fire drill at our child-care center, I asked the kids, "What would you do if I accidentally started a fire on the stove and your lunch was burning?"

One five-year-old knew: "I wouldn't eat that lunch."

—KAREN KIEFFER

My four-year-old grandson asked his mom why she couldn't drive him to day care. She said, "I have to breast-feed your little sister."

"Why can't Grandma do it?" he asked.

His mother explained that Grandma didn't have any milk.

"Then what's she got in there?" he asked. "Juice or something?"

—KIMBERLEY HOPPER

A young girl walked into her school library and asked the librarian—my daughter—for a particular book.

"Are you sure you want this book?" my daughter asked. "It's pretty scary."

"I'm not afraid of anything," said the girl. **"I've seen my grandmother naked."**

—ALFRED K. HARWELL

I was stepping out of the shower when my four-year-old daughter burst through the bathroom door.

"Excuse me!" I said. "I'm naked."

She responded, "Don't worry, I won't laugh at you."

—KODIE DAVIS

The teacher announced that to practice spelling, each member of the class would say what their father did for a living and then spell the occupation.

Mary went first. "My Dad is a baker, b-a-k-e-r, and if he were here, he would give everyone a cookie."

Next came Tommy. "My dad is a banker, b-a-n-k-e-r, and if he were here, he'd give each of us a quarter."

Third came Jimmy. "My dad is an electrician." But after struggling through a number of attempts to spell the word, the teacher asked him to sit and think about it for a moment while she called on someone else. She then turned to little Johnny.

"My dad is a bookie, b-o-o-k-i-e," Johnny said. "And if he were here, he'd lay you 8-to-5 that Jimmy ain't never gonna spell electrician."

—AL JENSEN

When my eight-year-old asked how I knew I was pregnant, I told her I had taken a pregnancy test.

"Oh," she said. "What questions were on the test?"

—LAUREL FALVO

I asked my three-year-old what she liked to eat.

"Nuts," she replied.

"Great," I said. "What kind? Pecans? Walnuts? Peanuts?"

"Donuts."

—B.L.

"My mom said I have to go to school if I want a house and a car, but frankly I don't think I'm ready for that much financial responsibility!"

My husband, a deputy district attorney, was teaching an antidrug class to a group of Cub Scouts. When he asked if anyone could list the gateway drugs, one Scout had the answer: "Cigarettes, beer and marinara."

—LORI WOLF

When my seven-year-old daughter was diagnosed with diabetes, a new diet regimen was called for.

"Do you think you could eat green beans?" I asked.

"No," she said. "I haven't liked green beans since the accident."

"What accident?"

"When I accidentally ate a green bean."

—MINDY KROPF

My five-year-old nephew has always happily answered to BJ. That ended when he came home from his first day of school in a foul mood. It seems his teacher took roll, and he never heard his name.

"Why didn't anyone tell me my name was William?!" he complained.

—GREG CLAUSER

A salesman rang the bell at a suburban home, and the door was opened by a nine-year-old boy puffing on a long black cigar. Hiding his amazement, the salesman asked the young man, "Is your mother home?"

The boy took the cigar out of his mouth, flicked ashes on the carpet and asked, "What do you think?"

—JONATHAN DINGLER

The topic for my third-grade class was genetics. Smiling broadly, I pointed to my dimples and asked, "What trait do you think I passed on to my children?"

**One student called out, "Wrinkles!"**

—LYNN GRAGG

While cleaning our bathroom, I noticed some spots on the wall next to the sink. I scrubbed the stains but didn't make much progress. Puzzled, I asked my son if he knew anything about them.

"Oh, sorry about that," he said. "I dyed my hair last week and didn't notice I'd splashed until the stains had already dried." Then he added, "But it's okay. I wash the stains every morning after my shower because the instructions on the box said it would clean up after 12 to 24 washings."

—BARRY WILSON

I am a lousy bow hunter, a fact that was driven home to me by my ten-year-old niece. Handing me an arrow that she found in the woods, Gina explained, "I figured it was yours. There's no deer on the end of it."

—MARK RUSZALA

Wondering why my niece, Charlotte was returning to college to get a master's in philosophy, I asked, "What can you do with a degree like that?"

"Well," she explained, "it will qualify me to deal with questions like, 'What is existence?' 'What is the essence of things?' and 'Do you want fries with that?'"

—MEL LOFTUS

I had to laugh when I first heard the greeting on my son's answering machine at West Virginia University: "Hi, this is Rick. If you are someone from the phone company, I've already sent the money. If this is one of my parents, please send money. If it's my financial institution, you didn't lend me enough money. If you're a friend, you owe me money. If you are a female . . . I have plenty of money!"

—KRISTIN CLAYTON

"Is this in HD?"

During dinner, I asked my three-year-old granddaughter if her meal was good. She picked over the plate before answering, "Not yet."

—WILLIAM YANNEY

A young French student is sent by his parents to spend a month with an English aristocratic family. His host, the lord of the house, shows him around the estate.

"Is that a golf course over there?" asks the boy. "Do you play often?"

"No," came the reply. "I tried once, but I didn't like it. Too tiring."

The student then sees two horses in a paddock. "I see you ride horses," he says.

"No," the lord replied, "I tried once, but I didn't like it. Too tiring."

The visit continues and they walk past a tennis court. "I suppose that . . ."

"Goodness, no," the lord answered, "I tried once, but I didn't like it. Too tiring."

At that point, a young man walks toward them. "Let me introduce my son, William, to you," says the lord.

The French boy shakes his hand and, turning toward the lord, quips, "An only child, I take it?"

—ROGER KISSEL

A teacher friend of my wife was discussing compound nouns with her class. "They're made up of two or more words," she explained. "For example, town house or boxcar. Can anyone think of another one?"

One boy raised his hand and offered, "Asphalt."

—JOSEPH R. VER BERG

Suffering a migraine attack one night, my sister, Debbie, lay down for a while, leaving her four children to do their homework. However, a short time later a fellow member of her church knocked on the door, and Debbie was horrified to hear one of her kids tell the visitor, "You can't come in. Mom's in bed with a migrant."

—SUE DALITZ

After being a widower for a few years, I was going to remarry. My daughter, with three young sons who had fond memories of their grandmother, tried to explain to them why I was getting married again. "Grandpa's lonely," she said. "He needs someone to talk to, go for walks with. He needs a companion at mealtime and company at home."

Doug, the middle boy, said, "Why doesn't he get a dog?"

—H. B. CLARKE

A few days before Mother's Day, my husband announced he had to work that Sunday and wouldn't be able to fix me dinner as he usually does. "I have an idea," my teenage daughter piped up. "I'll take you out to eat."

"But the restaurants will be so crowded with all the other mothers," I protested.

"Don't worry, Mom," she replied. "Most of them probably won't be eating at McDonald's."

—NANCY DEARBORN

## ? When do cows go to sleep?
When it's pasture bedtime.

HOSS ALLRED

Days after our youngest daughter was born, my family went for a drive. While my wife ran into a store, the baby started to cry. Not having anything else to give her, I let her suck on my finger while we waited for her mother to come back and breast-feed her. My eldest, age four, said, "Is that how you feed her—from your finger?"

—ADAM CAMPBELL

When I met five-year-old Timmy, he was in the hospital with broken legs. He'd chased a ball into the street and was hit by a car. Six weeks later, as his discharge nurse, I asked, "The next time your ball rolls into the street, what will you do?"

Timmy replied, "Send my sister."

—LINDA E. WILLIAMS

Blood may be thicker than water, but baseball beats them both. I learned this after explaining to my two boys that they were half-Lithuanian on their father's side and half-Yankee, meaning their other set of parents came from an old New England family.

My younger son looked worried. "But we're still a hundred percent Red Sox, right, Mom?"

—GAYLA BIEKSHA

"What does the word contemplate mean?" the college student asked his English professor.

"Think about it," the professor answered.

"Ugh!" the student groaned. "Can't you just tell me?"

—DANA THAYER

At a baby shower, everyone was asked to complete nursery rhymes. My 11-year-old daughter, Taylor, contributed this: "Jack Sprat could eat no fat. His wife could eat no carbs."

—DAVID HAM

A nursery-school teacher was driving a station wagon full of kids home one day when a fire truck zoomed past. Sitting in the front seat of the truck was a Dalmatian. The children started discussing the dog's duties.

"They use him to keep crowds back," said one child.

"No," said another. "He's just for good luck."

"No," said a third child. "They use the dogs to find the fire hydrants."

—RAYMONDE BOURGEOIS

When I was a teenager, my father caught me reading one of my older sister's magazines. "Son, why are you reading that sissy magazine?" he asked.

"There's an article that tells women where to meet men," I responded, pointing to the magazine's cover. "I need to know where I'm supposed to be."

—STEVEN C. VAUGHN

When I signed up our four-year-old for floor hockey at the YMCA, I reviewed the rules with him. Steven was used to playing with his older siblings, and I wanted to be sure he wouldn't be too rough when playing with other four-year-olds.

"Under no circumstances," I lectured, "are you allowed to hit anyone with your stick, no matter how mad they make you."

"Don't worry, Mommy," Steven replied. "I know that you drop your stick first and then fight!"

—SHELLEY M. SMITH

"**H**e's going to beat me up!" yelled my four-year-old.
"Why would your older brother do that?" I asked him.
"Because I accidentally dropped his toothbrush in the toilet."
"Just tell him and give him a new one."
"I can't."
"Why?"
"He's in the bathroom brushing his teeth!"

—KATRINA STANFORD

**A**s I was treating my daughter and her family to the buffet at a casino, all the bells and whistles for a winning slot machine began to go off. My seven-year-old grandson was awed. "Wow!" yelled Casey. "This is like Chuck E. Cheese for old people."

—PATRICIA KEYES

**W**hen my ten-year-old came home, I could tell something wasn't right.
"What's wrong?" I asked.
He sighed, "There's this kid who's trying to bully me."
"Trying?"
"Well, he's not very good at it."

—VALERIE BEVERLY

My five-year-old daughter, Rylee, was yelling at her younger brother for hitting her. "Troy, did you hit your sister?" I asked.
"No."
"Troy, Santa Claus can tell if you're lying."
He thought about the ramifications of this before asking, **"Can you?"**

—BRIAN SMITH

"Dave? I have big news.
I hope you're in the Lotus position."

# MODERN LIFE

When I went inside the station to pay for my tank of gas, I noticed a sign asking patrons to tell the cashier the number of their pump. Even though I was the only customer, I decided to be silly and tell him anyway.

"I'm Number One," I announced.

He smiled. "Well, now. Looks like those motivational tapes are really working for you."

—VIRGINIA WORZALLA

Mom was getting swamped with calls from strangers. The reason? A medical billing service had launched an 800 number that was identical to hers. When she called to complain, they told her to get a new number.

"I've had mine for twenty years," she pleaded. "Couldn't you change yours?"

They refused. So Mom said, "Fine. From now on I'm going to tell everyone who calls that their bill is paid in full." The company got a new number the next day.

—KIM DRAKE

Working on Capitol Hill, my husband was under constant pressure. After one late-night session, he came home exhausted and went straight to bed. When I turned out the light, he sat up in a panic.

"Is everything okay in the house?" he asked.

"Yes, honey," I answered. "I locked the doors and turned down the heat."

"That's good," he said, lying back down, his eyelids heavy. "What about the Senate?"

—MARILYN DAINES

The DVD player had conked out, and we weren't able to watch the movie we'd rented. Then my husband had a brilliant idea: "Why don't we use the PlayStation?"

We pushed all the buttons but couldn't get it to work, so we gave up and went upstairs.

We were reading in bed when our 17-year-old son appeared in our doorway. "Someone left a DVD in my PlayStation," he said.

"We were trying to watch a movie on it," my husband admitted, "but we couldn't get past the parental control screen."

"What a shame," our son said as he smiled and closed the door.

—CONNIE AMES

His residency complete, my friend's son, Dennis, thought about setting up practice in Great Falls, Montana. He liked the town but suggested his wife visit as well. Barely there a day, she came home and announced, "Let's move."

Surprised at her snap judgment, he asked, "Did you look at some homes or even go downtown?"

"Nope."

"What makes you so certain?" Dennis prodded.

"I pulled over to the side of the road outside of town and popped my hood," she explained. "Within a half-hour, a dozen people stopped to help."

—ROBERT KRAJEWSKI

My friend has a bad habit of overdrawing her bank account. One day before we went shopping, I complained about my lack of funds and lamented, "Guess I'll use plastic." Unconcerned, she whipped out her checkbook: **"I'm using rubber."**

—AMANDA HOWARD

A customer called our video-game service line looking for information regarding his console. So I directed him to our website.

"It's www.pan," I said. "That's p as in potato, a as in ant, n as in—"

"Wait!" he interrupted. "I haven't finished typing p as in potato yet."

—GAEL BUCKLEY

**Our friend was describing a couple he befriended at the Pentagon. "They're good people," he insisted. Then, by way of illustration:**

**"They both have security clearance."**

—VALERIE MUNNS GATHRIGHT

Maybe snow or sleet won't delay the mail, but there are other factors—like lack of faith in the system. The man ahead of me at the post office was getting forms for temporarily stopping mail delivery and change of address.

"When you've filled them out," suggested the clerk, " bring them here in person so they don't get lost in the mail."

—P. M. CLEPPER

A friend of mine got lost on the way to the Flat Rock Playhouse, a theater in a small North Carolina town. He stopped at a farmhouse where a woman gave him excellent directions. A week later he went back to see another play, got lost again and stopped at the same house. When the woman came to the door, she exclaimed, "You haven't found it yet?"

—TYSON BETTY

Of course I can keep secrets. It's the people I tell them to who can't keep them.

—ANTHONY HADEN-GUEST

We got lucky when we heard the old Piedmont Hotel in Atlanta was getting a facelift and its beautiful maple doors became available for sale as salvage items. We bought several and had them installed in our 19th-century home. Showing a friend around our house, I pointed out, "You know, many of these doors are from the Piedmont Hotel."

He raised an eyebrow. "Most people just take towels."

—BARBARA WOODALL

A big, burly man paid a visit to a pastor's home. "Sir," he said, "I wish to draw your attention to the terrible plight of a poor family. The father is unemployed, and the mother can't work because of the nine children she must raise. They are hungry and soon will be forced onto the street unless someone pays their $500 rent."

"How terrible!" exclaimed the preacher. Touched by the concern of a man with such a gruff appearance, he asked, "May I ask who you are?"

The visitor sobbed, "I'm their landlord."

While I waited outside for my wife to finish her shopping, my energetic toddler was zooming back and forth on the sidewalk, abruptly turning, then stopping.

An older man who'd just dodged her said, "She's a cutie. How old?"

"Two," I replied.

"Just think!" he offered. "In 14 years, she'll drive that way."

—AARON SANDLIN

"It's not that impressive now, but wait until Photoshop!"

While shopping in a supermarket in Florida, I heard over the PA system: "A wallet was found containing a large sum of cash but no identification. Will those laying claim to it please form a double line at the customer service counter."

—HARRY IANNARELLI

One afternoon I was in our living room reading the sports pages. "This pitcher earns $2.2 million a year just for throwing a ball straight," I ranted to my wife. "Anyone can do that." I picked up a rubber ball that was lying next to my chair and threw it at a couch cushion. "Look at that," I bragged. "Bullseye!"

My wife tossed the ball back, and I threw again, hitting dead center. "Two in a row," I cheered. My third toss went wild and ricocheted into one of my wife's favorite pictures, knocking it off the end table. She didn't even look up.

"And that," she said, "is why you make $22,000 a year."

—JIM CHANDLER

While sightseeing in Kentucky, we stopped to take a tour of Mammoth Cave. A visitor in our group, looking up at the huge domed ceiling, asked the guide, "Has there ever been a cave-in?"

"Never," he reassured us. "But if it did, look on the bright side. Where else could you get buried for $2.50?"

—DOUGLAS MAXSON

After a heart-transplant operation, a man was instructed by his doctor to go on a strict diet, give up smoking and get plenty of sleep.

The patient asked, "What about sex?"

"Only with your wife," the doctor replied. "We don't want you getting too excited."

—DERICK KELAART

In our busy household, meals had often consisted of frozen ready meals. Determined to give us a healthier diet, I decided to make a lamb casserole using fresh meat from the butcher, fresh vegetables from the greengrocer and herbs from the garden. After hours in the kitchen, I served it up to an expectant family.

Everyone agreed the food was delicious. "It tastes so good, Mum," declared my son, "that if you hadn't told me you made it yourself, I'd have thought it was one of the frozen ready meals."

—LUCY GRACE

My grandfather raided his savings account to buy himself an advanced satellite TV system. After the installation, he had two huge satellite dishes in his backyard and a monstrous remote control in his hand.

Our entire family was there for the unveiling. Grandpa sat down in his easy chair and started flipping through hundreds of channels from all over the world. We went outside and saw the dishes rotating until they finally came to rest. When we went back into the living room to see what he had decided to watch, we found that he had gone to sleep in his chair.

—MICHAEL C. STONE

Recently launched into the "real world" and shocked by the expenses that came with it, my brother Dustin was complaining about the high cost of auto insurance.

"If you got married," teased my dad, "the premium would be lower."

Dustin smiled. **"That would be like buying an airline just to get free peanuts."**

—AMY DOBBERSTEIN

"The system is down. Anybody remember how to do *anything?*"

**A**t the start of a week-long training class, a colleague was disappointed when he saw how small his hotel room was. He returned to the front desk. "I have a problem with my room," said my friend. "Do you possibly have a smaller one?"

A puzzled clerk asked for his room number, then checked her computer. "I'm sorry, sir, but we don't have a smaller room."

"I knew it!" he said. "I have the smallest room in this hotel!"

The clerk smiled and offered, "Let me see what I can do." My friend spent the week in a suite.

—DAWN RENWICK

A Texan, a Californian and a Seattle native were in a bar when suddenly the Texan grabbed a full bottle of tequila, tossed it into the air and shot it with a pistol. The other patrons shouted their disapproval, wondering why the Texan would waste good tequila. "It's just tequila," he said. "Where I come from, we have lots of it."

Not to be outdone, the Californian tossed a bottle of fine wine into the air and shot it. Again the patrons gasped at such wastefulness. "Where I come from," he told them, "we have plenty of wine."

Next, the Seattle native took out a bottle of beer and guzzled it. Then he threw the bottle into the air, shot the Californian and caught the falling bottle. "Why did you do that?" the hysterical people screamed.

"Where I come from, we have lots of Californians," the Seattle man explained. "But I really feel I should recycle this bottle."

—CHRISTINE LANTIN

During a congressional race in our district, a party loyalist took one of the candidates to a meeting of farm leaders. There he read off a laundry list of the man's qualifications: native Iowan, graduate of an Ivy League college, successful businessman, State Department staffer, and so on. When he finished, a farmer stood up.

"Seems to me it would be a mistake to send this man to Washington," he said. "We ought to keep him around for breeding purposes."

—A. J. PINDER

Every time I almost think humanity will be OK, I see someone struggle with the self-checkout for 20 minutes.

—CAPRICE CRANE, ON TWITTER

Needing to escape her hectic office, my friend fled to the mall, bought a candy bar and then relaxed on a bench next to a businessman. Soon, she heard the sound of a crumpling wrapper and realized that he was eating her candy bar. When he went to work on an ice-cream cone, she leaned over and took a huge lick.

"There!" she declared. She then stormed off to her car, reached into her purse for her keys and pulled out the candy bar she thought he'd eaten.

—ASHLEY OLIPHANT

### Airport security confiscated my Bengay.

### They accused me of packing heat.

—DAVE WEINBAUM

When my dad, a good ol' boy from the South, visited me in Manhattan, I treated him to dinner at an elegant French restaurant. Since he was out of his element, I ordered for him, choosing the beef bourguignon with a side of polenta, which he loved. That night, I overheard him on the phone with my stepmother. "Dinner was great," he raved. "But you won't believe how much they charge here for pot roast and grits."

—JULIE WEHMEYER

Believe it or not, I just received a check from Medicare for all of one cent. Why, I don't know, but concerned that some arcane regulation—complete with penalty—would apply for not cashing a government check, I took it to the bank. The teller looked at the amount, checked the endorsement and then asked, "How would you like this, heads or tails?"

—SHELDON LEVITAS

This guy is admitted to the hospital. Too weak to speak, he and his roommate sleep for days.

After two weeks, the first man gets the strength to point to himself and say, "American."

His roommate says, "Canadian." Exhausted, they pass out.

Two weeks later, the American summons the strength to speak again. "Shawn," he says in a frail voice.

"Dave," his roommate squeaks. They both fall back into a deep sleep.

Two weeks later, Shawn rouses himself enough to speak. "Cancer," he says.

Dave clears his throat and says, "Sagittarius."

—SHILPA SALGAONKAR

Stuck in traffic and bored out of my wits, I wiled away the time by staring at the back of the truck ahead of me. It belonged to a septic-tank company with a rather distinctive website: www.poophappens.com.

—LUKE SMITH

Nine months pregnant with twins, I bellied up to the supermarket meat bin in search of the perfect roast. The butcher appeared from the back and asked, "May I help you?"

"No, thank you," I said. "I'm just looking."

A minute later, he returned. "Can I help you?"

"No, I'm just looking," I repeated.

A few minutes later, he appeared yet again, asking the same annoying question.

"I'm just looking!" I said testily.

"In that case, ma'am," he said politely, "would you please step back a bit? Your stomach is pressing our service bell."

—SHIRLEY KRASELSKY

I was explaining to my daughter the changes in my political views over the years. When I was in college, I told her, I owned nothing and liked the idea of sharing the wealth, so I was a socialist. After I got married and bought a car, I became a Democrat. Then I got a good job and bought a house, so I became a Republican. As I got older, I invested my savings and made a fair amount of money and became a conservative. And now that I help my family and give money to church and charities, I concluded, I'm not sure what to call myself.

My daughter rolled her eyes and said, "How about *Your Majesty!*"

—BRUCE LAMKEN

# AT
# WORK

"It is impossible to live without failing at something, unless you live so cautiously that you might as well not have lived at all."

—J. K. ROWLING

# ON THE JOB

My 21-year-old granddaughter was being interviewed for a job. "What would you describe as your weakness?" she was asked.
"Um . . . shoes?"
She got the job.

—MURALI NARAYANAN

A job seeker at my office was filling out an application. After writing in his address, he was asked "Length of residence?"
The applicant wrote "One acre."

—JENNIFER MCNEIL

"Despite your university's outstanding qualifications and previous experience rejecting applicants, I find that your rejection does not meet my needs at this time. Therefore, I will assume the position of assistant professor in your department this August. Good luck rejecting future applicants."

After two stress-filled years of preparing for, then taking, a professional certification test, I got the results in the mail: I passed! Thrilled, I texted my family. My excitement waned somewhat after receiving this reply from my sister: "We are so excited about the news of your passing. Please let us know when the family will be celebrating!"

—REBECCA ATNIP

After I sent out résumés to universities regarding faculty positions, my husband asked if I'd caught the typo, the one where I addressed the cover letter: "Dear Faulty Search Committee."

—JENNIFER GOLBECK

"More applicants from Monster.com!"

The ad on Craigslist for this position explains why it opened up in the first place: **"We need a smart or more person to help un with our Company."**

My wife has been working as a temp in an office since the previous assistant retired. When she went to file some invoices, she was confused to find the M section of the filing cabinet almost full, while the other sections were practically empty. After checking, she realized that the last person had filed all the invoices under "Mr." or "Mrs."

—RAY HEYWOOD

Medical transcription requires a keen ear for technical jargon. But one applicant insisted she was singularly qualified for the position. After all, she wrote in her cover letter, "both of my sisters are nurses, and I watch the cable shows *Dr. G: Medical Examiner* and *Trauma: Life in the E.R.*"

—DONNA FORREST

The boss to one of his staff: "We've got a vacancy. Your twin brother could fill it."

"My twin brother?"

"Yes. The one I saw at the football game yesterday while you were attending your uncle's funeral."

When my sister applied for a job as a flight attendant, she was asked a battery of personal questions, including "Have you ever had a moving violation?"

"Yes," she answered. **"I was evicted two years ago."**

—MARGARET SYMINGTON

The client had a reputation for not paying his bills, but my brother-in-law George took the handyman's job anyway. And when he finished, sure enough, he left with a promise that the check would be in the mail soon. Days later, no check, but he did get called back by the client, who complained of an awful smell coming from the den.

"I have an idea what it might be," said George. "But before I do anything, I need to be paid for the first job."

Desperate, the man paid him on the spot. With that, George walked over to the fireplace and pulled out the dead fish he'd stashed there days earlier.

—WILLIAM LUDEWIG

I ran a store in a small town and often took calls from remote properties asking me to deliver food and other goods to them. On one occasion, I was asked to send a toothbrush.

"Do you want an expensive or a cheap one?" I asked.

"Make it a good one," was the reply. "There are five of us out here."

—JACK GENTLE

My neighbor Ernie pulled into his driveway after a tough day of repairing roofs. He got out of the truck and slammed the door. As his assistant jumped down from the passenger seat, Ernie let him have it.

"Dammit, Dave," he yelled. "I've taught you everything I know, and you still don't know anything!"

—CHRIS ERICKSON

The marquee at our neighborhood Mexican restaurant reads: "Open 24 hours in queso emergency."

—MARY MORA

"Our e-mail is down."

A sign prominently displayed at my workplace:
**"Is today the day you become complacent?"**

—W.P.

**W**hen my husband was a home builder, his thumb ended up on the business end of a sledgehammer, and our three-year-old daughter, Kiana, was eager to tell the entire world. When her caregiver asked how the accident had happened, Kiana shook her head sadly and said, "You know, sometimes at work, my daddy just gets hammered."

—STASIA UHLMANN

**S**oon after my accident, I went back to the classroom wearing a plaster cast round my chest that couldn't be seen under my shirt.

One day, I was having trouble reining in my rowdy tenth-grade class. Making matters worse, a stiff breeze coming from an open window kept blowing my tie into my face. That, at least, I could control: I stapled the tie onto my plaster cast.

It worked. The pupils' mouths fell open. For the rest of the day, I had no trouble from any of them.

—PAUL MADDOCKS

**M**y first job was at a fine-dining establishment. On the night we ran out of french fries, my boss handed me $100 and told me to run to the McDonald's next door and get $100 worth of fries. But when I came back with two huge greasy sacks, my boss looked confused.

"What's this?" she asked.

"The $100 worth of fries you asked for," I said.

Her eyes narrowed. "I told you $100 in fives!"

—KELLY SEMB

I visited my accountant to pick up an estate-planning form. His assistant was at lunch, so he hunted through the filing cabinet without success. When she returned, he asked for the form. She went straight to the filing cabinet and handed one over.

"How did you file them?" he asked.

"Under S for estate," she said.

—ALEX MCERVALE

**Overheard in the HR office: "I need my birth date to log on to my online benefits information.**

## But I can't remember what year I pretended I was born when you hired me."

—NICOLE HOLT

When I worked at a video store, I mentioned to a customer that her son already had a film out.

"What film?" she asked.

Realizing that it came from the adult section, and too embarrassed to tell her the title, I mumbled, "Uh . . . I'm not sure."

"That's all right," she said, putting her movie back. "I'll just watch whatever he got."

—PAUL BREON

Wanting to look my best for the office party, I splurged on a new dress, strappy high-heel shoes and, to add a fashion statement to my newly pedicured toenails, a toe ring.

That evening, I sashayed into the club, head high, and approached my boss's wife. Pointing to my painted, bejeweled toes, I asked, "Notice anything?"

"Yes," she gushed. "That's quite a bunion you have."

—ZOE SCHREIBMAN

At the end of my missionary work, where I served as the village doctor, the people bid me a warm and tearful farewell.

"Please don't go," an elderly villager pleaded.

Touched, I tried to reassure him. "Don't worry. You will soon get a much better doctor than me here."

"That's what the previous doctor told us."

—DR. A. LAXMINARAYANA RAO

Our supervisor, a saintly grandmother, was toiling away in her cubicle when the human relations specialist dropped by and asked her, in a voice loud enough for all to hear, "Do you have time to discuss your STD?" The room went uncomfortably silent, before she explained, "You know, your Short Term Disability."

—BERND SCHOLZ

After her election, the first Jewish woman president called her mother to invite her to the inauguration. The mother agreed to come, and when the great day arrived she was seated among Supreme Court justices and cabinet members.

Just a short time into the solemn ceremony, she nudged the man to her left. "You see that girl with her hand on the Bible?" the mother said with great excitement. "Her brother's a doctor!"

—PETER S. LANGSTON

While making my postal rounds, I delivered bulk mail from an insurance company addressed to "The safe driver at . . ."

The next day, one of my customers kicked the envelope back to me after having written on it, **"No such person at this address."**

—JOHN REDDY

Adding a funny hat to your pajamas at home—weird.
**Adding a funny hat to your pajamas at work—chef.**

—COMEDIAN JULIEANNE SMOLINSKI

The mayor of a city in a developing country invited the mayor of another municipality over for dinner. The visitor was very impressed with his host's affluent lifestyle and asked him how he managed to live so well. "See that bridge?" the first mayor said, pointing to a distant structure. "I skimmed five percent."

The visiting mayor went home and six months later invited the first mayor over to his new mansion. The first mayor was astounded and asked his friend the secret to his sudden wealth.

"See that bridge?" the second mayor said, gesturing out the window.

"What bridge?" asked the visitor.

"One hundred percent."

—ATUL T. SURAIYA

My father, who edited engineering proposals, got into a heated argument with an inflexible engineer. At the root of it was the latter's description of a harbor waterway project. He'd written: ". . . and there shall be three berths, each with its own berth control tower."

—DAVID USHER

*These businesses know it's all in how they sell themselves:*

- Ad from a local gym: "If you're not satisfied with the results at our club, we'll give you your old body back."

—ELEANOR GUYNN

- Sign spotted at a shoe store: "If we don't have your size, it's free!"

—STUART MCLENNAN

I think my fellow EMTs rely too heavily on abbreviation when they write their reports. One read: "Medic broke wind, and entered residence."

—D.B.

In the newsletters for the town house complex I manage, I always reiterate the rules, especially the one about cleaning up litter and debris. Unfortunately, my choice of words is not always the best. I once wrote "It is the resident's responsibility to keep their private area clean. Please refer to the rules and regulations if you don't know where your private area is."

—KELLY FRAMPTON

"How are things going?" one bee asked another.

"Terrible," the second bee replied. "I can't find any flowers or pollen anywhere."

"No problem," said the first bee. "Just fly down this street until you see all the cars. There's an outdoor bar mitzvah going on with lots of flower arrangements and fresh fruit."

"Thanks!" said the second bee, buzzing off.

Later, the two bees ran into one another, and the second bee thanked the first bee for the tip.

The first bee asked, "But what's that thing on your head?"

"My yarmulke," the second bee replied. "I didn't want them to think I was a wasp."

—LAURA BARILOTTI

**? What's gray, crispy and hangs from the ceiling?**

An amateur electrician.

— DOC BLAKELY

**Personally, I don't believe the world owes me a living— although for the amount I get, an apology would be nice.**

Carpenters from California, Missouri and New York showed up at the White House for a tour. The chief guard welcomed them with special enthusiasm because the front gates were in need of repair. He asked each person to come up with a bid. The California carpenter measured and figured and finally said, "Well, $400 for materials, $400 for my crew and $100 profit for me, $900 total." The guard nodded and turned to the carpenter from Missouri.

That man took out his tape measure and a pencil and after some calculating said, "It'll cost $700—$300 each for materials and my crew and $100 profit for me." The guard thanked the man and turned to the carpenter from New York.

Without hesitation, the New Yorker said, "This job will run $2700."

The guard gasped. "You didn't even measure or do any calculating," he replied. "How do you figure it'll be so expensive?"

"Simple," said the New York carpenter. "$1000 for me, $1000 for you, and we hire the guy from Missouri."

—DAN ANDERSON

Real estate agents are pulling out all the stops to sell homes. One particularly ingenious marketing ploy promised: "Free coffee with any purchase."

—MATTHEW KORNEGAY

A fellow teacher left the restroom and said, "You know you work in an elementary school when the graffiti on the bathroom wall says, 'I love my mom.' "

—LYNNETTE LOTT

"How's this for a severance package—five minutes to grab all you can get."

Four friends were arguing over whose dog was the smartest.

The first man, an engineer, called to his dog, "T Square, show your stuff." The dog trotted over to a desk, pulled out a paper and pencil and drew a perfect triangle.

The next guy, an accountant, called to his dog, "Slide Rule, go ahead." The canine went to the kitchen, nibbled open a bag of cookies and divided the contents into four equal piles.

The next man, a chemist, beckoned his dog, Beaker, to show what he could do. The dog went to the fridge, took out a quart of milk and poured out exactly eight ounces into a measuring cup.

The last man was a government worker. "Coffee Break," he hollered to his dog, "go to it." With that, the dog jumped to his feet, soiled the paper, ate the cookies and drank the milk.

—PAMELA JASON

While I was performing in a show outside Chicago, there was a gentleman who could often be found hanging around the lobby. Everyone called him the Marquis. One day, I asked the artistic director if he'd gotten the nickname because he looked so distinguished. "No," he replied. "We call him the Marquee because he hangs out in front of the theater and is usually lit."

—MARK REANEY

## Overheard:

**Sam:** I used to be a stand-up comedian before I worked here.
**Joe:** I never would have guessed that.
**Sam:** Ask me why I quit.
**Joe:** Why did you . . .
**Sam:** Timing!
**Joe:** . . . quit?

—MIKE SMITH

The insurance industry loves its acronyms. The first time I saw the term proof of ownership was in a client's file that read: "Insured has POO on damaged items."

—AMANDA SCHAEFER

How bad is business in our area?
A sign on an office building declared,

## "Buy one building, get one free."

—JAN PEARSON

The secretary to her boss on the intercom: "There's a gentleman on the line who would like to inquire into the secret of your success."

After a prolonged silence, the boss asks in a hoarse voice: "Is he a journalist or a policeman?"

—ALDA FERREIRA ANTUNES

One coworker's advice to another: "It's one thing to stick your neck out for a person, but when you stick your neck out for a system, it's just a waste of neck."

—KATHRYN HARGROVE

Two friends were discussing their family histories when one of them lamented that he knew precious little about his roots. "I've always wanted to have my family history traced," he said, "but I can't afford to hire someone. Any suggestions?"

"Sure," replied his friend. **"Run for public office."**

—EARLE HITCHNER

## Why teachers take the summer off . . .

**Teacher:** What does the word plummet mean?

**Eight-year-old student:** A girl plumber.

—JACLYN TISCHHAUSER

Our cable customer complained that his service was acting up. When I asked what the trouble was, he explained, "Connectile dysfunction."

—ROBERT MCCULLOUGH

While my brother, a helicopter pilot, was attending a training exercise, another chopper pilot prematurely released his payload and dropped it 300 feet to the ground. No one was hurt, but the next morning, this label was placed next to the release switch on all the copters: For Desk Job, Push Here.

—VIRGINIA SPENCER

"Do you believe in life after death?" the boss asked one of his employees.

"Yes," replied the employee.

"That's okay then," said the boss. "Because while you were at your grandmother's funeral yesterday, she popped in to see you."

—GERALD MCDADE

After a long day at the office, I couldn't wait to get home. "Once I leave here, I never think about work," I told a colleague. "Have you ever felt that way?"

"No," he said. **"It doesn't take me that long."**

—STEVE BENNETT

# QUOTABLE QUOTES

**"WHEN A MAN TELLS YOU THAT HE GOT RICH THROUGH HARD WORK, ASK HIM: 'WHOSE?'"**

—DON MARQUIS

"You go to your TV to turn your brain off. You go to the computer when you want to turn your brain on."

—STEVE JOBS

"Confidence is 10 percent hard work and 90 percent delusion."

—TINA FEY, IN *VOGUE*

"A professional is one who does his best work when he feels the least like working."

—FRANK LLOYD WRIGHT

"I read about a new 24-hour daycare that's opening in India. Yeah, it's pretty cute: Instead of playing telephone, the kids just play tech support."

—JIMMY FALLON, ON *LATE NIGHT*

"I couldn't wait for success, so I went ahead without it."

—JONATHAN WINTERS

**"I USED TO WANT TO BE A LAWYER, BUT I DIDN'T WANT TO HAVE HALF MY BRAIN SUCKED OUT."**

—MAX WALKER

"Be nice to nerds. Chances are you'll end up working for one."

—CHARLES SYKES

"Hard work never killed anybody, but why take a chance?"

—EDGAR BERGEN

**"IN THE BUSINESS WORLD, THE REARVIEW MIRROR IS ALWAYS CLEARER THAN THE WINDSHIELD."**

—WARREN BUFFET

" 'PUL OVR.' You mean that was from you?"

# LAW AND DISORDER

A cop stops a drunk late at night and asks where he's going.

"I'm going to a lecture about alcohol abuse and the effects it has on the human body," slurs the drunk.

"Really? Who's giving that lecture at one in the morning?"

"My wife."

—ALFRED MANSOOR

Recently, my husband was pulled over for not wearing his seat belt. But Irv was convinced he was being railroaded.

"Officer," he said in his most condescending voice. "How do you know I'm not wearing a seat belt if my windows are tinted?"

"Because, sir," replied the officer, "it's hanging out the door."

—JUDITH FINKLER

A man went to the police station and asked to speak to the burglar who had broken into his house the previous night.

"You'll get your chance in court," the desk sergeant told him.

"I have to know how he got into the house without waking my wife," pleaded the man. "I've been trying to do that for years!"

—SUZANNE DEVONSHIRE

The police stops a car on the freeway and asks the driver: "Sir, may I ask for how long have you been driving with defective back lights?"

The driver gets out, looks at the back of his car, then falls on his knees and begins to sob.

"Oh come on," the policeman consoles him, "it's not so serious as that."

"Oh no? And my trailer and motorboat? Where are they?"

—ERIKA ANTALNÉ FILUS

A police officer at the scene of a car accident saw a horrible sight smashed against the inside of the windshield. Quickly he called for help and then ran over to the car.

"Are you badly hurt?" the officer asked the man in the front seat.

"Nah," replied the driver, "but this pizza is a mess."

—TIM CARVER

The irate driver waved his speeding ticket in the air at the police officer who'd just written him up.

"What am I supposed to do with this?" the man yelled.

"Hang on to it," the cop replied.

## "When you collect four, you get a bicycle."

—MARILYN MACDONALD

The police stop a motorist for a roadside check.

"What are all those daggers in your car?" the trooper asks.

"I'm a juggler."

"I don't believe it," the policeman says, "show me something."

The juggler gets out and starts tossing the daggers.

Another car passes by with two buddies in it. Says one: "Boy, I'm glad I quit drinking. Look what they've come up with in place of a breathalizer."

—MARGIT MOLNÁR

When a neighbor's home was burglarized, I decided to be more safety conscious. But my measly front-door lock wasn't going to stop anyone, so I hung this sign outside: "Nancy, don't come in. The snake is loose. Mom."

—SHARON BOUSCHER

A male and female driver are involved in a horrific collision. Amazingly, both escape unhurt, though their cars are written off.

As they crawl from the wreckage, the man sees the woman is blonde and beautiful. She turns to him and gushes breathily: "We shouldn't have survived that. Maybe it's a sign from God that we're meant to be together!"

Sensing he could be on to a good thing, the man stammers back, "Oh yes, I agree completely!"

"And look," she continues. "Though my car was destroyed, this bottle of wine is intact, too! It's another sign. Let's drink to our love!"

"Well, okay!" says the man, going with the moment. She offers him the bottle, so he downs half and hands it back. "Your turn," he says.

"No, thanks," says the woman, "I think I'll just wait for the police."

A man notices that his wife is missing. He goes to the police station to file a report. The officer on duty asks him to describe her.

"Okay," he says, "but only on one condition. You cannot show it to her afterward."

—TÍMEA LÁDI

A report came into the police station about a house break-in and the theft of five bagpipes. The desk sergeant took the information and said, "We'll send out an investigator." Then, turning the complaint over to one of his officers, he suggested, **"I'd check out the neighbors on either side."**

—JACK TRACY

The police arrived and found a woman dead on her living room floor with a golf club next to her body.

An officer asked the husband, "Is this your wife?"

"Yes," he replied.

"Did you kill her?"

"Yes," he replied.

"It looks like you struck her eight times with this 3-iron. Is that correct?"

"Yes," the husband replied, "but put me down for a five."

—GRAHAME JONES

I was prosecuting a case involving a man charged with driving under the influence. The defense counsel was beginning to lose his cool with the police witnesses and implied that they had gotten their facts wrong.

"People do make mistakes, don't they, Officer Lock?" he demanded of one witness.

"Yes, sir," came the reply. "I'm Officer Webster."

The defense lost.

—ROGER GRAY

While fishing off a beach in the Caribbean, a lawyer struck up a conversation with an engineer. The lawyer explained that his house had burnt down and he had lost everything. Happily, though, the insurance company had paid out a sizeable sum for the damage.

"That's a coincidence," remarked the engineer. "My house and all my belongings were destroyed in a flood, and my insurance company also coughed up for everything."

The lawyer looked confused. "How do you start a flood?" he asked.

—ROHAN CHOPRA

"It's bad enough I get overruled at home—
but here also, Sharon?"

The prosecutor was relentless as he badgered the witness. "What did the accused do when he learned the jewelry was part of a stolen hoard?" he demanded.

"He did what any honest man would do," said the witness.

"And what was that?"

"I didn't think you'd know."

—GENE NEWMAN

Walking into a lawyer's office, a man asked what the barrister's rates were.

"Fifty dollars for three questions," the lawyer stated.

"Isn't that awfully expensive?" the man asked.

"Yes," the lawyer replied. **"What's your third question?"**

—MATT FRANKLIN

The murder suspect's trial wasn't going well, so his attorney resorted to a trick. "Ladies and gentlemen of the jury," he said, "I have a surprise for you. In one minute, the real murderer will walk into this courtroom."

Stunned, the jurors looked toward the door, but nothing happened. The lawyer chuckled.

"I lied. But because you all looked with anticipation, that proves there is reasonable doubt as to my client's guilt, and I insist that you find him not guilty."

The jury retired to deliberate, then returned a verdict of guilty.

"But you must have had some doubt," bellowed the lawyer. "You all stared at the door."

"Oh, we looked," said the jury foreman. "But your client didn't."

—SARAH BROWN

I mentioned to an unmarried friend of mine—an attorney—that he should attend a singles mixer for lawyers. He hated the idea.

"Why," he asked, "would I want to date someone who's been trained to argue?"

—AUGUST MURPHY

It had been a nerve-wracking experience for my attorney husband. He was working with the FBI on a federal sting operation. Worried for his safety, they put him under protective surveillance. Finally the agency told him they had rounded up all the criminals and were lifting the surveillance. A few days later my relieved spouse was on the phone, telling his brother about the whole adventure.

"Did you happen to mention to the FBI that you have an identical twin?" his horrified brother interrupted. "Who lives next door?"

—J.D.

At a courtroom, the judge interrogates the defendant, "So, you declare you suffer from a disease that affects your memory?"

"That's right," answers the defendant.

"And how does this disease affect you?"

"It makes me forget things."

"So, could you give us an example of something you've forgotten?"

—CARMEM MARIA F. LIMA

I work in a courthouse, so when I served jury duty, I knew most of the staff. As I sat with other prospective jurors listening to a woman drone on about how long the process was taking, a judge and two lawyers passed by, giving me a big hello. A minute later, a few maintenance workers did the same. That set off the malcontent: "Just how long have you been serving jury duty?"

—KATHLEEN DERBY STURDIVANT

**? Where do vampires learn to suck blood?**
Law school.

MARILYN MILLER

A group of prospective jurors was asked by the judge whether any of them felt they had ever been treated unfairly by an officer of the law.

"I once got a ticket for running a stop sign," offered one woman, "even though I definitely came to a complete stop."

"Did you pay the ticket?" the judge questioned.

"Yes."

"If you thought you were innocent," the judge went on, "why didn't you contest it?"

"Your Honor," she replied, "there have been so many times I didn't get a ticket for running a stop sign that I figured this evened things out a little."

—CHARLES KRAY

JURY OF ONE'S PEARS

**My father still keeps the first dollar he ever made—
and the police still keep the machine he made it with.**

—NATALIA SKORUBSKI

I was in small-claims court when I listened in on the case of a woman who held a good job but still had trouble paying her bills on time. "Can't you live within your income?" asked the judge.

"No, Your Honor," she said. "It's all I can do to live within my credit."

—RALPH WARTH

A woman is brought to court after stealing from a supermarket.

"Mrs. Krupnick," says the judge, "what did you take?"

"Just a small can of peaches," she answers. "There were only six peaches in the can."

"Six peaches . . . hmm . . . I sentence you to six nights in jail, a night for each peach."

The woman is crushed. She's about to collapse to the floor when her husband, seated in the gallery, leaps to his feet.

"Your Honor," he shouts, "she also stole a can of peas!"

Farmer Joe is suing a trucking company over injuries he suffered in an auto accident.

The company's lawyer begins his cross-examination. "Is it true that at the accident scene you said, 'I'm fine'?"

"Let me explain," pleads the farmer. "I had loaded my mule Bessie into the trailer and was driving down the road when this truck crashed into us. I was hurt bad. When the trooper came on the scene, he heard Bessie moaning. He took one look at her, pulled out his gun and shot her right between the eyes.

"Then he walked over to me with his gun and asked, 'Your mule was in such bad shape I had to shoot her. How are you?' "

I grew up in the Midwest and was very unsure of myself when I went to take the road test for my driver's license. The examiner was a woman who said nothing to me the entire time, except for giving terse instructions to turn left, right and parallel park.

When we returned to the parking lot, she looked at me. "I'm going to give you your license," she said. "But don't ever ask to borrow my car."

—MARILYN CASEY

A priest, a doctor and a lawyer were stuck behind a particularly slow group of golfers. After three holes, they complained to the greenskeeper.

"Sorry, guys. That's a group of blind firefighters," the man explained. "They lost their sight saving our clubhouse from burning down last year, so we let them play here anytime for free."

"That's so sad," the priest said. "I'll say a special prayer for them tonight."

"Good idea," the doctor agreed. "I'm going to contact my ophthalmologist buddy and see if there's anything he can do for them."

"I guess," the lawyer said. "But why can't they play at night?"

"There's good news and bad news," the divorce lawyer told his client.

"I could sure use some good news," sighed the client. "What is it?"

"Your wife isn't demanding that your future inheritances be included in the settlement."

"And the bad news?"

"After the divorce, she's marrying your father."

—STEVE KEUCHEL

"Why do you want to divorce your wife?" demands the judge.

"Because every night she whispers in my ear: 'It's time for you to go home.'"

—FERENC L.

An airliner was having engine trouble, and the pilot instructed the cabin crew to have the passengers take their seats and prepare for an emergency landing. A few minutes later the pilot asked the flight attendants if everyone was buckled in and ready.

"All set back here," came the reply, "except for one lawyer who's still passing out business cards."

—BRYAN STINCHFIELD

One day, First Lady Eleanor Roosevelt visited a penitentiary. When FDR asked where she was, he was told, "She's in prison."

"I'm not surprised," Roosevelt responded. "But what for?"

A letter I received while presiding over traffic court: "Dear Judge, I am sorry to be so slow in sending in the money for my traffic ticket. But having gotten recently married, I am just getting back on my feet."

—JAMES R. WALTON

During his spare time my brother, an attorney, volunteers on his town's fire and rescue squad. When I mentioned this to a friend, he smiled and said, "Let me get this straight. Your brother is a lawyer and an EMT? **So he doesn't have to chase the ambulance—he's already in it?**"

—DALE BIRCH

# TECH TALK

The computer in my high school classroom was acting up. After watching me struggle with it, a student explained that my hard drive had crashed. So I called IT. "Can someone look at my computer?" I asked. "The hard drive crashed."

"We can't just send people down on your say-so," said the specialist. "How do you know that's the problem?"

"A student told me."

"We'll send someone right over."

—THOMAS ELLSWORTH

My heart sank as I read the spam that began, "By opening this e-mail, you have activated the Amish computer virus." Then I realized that not only was my computer in jeopardy, so was my reputation, as it continued, "Since the Amish don't have computers, this works on the honor system. Please delete all your files. Thank you."

—TRACIE WALKER

Outraged by the high fees her computer consultants charged, a friend asked my dad which service he used. "My sons," he said. "They both have degrees in computer science."

"So you get that kind of work done for nothing," the friend marveled.

Dad smiled. "Actually, I figured it cost me about $40,000 for my kids to fix my computer for free."

—RYAN GILLESPIE

A computer once beat me at chess, but it was no match for me at kickboxing.

—EMO PHILIPS

I finally convinced my mother that it was a good idea for her to learn to text. Her first message to me: "Whereisthespacebar?"

—CINDY RODEN

Using my cell phone to access the Internet, I was plagued by pop-up ads. Blocking them required a confusing process that ended with this confirmation: "Your cell phone number has been added to be removed."

—CRAIG YOUNG

A fuming customer called the shop from where he'd bought his new laptop. "You've cheated me," he told the salesgirl. "I can't transfer a single file from my old PC to this one."

"Please tell me what you did," said the salesgirl.

"Oh, you think I don't know?" said the customer. "Okay . . . I right-clicked the mouse on the filename in my old PC and selected the Copy option. I then clicked Paste on the new laptop."

"So did you first get the file into a pen-drive or something?" the confused salesgirl enquired.

"No. I disconnected the mouse and plugged it into the lousy laptop you sold me."

—ISHITA JAIN

I took a two-year-old computer in to be repaired, and the guy looked at me as though he was a gun dealer and I'd brought him a musket. In two years, I'd gone from cutting-edge to Amish.

—JON STEWART

Heating water for pasta, I kept checking to see if it had begun to boil. My 13-year-old son shook his head. "Stop doing that, Mom. It's like that saying: 'A watched website never loads.'"

—JANIE HANSON

While lobbying for her very own computer, my 12-year-old niece asked her father, "When you were a kid, how old were you when you got your own computer?"

"There were no computers when I was a kid," he said.

She was aghast. **"Then how did you get on the Internet?"**

—HERBERT BUETOW

**?** **What is a computer's first sign of old age?**
Loss of memory.

---

As a debate arose over a question in our literature class, my professor turned to his iPhone. Scrolling through the search results, he wondered aloud, "What did professors do before Wikipedia?"

A fellow student shouted out, "Know things."

—DANIEL MITCHELL

"I'm thinking of buying a tanning bed," I told my mother-in-law.

"You should talk to my son's friend Craig to see if he has one. Apparently, he's selling all his belongings on the Internet."

Confused, I walked away, wondering, Who do we know named Craig? Then it hit me—Craigslist.

—JENNIFER GILBERT

I've invented Twofacebook, the antisocial network. You start being friends w/entire world & defriend people one by one.

—ANDY BOROWITZ, ON *TWITTER*

My mother is still having trouble understanding just how her iPhone works. Upon receiving a text, she said to me, "Quick, give me a pencil so I can write this down."

—SANDRA NOVELLA

A man tells his doctor, "Doc, help me. I'm addicted to Twitter!"

The doctor replies, "Sorry, I don't follow you . . ."

—CHRISTINE SCHRUM

**"Don't look now . . . I think we're being followed!"**

One of my third graders came to school sobbing.

"My son's upset because he couldn't complete his math homework," explained his mother, holding his hand.

"Why?" I asked.

"Unfortunately," she said, "Our computer doesn't have Roman numerals."

—MARSHALL LERESCHE

During the Cold War, I was an interpreter in the air force. We were testing a computer that purportedly could translate Russian into English, and vice versa. We began by uttering this English phrase, "The spirit is willing, but the flesh is weak."

The Russian translation came out, "Vodka horosho, no myaca slabie." Or, in English, "The alcohol is good, but the meat is poor."

—SAM CONNOR

## FACEBOOK VS. DAD

**David D.:** Where to buy chicken casserole supplies

**Stephen D.:** Dad, this is Facebook, not Google. Try again.

**David D.:** Where to buy chicken casserole supplies

**Stephen D.:** Dad, no.

**David D.:** Where to buy supplies for chicken casserole

**Stephen D.:** Are you serious?

**David D.:** Chicken casserole supply store

**Stephen D.:** Fiesta Mart, 8130 Kirby Drive.

Saddam Hussein decided that he wanted to document his memoirs, so he asked his guard for a stenographer.

The guard came back a little while later with a laptop computer instead.

"No thanks," Saddam said. "I'm a dictator."

—GORDON HALSEY

The Department of Defense has a Contact Us link on its website, inviting readers to pose any question they want. One guy did just that: "So do you have any top secret information you would like to tell me? I am doing a project for my senior economics class and was just wondering. . . . E-mail me back."

—CHRIS PIETRAS

I recently found this great website that conducts cyber garage sales. You list the stuff you want in the subject line of an e-mail, send it off and wait for a response. Recently, I sent a note saying I was in the market for three particular items. In short order, I got three responses. Nobody had any of the items I'd listed. But they all found what I'd written amusing: "Wanted—Envelopes, piano bench and one night stand."

—SANDI SIMMONS

*Recently, I eavesdropped on two women chatting.*

**Woman 1:** I just joined an online dating website.
**Woman 2:** Really? Did you find any matches?
**Woman 1:** Yeah, my ex-husband.

—YOLANDA GOMEZ

After a minor accident, my mother accompanied me to the emergency room. Now, I'm five feet, three inches tall and pleasantly plump—not exactly Brad Pitt. But when the nurse asked for my height and weight, I blurted out, "Five-foot-eight and 125 pounds."

As the nurse paused to check her eyesight, Mom leaned over to me. "Sweetheart," she gently chided, "this isn't the Internet."

—BOB MEYERSON

Not only am I getting better at Tetris, but I'm loading more dishes into my dishwasher than I ever thought possible.

—COMEDIAN PEGGY O'BRIEN

My wife and I had been texting back and forth when unbeknownst to her, I had to stop for a few minutes. When I returned to my cell phone, I found this text message awaiting me: "CGYT?"

"Huh?" I responded.

She shot back: "Cat Got Your Thumb?"

—PAUL BROUN

A customer stepped up to my bank window requesting her account balance.

"Sorry," I told her, "but I'm afraid our computer is down."

"Ah," she said understandingly. **"Terminal depression."**

—ADAM PARRY

Some texts should not be abbreviated. Case in point, this message from my cousin, which simply read "A J D." I was confused until my father called to tell me, "Aunt June died."

—MELODIE DIAZ CRUZ

My niece in college posted her latest Facebook status: "I am going home so Mom can take me to the doctor and tell him what's wrong with me."

—VIKKI SMITH

*The Last Facebook status update:*

- . . . standing over a patient in the operating room, scalpel in hand, wishing he hadn't lied on his résumé about being a surgeon. Here goes nothing . . .

- . . . in a marriage-counseling session with his wife, wondering what the score of the football game is. Go, Eagles!

- . . . thinks that if his boss doesn't like him sleeping on the floor of the office, then his boss shouldn't have gotten such comfy carpets.

- . . . needs help robbing the bank over on the corner of Main and Willow. Any takers? Be there around noonish.

—FRANK FERRI

My ex and I had a very amicable divorce. I know this because when I wrote the Facebook status "I'm getting a divorce," he was the first one to click Like.

—COMEDIAN GIULIA ROZZI

Usually there's no computer problem I can't solve.
But I met my match when I turned on my machine and was greeted with the message
**"Keyboard not detected. Hit any key to continue."**

—ALEX HU

"Wow!" said my tween daughter. She was reading the nutritional label on a bag of cheese curls. "These must be loaded with cholesterol. The label lists it as Omg!"

My tween son took a look. "That's zero milligrams, not 'Oh My God.'"

—KATHY TORRENCE

Soon after texting a girl I liked, I received this response: "ERROR 3265 SWRVICE UNAVAILABLE." She never could spell.

—CHRISTOPHER THOMPSON

I just read a great novel on my Kindle. It was a real button-presser.

—PETER BACANIN

**?** **How do you make friends with a computer?**
Bit by bit.

**"Let's face it . . . we're dial-up people in a broadband world."**

**"W**hat are those?" asked my younger sister. She had just spotted the old encyclopedias our mother had unearthed in the basement.

Mom tried to explain the concept of an encyclopedia to her, but it just wasn't clicking. She finally blurted out, "It's like Google, but in a book."

—AMBER SANDOE

**M**y father just e-mailed me a note: "This e-mail is from my new computer. Does it look better? Love, Dad."

—JANICE KYLE

I didn't realize how good I was with computers until I met my parents.

—COMEDIAN MIKE BIRBIGLIA

*What's the biggest problem Facebookers are confronting? Parents signing up. Here's how one writer's Facebook status updates now read, ever since he was friended by his mom:*

- Scott is making good, well-informed decisions.

- Scott is going to bed at a very reasonable hour.

- Scott is drinking only on occasion, and even then it's just one or two.

- Scott quit smoking several months ago without any apparent difficulty.

- Scott is making large, regular contributions to his savings account.

- Scott is making yet another home-cooked meal, avoiding fast food as usual.

- Scott is not gaining weight, and his clothes fit just fine.

—SCOTT A. HARRIS

# LIFE
## and
# DEATH

"All the art of living lies in a fine mingling of letting go and holding on."

—HAVELOCK ELLIS

# WHAT'S UP, DOC?

The man goes to see his doctor because he has a lettuce leaf sticking out of his ear.

"Hmmm," the doctor says. "That's strange."

The guy replies, "I know. And that's just the tip of the iceberg."

—GREG COX

Carpooling to work, a man got increasingly stressed with each trip. After a week of panic attacks, he went to the doctor. "I'm fine on the bridges, in the traffic and even in the dark after a long day," the man explained. "But when I go through tunnels with those four other guys, I feel like I'm gonna explode. Am I crazy?"

"Not at all," the doc said. "You just have Carpool Tunnel Syndrome."

—NOAH HART

Two surgeons and a dermatologist were having lunch in the hospital cafeteria when the first two doctors began to laugh hysterically.

"What's so funny?" the dermatologist asked, confused.

"Sorry, you wouldn't understand," one of the surgeons said. "It's an inside joke."

—ANDREW HARGADO

I sat in the doctor's waiting room watching a young mother try desperately to control her three loud children.

"They're not a very good advertisement, are they?" she groaned apologetically.

A man muttered, "Only if you're advertising contraceptives."

—BARBARA WOOTTON

"You're right. Without fail, it's tied inversely proportionally to the Dow."

To treat my bronchitis, the doctor pulled out his prescription pad.

"This is for Zithromax," he said as he wrote, then muttered, "Mypenzadyne."

I was familiar with the antibiotic Zithromax but not the other drug. "What's Mypenzadyne?"

He looked confused for a second, then enunciated slowly, "My pen is dying."

—JASON ARMSTRONG

Did you hear about the student who flunked medical school? **His handwriting was legible.**

—SAMUEL SILVER

**Q**uasimodo goes to a doctor for his annual checkup. "I think something is wrong with your back," the doctor says.

"What makes you say that?" Quasimodo asks.

"I don't know," the doctor replies. "It's just a hunch."

**W**hile making rounds, a doctor points out an X-ray to a group of interns. "As you can see," she says, "the patient limps because his left fibula and tibia are radically arched. Michael, what would you do in a case like this?"

"Well," ponders the intern, "I suppose I'd limp too."

—TRAVIS CRAM

**D**ad arrived promptly at 9:30 for his appointment with the proctologist. An hour and a half later, he finally saw the doctor. Afterward, the doctor gave him this advice: Avoid sitting for a long time. Dad grumbled, "The only time I do that is when I come here for an appointment."

—MARK GOULDING

**W**e brought our newborn son, Adam, to the pediatrician for his first checkup. As he finished, the doctor told us, "You have a cute baby."

Smiling, I said, "I bet you say that to all new parents."

"No," he replied, "just to those whose babies really are good-looking."

"So what do you say to the others?" I asked.

"He looks just like you."

—MATT SLOT

It had been a long time—seven years to be exact—since my friend Brian had been to see his doctor. So the nurse told him that if he wanted to make an appointment, he would have to be reprocessed as a new patient.

"Okay," said Brian, "reprocess me."

"I'm sorry," she told him. "We're not accepting any new patients."

—BARBARA SAMPSON

Five years had passed since my last eye exam, and I could tell it was definitely time for another. My vision was getting fuzzier. The eye doctor's receptionist gave me a pre-examination form. One entry was "Reason for visiting the doctor." I couldn't resist. I wrote, "Long time no see."

—DAWN ARTESE

In hindsight, I should have been more specific. I was visiting my doctor as part of a checkup after surgery. "When can I resume regular activities?" I asked.

He blushed slightly. "You mean like sex?"

"Actually, I was thinking of vacuuming."

—PATTY KEBERLE

Just before I was to have a physical, my doctor handed me an examining gown.

"I can never remember with these things," I commented. "Does the opening go in the front or the back?"

He shrugged. **"Doesn't matter. You can't win either way."**

—KATHRYN FOLSOM

"He came out of the surgery okay, but Mr. Sims is on his way back to the recovery room after seeing the *BILL*."

As soon as I stepped into the urgent-care facility in my hometown, I could see the place was packed with patients. The nurses and doctors all seemed frazzled. Just how frazzled I discovered when a doctor walked into the room, pulled out his examination light, pointed it in my ear and instructed, "Say, 'Ah.'"

—KRISTIN EGERTON

The huge backlog in the doctor's waiting room was taking its toll. Patients were glancing at their watches and getting restless.

Finally, one man walked to the receptionist's station and tapped on the glass.

She slid back the window, saying, "Sir, you'll have to wait your turn."

"I just had a question," he said dryly. "Is George W. Bush still president?"

—DICK FLOERSHEIMER

Panicking when her two-year-old swallowed a tiny magnet, my friend Phyllis rushed him to the emergency room.

"He'll be fine," the doctor promised her. "The magnet should pass through his system in a day or two."

"How will I be sure?" she pressed.

"Well," the doctor suggested, "you could stick him on the refrigerator, and when he falls off, you'll know."

—MARIE THIBODEAU

**?** **What did the green grape say to the purple grape?**
Breathe! Breathe!

PAUL LEWIS

I was dancing at a party when I tripped and stubbed my toe. A few days later, my toe swollen and purple, I went to see a podiatrist. I told him how I hurt myself and admitted to feeling foolish at how clumsy I was. X-rays showed my toe was not broken, and the doctor said he didn't need to do anything. Anxious to speed the healing, though, I asked whether there was something I could do: "Should I soak it? Put it on ice? Is there anything you recommend?"

He smiled: "Take dancing lessons."

—BARBARA NANESS

The cardiologist at the ER had bad news for me: "You're going to need a pacemaker."

Later, the nurse filling out the admission form began to ask me the standard questions: "Have you ever had mumps, measles, etc.?"

Seeing how upset I was, she put down the clipboard and took my hand. "Don't worry," she said soothingly. "This kind of heart problem is easily fixed, and your life will be much better as a result."

I felt reassured until she continued: "Do you have a living will?"

—ROBERT PORTER

Doing rounds, a new nurse couldn't help overhearing the surgeon yelling, "Typhoid! Tetanus! Measles!"

"Why does he keep doing that?" she asked a colleague.

**"Oh, he likes to call the shots around here."**

—HEATHER BRESS

After I warned the nurse taking blood that it would be very hard to find a vein on me, she said, "Don't worry. We've seen worse. Last year we had a girl come in to get a blood test for her marriage license, and we had to stick her six times in four places before we got anything."

"Yes, I know," I said. "That was me!"

—CONNIE DOWN

A man is recovering from minor surgery when his nurse comes in to check on him.
"How are you feeling?" she asks.
"I'm okay," he says, "but I didn't like the four-letter word the doctor used during surgery."
"What did he say?" the nurse asks.

"Oops."

—ROBERT REA

While attending a convention, three psychiatrists take a walk. "People are always coming to us with their guilt and fears," one says, "but we have no one to go to with our own problems."

"Since we're all professionals," another suggests, "why don't we hear each other out right now?" They agree this is a good idea.

The first psychiatrist confesses, "I'm a compulsive shopper and deeply in debt, so I overbill patients as often as I can."

The second admits, "I have a drug problem that's out of control, and I frequently pressure my patients into buying illegal drugs for me."

The third psychiatrist says, "I know it's wrong, but no matter how hard I try, I just can't keep a secret."

—AMY BERTMAN

I was at a sporting event when a gentleman behind me gasped and fell over. I climbed over the seat and first established that he was breathing. As I checked the man's pulse rhythm, a woman stormed over and pushed me away.

"Step aside! I'm a nurse!" she shouted. She then proceeded to examine the man.

As I retreated to my seat, I announced, "When you get to the part about 'Call a doctor,' I'll be here."

—KARL J. PIZZOLATTO, MD

Helen goes to a psychiatrist and says, "Doctor, you've got to do something about my husband—he thinks he's a refrigerator!"

"I wouldn't worry too much about it," the shrink replies. "Lots of people have harmless delusions. It will pass."

"But, Doctor, you don't understand," Helen insists. "He sleeps with his mouth open, and the little light keeps me awake."

—JOHN R. LOPEZ, JR.

Shorthand is the norm in the medical field when taking notes. For example, HTN stands for "hypertension." I did a double take, though, when a diabetic patient came into the ER suffering from high blood sugar levels. The nurse had charted the complaint as "Out of control BS."

—SHERRELL LAM

As my friend, an anesthesiologist at a hospital, passed by an operating room, she noticed it was being set up for a breast augmentation procedure. So she popped her head inside.

"What's going on?" she asked a nurse.

The nurse's reply: "They're making a mountain out of a molehill."

—YO KLEIN

**My doctor told me to stop having intimate dinners for four. Unless there are three other people.**

—ORSON WELLES

**A** man was very skeptical of chiropractors, but when no other treatment seemed to relieve the chronic pain in his back, he decided to give it a try. Before his first appointment, he told the chiropractor of his reservations, but after a few adjustments, he felt better than he had in years.

"What do you think now?" the chiropractor asked.

"Well," the man replied, "I guess I stand corrected."

—CHRIS J. DEIGHAN

## Doctor, Doctor

*. . . I keep having déjà vu.*
**Doc:** Didn't I see you yesterday?

*. . . my son swallowed a roll of film.*
**Doc:** Let's wait and see what develops.

**O**ur nine-year-old son had hurt his leg, and my husband, an automobile engineer, took him to the family doctor. "Please repair him," my husband said to the doctor. Then realizing he hadn't used the right words, he tried again, "I mean, fix him right . . . I mean, do whatever you like to call it, but put him back on the road!"

—BELA AGARWAL

**A**lthough my doctor stopped by my hospital room to see me every day while I was recuperating from an operation, he hardly said two words to me. But once, after being unusually chatty, he remarked, "It sure has been nice talking to you. All my other patients are in comas."

—LILLIAN B. MCDADE

The doctor was trying to encourage a gloomy patient.

"You're in no real danger," he said. "Why, I've had the same complaint myself."

"Yes," the patient moaned, "but you didn't have the same doctor!"

—LILLIAN M. DECKER

After a checkup, a doctor asked his patient, "Is there anything you'd like to discuss?"

"Well," said the patient, "I was thinking about getting a vasectomy."

"That's a big decision. Have you talked it over with your family?"

"Yes, we took a vote . . . and they're in favor of it 15 to 2."

Waiting in the ER for test results, I overheard a doctor talking to another patient. "So," he said, "I understand you've lost the ability to speak. When did this happen?"

—ANNA GOODBERLET

As a student nurse, I had to give an injection to a 79-year-old male patient. I asked which hip he preferred the shot in. He wanted to know if he really had a choice. I told him he did. He looked me straight in the eye and said, "yours!"

—KAY NYLAND

**? Why is a hospital gown like health insurance?**

You're never as covered as you think you are.

At the podiatrist's office, my mother listed all her ailments.

"I have a lot of health issues," she told him. "Crohn's disease, thyroid problems, high cholesterol—that's just the tip of the iceberg. But I have one saving grace: I don't drink."

The doctor nodded understandingly: **"You should."**

—GREGORY MARK SPITZER

Joe was suffering from excruciating headaches. The doctor told him he could cure the headaches, but it would require castration. "You have a rare condition that causes pressure to build up against your spine," the doctor explained. "This, in turn, causes headaches. The only cure is surgery." Joe was shocked but had the operation.

When he left the hospital, Joe was depressed, so he stopped at a men's shop for a new suit. The salesman eyed him and said, "44 long?"

"That's right," Joe said. He tried on the suit, and it fit perfectly.

"How about a new shirt?" the salesman asked. "Let's see, a 34 sleeve and 16½ neck ought to do it."

"Right again," Joe said. "You're simply amazing."

"While we're at it, how about some new underwear?" the salesman suggested. He eyed Joe's waist and said, "Size 36."

"Nope, you finally missed one," Joe said, chuckling. "I wear size 34."

"You couldn't possibly," replied the salesman. "Underwear that tight would create a great deal of pressure against your spine and cause one heck of a headache."

—BRYAN ELDRING

**"I suggest you just call yourself a white horse with black stripes and avoid years of expensive therapy."**

**W**hile my friend Cheryl was working as a receptionist for an eye surgeon, a very angry woman stormed up to her desk.

"Someone stole my wig while I was having surgery yesterday," she complained. The doctor came out and tried to calm her down.

"I assure you no one on my staff would have done such a thing," he said. "Why do you think it was taken here?"

"After the operation, I noticed the wig I had on was ugly and cheap-looking."

"I think," explained the surgeon gently, "that means your cataract operation was a success."

—RAHEELA A. SHAIKH

A doctor was addressing a large audience in the Grange Hall.

"The material we put into our stomachs is enough to have killed most of us sitting here years ago. Red meat is awful. Soft drinks corrode your stomach lining. High-fat diets can be dangerous. But there is one food that causes the most grief and suffering for years after eating it. Can anyone tell me what that is?"

After several seconds of quiet, a 75-year-old man in the front row raised his hand and softly said, "Wedding cake."

—CHARLES NICKEL LACEY

John tells his shrink, "Last night I dreamed you were my mother."

"How do you feel about that?" asks the psychiatrist.

"I haven't had time to think about it," says John. "I overslept this morning. Then I remembered I had an appointment with you, so I gobbled down a Coke and a cookie and came straight here."

"A Coke and a cookie?" the doc replies. "You call that breakfast?"

A young doctor friend, a newcomer to Maine, reported that the famous New England reticence was more powerful even than he had anticipated. Called to the home of an elderly woman who had pneumonia, he asked her if she had ever had penicillin. "Oh, yes," she replied. Thus reassured, he gave her a shot. Later that night, his patient was admitted to the hospital with a severe penicillin reaction. After several hours, the danger passed. Standing at the patient's bedside, our relieved friend was discussing with another doctor the sheer bad luck of encountering such a major reaction in one who had taken the drug before.

Suddenly the patient interrupted him. "Now, Doctor, you don't need to feel bad about this. Why, the last time I had a penicillin shot, the very same thing happened."

—JANE HUNT

**Patient:** Lately I feel that everyone takes advantage of me.
**Psychiatrist:** Don't worry about it. That's perfectly normal.
**Patient:** Really? Thanks a lot, Doc. How much do I owe you?
**Psychiatrist:** How much do you have?

—TOM MCQUEEN

Looking down at his patient, the doctor decided to tell him the truth: "I feel I should tell you that you are a very sick man. The situation is complex and confusing, and things don't look too promising. Now, is there anyone you would like to see?" Bending down toward the man, the doctor heard a feeble yes. "Who is it?" asked the doctor. In a slightly stronger tone, the sufferer said, "Another doctor."

—CHARLES WADSWORTH

## DIVINE LAUGHTER

My teenage daughter is not the most knowledgeable Catholic. After my husband bought me a gorgeous cross pendant, Michelle gushed, "It looks like something the Pope's wife would wear!"

—BECKY O'NEILL

When my elderly friend told me about a lesbian she knew and how wonderful she thought she was, I figured it was the perfect time to fess up to her.

"You know, I'm a lesbian too," I said. "And so is the gal I live with."

"I didn't know that," she said, and then, shrugging, added, "but everyone has a right to their own religion."

—DIANE ROBINETTE

**Why there aren't church hecklers.**

**W**hen my brother was a pastor in Thunder Bay, he usually put the title of his upcoming sermons on a street-side bulletin board. One week, his sermon was "Hell, the Forgotten Horror." Underneath was the permanent message printed at the bottom of the sign: "A Warm Welcome to All."

—JUDY MAJOR

As our priest went along the line of worshippers, giving them Holy Communion, he saw what he thought was a communion wafer lying on the floor. Because, as blessed bread, it had to be consumed, he popped it into his mouth.

"Mummy, Mummy," the small boy next to me cried out. "The vicar's eaten my *Save the Children* badge."

—PAM DAVIES

The high school was using our church's Family Life Center for its annual spring banquet. Since we wanted to keep the teenagers confined to the gym and out of the main building, someone suggested posting a Do Not Enter sign on the door. I knew that wouldn't work, so I put up another sign that did the job. It read, Prayer Room.

—BILL DENHAM

A businessman who needed millions of dollars to clinch an important deal went to church to pray for the money. By chance he knelt next to a man who was praying for $100 to pay an urgent debt. The businessman took out his wallet and pressed $100 into the other man's hand. Overjoyed, the man got up and left the church. The businessman then closed his eyes and prayed, "And now, Lord, that I have your undivided attention . . ."

—BRENDAN P. EDET

As church secretary, I prepare the bulletin for each week's services. One Sunday morning, I heard snickering from the pews. Quickly grabbing the bulletin, I found the cause. The sermon title for that day was: **"What Makes God Sick: Pastor Joe Smith."**

—DEANNE BLAND

Spotted on a church marquee: **"Love your enemies;
After all, you made them."**

—BARBARA TELECSAN

A doctor, an engineer and a lawyer were arguing over whose profession was the oldest.

"On the sixth day, God took one of Adam's ribs and created Eve," said the doctor. "So that makes him a surgeon first."

"Please," said the engineer. "Before that, God created the world from chaos and confusion, so he was first an engineer."

"Interesting," said the lawyer smugly, "but who do you think created the chaos and confusion?"

—LYNDELL LEATHERMAN

It was Easter Sunday at our military chapel. The pastor called the children to the front and told them the story of how Jesus was crucified by the Romans, his body placed in a tomb and the front covered by a stone.

"But on the third day," he said, "the stone was rolled away, and Jesus was not there. Do you know what happened next?"

One kid shouted, "Jesus turned into a zombie and went after the Romans!"

—LOU DELTUFO

At a church social one evening, as the secretary's husband served me a cup of coffee, I noticed a nasty-looking purplish bruise under one of his fingernails. "Dave," I asked teasingly, "just what did you say when that happened?"

"Hoover," he answered.

"Hoover?" I repeated.

"Yes," he said. "That was the biggest dam I could think of."

—NOREEN WEBSTER

"I need to speak to you about these emoticons you keep slipping into the scriptures."

One Sunday my teenage son was in church. When the collection plate was passed around, he pulled a dollar bill from his pocket and dropped it in.

Just at that moment, the person behind him tapped him on the shoulder and handed him a $20 bill. Secretly admiring the man's generosity, my son placed the $20 in the plate and passed it on. Then he felt another tap from behind and heard a whisper: "Son, that was your $20. It fell out of your pocket."

—MARY C. LOWE

In my role as a pastor of a Baptist church, I visited a woman with a bad back. She was down on the floor, the most comfortable position she could find. I asked if she would like me to lay my hands on her back and pray, to which she said "yes."

I quickly felt a significant surge of warmth from her back, and I excitedly explained that this could be God performing the healing process.

"I'm sorry to disappoint you," she said, "but that is my hot water bottle."

—DAVID HILL

By the time the morning service was to begin, only one man was in the church. The minister said to him, "It looks like everyone has slept in. Do you want to go home or should I preach the sermon?"

The man replied, "When I go to feed the chickens and only one comes, I still feed it."

The minister took that as a yes, mounted the pulpit and delivered an hour-long sermon. At the end, he asked the man what he thought. His answer: "When I go to feed the chickens and only one comes, I don't give it the whole bucket!"

—RENEE DAGG

A young boy arrived late to his Sunday school class. He was normally punctual so the teacher asked him if anything was wrong.

"No," said the boy. "I had planned to go fishing, but my father told me that I had to go to church instead."

Impressed, the teacher asked the boy if his father had explained why it was more important to go to church than to go fishing.

"Yes," the boy replied. "He said he didn't have enough bait for both of us."

—CHAU PEI YING

Many years ago, we had a beloved archdeacon in our parish church. His wife was very supportive and sometimes, when he was preaching from the pulpit, she would hand him a note. It might have been about a thought that had just occurred to her or something she wanted to make sure he hadn't forgotten. He would often read these notes to the congregation.

I remember one Sunday when the rector read the note his wife had just handed to him: "Dear, your wig is crooked."

—ALBERT JAMES

After 48 years in the priesthood our elderly parish priest was due to retire.

Throughout the months leading up to his retirement there were celebrations at the church as well as at the elementary school where my children were in attendance.

On the Sunday of Father's second last Mass my nine-year-old daughter, Meagan, whispered to me, "Father must be getting really excited."

"Why?" I asked.

"Because NOW he can get married!" Meagan replied.

—ELAINE KIRBYSON

Sam shows up at a revival meeting, seeking help.

"I need you to pray for my hearing," he tells the preacher.

The preacher puts his fingers on Sam's ears and prays and prays. When he's done, he asks, "How's your hearing now?"

"I don't know," says Sam. **"I don't go to court till next Tuesday."**

—JAMES HOSKIN

A woman I know quite well told me outside church, "I'm ashamed to admit it, but I can never remember your husband's name."

"It's Neville," I said, adding jokingly, "just remember it rhymes with devil."

The next time we met, she called, "Good morning, Nathan."

"Where did you get Nathan from?" I asked, bemused.

"You told me it rhymed with Satan," she replied.

—JANE DAVIS

My husband, who is a pastor, was having a conversation with our children about the differences between religions.

My daughter, Sarah, wanted to know the differences between a Roman Catholic priest and a minister. He explained that one of the biggest differences is that priests do not marry. My husband also said that a priest devotes his life to God, and that marriage and a family would distract him from his duties. But a pastor, who also dedicates his life to serve God, can marry. "It's like having your cake and eating it too," he said.

Sarah's response: "Priests can't eat cake?"

—JO-ANNE TWINEM

Spotted in my church bulletin: "**The church will host an evening of fine dining, super entertainment and gracious hostility.**"

—SHARON OWEN

Two old friends, Quinn, a Christian, and Sophie, a Jew, are having lunch when Sophie says to her friend, "Don't take this personally, but how can you honestly believe that Jesus walked on water, turned water into wine or made the infirm walk?"

"Well, look at it this way," says Quinn, "maybe there were rocks beneath the water's surface, and he crossed over them. Or maybe there was a little wine in the water, and that's what someone tasted. As for healing the sick, maybe they just needed his guidance. But who are you to question my beliefs? What about Moses parting the Red Sea?"

Sophie nods thoughtfully. "Wasn't that something?"

—PATTI BROWNE

An angel appears at a faculty meeting and tells the dean, "In return for your unselfish and exemplary behavior, the Lord will reward you with your choice of infinite wealth, wisdom or beauty."

"Give me infinite wisdom!" declares the dean, without hesitation.

"Done!" says the angel before disappearing in a cloud of smoke.

All heads now turn to the dean, who sits surrounded by a faint halo of light. "Well," says a colleague, "say something brilliant."

The dean stands and, with the poise of Socrates, opines, "I should have taken the money."

—HENRY MIXON

"Not another Powerpoint sermon!"

Once a year our church group holds a sale to raise money for its youth group. At our last sale, just as we finished putting everything out, a middle-aged man arrived in a huff. Growling, he yanked two sports coats and a few suits off the clothes rack, then stomped over to the cash, where a puzzled volunteer asked if everything was all right.

"I don't know what the world is coming to," the man said in an injured tone. "This is the third year my wife's given my favorite clothes to this church sale!"

—MAGGIE THEISS

Shortly after the evening service at my local church began, there was a torrential downpour.

After the rain stopped, I heard the persistent drip of water as it trickled through the roof.

This was very distracting, and at the end of the service I told the minister: "I have just spent the evening listening to the most annoying drip I've ever heard!"

I only realized what I had said when I saw the shock on the minister's face.

—ISHBEL MACKAY

My church choir was in the middle of rehearsing a requiem for an upcoming concert and, with the concert date fast approaching, our director was getting a little more picky about various elements of our performance. During one rehearsal he interrupted us to comment on the fact that we were breathing in the wrong spot.

"No, no, no!" he said. "There is to be no breathing after death."

—TRACY BAXTER

An elderly Frenchman is in his local church's confessional.

"Forgive me Father, for I have sinned," he says. "During the Second World War a beautiful woman knocked on my door and asked me to hide her from the enemy. I put her in the attic."

"No need to ask forgiveness for that, my son," says the priest. "It was a wonderful thing to do."

"Yeah," says the man, "But she started offering me sexual favors in return, and I went along with it."

"People in wartime situations do funny things. If you are truly sorry for your actions, you are forgiven."

"That's a great load off my mind," says the pensioner. "May I ask you a question?"

"Of course."

"She's getting on a bit now. Should I tell her the war is over?"

—WAYNE EVANS

One night, the lights went out in the church I used to attend right when the minister was reading the Bible. He then recommended that those present pray in silence until the situation was resolved.

Among the faithful was an elderly gentleman who slept regularly during service. In this precise moment of silence and darkness, he woke up and yelled, "Damn them all! They went away and left me here alone!"

—SAMUEL SCHULKA

A few years ago, I successfully completed the process and was about to be ordained as a pastor in our church. We shared this joyous news with my mother-in-law who took great pride telling her friends.

We laughed, however, when we heard what she was saying to them: "Bob is being pasteurized."

—BOB BADDELEY

After a frustrating morning of getting our four children packed up and off to church, we attempted to get everybody into the front pew with minimal disruption. We were sitting down when the pastor mentioned a scripture that said children were a blessing, like a quiver full of arrows.

"Yeah," my wife replied,

## "Sometimes I just can't wait to shoot them."

—THOMAS ZIMMERMANN

Our new minister pleaded with the congregation for help on a church project. After weeks with few takers, he called our house with this deeply felt, if not diplomatic, request: "I am scraping the bottom of the barrel for volunteers and wonder if you might be able to help?"

—VIRGINIA NIFONG

A young parish minister about to deliver his first sermon asked a retired cleric for advice on how to capture the congregation's attention.

"Start with an opening line that's certain to grab them," the older man said. "For example: 'Some of the best years of my life were spent in the arms of a woman who was not my wife.'" He smiled at the younger man's shocked expression before adding, "She was my mother."

The next Sunday, the young clergyman nervously clutched the pulpit rail in front of the congregation. Finally he said, "Some of the best years of my life were spent in the arms of a woman." He was pleased at the instant reaction—then became panic-stricken. "But for the life of me, I can't remember who she was!"

—GIL HARRIS

# QUOTABLE QUOTES

"How can I believe in God when just last week I got my tongue caught in the roller of an electric typewriter?"

—WOODY ALLEN

**"IF THERE IS NO GOD, WHO POPS UP THE NEXT KLEENEX?"**

—ART HOPPE

"They say such nice things about people at their funerals that it makes me sad that I'm going to miss mine by just a few days."

—GARRISON KEILLOR

"The secret to a good sermon is to have a good beginning and a good ending, then having the two as close together as possible."

—GEORGE BURNS

**"CLOUD NINE GETS ALL THE PUBLICITY, BUT CLOUD EIGHT ACTUALLY IS CHEAPER, LESS CROWDED AND HAS A BETTER VIEW."**

—GEORGE CARLIN

"To lose one parent may be regarded as a misfortune; to lose both looks like carelessness".

—OSCAR WILDE

**"I DON'T PRAY BECAUSE I DON'T WANT TO BORE GOD."**

—ORSON WELLES

"When did I realize I was God? Well, I was praying, and I suddenly realized I was talking to myself."

—PETER O'TOOLE

"What I look forward to is continued immaturity followed by death."

—DAVE BARRY

"According to our records, you once Googled God's name in vain."

# PASSING ON

Carl and Abe are two old baseball fanatics. They agree that whoever dies first will try to come back and tell the other one if there's baseball in heaven.

One evening, Abe passes away in his sleep. A few nights later, Carl hears what sounds like Abe's voice. "Abe, is that you?" he asks.

"Of course it's me," Abe replies.

"I can't believe it," Carl whispers. "So tell me, is there baseball in heaven?"

"Well, I have good news and bad news," Abe says. "The good news is, yes, there's baseball in heaven. The bad news is you're pitching tomorrow night!"

—DAVID DANGLER

An old lady visits her recently deceased husband at the funeral parlor. When she sees him, she starts crying.

"He's wearing a black suit," she tells the undertaker. "It was his dying wish to be buried in blue."

The undertaker apologizes, saying that it's normal practice to put bodies in a black suit, but he'll see what he can arrange.

Next day, the woman returns and there is her husband resplendent in a blue suit. "That's wonderful," she says. "Where did you get it?"

"Well," explains the undertaker, "After you left, a man about your husband's size was brought in wearing a blue suit. His wife said that he wanted to be buried in black and was there anything we could do?"

The old lady smiles at the undertaker.

"After that," he continues, "It was simply a matter of swapping the heads."

—ROBERT A'COURT

The flyer invited me to a seminar entitled: **"Everything You Ever Wanted to Ask About Cremation."** The location: **Smokehouse BBQ.**

—L.J.

My wife's mother had a great sense of humor and was "Grama" to everyone in our extended family. When she died at 87 after a lingering illness, three generations of the family gathered at the funeral home.

When the visitors had left, my wife approached the casket with three of our grandchildren and told them that they could touch Grama if they wished.

The two older children timidly touched Grama's arm and quickly pulled away. But when two-year-old Keiran was lifted up, she firmly placed both hands on Grama and declared, "Yup, she's dead all right!"

Grama would have just loved it.

—PERCY AFFLECK

Sue passed away, so her husband, Bubba, called 911. The operator said they'd send someone out right away. "Where do you live?" asked the operator.

Bubba replied, "At the end of Eucalyptus Drive."

The operator asked, "Can you spell that for me?"

There was a long pause. Finally Bubba said, "How 'bout if I drag her over to Oak Street, and you pick her up there?"

On our way to a funeral home for the viewing of a friend's father, I reminded my three-year-old daughter to be quiet and respectful. And she was—right up to the end, when she asked, "Mommy, who's the man in the treasure chest?"

—JENNIFER TURK

**A**s an Anglican priest, I was asked one Sunday to inter the ashes of an elderly couple who had died just weeks apart. The service was held in a small, rural cemetery that I wasn't familiar with, so after the service, I wandered around, looking at headstones. Most carried the usual epitaphs: "Safe in the arms of Jesus," "At rest." One stood out, though. Its message: "This was not my idea!"

—REV. KEN BOND

**P**atrons of a pub mourned the passing of the bar's mutt, Spot. They cut off his tail and framed it as a memorial. Spot was about to enter heaven when St. Peter stopped him. "Heaven's a place of perfection," said the saint. "You deserve to enter, but not without your tail. Go back and retrieve it."

In the middle of the night, Spot scratched on the door of the pub.

"It's the spirit of our dear Spot!" exclaimed the bartender. "What can I do for you?"

Spot said he needed his tail to enter heaven.

"Oh, sorry," the barkeeper replied, "but my liquor license doesn't allow me to retail spirits after hours."

—CRAIG IAN DUFT

Losing my father was bad enough. So imagine my surprise when I spotted my name in the obituaries instead of his. I had to phone a friend.

"Did you see the report of my death in the paper?" I asked.

"Yes," he said. **"Where are you calling from?"**

—RALPH WARTH

**"** I'm afraid of the dark, so could I get one with a night light?**"**

A man walked into a bar and saw an old friend dejectedly nursing a drink. "You look terrible," the man said.

"My mother died in March and left me $10,000," the friend replied. "Then in April my father died and left me $20,000."

"Gee, that's tough, losing both parents in two months."

"Then to top it off," the friend said, "my aunt died last month and left me $50,000."

"How sad."

"Tell me about it," the friend continued. "So far this month, nothing."

—RACHEL SIDELL

A preacher was contacted by the local funeral director to hold a graveside service for someone with no family or friends. The preacher started out early for the cemetery but quickly got lost, making several wrong turns.

He arrived a half hour late, and the hearse was nowhere in sight. Seeing some workmen eating lunch, the preacher went to the open grave nearby and found the casket already in the ground. Taking out his prayer book, he read the service.

As he was returning to his car, he overheard one workman ask another: "Should we tell him it's a septic tank?"

—COLIN ENGLISH

I accidentally rear-ended a car while driving our funeral home van. The couple was unhurt, but the driver seemed shaken. When we exchanged information, I remarked that her name sounded familiar. "That's because we made our funeral arrangements with you six months ago," she said, "but we never thought you'd come looking for us!"

—DAVID K. SHEWCHUK

A teacher, a petty thief and a lawyer all died and went to the Pearly Gates. Because of crowding, St. Peter told them they had to pass a test before ascending any further. Addressing the teacher, he asked, "What was the name of the famous ship that hit an iceberg and sank?"

"The Titanic," she answered, and St. Peter motioned her into heaven.

The thief was next. "How many people died on that ship?" St. Peter asked.

"Gee, that's tough," the man replied. "But luckily I just saw the movie. The answer is 1500." St. Peter let him through.

Then St. Peter turned to the lawyer. "Name them."

—LYNDELL LEATHERMAN

One of the deceased at our funeral home was a farmer who had suffered a heart attack while helping a cow in labor. The headline on his obituary read **"Mr. Jones Dies While Giving Birth to a Calf."**

—DEBORAH HUDSON

**A** man died and went to hell. As he passed sulfurous pits and shrieking sinners, he saw his town's most notorious lawyer snuggling up to a beautiful model. "This is so unfair," the man bellowed to the devil. "I have to roast and suffer for all eternity, and that sleazy lawyer gets to spend it with her?"

"Silence!" the devil demanded, jabbing his trident at the man. "You must pay your penance, and the model must pay hers!"

—ANGELA M. SALIANI

**I** sat down at the computer to prepare the order of service for my much-loved uncle's funeral. After the opening prayers came the first hymn. As I typed in, "Dear Lord and Father of Mankind," the little computer man on Microsoft Word popped up: "It looks like you're writing a letter. Would you like help?"

—LYN MCCULLOCH

**W**hile my parents were making their funeral arrangements, the cemetery salesman pointed out a plot that he thought they would like. "You'll have a beautiful view of the swan pond," he assured them.

Dad wasn't sold: "Unless you're including a periscope with my casket, I don't know how I'm going to enjoy it."

—CAROL BEACH

A few weeks after the death of my father-in-law, I found my seven-year-old son crying in bed. His grandmother had died the previous year, and he was taking it all very hard.

"You know, Kyle," I said, "when we die, we'll get to see Grandma and Grandpa again in heaven."

With tears spilling down his face, Kyle cried, "That's easy for you to say. You don't have that long!"

—FARREL CHAPMAN

On the way to the funeral home to confirm arrangements for my mother's funeral, my dad, my sister and I were trying to decide on appropriate music for the visitation. Dad said that Mom loved the Bee Gees, so I said we could have their music playing softly in the background.

Laughing, my sister said, "I think we should skip 'Stayin' Alive.'"

—KAREN HOLTZ

An undertaker friend organized the funeral of a man who was to be buried on his birthday. To mark the sad irony, the man's young grandson asked if he could put a card in the coffin.

My friend happily agreed—not realizing it was a musical card. As the coffin was carried through the church, the movement knocked the card off the departed's chest and triggered its mechanism.

The service remained dignified, but its solemnity was somewhat undermined by a tinny voice singing "Happy birthday to you, happy birthday to you" from somewhere inside the coffin.

—ALAN HASKEY

**In hell, you have to find the start to Scotch tape over and over.**

—MOLLY_KATS, ON TWITTER

As director of a small funeral home I handle most functions, including answering the telephone. One day, I picked up the phone and said: "Funeral services. This is Wayne speaking. How may I help you?"

"I think I have the wrong number," the woman replied. "I was calling a travel agency, but I don't want to go where you'd send me!"

—WAYNE BOYLAN

My mom was telling me about her prearranged funeral and about the urn she chose, which cost more than the cremation itself. She described it in great detail, then added,

## "Wait 'til you see me in it!"

—KATHY SMITH

On returning home from a funeral, I told my daughter and son-in-law that I didn't want a service when I died, just a tea. "A nice tea," I added.

There was a pause, then my son-in-law piped up, "Would it be possible for you to do some baking and put it in the freezer?"

—FLOSS THOMSON

Lying on his deathbed, a loving husband was wavering between life and death when he thought he smelled chocolate chip cookies baking. They were his favorite, so he dragged himself out of bed, crawled to the kitchen and was just reaching up to take a cookie off the plate when his wife slapped his hand with a spatula.

"Don't touch!" she commanded. "They're for the funeral."

—COLIN TAYLOR

When my quiet grandfather, Jack, passed away, my family gathered at the funeral parlor to pay their respects. Since we are a large family spread out over much of the continent, the atmosphere became quite festive as family members reunited. My grandmother, who always loved a party, could not help but comment: "Well, isn't this just like old times; we're all here having a great time, and there's Jack, over in the corner, not saying a word!"

—DARREN WHITE

I was passing a funeral parlor with my four-year-old daughter just as the hearse pulled in.

"What's that funny-looking car?" she asked.

"It's used to take dead people to the cemetery," I explained.

She glanced at the driver and his stern-looking assistant dressed in black and replied, "Oh, yes, I can see one sitting in the front."

—SUSAN FITCH

*You'd die of embarrassment if these phrases appeared in your obituary:*

- "She leaves behind a brother and 117 cats."
- "Passed away in a failed stunt that has already been viewed more than 40 million times on YouTube."
- "Was always quick to point out others' grammatical errors."
- "Survived by his parents and his animatronic wife, Elizabot."

—CHRIS WHITE

My husband, a funeral director, was at work one day when our daughter, Patricia, was in a car accident. Coming out of shock, Patricia found a woman hovering over her.

"Is there anything I can do?" the woman asked.

"Call Anderson's Funeral Home," Patricia moaned.

The woman looked surprised. "Oh, you'll be all right, dear," she reassured her.

—KAY ANDERSON

# JUST for LAUGHS

The world has always been fragile. Just ask the dinosaurs.

—MICHAEL SHANNON

# HUMOR IN UNIFORM

**S**oon after being transferred to a new duty station, my marine husband called home one evening to tell me he would be late. "Dirty magazines were discovered in the platoon quarters," he said, "and the whole squad is being disciplined."

I launched into a tirade, arguing that marines should not be penalized for something so trivial.

My husband interrupted. "Honey, when I said 'dirty magazines,' I meant the clips from their rifles hadn't been cleaned."

—MILLIE COURTIS

**A** navy man and new to town, I found a barbershop with a sign in the window that read "Military Cuts Our Specialty."

I walked in and told the barber exactly what I wanted: "A standard Naval Aviator. Do you know what that is?"

"Sure," he said. "Blocked in the back, 2.5 inches on the sides, and you expect me to make you better-looking than you actually are."

—CHRIS FARRINGTON

**M**y brother was vacationing on a beach when he heard someone call to him using an old nickname from his navy days. My brother couldn't place the face, but the man insisted they had served together, and he even told stories of their days on the high seas.

Soon the memories came flooding back. As they reminisced, the friend revealed that he had received a medical discharge.

"What was wrong?" my brother asked.

His friend replied dolefully, "The doctor said that I suffer from amnesia."

—RUTH FALCÃO

**H**ome on leave from Iraq, my step-grandson was showing off his abs. Not to be outdone, my husband thumped his prodigious stomach and bragged, "I still have my six-pack. It's just six inches deeper."

—K.H.

**O**n his first day of army basic training, my husband stood with the other recruits as the sergeant asked, "How many of you are smokers?"

Several men raised their hands.

"Congratulations!" he said. "You just quit."

—CHRISTINA KOSATKA

When I invited an army friend to a party, I offered to give him directions. He declined, saying, "I've invaded three countries in five years. I think I can find your house."

—RITA BRISTOL

I taught a class on human relations to basic trainees, where we discussed how everyone deserves respect. At the end of one class, their training instructor stuck his head in and shouted, "Okay, you babies, let's get out of here. We have places to go!"

As he passed me, an airman mumbled, "Now back to reality."

—PAT FERRY

A sign your child has been raised in a military family: My daughter was playing with Barbie dolls. Seeing a lone Ken doll among all those women, I said, "Poor Ken, he's the only guy."

"Yeah," she said. "All the rest of the dads are deployed."

—MELINDA KUNZ

Have you heard of World War II?" my husband asked our six-year-old grandson.

"Well, I've heard of it," Bronson said tentatively. "But I can't remember what game it is."

—LORNA PACKARD

"You have four cavities!" barked the naval dentist, looking at my X-rays. He grabbed a huge steel syringe and shot both sides of my mouth full of novocaine. He then looked at the X-rays and then my mouth. Then back at the X-rays and again at my mouth. Then he sat down.

"I have good news and bad news," he said. "The bad news is, these are not your X-rays. The good news is, you're cured."

—PAUL STANIC

During Operation Iraqi Freedom, the marines in my squadron went out of their way to make themselves feel at home. In front of the trailers that served as our administrative offices, the gravel front "lawn" was carefully groomed and lined with a border of sandbags. In the center was a wooden sign: "Keep Off the Grass!"

—BETHANY KOSHUTA

On my grandfather's first day of boot camp, his drill sergeant brought the unit to attention and asked, "Is anyone here musically inclined?"

Seeing an easy job in the offing, three soldiers, including Grandpa, raised their hands.

"Good," said the sergeant. "You three will move the commander's piano."

—BRANT DEICHMANN

Being color-blind excluded me from certain jobs in the marines. But my recruiter took pity on me and gave me a color vision test book to memorize before taking the eye test. Later that week, I took the test and successfully recited each color in the book. The doctor was impressed.

"Excellent," he said. "Just one thing: I opened the book on page two."

—DAN KEHL

My sister had her kindergarten class write to my nephew Nate and his marine buddies serving in Afghanistan. Nate's favorite letter was this one: **"Dear Marine, thank you for being in the army."**

—ANNE KOPP

In Iraq, my sergeant was not happy with the speed with which I was moving MREs (Meals Ready to Eat) from a non-air-conditioned building into an air-conditioned tent.

"Hurry up," he yelled. "The sun's going to ruin those MREs. Have you ever had a bad MRE?"

Moving a pallet, I grunted, "You ever had a good one?"

—CHRIS NEWTON

"Before we launch an attack, let's make sure we unfriend them first."

I took my four-year-old great-grandson to the Leavenworth
National Cemetery, where my husband is buried.
While there, we heard the sound of a bugle.

"What's that?" asked Jeremiah.

"'Taps.' They play it at a soldier's burial," I explained.

A minute later came the honorary rifle salute.
With eyes bugging out, Jeremiah asked,

## "Did they shoot him?!?"

—JACKI CAHILL

After a snowstorm buried our neighborhood, my wife called the hospital and said she could not make it to work because all the roads were blocked.

"We'll send the National Guard," she was told. "They'll get you out."

"Good luck with that," she said. "My husband's in the National Guard, and he can't get out either."

—BRIAN WOOLSHLEGER

On the first morning of boot camp, our unit was dragged out of bed by our drill sergeant and made to assemble outside. "My name is Sergeant Jackson," he snarled. "Is there anyone here who thinks he can whip me?"

My six-foot-three, 280-pound brother, who had enlisted with me, raised his hand. "Yes, sir, I do."

Our sergeant grabbed him by the arm and led him out in front of the group. "Men," he said, "this is my new assistant. Now, is there anyone here who thinks he can whip both of us?"

—ROBERT NORRIS

As we set out on patrol in Afghanistan, my platoon leader was torn between which route to take.

"One road will probably get us ambushed," he said. "But if we take the second, we'll likely run into IEDs. What do you think?"

I considered our options, then gave him my suggestion: **"I say we take a couple of days off."**

—RYAN HENDRICKS

**A**s a dental officer in the air force, I was treating a recruit. As he lay prone in the chair, I asked him a question about his pain level. He responded, "Yes."

"Yes is not enough," I said.

With that, he leaped out of the chair, stood at attention and shouted, "Yes, sir!"

—DOUGLAS C. BOYD, DMD

**W**ith the help of a balky 16-ton forklift, I was loading containers onto an aircraft bound for Afghanistan. Our sergeant major stopped by to ask how I was doing.

"It would be easier if the idiot who owns the red truck would move it," I complained.

"Okay," he replied. "I will."

—CPL. DEBBIE MACNEIL

**A** sergeant was trying to sell us new soldiers on the idea of joining the airborne division. His pitch clearly needed work.

"The first week, we separate the men from the boys," he began. "The second week, we separate the men from the idiots. The third week, the idiots jump."

—JIMMY RONEY

While standing watch in the coast guard station in Juneau, Alaska, I got a call from the navy. They had lost contact with one of their planes and needed us to send an aircraft to find it. I asked the man where the plane had last been spotted so we would know where to search.

"I can't tell you," he said. "That's classified."

—ALFRED MILES

My son, stationed in Japan, dated a Japanese girl who spoke little English. That didn't faze him until the night she announced, "I have chicken pox."

My son didn't know whether to run or get her to the hospital. Then he noticed her shiver.

"You don't have chicken pox," he said. "You have goose bumps."

—NEJLA WILLIAMS BODINE

During inspection, a female officer asked our very nervous corporal what his first general order was.

"Sir, this cadet's first general order is to take charge of this post and all government property in view, sir!"

Excellent response, except for one detail.

"Do I look like a ma'am or a sir?" the officer demanded.

The startled corporal bellowed back, "Sir, you're a ma'am, sir!"

—MATT WAKEFIELD

*Overheard: Two veterans chatting about the Korean War.*

**First Guy:** What knife did you use over there?

**Second Guy:** I didn't have a knife. I figured that if I needed to use it, I was too close to the enemy.

—KAITLYN WILDE

When a coworker from my old firm was deployed abroad, the boss placed this sticky note on his door: "Stepped out. Back in 12 months."

—JOYCE HUANG

The five-year-old boy at our school was from a military family: His mother was a fighter pilot, and his father served in Afghanistan.

"Do you know my full name?" he asked me.

"No, I don't," I said.

"It's James Phillip Thomas Steven Harold Jackson the Third. But my mother calls me Steven. My father's full name is James Phillip Thomas Steven Harold Jackson the Second."

"And what does your mother call him?"

"Cupcake."

—M. JACKSON

When my very pregnant niece, a sergeant in the New York Army National Guard, accidentally knocked over a glass of water, one of her soldiers volunteered to help clean it up. As he was mopping up the mess, an officer walked in.

"Private, what's going on in here?" he asked.

To the officer's horror, the private replied, "Sir, the sergeant's water broke, and I'm helping her clean up."

—DAVID HEATON

During my time in the navy, everyone was getting KP or guard duty except me. Not wanting to get in trouble, I asked the ensign why.

"What's your name?" he asked.

"Michael Zyvoloski."

"That's why. I can't pronounce it, much less spell it."

—MICHAEL J. ZYVOLOSKI

"The war games are going well, sir. We've just reached level four, where our M-16s turn into fire-breathing, tank-eating dragons."

**M**y boot camp platoon was last in line to eat, and our impatient drill sergeant was in such a hurry that he ran up to each of us, shouting, "Don't waste time tasting . . . just swallow!"

—NELSON GOULD

**S**oon after my son, a marine, was deployed to Afghanistan, he called and spent much of the time describing the abject poverty of the people who lived there. When he calmed down, I asked what I thought was a simple question: "What time is it there now?"

That set him off again. "I'm ten and a half hours ahead of you," he replied. "That's how poor this country is. It can't even afford a full time zone."

—ROBIN LYNN MULL

**M**y Afghan interpreter loved using American idioms, even though he rarely had a firm grasp of them. One day, during a meeting with village elders, I asked him to leave out the chitchat and get to the point.

"I understand, sir," he said. "You want me to cut the cheese."

—PATRICK HAWS

**D**uring World War II, my friend and I were in a nightclub when two men in uniform asked us to dance. Feeling it was our patriotic duty, we joined them on the dance floor. "So," I asked my partner, "what branch of the service are you in?"

He mumbled, "The Greyhound bus service."

—MARGIE SCHATZ SHEEHAN

**M**y second graders were assigned the task of writing thank-you cards to soldiers serving in the Middle East. One of them wrote, "Thank you for protecting us! I hope we win!"

—GEORGINA MCCARTHY

**O**ne of my soldiers in Afghanistan wanted to surprise his wife with flowers for Valentine's Day, but he was afraid she would see the bill before the flowers arrived. So I offered to put the flowers on my credit card and have him pay me in cash. The plan worked beautifully until after Valentine's Day, when my wife received a $120 florist bill but no flowers.

—MICHAEL MERRILL

**K**etchikan, Alaska, gets more than 12 feet of rain each year. But the day we visited our grandson Josh, who is stationed at the coast guard base there, the sun decided to shine.

"It's so sunny," I marveled.

"We don't say it's sunny here," corrected Josh. "We refer to it as 'cloud failure.' "

—PATRICIA HARPER

**M**ail delivery at our base in Japan was irregular at best, so everyone would call the post office to see if the mail had arrived. Tired of the constant calls, the post office manager announced that he would raise a white flag to signal that mail had arrived. That idea was scrapped after soldiers kept calling to ask if the white flag was up.

—DONALD DEREADT

I stood next to a retired Marine Corps general at a military trade show, watching a cutting-edge robot navigate an obstacle course.

"I bet you didn't have these back in your day," I said.

"Oh, we did," he answered. **"They were called privates."**

—CHARLIE BAISLEY

# QUOTABLE QUOTES

"I wanted to join the army. The sign said 'Be All That You Can Be.' They told me it wasn't enough."

—JAY LONDON

"I was in the army, and to me it was like a newsreel."

—MEL BROOKS

"Leaders can let you fail and yet not let you be a failure."

—STANLEY MCCHRYSTAL, RETIRED U.S. ARMY FOUR-STAR GENERAL

"Seeing your name on the list for KP or guard duty when you're in the army is like reading a bad review."

—ROBERT DUVALL

"I WAS IN THE ROTC. OF COURSE, ROTC STOOD FOR 'RUNNING OFF TO CANADA.'"

—JAY LENO

"YOU, YOU, AND YOU . . . PANIC. THE REST OF YOU, COME WITH ME."

—U.S. MARINE CORPS GUNNERY SGT.

"Whoever said the pen is mightier than the sword obviously never encountered automatic weapons."

—GEN. DOUGLAS MACARTHUR

"When I lost my rifle, the army charged me $85. That's why in the navy, the captain goes down with the ship."

—COMEDIAN DICK GREGORY

My 11-year-old granddaughter was helping me sort through a pile of papers on my desk. After flipping through page after page of letters from the Department of Veterans Affairs, she turned to me with, I believe, a new appreciation.

**"Grandma," she asked, "exactly how many affairs did you have with veterans?"**

—SYLVIA FORCE

I was in our local VA hospital when a clerk began scolding a veteran who'd lit up a cigarette in a no-smoking area.

"Sir!" she barked. "When did you start smoking?"

The conversation came to a halt when he replied, "In Vietnam, right after that first bomb dropped."

—DOROTHY KREIPKE-MILLER

My unit was building shelves in the USO at an army camp in Kuwait with the help of a very gruff marine sergeant.

"Sergeant, where do you want this?" I asked, holding up his tape measure.

"Put it with my hat," he said.

"'Hat'? Don't you marines call it a 'cover' or a 'lid'?"

With a look of contempt, he asked, "Do I look like a Crock-Pot to you?"

—BONAH BACHENHEIMER

After my husband, a veteran, spoke at an elementary school, a student asked what he ate during battle.

"C rations," he replied.

"Ooh!" she squealed. "I love seafood."

—DOTTY BOEZINGER

Lt. Gen. William "Gus" Pagonis told the story of going to a movie shortly after retiring. When he and his wife walked into the near-empty theater, a young man stood up and pointed at them. Used to the attention, General Pagonis launched into a speech, thanking the young man and saying how pleased he and his wife were to be there and how—

"Uhh . . ." interrupted the confused usher. "I'm just counting customers. We need ten people before they can start the film."

—TERRI KOYL

Upon returning from a stint in Iraq, my sister insisted that the best part about being home was having real food again: "The Lunchables I had for breakfast was great!"

—GARRETT LEE THORNE

After 29 years of military service, I figured some of my interest in military history would have rubbed off on my 14-year-old son. Wrong! While helping him prepare for his Civil War exam, I asked, "Why did General Lee take his army north to Gettysburg?"

His response: "To listen to Lincoln's speech."

—DONNA WILLIAMS

It was the '60s, and our unit command decided to let us have mustaches, something our first sergeant clearly opposed. Nevertheless, he told us to go ahead and grow one. A week later, he appeared before the morning formation with a razor. He proceeded to shave off each of our mustaches and let the hairs fall into individual envelopes on which he wrote our name. "Now," he announced, "if anyone asks where your mustache is, tell him it's in the sergeant's safe."

—GARY MUFFITT

**A**t a formal NATO dinner, a British officer commented on my ceremonial spurs. "Wearing them is a tradition for U.S. Cavalry officers," I explained.

He smiled with more than a bit of condescension. "My dear boy, the United States Army doesn't have traditions. It has habits."

—STEVEN EDEN

**B**ase rules required that everything around the aircraft hangar at our air force base be painted a bright yellow. When our sergeant noticed that the newly issued trash cans were not yellow, he snarled to an airman, "When I come back tomorrow, I better not see those trash cans unpainted." He got his wish. The next morning, all the new trash cans were gone.

—JOHN LEARD

**W**hile serving in Vietnam, I met some camouflaged soldiers sitting in a converted fishing boat that had a camouflaged engine and machine gun.

"Great camo job," I told them. "No one will ever spot you."

"There's one slight flaw," one of the soldiers said, lifting up a life vest. "We're required to wear these bright orange life preservers when under way."

—WILLIAM KAY

**E**ggs in the military rarely come from chickens. Instead, they're hatched in powder form. As I prepared to make scrambled eggs during KP duty, I filled a large tub with water and poured in a 25-pound bag of the stuff. As I stirred, my mess sergeant threw four whole eggs in, shells and all.

"Why'd you do that?" I asked.

His reply: "So when they bite into a shell, they'll think it's real."

—JASON MICKOLIO

"Look at it this way:

Most people have to pay to go on a cruise."

My father served in the Seabees, which meant he was more likely to handle a cement mixer than a rifle. I tried to explain this to my six-year-old son.

"Grandpa didn't fight in any battles," I said. "He wasn't that kind of soldier."

"Oh," said my son. "He was in the Salvation Army."

—JODI WEBB

A woman called our restaurant. "I want to treat my husband to breakfast for Veteran's Day," she said. "Do you still offer free meals to veterans?"

—JOHN BARTUSKA

**W**hen I was stationed in Naples with the U.S. Navy, my wife and I became parents of a baby girl, the first grandchild on both sides of the family. Soon after, my in-laws were out to dinner with another couple who were also new grandparents. My mother-in-law listened patiently as the other woman detailed what a joy it was babysitting for her new granddaughter. Not to be outdone, my mother-in-law said, "Well, my granddaughter is touring Europe."

—MARK NOVAK

**D**iscussing phone etiquette for naval recruits, our lieutenant recalled a cautionary tale about the time he thought he was calling the ship's chart house.

A sleepy voice answered, "Yeah, whaddaya want?"

"That's no way to answer a phone when an officer calls," he snarled. "Now let's start over. Pretend I just called you."

"Okay. Captain's cabin, captain speaking!"

—HERM ALBRIGHT

**W**hen I was a convoy commander in Iraq, my radio call signal was Rolling Thunder Five. Eventually, I shortened it and would just state, "This is Thunder Five. Over." But I went back to using my full call sign a few days later after an honest sergeant clued me in to something.

"You know, ma'am," he said, "it sounds like you're saying, 'This is Thunder Thighs' over the radio."

—LEANNE D. WELDIN

**A** truck we were towing back to Rhein-Main Air Base in Germany crashed, and the senior airman had to fill out an accident report, per regulations. He began, "In the process of towing, we heard a loud noise in the rear. I became concerned when the vehicle in tow passed me with no driver in it."

—GEORGE DESPIRITO

**C**omedian Paul Gilmartin has trouble imagining what our soldiers have to deal with in Afghanistan: "Desert combat? I can't even stand the walk back from the beach to the car."

**D**ue to a manpower shortage at our air force base in England, the commander nixed all afternoons off. That same day, an airman broached the subject with him.

"Didn't you hear what I said this morning?" our commander snapped. "You'd better have a great reason."

"Sir," said the airman, "my wife is expecting to get pregnant this afternoon, and I want to be there when it happens."

He got the afternoon off.

—PAT FERRY

It was nighttime in Vietnam. All was quiet in our forward outpost when a perimeter guard opened up with grenades and automatic rifle fire. It sounded like all of North Vietnam was attacking. I sprinted over to him.

"What is it?!" I hollered.

The pandemonium stilled, and a small, frightened voice replied, **"Big snake, sir."**

—CRAIG MACNAB

**P**ulling guard duty is dull work. But I never realized just how dull until one night when, with nothing else to do, I looked underneath my desk. There I found these words scrawled by a predecessor: "Man, you must really be bored!"

—MICHAEL BIELARSKI

**W**hen my ex-marine father-in-law was at my house, our six-year-old neighbor came by to play with my kids.

I asked her if she knew who he was. She looked up at him with her big blue eyes and said, "I don't remember what his name is, but I know he used to be a submarine."

—JANELLE RAGLAND

**A**fter serving 11 years in the navy, I was discharged with—shall we say—a vastly increased vocabulary. This became evident one day as I drove with my five-year-old daughter. Everyone on the road was annoying me, and I let each of them know it.

Eventually, my daughter asked, "Daddy, why are all the bad drivers around you and not Mommy?"

—JOHN ERNEST SWAPP

**A** general walked into an elevator on base that was occupied by a specialist. "What are you doing to prepare for your deployment to Afghanistan, Specialist?" he asked.

Flustered, the specialist simply shrugged.

This didn't sit well with the general. He went to the officer in charge and demanded to know why his soldiers seemed unprepared. The officer assembled his staff in an attempt to figure out the problem, and soon we all received this memo: "As of today, specialists are no longer allowed to take the elevator."

—LT. GALEN P. MAHON

# LAST LAUGHS

**W**e were headed to a resort when my father got hopelessly lost. Spotting a farmer in his field, Dad pulled over and asked for directions to Lake Ronkonkoma.

"Never heard of it," said the farmer. "But you're going the wrong way."

—NICK DEMARTINO

**S**hopping in a supermarket, my friend spotted a pregnant woman who looked ready to give birth. She ran to the manager's office and screamed, "Do something! Her water's broken! I can see water at her feet!"

Returning a week later, she bumped into the manager. "So did the woman give birth?" she asked.

"Yes," he replied. "To a large frozen chicken that was hidden up her shirt."

—BRENDA BRENNAN

**I** want to take one of those English as a Second Language courses—just go in and blow everybody away on the first day.

—COMEDIAN CRAIG ANTON

**T**he plan: to build a garden walkway made up of dozens of wooden squares. I decided I'd slice railroad ties into two-inch thick pieces for the sections. That's what I told the clerk at the lumber yard.

"You got a power saw?" he asked.

"No," I said. "Can't I just use my hand saw?"

He nodded slowly. "You could. But I just have one question. How old do you want to be when you finish?"

—JUDY MYERS

"Are you the one who called about the leaky faucet?"

My father is a glass-half-empty-and-probably-polluted kind of guy. So during a trip to the zoo, I wasn't surprised by his reaction when a magnificent peacock strutted past. As my family admired the polychromatic feathers, Dad wondered, "Can you imagine what that thing would look like without feathers?"

—CHRIS LOUGHRAN

Finding a bottle on the beach, Jake uncorks it and releases a genie. "Ah, now you get three wishes," says the genie.

"Great!" Jake replies. "First, I want one billion dollars." Poof! There's a flash, and a paper with Swiss bank account numbers appears in Jake's hand.

"Next, I want a Ferrari." Poof! Another flash, and a shiny red Ferrari is parked next to him.

"Finally," Jake says, "I want to be irresistible to women." Poof! There's another blinding flash, and Jake turns into a box of chocolates.

—RICHARD A. WRIGHT

While we were visiting Block Island, off the New England coast, my friend, who'd had a few, called to ask me for a ride home. "I'm outside Iggi's Inn," he slurred.

After many hours—and even more miles—driving around looking for Iggi's Inn, I finally found him. He was leaning against a large sign for the 1661 Inn.

—CLAYTON LUCE

As I shopped, the following announcement came over the department store's PA system: "If someone here has a convertible with the top down, it just started raining. Towels are located in aisle five."

—SHERRY BAILEY

**A**s I stepped out of the shower, I heard someone in my kitchen downstairs. Knowing that my wife was out, I grabbed my 1903 heirloom rifle—which no longer works—and crept downstairs, forgetting the fact that I was in my birthday suit.

I came around the corner with the gun raised, only to find my wife loading the dishwasher.

"What are you doing?" she asked.

"I thought I heard an intruder. I came down to scare him."

Scanning the contours of my doughy, naked body, she mumbled, "You didn't need the gun."

—KURT EPPS

**W**orking on a new trick, a magician turned his wife into a couch and his kids into chairs, but he couldn't turn them back. What have I done? he wondered. How can I bring back my family? Out of ideas, he loaded everybody into his van and rushed to the hospital. He explained the situation, and his family was whisked off to surgery. Hours later, the surgeon emerged.

"How are they?" the magician asked.

"Comfortable."

—BOB MEYERSON

I entered an auction at an out-of-town convention and won a large Queen Anne wingback chair. Getting it back to my seventh-floor hotel room proved a challenge. I got it in the elevator, but there wasn't enough room for everyone, so I invited another woman to take a seat. We stopped on the third floor, and a drunk started to enter. He looked at the woman on the chair for a second before suggesting, **"If I were you, I'd ask for a bigger room."**

—THAYER DONOVAN

My husband and I love that nearly every flashing construction sign we pass has some sort of typo. Our favorite: "Caution! Loose Gravey Ahead!"

—TERRA COSTIN

I was at the drugstore and noticed a young male cashier staring at the pretty girl in front of me. Her total came to $14.62, and after handing over a $100 bill, she waited for change. "Here you go," said the cashier, smiling as he returned the proper amount. "Have a great day!"

Now I placed my items on the counter. The tally was $32.79, and I, too, gave the cashier a $100 bill. "I'm sorry, ma'am. We can't accept anything larger than a fifty," he told me, pointing to a sign stating store policy.

"But you just accepted that last girl's hundred," I reasoned.

"I had to," he said. "It had her phone number on it."

—KAREN REHM

In ancient Greece, a man came running up to Socrates with gossip he'd heard about Diogenes.

"Before you tell me," interrupted Socrates, "are you sure that what you are about to tell me is true?"

"No," admitted the man.

"Is what you are about to tell me about Diogenes something good?"

"No, but he . . ."

"Will this news benefit me?"

"No, but Diogenes . . ."

"If what you want to tell me is not true, not good, and of no benefit, why tell it to me at all?"

The man walked away in shame. And that's how Socrates never found out that Diogenes was fooling around with his wife.

# QUOTABLE QUOTES

"I'VE NEVER BEEN SWIMMING. THAT'S BECAUSE IT'S NEVER BEEN MORE THAN HALF AN HOUR SINCE I LAST ATE."

—COMEDIAN ARTIE LANGE

"A person without a sense of humor is like a wagon without springs. It's jolted by every pebble on the road."

—HENRY WARD BEECHER

"I never sing in the shower. It's very dangerous."

—JIMMY FALLON

"THE TROUBLE WITH JOGGING IS THAT THE ICE FALLS OUT OF YOUR GLASS."

—MARTIN MULL

"Three groups spend other people's money: children, thieves, politicians. All three need supervision."

—DICK ARMEY

"Always buy a good bed and a good pair of shoes. If you're not in one, you're in the other."

—GLORIA HUNNIFORD

"I BELIEVE IN LOOKING REALITY STRAIGHT IN THE EYE AND DENYING IT."

—GARRISON KEILLOR

"Just dialed the wrong person on Skype. Guess I made a Skypo."

—ALLEN KLEIN

"My grandmother started walking five miles a day when she was sixty. She's ninety-seven now, and we don't know where the hell she is."

—ELLEN DEGENERES

Every year on my birthday, I looked forward to my aunt's gift—a scarf, hat or sweater knitted by hand. One year, she must have had better things to do because I received a ball of yarn, knitting needles and a how-to-knit book. Her card read **"Scarf, some assembly required."**

—DIONNE OBESO

An 80-year-old man goes to a doctor for a checkup. The doctor is amazed at his shape. "To what do you attribute your good health?"

"I'm a turkey hunter, and that's why I'm in good shape. Get up before daylight, chase turkeys up and down mountains."

The doctor says, "Well, I'm sure it helps, but there have to be genetic factors. How old was your dad when he died?"

"Who says my dad's dead?"

"You're 80 years old and your dad's alive? How old is he?"

"Dad's 100. In fact, he turkey hunted with me this morning."

"What about your dad's dad—how old was he when he died?"

"Who says my grandpa's dead?"

"You're 80 years old and your grandfather's still living? How old is he?"

"Grandpa's 118."

"I suppose you're going to tell me he went turkey hunting this morning?"

"No. He got married."

The doctor looks at the man in amazement. "Got married? Why would a 118-year-old guy want to get married?"

The old-timer answers, "Who says he wanted to?"

—ARDELL WIECZOREK

**A** hunter sneaked up on a duck and was about to fire when the duck yelled, "Don't shoot, and I'll give you a hot stock tip!"

"Okay," the hunter replied. "What's the stock?"

"It's a company called Sounds Like a Duck," the fowl said. "It manufactures a duck call, and the share price went up two points last week."

The hunter immediately went home and bought a thousand shares, figuring if anyone could determine an effective duck call it would be a duck. But just two weeks later, the company went out of business. Furious, the hunter drove back to the pond to get an explanation.

"I just lost thousands of dollars because of your lousy tip," the hunter said angrily.

"Big deal," the duck replied. "We just lost our early warning system."

—DONALD F. NIGRONI

**W**ith a new book on handwriting analysis, I began practicing on colleagues at work. One skeptical woman asked if she could bring in a sample of her daughter's writing. "Of course," I replied.

Next day, the woman handed me an envelope. I opened it, read the contents, then dramatically told her, "Your daughter is 14 years old. She's an A student. She loves music and horses."

Amazed, the woman ran off to tell her friends before I could show her the note. It read: "I'm 14 years old and an A student. I love music and horses. My mother thinks you're a fake."

—BILL WHITMAN

**?** **What do you get if you divide the circumference of your jack-o'-lantern by its diameter?**

Pumpkin pi.

BEN ARNOLD-BIK

**O**n our first visit together to a nearby amusement park, my husband immediately fell in love with a big, colorful Dr. Seuss hat he saw many people wearing. Soon we found out that the hats were given away to winners at one of the park's more difficult arcade games. That day, and on each of our following four trips to the park, we spent ridiculous amounts of money trying to win the hat but never succeeded.

On our fifth visit, our friend Gerard came with us. When told of our frustrating hat saga, he said, "No problem. Give me a few minutes, and I'll get one."

My husband and I snickered to ourselves as Gerard left. But sure enough, just a few minutes later, he was back with the beloved hat in hand. "I can't believe it," my husband said as he triumphantly placed the hat atop his head. "Have you played that game before?"

"What game?" Gerard replied. "I bought the hat at the souvenir store."

—MARLA SARINO

**W**hile sightseeing at George Washington's home in Mount Vernon, Virginia, a family friend became nervous when she thought she had lost two of my cousins. She looked everywhere and called out their names repeatedly. Soon our friend grew perturbed that not one of the Mount Vernon employees had joined in the search. Instead, they simply stood around, staring at her as if she were crazy. Finally, just a few moments later, my cousins—George and Martha—came out from hiding.

—TRACY NELSON

Sign spotted on a telephone pole in my neighborhood: "Garage Sale this Saturday—7 a.m. until 100 degrees."

—KATHY RICHEY

"I took the road less traveled."

**A** pig walks into a bar, orders 15 beers and knocks them back. "You've had a lot to drink. Would you like to know where the bathroom is?" asks the bartender.

"No," says the hog. "I'm the little pig that goes wee-wee-wee all the way home."

A man noted for his tact was awakened one morning
at four o'clock by his ringing telephone.
"Your dog's barking and it's keeping me awake,"
said an irate voice.
The man thanked the caller and politely asked his name
before hanging up. The next morning at four o'clock,
he called back his neighbor.

### "Sir," he said, "I don't have a dog."

—RUTH MEYERS

**T**he last thing my friend Christy was prepared for was an invitation to a costume party. Eight and a half months pregnant, she was in no shape for any conventional costume. Still, she wanted to go, so she painted a big yellow circle on an extra-extra large white T-shirt, dug a pair of red devil horns out of her kids' Halloween junk pile . . . and went as a deviled egg.

—BETTY C. HATCHER

**B**eing Korean, I asked my Tennessean friend, "What's the difference between whiskey and moonshine?"
His reply: "Tax."

—KISU KIM

Bored during a long flight, an eminent scholar leaned over and woke up the sleeping man next to him to ask if he would like to play a game. "I'll ask you a question," the scholar explained, "and if you don't know the answer, you pay me $5. Then you ask me a question, and if I don't know the answer, I'll pay you $50."

When the man agreed to play, the scholar asked, "What's the distance from the earth to the moon?"

Flummoxed, the man handed him $5. "Ha!" said the scholar. "It's 238,857 miles. Now it's your turn."

The man was silent for a few moments. Then he asked, "What goes up a hill with three legs and comes down with four?"

Puzzled, the scholar racked his brains for an hour—but to no avail. Finally, he took out his wallet and handed over $50. "Okay, what is the answer?" the scholar asked.

The man said, "I don't know," pulled out a $5 bill, handed it to the scholar and went back to sleep.

—KRIS UEBERRHEIN

My husband, who uses a wheelchair, showed up at his eye doctor's for an appointment. The receptionist checked the schedule, then said, "The nurse will call you in a moment. Have a seat."

He smiled. "Done."

—KIM FRIEDMAN

I never realized just how small my grandparents' town was until we decided to see a movie on Main Street. We called the theater and asked what time the film started. The manager replied, **"When can you get here?"**

—ELISE JONES

WICCAPEDIA

IAN BAKER.

**A**bout an hour after our son Noah was born, and while my parents were getting acquainted with him, our minister stopped in to visit. Noah, who had been quiet until then, cried as soon as the pastor spoke.

"That's odd," the pastor said, "he should be used to my voice. He's been hearing my sermons for nine months."

"Yes," Dad retorted, "but this is the first chance he's had to comment on them."

—TARA RUEL

Late one night, Norm's doorbell rang. When he answered the door, he found a six-foot cockroach standing there. The bug grabbed Norm by the collar, punched him in the eye, threw him across the living room and then ran off.

The next day, Norm went to see his doctor to have his bruised eye examined.

"Ah, yes," the doctor said when Norm explained what had happened.

"There's a nasty bug going around."

—DONALD GEISER

## Revenge of the blondes . . .

**Q:** Why are so many blonde jokes one-liners?
**A:** So brunettes can remember them.

**Q:** What do brunettes miss most about a great party?
**A:** The invitation.

**Q:** What do you call a good-looking man with a brunette?
**A:** A hostage.

**Q:** What's black and blue and brown and lying in a ditch?
**A:** A brunette who has told too many blonde jokes.

"You've gotta help me," the man said to the psychiatrist. "Every night this week I've dreamed I'm playing in a badminton tournament. Then I wake up tired and sweaty."

"Okay, here's your medicine," the doctor said. "Drink this right away, and you'll be cured in no time.

"Can't I wait and drink it tomorrow?" the dreamer wanted to know.

"Why?" the doctor asked.

"It's our championship game tonight."

—EMILY LEYBLE

**R**ecently, my girlfriend, Karen, got a job at a local hardware store. "The owners don't want us hanging out with our friends," she said. "If you stop by, tell them you're my brother."

On my first visit, I walked to the customer service desk and asked the older woman there, "Is Karen around?" When she looked at me quizzically, I added, "I'm her brother."

She smiled. "What a nice surprise. I'm Karen's mother."

—ANAND MAHARAJ

**D**uring a state visit to Great Britain, President Ronald Reagan purportedly went horseback riding with Queen Elizabeth. At one point, one of the horses passed gas quite loudly. The queen apologized, saying, "There are some things even royalty can't control."

Reagan replied, "I'm glad you told me, or I would have thought it was the horse."

**T**he new phone book arrived with a handy blank emergency-number form attached to the front page. I guess everyone's notion of an emergency is different. The categories for phone numbers were listed in this order: 1. Pizza 2. Takeout Restaurants 3. Taxi 4. Poison Control 5. Doctor.

—MEGHAN HUNSAKER

As I helped my elderly neighbor clean out his garage, I stumbled upon an ax in the corner.

"That was my grandfather's," he said, picking it up and running his fingers along the blade. **"Of course, it's been through three new heads since he last used it."**

—BEN KREUSSER

## ?  Why did the new race-car driver make so many stops?

Because some guy on the side of the road kept flagging him down.

— STEVE JOHNSON

---

**O**ne afternoon I rushed out of the house, forgetting my keys, and found myself locked out. There was nothing I could do but wait for my husband to come home, so I went over to a neighbor who was outside raking leaves.

"You locked yourself out?" he said.

"Yeah. This is the second time since we moved in. After the first time we took an extra key and put it in a jar, then stuck it in a potted plant on the back deck."

"So what's the problem?"

"I took the plants in for the winter."

—ADRIANA DESIMONE

**A** man walked into his backyard one morning and found a gorilla in a tree. He called a gorilla-removal service, and soon a serviceman arrived with a stick, a Chihuahua, a pair of handcuffs and a shotgun.

"Now listen carefully," he told the homeowner. "I'm going to climb the tree and poke the gorilla with this stick until he falls to the ground. The trained Chihuahua will then go right for his, uh, sensitive area, and when the gorilla instinctively crosses his hands in front to protect himself, you slap on the handcuffs."

"Got it," the homeowner replied. "But what's the shotgun for?"

"If I fall out of the tree before the gorilla," the man said, "shoot the Chihuahua."

—TIMOTHY SLEDGE

One would be hard-pressed to pass on this ad, spotted on Craigslist: "1990 Ford Escort $250. Could be driven. Should be towed."

—RYAN MALLOY

**A**pparently I tend to brag too much about my home state of Ohio. One day I told a long-suffering friend, "You know, the first man in powered flight was from Ohio. The first man to orbit the earth was from Ohio. And the first man on the moon was from Ohio."

"Sounds like a lot of people are trying to get out of Ohio."

—JEAN NEIDHARDT

**F**eeling sick, my sister grabbed the thermometer from the medicine cabinet and popped it into her mouth.

"Uh, Julie, that's the dog's thermometer," said my mother.

Julie spit out the thermometer. "Ewww, that was in Fitzie's mouth?!"

Mom hesitated before replying, "Not exactly."

—JANET GALLO

**A**fter my parents passed away, my wife and I transferred thousands of their 35-mm slides to videotape, using freezer bags to organize the project. After the videotape was complete, my stepdaughter came for a visit and did a double take when she noticed a bag of turkey meat that my wife was defrosting on the counter. It was labeled "Dave's Folks."

—DAVID HYRE

**T**o me, boxing is like ballet, except there's no music and no choreography, and the dancers hit each other.

—JACK HANDEY

I'm a stickler about people spelling my first name correctly: K-A-T-H-Y. One day, I went to an electronics store where they ask for your name when you buy something. I told the clerk my name is Kathy with a K. He didn't say anything as I paid for my goods and left the store. Later, when I looked at my receipt, I saw that he had noted my name: Cathy Withakay.

—KATHY LANDERKIN

**"Every year I say, 'Just a little off the top,' but they never listen!"**

During a game of Scrabble, my aunt decided to pass. "I simply can't move my vowels," she complained.

My uncle replied, **"Does that mean you're consonated?"**

—SUZANNE CARLSON

I just watched my dog chase his tail for ten minutes, and I thought to myself, *Wow, dogs are easily entertained.* Then I realized: I just watched my dog chase his tail for ten minutes.

—ADAM JOSHUA SMARGON

Since I was a new patient, I had to fill out an information form for the doctor's files. The nurse reading it over noticed my unusual name.

"How do you pronounce it?" she asked.

"Na-le-Y-ko," I said, proud of my Ukranian heritage.

"That sounds real nice," she said, smiling.

"Yes, it is melodious," I agreed.

"So," she asked sweetly, "what part of Melodia is your family from?"

—ANN NALYWAJKO

In an attempt to balance work and motherhood, I delegated the grocery shopping to my young babysitter. But the job proved a tad daunting. One day while I was at work, she texted me from the supermarket.

"Can't find Brillo pads," she wrote. "All they have are Tampax and Kotex."

—KIMBERLY CLARK

Vacationing in Hawaii, two priests decide to wear casual clothes so they won't be identified as clergy. They buy Hawaiian shirts and sandals and soon hit the beach. They notice a gorgeous blonde in a tiny bikini.

"Good afternoon, Fathers," she says as she strolls by.

The men are stunned. How does she know they're clergy? Later they buy even wilder attire: surfer shorts, tie-dyed T-shirts and dark glasses.

The next day, they return to the beach. The same fabulous blonde, now wearing a string bikini, passes by, nods politely at them and says, "Good morning, Fathers."

"Just a minute, young lady," says one of the priests. "We are priests and proud of it, but how in the world did you know?"

"Don't you recognize me? I'm Sister Kathryn from the convent."

—MICHAEL RANA

After she fainted, my mother was raced to the hospital. Her doctor asked, "Why do you think you passed out?" Looking at him oddly, Mom replied,

"Because I woke up on the floor."

—JEFFREY WARD

My mother enjoys shopping at those dollar stores where almost everything costs just a buck. Recently Mom commented to a cashier that she loves shopping at the store when she is depressed because you can buy so much for so little. When the cashier rang up her purchases and the total came to $99.58, a woman behind her quipped, "You must have been on the verge of suicide!"

—DAVID SINGH

"Looks like somebody's using your Rogaine."

A friend of mine had been wanting new kitchen cabinets for a long time, but her husband insisted they were an extravagance. She went to visit her mother for two weeks, and when she returned, she was overjoyed to find that beautiful new cabinets had been installed.

A few days later, a neighbor came over to visit my friend. After admiring the new cabinets, the neighbor added, "All of us were so glad that the fire your husband had while you were gone was confined to the kitchen."

—MARGARET GUNN

Two great white sharks swimming in the ocean spy some surfers. The younger one licks his lips and makes a beeline for them.

"Just a minute," says his father, stopping him. "First we swim around them with just the tip of our fins showing."

And they do.

"Now we swim around them a few times with all our fins showing."

And they do.

"Now we eat everybody."

When they are both gorged, the son asks, "Dad, why didn't we just eat them when we first saw them?"

"Because they taste better without all the poop inside."

—FRANK JOHNSTON

Eight and a half months very pregnant with twins, I was used to getting nervous glances from strangers. But I never realized how imposing I was until my husband and I went out to dinner at a new restaurant. The hostess sat us at our table, took a long look at my stomach and asked, "Would you like me to get you a high chair just in case?"

—CARISSA LUCYK

My friend's ad: "For Sale: '96 Mitsubishi Eclipse Spyder. Brand-new convertible top and tires. Needs minor work. Serious injuries only!"

—DR. NAVJOT GILL

I recently visited my son while he was doing some remodeling at his house. As he left one morning, he told me I'd need to let the plumber in to do some work in the bathroom. Thinking I wouldn't want to let just anyone into the house, I asked how I could recognize him.

Without missing a beat, my son replied, "He'll be carrying a toilet."

—AVA C. SHAUGHNESSY

The local wholesale warehouse sells everything from tires to tuna fish. I was there around noon and stopped at the lunch counter for a slice of pizza. I ate only half of it and threw my leftovers in a nearby trash can.

Then I turned to see a man standing there, hot dog in one hand, ketchup in the other, with a look of horror on his face. I asked him what was wrong. He said, "I just purchased that trash can!"

—CHRIS BIRCH

Sometimes I'll stand up in a meeting and say, "You just gave me an idea!" Then I leave the room, drive home and go to bed.

—TIM SIEDELL

## What does it mean when you find a bear with a wet nose?

It means you're too close to the bear.

DAVID GAY

The topic of conversation at our neighbors' barbecue was their beautiful new lawn. It especially sparkled next to the dying brown patch of earth on our side of the fence. My husband, Bob, had a ready excuse.

"Look at what our gardener did!" he said. **"He put the sod in upside down."**

—PAMELA WIEBUSCH

After one of my students acted up, I took him to our school psychiatrist, who asked if he had ADHD.

"No," said the boy. "I just have a normal TV."

—MATTHEW HUGHES

One weekend, a doctor, a priest and an attorney were out in a fishing boat. Their motor had conked out and one of the oars had drifted off. Just as the doctor was about to dive in to retrieve the oar, the boat was surrounded by sharks.

"I can't go now," the doctor said. "If someone gets bitten, you'll need my services."

"I can't go either," said the priest. "If the doctor fails, I'll need to give last rites."

"Fine," said the attorney. "I'll get it." He dove in, the sharks moved, he retrieved the oar and climbed back into the boat. The doctor and priest looked flabbergasted. The attorney just smiled and said, "Professional courtesy."

—MELODY LEE

# Also Available from Reader's Digest

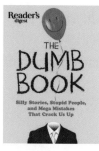

## The Dumb Book

The old adage "truth is stranger than fiction" can also be construed as "truth is funnier than fiction." In our first collection of silly (but true!) stories, the editors of *Reader's Digest* poke a little fun at the unbelievably dumb things that happen—and make us laugh—every day.

**ISBN 978-1-62145-138-9** • **$9.99** paperback

## Reader's Digest's Funny Family Jokes

*Reader's Digest* has a long tradition of providing readers with laughter. Here we have compiled some of the funniest jokes, riddles, and one-liners that can be shared across generations, around the dinner table or the campfire. There's something for everyone from age 9 to 99.

**ISBN 978-1-62145-189-1** • **$9.99** paperback

## How to Write a Memoir in 30 Days

Everyone has a story to tell. If you've ever thought of sharing yours but don't know where to begin, this is the book for you. Step-by-step techniques are presented in a welcoming, non-intimidating style, and information and advice about different publishing paths is also included.

**ISBN 978-1-62145-145-7** • **$14.99** paperback

## Quotable Quotes

An update of the bestselling Reader's Digest timeless classic, this new twenty-first-century collection features words of wisdom, wry witticisms, provocative opinions, and inspiring reflections from both history's greatest figures and our beloved modern celebrities.

**ISBN 978-1-62145-004-7** • **$14.99** hardcover

E-book editions are also available.

For more information, visit us at RDTradePublishing.com

Reader's Digest books can be purchased through retail and online bookstores.